Fodor's 96
Chicago

"When it comes to information on regional history, what to see and do, and shopping, these guides are exhaustive."

—*USAir Magazine*

"Usable, sophisticated restaurant coverage, with an emphasis on good value."

—Andy Birsh, *Gourmet Magazine* columnist

"Valuable because of their comprehensiveness."

—*Minneapolis Star-Tribune*

"Fodor's always delivers high quality...thoughtfully presented...thorough."

—*Houston Post*

"An excellent choice for those who want everything under one cover."

—*Washington Post*

D1165963

Fodor's Travel Publications, Inc.
New York • Toronto • London • Sydney • Auckland

Fodor's Chicago

Editor: Hannah Borgeson

Editorial Contributors: Steven Amsterdam, Robert Andrews, Robert Blake, Don Davenport, Elizabeth Gardner, Julie Ann Getzlaff, Tracy Patruno, Mark Kollar, Mary Ellen Schultz, M.T. Schwartzman (Gold Guide editor), Dinah Spritzer, Phil Vettel

Creative Director: Fabrizio La Rocca

Cartographer: David Lindroth

Cover Photograph: John Ivanko

Text Design: Between the Covers

Copyright

Special Sales

Fodor's Travel Publications are available at special discounts for bulk purchases for sales promotions or premiums. Special editions, including personalized covers, excerpts of existing guides, and corporate imprints, can be created in large quantities for special needs. For more information, contact your local bookseller or write to Special Markets, Fodor's Travel Publications, 201 East 50th Street, New York, NY 10022. Inquiries from Canada should be directed to your local Canadian bookseller or sent to Random House of Canada, Ltd., Marketing Dept., 1265 Aerowood Drive, Mississauga, Ontario L4W 1B9. Inquiries from the United Kingdom should be sent to Fodor's Travel Publications, 20 Vauxhall Bridge Road, London SW1V 2SA England.

PRINTED IN THE UNITED STATES OF AMERICA

10 9 8 7 6 5 4 3 2 1

CONTENTS

ON THE ROAD WITH FODOR'S

A GOOD TRAVEL GUIDE is like a wonderful traveling companion. It's charming, it's brimming with sound recommendations and solid ideas, it pulls no punches in describing lodging and dining establishments, and it's consistently full of fascinating facts that make you view what you've traveled to see in a rich new light. In the creation of *Chicago '96*, we at Fodor's have gone to great lengths to provide you with the very best of all possible traveling companions—and to make your trip the best of all possible vacations.

About Our Writers

The information in these pages is a collaboration of a number of extraordinary writers.

Freelance writer **Julie Ann Getzlaff,** a native Chicagoan, learned a few things about her hometown by updating the Exploring and Shopping chapters, as well as the Gold Guide. Recently relocated to the San Francisco Bay Area, she misses Chicago's stunning architecture and fantastic museums—but not its climate!

Mark Kollar, updater of the Sports, Arts and Nightlife, and Excursions chapters of this edition, covers Wall Street as a financial reporter in New York. He has spent most of his life in the Chicago area and has written a book about the futures markets there. Family and friends—and the Cubs—keep him coming back to Lake Michigan regularly.

Phil Vettel has been covering the Chicago-area entertainment and dining scene for 16 years, the last six of them as restaurant critic for *The Chicago Tribune*. His weekly reviews appear in the *Tribune,* America Online, and CLTV News. He lives with his wife, two sons, and a dog, some of whom accompany Phil on his restaurant visits.

Steven Amsterdam, who updated this book's lodging chapter, has stayed in some of the world's finest hotels. He's also experienced plenty of dives. A former Chicago resident, Steven now lives in Manhattan and works in Fodor's map department.

We'd also like to thank Sylvia Nelson, familiarization trip coordinator for the Chicago Office of Tourism. More thanks go to Al Becker and the crew of American Airlines for smooth flights to and from Chicago.

What's New

A New Design

If this is not the first Fodor's guide you've purchased, you'll immediately notice our new look. More readable and easier to use than ever? We think so—and we hope you do, too.

Let Us Do Your Booking

Our writers have scoured Chicago to come up with an extensive and well-balanced list of the best B&Bs, inns, and hotels, both small and large, new and old. But you don't have to beat the bushes to come up with a reservation. Now we've teamed up with an established hotel-booking service to make it easy for you to secure a room at the property of your choice. It's fast, it's free, and confirmation is guaranteed. If your first choice is booked, the operators can line up your second right away. Just call 1–800/FODORS–1 or 1–800/363–6771 (0800–89–1030 in Great Britain; 0014–800–12–8271 in Australia; 1–800/55–9101 in Ireland).

Travel Updates

In addition, just before your trip, you may want to order a Fodor's Worldview Travel Update. From local publications all over Chicago, the lively, cosmopolitan editors at Worldview gather information on concerts, plays, opera, dance performances, gallery and museum shows, sports competitions, and other special events that coincide with your visit. See the order blank at the back of this book, call 800/799–9609, or fax 800/799–9619.

And in Chicago

The biggest new development in Chicago is the renovation of **Navy Pier,** which officially opened in July of 1995. The 1916 facility has hosted performances, housed college classes, and served as a training center; after the pier sat derelict throughout most of the 1970s and 80s, the state and city launched an ambitious project to turn it into a multi-use recreation and convention complex. In addition to the fleet of dinner-cruise vessels that now use the pier as home port during the summer months, Navy Pier is also home to the vaulted-roofed Skyline Stage, a 1,500-seat outdoor theater; Crystal Gardens, one of the country's largest indoor botanical parks; the Chicago Children's Museum; an IMAX Theater; an outdoor beer garden; and numerous shops, restaurants, and bars. The summer-season amusement park, with its old-fashioned carousel and 150-foot lighted Ferris wheel, is already a big hit; the ice-skating rink will debut during the winter.

The renaissance of the pier also adds to Chicago's myriad **dining options;** scheduled to open are Riva, a 300-seat Italian seafood and steak restaurant with breathtaking skyline views; Widow Newton's Tavern, a playful concept from the creator of Old Carolina Crabhouse on North Pier; Charlie's Ale House, a casual, comfortable pub; and a food court.

McCormick Place, Chicago's main convention and exposition center, is undergoing $987 million of expansions and remodeling, intended for completion in 1997. An 11-story, glass-enclosed grand concourse will serve as a striking new entrance and will connect the convention buildings. The two existing buildings are receiving new carpeting and are being repainted, and a third structure with more than 1 million square feet of meeting and exposition space is planned.

The Navy Pier development includes **Festival Hall,** for events that are too small for McCormick Place but too big for most hotels; it has 48,000 square feet of meeting rooms and 170,000 square feet of exhibit space.

The **1996 Democratic National Convention** will take place in Chicago's new United Center in August, from the 26th to the 29th, drawing approximately 35,000 visitors to the city. For information on its series of free public events, call Chicago '96 (☎ 312/214–1996), the host committee.

In museum news, the **Art Institute of Chicago** will offer a host of new exhibits during 1996, including: *Annette Massager* (Feb. 17–May 5) a photography exhibit

exploring the contemporary European artist's work; *Worlds Seen and Imagined: Japanese Screens from the Idemitsu Museum of Arts* (Feb. 17–Apr. 28), featuring 55 rare screen paintings from the Idemitsu Museum of Arts in Tokyo; *American Textiles from the Permanent Collection* (Mar. 6–July 21), highlighting the Art Institute's collection of quilts, coverlets, and other textiles; *Galleries of Modern Art: 1950–1970* (opens Apr.), the second phase of the highly acclaimed renovation of the *Galleries of Modern Art: 1900–1950* that opened in 1991, featuring American and European painting and sculpture dating from 1950 to 1970; *Alone in a Crowd: Prints by African-American Artists of the 1930s–1940s* (May 17–July 14), which displays approximately 100 rare prints by a group of relatively unrecognized but highly influential African-American artists who were active during the era of New Deal federal arts projects; and *Degas: The Late Work* (Sept. 28–Jan. 5), which focuses on his work from 1886 until he died in 1917. Among the special exhibits at the **Museum of Science and Industry** is *Movie Special Effects* (June–Oct.).

How to Use This Book

Organization

Up front is the **Gold Guide,** comprising two sections on gold paper that are chock-full of information about traveling within your destination and traveling in general. Both are in alphabetical order by topic. **Important Contacts A to Z** gives addresses and telephone numbers of organizations and companies that offer destination-related services and detailed information or publications. Here's where you'll find information about how to get to Chicago from wherever you are. **Smart Travel Tips A to Z,** the Gold Guide's second section, gives specific tips on how to get the most out of your travels, as well as information on how to accomplish what you need to in Chicago.

At the end of the book you'll find **Portraits,** including a great Studs Terkel piece about life in Chicago and wonderful essays about the city's architecture and neighborhoods. These are followed by suggestions for pre-trip reading, both fiction and nonfiction.

Stars

Stars in the margin are used to denote highly recommended sights, attractions, hotels, and restaurants.

Credit Cards

The following abbreviations are used: **AE,** American Express; **D,** Discover; **DC,** Diners Club; **MC,** MasterCard; and **V,** Visa.

Please Write to Us

Everyone who has contributed to *Chicago '96* has worked hard to make the text accurate. All prices and opening times are based on information supplied to us at press time, and Fodor's cannot accept responsibility for any errors that may have occurred. The passage of time will bring changes, so it's always a good idea to call ahead and confirm information when it matters—particularly if you're making a detour to visit specific sights or attractions. When making reservations at a hotel or inn, be sure to mention if you have a disability or are traveling with children, if you prefer a private bath or a certain type of bed, or if you have specific dietary needs or any other concerns.

Were the restaurants we recommended as described? Did our hotel picks exceed your expectations? Did you find a museum we recommended a waste of time? We would love your feedback, positive and negative. If you have complaints, we'll look into them and revise our entries when the facts warrant it. If you've happened upon a special place that we haven't included, we'll pass the information along to the writers so they can check it out. So please send us a letter or postcard (we're at 201 East 50th Street, New York, New York 10022.) We'll look forward to hearing from you. And in the meantime, have a wonderful trip!

Karen Cure

Editorial Director

Chicago

800W

Crosby

North

400W

Hudson Ave.

Walton

NEAR NORTH

Locust

Chestnut

John H
B

Institute Pl.

Tower

Branch Chicago

Kingsbury

Larrabee

Chicago Ave.

Orleans

Evanston/Ravenswood

Franklin

Wells

La Salle

Clark

Dearborn

State

Howard-Dan Ryan

Superior

Huron

Erie

Ontario

Ohio

River

Ohio

Grand Ave.

Grand Ave.

RIVER NORTH

Rush

001W

001E

Rush

Wabash Ave.

Ontario

Ohio

Grand Ave

Illinois

Hubbard

Kinzie

Wrigl
Buildi

Kinzie

400N

O'Hare-Congress-Douglas

Union Ave.

Milwaukee Ave.

Fulton

W. Wacker Dr.

S. Wate

O'HARE
INTERNATIONAL
AIRPORT

Lake-Englewood-Jackson Park

Lake

Lake

Randolph

Despaines

Jefferson

Clinton

Canal

State of
Illinois
Center

State

Lake

Washington Blvd.

John F. Kennedy Expwy

Northwestern
Station M

Washington

Daley
Center

THE LOOP

Marsh
Field &

Madison

Madison

La Salle

Wabash

Street

Mall

Peoria

Green

Halsted

Monroe

S. Wacker Dr.

Franklin

Wells

Monroe

Clark

Dearborn

Carson Pirie
Scott & Co.

Ave.

Madison

Adams

Jackson Blvd.

Adams

Sears
Tower

Quincy

Orches

400S

Van Buren

Chicago
Board
of Trade

Fine A
Build

Van Buren

I 290

90
94

O'Hare-Congress-Douglas

La Salle St.
Station M

Harold Washington
Library Center

NEAR

Dwight D.
Eisenhower Expwy.

Congress Pkwy.

Plymouth Ct.

State

Au
The

WEST

Harrison

Harrison

Jackson Park/Midway:
Dan Ryan

Harris

SIDE

Dan Ryan Expwy

S. Branch

Wells

Financial Pl.

Clark

La Salle

Federal

Lake-Englewood-
Howard-
Dan Ryan

E.

800S

TO
MIDWAY
AIRPORT

Polk

Chicago River

SOUTH
LOOP

Polk

001W

001E

Wabash Ave.

8th

Taylor

800W

500W

Taylor

9th St.

11th S

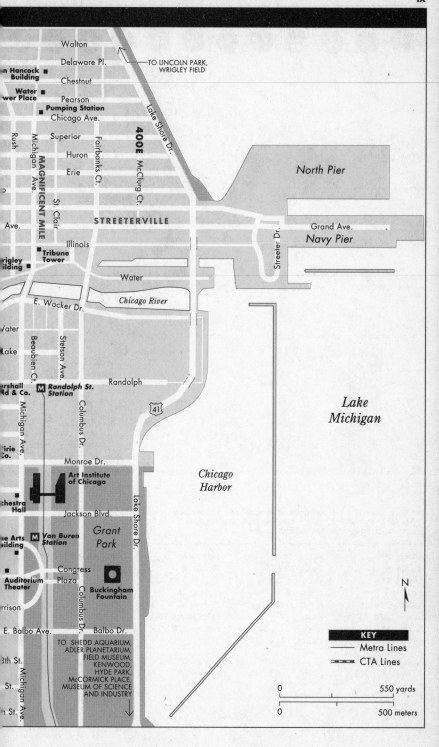

Walton

Delaware Pl.

n Hancock
Building

Chestnut

Water
wer Place

Pearson

Pumping Station

Chicago Ave.

TO LINCOLN PARK,
WRIGLEY FIELD

Lake Shore Dr.

Superior

Huron

Erie

Rush

Michigan Ave.

MAGNIFICENT MILE

400 E

McClurg Ct.

Fairbanks Ct.

St. Clair

STREETERVILLE

Ave.

Illinois

rigley
ilding

Tribune
Tower

Streeter Dr.

North Pier

Grand Ave.

Navy Pier

Water

E. Wacker Dr.

Chicago River

Vater

Lake

Beaubien Ct.

Stetson Ave.

Randolph

Lake
Michigan

rshall
d & Co.

M Randolph St.
Station

Columbus Dr.

41

irie
Co.

Michigan Ave.

Monroe Dr.

Art Institute
of Chicago

Chicago
Harbor

chestra
Hall

Jackson Blvd.

Lake Shore Dr.

e Arts
ilding

M Van Buren
Station

Grant
Park

Congress
Plaza

Columbus Dr.

Auditorium
Theater

Buckingham
Fountain

rrison

E. Balbo Ave.

Balbo Dr.

N

3th St.

TO SHEDD AQUARIUM,
ADLER PLANETARIUM,
FIELD MUSEUM,
KENWOOD,
HYDE PARK,
McCORMICK PLACE,
MUSEUM OF SCIENCE
AND INDUSTRY

St.

Michigan Ave.

h St.

KEY

Metra Lines

CTA Lines

0   550 yards

0   500 meters

Numbers below vertical bands relate each zone to Greenwich Mean Time (0 hrs.).
Local times frequently differ from these general indications,
as indicated by light-face numbers on map.

Algiers, **29**
Anchorage, **3**
Athens, **41**
Auckland, **1**
Baghdad, **46**
Bangkok, **50**
Beijing, **54**

Berlin, **34**
Bogotá, **19**
Budapest, **37**
Buenos Aires, **24**
Caracas, **22**
Chicago, **9**
Copenhagen, **33**
Dallas, **10**

Delhi, **48**
Denver, **8**
Djakarta, **53**
Dublin, **26**
Edmonton, **7**
Hong Kong, **56**
Honolulu, **2**

Istanbul, **40**
Jerusalem, **42**
Johannesburg, **44**
Lima, **20**
Lisbon, **28**
London
(Greenwich), **27**
Los Angeles, **6**
Madrid, **38**
Manila, **57**

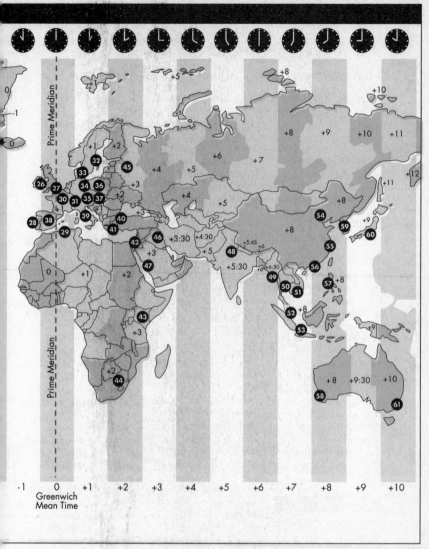

IMPORTANT CONTACTS A TO Z

An Alphabetical Listing of Publications, Organizations, and Companies That Will Help You Before, During, and After Your Trip

No single travel resource can give you every detail about every topic that might interest or concern you at the various stages of your journey—when you're planning your trip, while you're on the road, and after you get back home. The following organizations, books, and brochures will supplement the information in Fodor's *Chicago '96*. For related information, including both basic tips on visiting Chicago and background information on many of the topics below, study Smart Traveling A to Z, the section that follows Important Contacts A to Z.

A

AIR TRAVEL

The major gateway to Chicago is **O'Hare International Airport** (☎ 312/686–2200). One of the world's busiest airports, it is located 20 miles from downtown in the far northwestern corner of the city. **Midway Airport** (☎ 312/767–0500), on Chicago's Southwest Side, about 7 miles from downtown, is smaller, relatively uncrowded, and lacks O'Hare's confusion. **Meigs Field** (☎ 312/744–4787), just south of downtown, serves commuter airlines with flights to downstate Illinois and Wisconsin.

Flying time is about 2 hours from New York and about 4 hours from Los Angeles.

CARRIERS

Carriers serving Chicago include every U.S. airline, most international airlines, and a number of regional carriers.

American Airlines (☎ 800/433–7300) flies into O'Hare direct from more than 100 cities in the United States and abroad. For inexpensive, no-frills flights, contact **Kiwi International** (☎ 800/538–5494), based in Newark and New York, serving Atlanta, Chicago, Orlando, San Juan, Tampa, and West Palm Beach; **MarkAir** (☎ 800/627–5247), based in Anchorage, Alaska, which serves Atlanta, Chicago, Cincinnati, Colorado, Dallas, Kansas City, Minneapolis, Newark, Phoenix, and Washington DC; **Midwest Express** (☎ 800/452–2022), based in Milwaukee, which serves 45 U.S. cities in the Midwest and on both coasts, including Appleton, Atlanta, Boston, Cleveland, Columbus, Dallas/Ft.

Worth, Dayton, Denver, Des Moines, Detroit, Flint, Ft. Lauderdale, Ft. Myers, Grand Rapids, Green Bay, Indianapolis, Kalamazoo, Kansas City, La Crosse, Lansing, Las Vegas, Los Angeles, Madison, Midland/Bay City/Saginaw, Milwaukee, Muskegon, New York, Newark, Omaha, Philadelphia, Phoenix, Rochester, Rockford, St. Louis, San Diego, San Francisco, South Bend, Tampa, Toronto (Ontario, Canada), Traverse City, Washington DC, and Wausau/Stevens Point (Wisconsin); **Private Jet** (☎ 404/231–7571, 800/546–7571, or 800/949–9400), based in Atlanta, serving Cancún, Chicago, Cincinnati, Dallas, Las Vegas, Los Angeles, Miami, Orlando, St. Louis, St. Thomas, San Francisco, and Washington DC; **Southwest Airlines** (☎ 800/444–5660), based in Salt Lake City and serving Alabama, Arizona, Arkansas, California, Idaho, Illinois, Indiana, Kentucky, Louisiana, Maryland, Michigan, Missouri, Nevada, New Mexico, Ohio, Oklahoma, Oregon, Tennessee, Texas, Utah, and Washington; and **ValuJet** (☎ 404/994–8258 or 800/825–8538), also based in Atlanta and serving Chicago, Dallas, Ft. Myers, Indianapolis, Jacksonville, Louisville, Memphis, Nashville, New Orleans, Savannah, Tampa, Washington DC, and West Palm Beach.

COMPLAINTS

To register complaints about charter and scheduled airlines, contact the U.S. Department of Transportation's **Office of Consumer Affairs** (400 7th St. NW, Washington, DC 20590, ☎ 202/366–2220 or 800/322–7873).

CONSOLIDATORS

An established consolidator selling to the public is **TFI Tours International** (34 W. 32nd St., New York, NY 10001, ☎ 212/736–1140 or 800/745–8000). **FLY–ASAP** (3824 E. Indian School Road, Phoenix, AZ 85018, ☎ 800/359–2727) isn't a discounter but gets good deals from among published fares, and gets discount tickets from consolidators.

PUBLICATIONS

For general information about charter carriers, ask for the Office of Consumer Affairs' brochure **"Plane Talk: Public Charter Flights."** The Department of Transportation also publishes a 58-page booklet, **"Fly Rights"** ($1.75; Consumer Information Center, Dept. 133-B, Pueblo, CO 81009).

For other tips and hints, consult the Consumers Union's monthly **"Consumer Reports Travel Letter"** ($39 a year; Box 53629, Boulder CO 80322, ☎ 800/234–1970) and the newsletter **"Travel Smart"** ($37 a year; 40 Beechdale Rd., Dobbs Ferry, NY 10522, ☎ 800/327–3633); *The Official Frequent Flyer Guidebook,* by Randy Petersen ($14.99 plus $3 shipping; 4715-C Town Center Dr., Colorado Springs, CO 80916, ☎ 719/597–8899 or 800/487–8893); *Airfare Secrets Exposed,* by Sharon Tyler and Matthew Wonder (Universal Information Publishing; $16.95 plus $3.75 shipping from Sandcastle Publishing, Box 3070-A, South Pasadena, CA 91031, ☎ 213/255–3616 or 800/655–0053); and *202 Tips Even the Best Business Travelers May Not Know,* by Christopher McGinnis ($10 plus $3.00 shipping; Irwin Professional Publishing, 1333 Burr Ridge Parkway, Burr Ridge, IL 60521, ☎ 800/634–3966).

AIRPORT TRANSFERS

BY PUBLIC TRANSIT

For information contact the **Chicago Transit Authority** (CTA; ☎ 312/836–7000).

BY BUS

Continental Airport Express (☎ 312/454–7799) coaches provide service from both airports to major downtown and Near North hotels; call for reservations. The trip downtown from O'Hare takes an hour or longer, depending on traffic conditions and your destination; the fare is $14.75. The trip downtown from Midway takes about half an hour; the fare is $10.75.

CW Limo (☎ 312/493–2700) offers moderately priced express van service from both airports to locations in Hyde Park and the South Side. Vans leave O'Hare about every hour; the fare is $14 and travel time to Hyde Park is roughly an hour. CW also serves Midway during peak traffic times; the fare is $10.50.

B

BETTER BUSINESS BUREAU

Contact the **Chicago Better Business Bureau** (211 West Wacker Dr., 60606-1217, ☎ 312/444–1188). For other local contacts, consult the **Council of Better Business Bureaus** (4200 Wilson Blvd., Arlington, VA 22203, ☎ 703/276–0100).

BUS TRAVEL

Greyhound Lines (630 W. Harrison St., ☎ 312/408–5971 or 800/231–2222) has nationwide service to its main terminal in the Loop and to neighborhood stations at the 95th Street and Dan Ryan Expressway CTA station, and at the Cumberland CTA station near O'Hare Airport. The Harrison Street terminal is far from most hotels, so plan on another bus or a cab to your hotel.

WITHIN CHICAGO

See Public Transportation, *in* Smart Travel

Tips A to Z, *below,* for information on CTA buses.

AUDIO VISUAL RENTALS

AVS (955 W. Washington Blvd., ☎ 312/733–3370), **Midwest Visual** (820 N. Orleans St., ☎ 312/787–1644), **Video Replay** (118 W. Grand Ave., ☎ 312/822–0221).

CATERERS

Corner Bakery Catering (516 N. Clark St., ☎ 312/527–1956), **Lettuce Catering in the Loop** (440 S. La Salle St., ☎ 312/663–8835), **The Bountiful Board** (2826 N. Lincoln Ave., ☎ 312/549–1999).

CHAMBER OF COMMERCE

Chamber of Commerce (330 N. Wabash Ave., Suite 2800, ☎ 312/494–6700).

COMPUTER RENTALS

Computer Access (175 W. Jackson Blvd., Suite 644, ☎ 312/735–1022), **GE Computer & Workstation Rentals** (4000 Sussex Ave., Aurora, ☎ 312/759–0066).

CONVENTION AND EXHIBITION CENTERS

McCormick Place (2300 S. Lake Shore Drive, ☎ 312/791–7000), **Navy Pier** (600 E. Grand Ave., ☎ 312/791–7000), **United Center** (1901 W. Madison St., ☎ 312/455–4500).

FORMAL WEAR

Gingiss Formal Wear (151 S. Wabash Ave., ☎ 312/263–7071), **Seno Formal Wear** (6 E. Randolph St., ☎ 312/782–1115).

LIMOUSINES

American Limousine (☎ 312/920–8888), **Chicago Limousine Service** (☎ 312/726–1035), **Presidential Limousine** (☎ 312/278–9900).

OVERNIGHT DELIVERY

Federal Express (☎ 312/559–9000), **UPS** (☎ 708/990–2900), **U.S. Post Office Express Mail** (☎ 800/222–1811).

MESSENGERS

Arrow (☎ 312/489–6688), **Cannonball** (☎ 312/829–1234).

NOTARY PUBLICS

Around the Clock Notary (☎ 312/477–2400), **Chicago & La Salle Currency Exchange** (755 N. La Salle St., ☎ 642–0220).

PHOTOCOPYING

Copies Now By Sir Speedy (28 N. Clark St., ☎ 312/236–5587), **Kinko's** (6 W. Lake St., ☎ 312/251–0441 and 444 N. Wells St., ☎ 312/670–4460).

SECRETARIAL SERVICES

A-EC Secretarial Services (39 S. La Salle St., ☎ 312/236–6847), **HQ Business Centers** (70 W. Madison St., ☎ 312/214–3100), **Kinko's** (6 W. Lake St., ☎ 312/251–0441 and 444 N. Wells St., ☎ 312/670–4460).

Major car-rental companies represented in Chicago include **Alamo** (☎ 800/327–9633, 0800/272–2000 in the U.K.), **Avis** (☎ 800/331–1212, 800/879–2847 in Canada), **Budget** (☎ 800/527–0700, 0800/181–181 in the U.K.), **Dollar** (known as Eurodollar outside North America, ☎ 800/800–4000, 0181/952–6565 in the U.K.), **Hertz** (☎ 800/654–3131, 800/263–0600 in Canada, 0181/679–1799 in the U.K.), and **National** (☎ 800/227–7368, 0181/950–5050 in the U.K., where it is known as Europcar). Rates in Chicago begin at $48 a day and $106 week for an economy car with unlimited mileage.

BABY-SITTING

Make child-care arrangements with your hotel or through **American Registry for Nurses and Sitters** (3921 N. Lincoln Ave., Chicago, IL 60613, ☎ 312/248–8100) and **Art Resource Studio** (2755 N. Pine Grove St., Chicago, IL 60614, ☎ 312/975–1671), with weekday craft workshops and drop-off care on weekends. Call ahead, as hours vary.

FLYING

Look into **"Flying With Baby"** ($5.95 plus $1 shipping; Third Street Press, Box 261250, Littleton, CO 80126, ☎ 303/595–5959), cowritten by a flight attendant. **"Kids and Teens in Flight,"** free from the U.S. Department of Transportation's Office of Consumer Affairs, offers tips for children flying alone. Every two years the February issue of *Family Travel Times* (*see* Know-How, *below*) details children's services on three dozen airlines.

GAMES

The gamemeister, Milton Bradley, has games to help keep little (and not so little) children from getting fidgety while riding in planes, trains, and automobiles. Try packing the *Travel Battleship* sea battle game ($7), *Travel Connect Four,* a vertical strategy game ($8), the *Travel Yahtzee* dice game ($6), the *Travel Trouble* dice and board game ($7), and the *Travel Guess Who* mystery game ($8).

KNOW-HOW

Family Travel Times, published four times a year by Travel With Your Children (TWYCH, 45 W. 18th St., New York, NY 10011, ☎ 212/206–0688; annual subscription $40), covers destinations, types of vacations, and modes of travel.

The *Family Travel Guides* catalogue ($1 postage; Box 6061, Albany, CA 94706; ☎ 510/527–5849) lists about 200 books and articles on family travel. Also check *Take Your Baby and Go! A Guide for Traveling with Babies, Toddlers and Young Children,* by

Sheri Andrews, Judy Bordeaux, and Vivian Vasquez ($5.95 plus $1.50 shipping; Bear Creek Publications, 2507 Minor Ave., Seattle, WA 98102, ☎ 206/322–7604 or 800/326–6566). Also from Globe Pequot are *The 100 Best Family Resorts in North America,* by Jane Wilford with Janet Tice ($12.95), and the two-volume (eastern section and western editions) set of *50 Great Family Vacations in North America* ($18.95 each plus $3 shipping).

LOCAL INFO

Chicago Parent (139 S. Oak Park Ave., Oak Park, IL 60302, ☎ 708/386–5555) is a monthly publication with events and resource listings that is available free at locations throughout the city.

LODGING

The Ritz-Carlton (160 E. Pearson St., Chicago, IL 60611, ☎ 312/266–1000 or 800/621–6906) provides many children's services, from complimentary strollers to a children's menu, and kids stay free in their parents' room. At the **Drake** (140 E. Walton Place, Chicago, IL 60611, ☎ 312/787–2200), children under 18 stay free, and the restaurant has a children's menu. Most **Days Inn** hotels (☎ 800/325–2525) charge only a nominal fee for children under 18 and allow kids 12 and under to eat free; many offer efficiency-type apartments, too.

CANADIANS

Contact **Revenue Canada** (2265 St. Laurent Blvd. S, Ottawa, Ontario, K1G 4K3, ☎ 613/993–0534) for a copy of the free brochure **"I Declare/Je Déclare"** and for details on duties that exceed the standard duty-free limit.

U.K. CITIZENS

HM Customs and Excise (Dorset House, Stamford St., London SE1 9NG, ☎ 0171/202–4227) can answer questions about U.K. customs regulations and publishes **"A Guide for Travellers,"** detailing standard procedures and import rules.

COMPLAINTS

To register complaints under the provisions of the Americans with Disabilities Act, contact the U.S. Department of Justice's **Public Access Section** (Box 66738, Washington, DC 20035, ☎ 202/514–0301, TDD 202/514–0383, FAX 202/307–1198).

ORGANIZATIONS

Access Living (310 S. Peoria, Suite 201, Chicago, IL 60607) offers personal-attendant referrals for travelers with disabilities.

FOR TRAVELERS WITH HEARING IMPAIRMENTS➤ Contact the **American Academy of Otolaryngology** (1 Prince St., Alexandria, VA 22314, ☎ 703/

836–4444, FAX 703/
683–5100, TTY
703/519–1585).

FOR TRAVELERS WITH
MOBILITY PROBLEMS➣
Contact the **Information
Center for Individuals
with Disabilities** (Fort
Point Pl., 27–43 Worm-
wood St., Boston, MA
02210, ☎ 617/727–
5540, 800/462–5015 in
MA, TTY 617/345–
9743); **Mobility International USA** (Box 10767,
Eugene, OR 97440, ☎
and TTY 503/343–
1284, FAX 503/343–
6812), the U.S. branch
of an international
organization based in
Belgium (*see below*)
that has affiliates in 30
countries; **MossRehab
Hospital Travel Informa-
tion Service** (1200 W.
Tabor Rd., Philadel-
phia, PA 19141, ☎
215/456–9603, TTY
215/456–9602); the
**Society for the Advance-
ment of Travel for the
Handicapped** (347 5th
Ave., Suite 610, New
York, NY 10016, ☎
212/447–7284, FAX
212/725–8253); the
**Travel Industry and
Disabled Exchange**
(TIDE, 5435 Donna
Ave., Tarzana, CA
91356, ☎ 818/344–
3640, FAX 818/344–
0078); and **Travelin'
Talk** (Box 3534,
Clarksville, TN 37043,
☎ 615/552–6670, FAX
615/552–1182).

FOR TRAVELERS WITH
VISION IMPAIRMENTS➣
Contact the **American
Council of the Blind**
(1155 15th St. NW,
Suite 720, Washington,
DC 20005, ☎ 202/
467–5081, FAX 202/
467–5085) or the
**American Foundation
for the Blind** (15 W.

16th St., New York,
NY 10011, ☎ 212/
620–2000, TTY
212/620–2158).

IN THE U.K.

Contact the **Royal
Association for Disabil-
ity and Rehabilitation**
(RADAR, 12 City
Forum, 250 City Rd.,
London EC1V 8AF, ☎
0171/250–3222) or
Mobility International
(Rue de Manchester 25,
B1070 Brussels, Bel-
gium, ☎ 00–322–
410–6297), an
international clearing-
house of travel informa-
tion for people with
disabilities.

PUBLICATIONS

Several free publications
are available from the
**Consumer Information
Center** (Box 100,
Pueblo, CO 81009, ☎
719/948–3334). Call or
write for a free cata-
logue of current titles.

Fodor's **Great American
Vacations for Travelers
with Disabilities** ($18;
available in bookstores,
or call 800/533–6478)
details accessible attractions, restaurants, and
hotels in U.S. destina-
tions. The 500-page
Travelin' Talk Directory
($35; Box 3534,
Clarksville, TN 37043,
☎ 615/552–6670) lists
people and organiza-
tions who help travelers
with disabilities. For
specialist travel agents
worldwide, consult the
**Directory of Travel
Agencies for the Dis-
abled** ($19.95 plus $2
shipping; Twin Peaks
Press, Box 129, Van-
couver, WA 98666, ☎
206/694–2462 or
800/637–2256) and the
**Directory of Travel
Agencies for the Dis-**

abled, by Helen Hecker
($19.95 plus $3.50
handling; Disability
Bookshop, Box 129,
Vancouver, WA, 98666;
☎ 206/694–2462).

**TRAVEL AGENCIES,
TOUR OPERATORS**

The Americans with
Disabilities Act requires
that travel firms serve
the needs of all travel-
ers. However, some
agencies and operators
specialize in making
group and individual
arrangements for travel-
ers with disabilities,
among them **Access
Adventures** (206 Chest-
nut Ridge Rd.,
Rochester, NY 14624,
☎ 716/889–9096), run
by a former physical-
rehab counselor. In
addition, many of the
operators and agencies
listed below (*see* Tour
Operators, *below*) can
also arrange vacations
for travelers with dis-
abilities.

FOR TRAVELERS WITH
MOBILITY PROBLEMS➣ A
number of operators
specialize in working
with travelers with
mobility problems:
Hinsdale Travel Service
(201 E. Ogden Ave.,
Suite 100, Hinsdale, IL
60521, ☎ 708/325–
1335 or 800/303–
5521), a travel agency
that will give you access
to the services of
wheelchair traveler
Janice Perkins;
Wheelchair Journeys
(16979 Redmond Way,
Redmond, WA 98052,
☎ 206/885–2210),
which can handle
arrangements world-
wide.

FOR TRAVELERS WITH DEVELOPMENTAL DISABILITIES> Contact the nonprofit **New Directions** (5276 Hollister Ave., Suite 207, Santa Barbara, CA 93111, ☎ 805/967–2841), for travelers with developmental disabilities and their families as well as the general-interest operations above.

DISCOUNT CLUBS

Options include **Entertainment Travel Editions** (fee $28–$53, depending on destination; Box 1068, Trumbull, CT 06611, ☎ 800/445–4137), **Great American Traveler** ($49.95 annually; Box 27965, Salt Lake City, UT 84127, ☎ 800/548–2812), **Moment's Notice Discount Travel Club** ($25 annually, single or family; 163 Amsterdam Ave., Suite 137, New York, NY 10023, ☎ 212/486–0500), **Privilege Card** ($74.95 annually; 3391 Peachtree Rd. NE, Suite 110, Atlanta GA 30326, ☎ 404/262–0222 or 800/236–9732), **Travelers Advantage** ($49 annually, single or family; CUC Travel Service, 49 Music Sq. W, Nashville, TN 37203, ☎ 800/548–1116 or 800/648–4037), and **Worldwide Discount Travel Club** ($50 annually for family, $40 single; 1674 Meridian Ave., Miami Beach, FL 33139, ☎ 305/534–2082).

E

EMERGENCIES

Police, fire, ambulance (☎ 911).

HOSPITALS

In the Near North or north, **Northwestern Memorial Hospital** (250 E. Superior St. at Fairbanks Ct., ☎ 312/908–2000). In the Loop, **Rush Presbyterian St. Luke's** (1750 W. Harrison St., ☎ 312/942–5000). In Hyde Park and the South Side, **Michael Reese Hospital** (2929 S. Ellis Ave., ☎ 312/791–2000), or the **Bernard Mitchell Hospital at the University of Chicago** (5841 S. Maryland Ave., ☎ 312/702–1000). Michael Reese and other hospitals sponsor storefront clinics for fast treatment of minor emergencies. Call the hospitals for information, or check the Chicago Consumer Yellow Pages under "Clinics."

DENTISTS

The **Chicago Dental Society Emergency Service** (☎ 312/726–4321 or 312/836–7300) makes referrals at all hours.

24-HOUR PHARMACIES

Osco (call 800/654–6726 for nearest location). **Walgreen's** (757 N. Michigan Ave., at Chicago Ave., ☎ 312/664–8686).

G

GAY AND LESBIAN TRAVEL

ORGANIZATIONS

The **International Gay Travel Association** (Box 4974, Key West, FL 33041, ☎ 800/448–8550), a consortium of 800 businesses, can supply names of travel agents and tour operators.

PUBLICATIONS

The premier international travel magazine for gays and lesbians is **Our World** ($35 for 10 issues; 1104 N. Nova Rd., Suite 251, Daytona Beach, FL 32117, ☎ 904/441–5367). The 16-page monthly "Out & About" ($49 for 10 issues; ☎ 212/645–6922 or 800/929–2268), covers gay-friendly resorts, hotels, cruise lines, and airlines.

TOUR OPERATORS

For mixed gay and lesbian travel, contact **Toto Tours** (1326 W. Albion Suite 3W, Chicago, IL 60626, ☎ 312/274–8686 or 800/565–1241).

TRAVEL AGENCIES

The largest agencies serving gay travelers are **Advance Travel** (10700 Northwest Freeway, Suite 160, Houston, TX 77092, ☎ 713/682–2002 or 800/695–0880), **Islanders/ Kennedy Travel** (183 W. 10th St., New York, NY 10014, ☎ 212/242–3222 or 800/988–1181), **Now Voyager** (4406 18th St., San Francisco, CA 94114, ☎ 415/626–1169 or 800/255–6951), and **Yellowbrick Road** (1500 W. Balmoral Ave., Chicago, IL 60640, ☎ 312/561–1800 or 800/642–2488). **Skylink Women's Travel** (746 Ashland Ave., Santa Monica, CA 90405, ☎ 310/452–0506 or 800/225-5759) works with lesbians.

I

INFORMATION
HOT LINES

Fine Arts Hotline (☎ 312/346–3278), **Live Concert Hotline** (☎ 312/666–6667), **Sports Information** (☎ 312/976–4242), **Stock Market** (☎ 312/976–3434), **Time** (☎ 312/976–1616), **Weather** (☎ 312/976–1212).

INSURANCE

Travel insurance covering baggage, health, and trip cancellation or interruptions is available from **Access America** (Box 90315, Richmond, VA 23286, ☎ 804/285–3300 or 800/284–8300), **Carefree Travel Insurance** (Box 9366, 100 Garden City Plaza, Garden City, NY 11530, ☎ 516/294–0220 or 800/323–3149), **Near Sevices** (Box 1339, Calumet City, IL 60409, ☎ 708/868–6700 or 800/654–6700), **Tele-Trip** (Mutual of Omaha Plaza, Box 31716, Omaha, NE 68131, ☎ 800/228–9792), **Travel Insured International** (Box 280568, East Hartford, CT 06128-0568, ☎ 203/528–7663 or 800/243–3174), **Travel Guard International** (1145 Clark St., Stevens Point, WI 54481, ☎ 715/345–0505 or 800/826–1300), and **Wallach & Company** (107 W. Federal St., Box 480, Middleburg, VA 22117, ☎ 703/687–3166 or 800/237–6615).

IN THE U.K.

The **Association of British Insurers** (51 Gresham St., London EC2V 7HQ, ☎ 0171/600–3333; 30 Gordon St., Glasgow G1 3PU, ☎ 0141/226–3905; Scottish Provident Bldg., Donegall Sq. W, Belfast BT1 6JE, ☎ 01232/249176; and other locations) gives advice by phone and publishes the free **"Holiday Insurance,"** which sets out typical policy provisions and costs.

L

LODGING

APARTMENT AND VILLA RENTALS

Principal clearinghouses include **Intervac International** ($65 annually; Box 590504, San Francisco, CA 94159, ☎ 415/435–3497), which has three annual directories; and **Loan-a-Home** ($35–$45 annually; 2 Park La., Apt. 6E, Mount Vernon, NY 10552-3443, ☎ 914/664–7640), which specializes in long-term exchanges. In Chicago, the **Belden-Stratford** (☎ 312/281–2900 or 800/800–8301; *see* Chapter 6, Lodging), a 1920s landmark building overlooking Lincoln Park, offers particularly plush rentals.

M

MONEY MATTERS

ATMS

For specific **Cirrus** locations in the United States and Canada, call 800/424–7787. For U.S. **Plus** locations, call 800/843–7587 and enter the area code and first three digits of the number you're calling from (or of the calling area where you want an ATM).

WIRING FUNDS

Funds can be wired via **American Express MoneyGram**^{SM} (☎ 800/926–9400 from the U.S. and Canada for locations and information) or **Western Union** (☎ 800/325–6000 for agent locations or to send using MasterCard or Visa, 800/321–2923 in Canada).

P

PASSPORTS
AND VISAS

U.K. CITIZENS

For fees, documentation requirements, and to get an emergency passport, call the **London Passport Office** (☎ 0171/271–3000). For visa information, call the **U.S. Embassy Visa Information Line** (☎ 0891/200–290; calls cost 49p per minute or 39p per minute cheap rate) or write the **U.S. Embassy Visa Branch** (5 Upper Grosvenor St., London W1A 4JB). If you live in Northern Ireland, write the **U.S. Consulate General** (Queen's House, Queen St., Belfast BTI 6EQ).

PHOTO HELP

The **Kodak Information Center** (☎ 800/242–2424) answers consumer questions about film and photography.

R

RAIL TRAVEL

Amtrak (☎ 800/872–7245) offers nationwide service to Chicago's

Union Station (Jackson and Canal Sts., ☎ 312/558–1075). Some trains travel overnight, and you can sleep in your seat or book a roomette at additional cost. Most trains have attractive diner cars with acceptable food, but you may prefer to bring your own.

WITHIN CHICAGO

Chicago's extensive public transportation network includes buses and rapid transit trains, both subway and elevated. The **CTA** publishes an excellent map of the transit system, available on request from the CTA (Merchandise Mart, Chicago, IL 60654). The **RTA Travel Information Center** (☎ 312/836–7000) provides information on how to get around on city, suburban, and commuter transit and bus lines.

S

EDUCATIONAL TRAVEL

The nonprofit **Elderhostel** (75 Federal St., 3rd Floor, Boston, MA 02110, ☎ 617/426–7788), for people 60 and older, has offered inexpensive study programs since 1975. The nearly 2,000 courses cover everything from marine science to Greek myths and cowboy poetry. Fees for programs in the United States and Canada, which usually last one week, run about $300, not including transportation.

ORGANIZATIONS

Contact the **American Association of Retired Persons** (AARP, 601 E St. NW, Washington, DC 20049, ☎ 202/434–2277; $8 per person or couple annually). Its Purchase Privilege Program gets members discounts on lodging, car rentals, and sightseeing, and the AARP Motoring Plan furnishes domestic trip-routing information and emergency road-service aid for an annual fee of $39.95 per person or couple ($59.95 for a premium version).

For other discounts on lodgings, car rentals, and other travel products, along with magazines and newsletters, contact the **National Council of Senior Citizens** (membership $12 annually; 1331 F St. NW, Washington, DC 20004, ☎ 202/347–8800) and **Mature Outlook** (subscription $9.95 annually; 6001 N. Clark St., Chicago, IL 60660, ☎ 312/465–6466 or 800/336–6330).

PUBLICATIONS

The 50+ Traveler's Guidebook: Where to Go, Where to Stay, What to Do, by Anita Williams and Merrimac Dillon ($12.95; St. Martin's Press, 175 5th Ave., New York, NY 10010, ☎ 212/674–5151 or 800/288–2131), offers many useful tips. **"The Mature Traveler"** ($29.95; Box 50400, Reno, NV 89513, ☎ 702/786–7419), a monthly newsletter, covers travel deals.

ORIENTATION TOURS

BY LAND➤ **American Sightseeing's** (☎ 312/427–3100) North tour along State Street and North Michigan Avenue includes the John Hancock Center, Water Tower Place, and the Lincoln Park Conservatory. The South tour covers the financial district, Grant Park, the University of Chicago, the Museum of Science and Industry, and Jackson Park. They offer African-American–history and other ethnic-history tours, too. Tours leave from the Palmer House (17 E. Monroe St.), or you can arrange to be picked up at your hotel (downtown or Near North only). The cost is $15 adults, $7.50 children 5–14; for a combined 4-hour tour of north and south, the cost is $25 adults, $12.50 children 5–14. Two-hour tours leave daily 9:30, 11:30, 1:30, and 3:30 in summer, 10, noon, and 2 in winter.

The double-decker buses of **Chicago Motor Coach Co.** (☎ 312/922–8919) take visitors on one-hour narrated tours of Chicago landmarks. Climb on at the Sears Tower (Jackson Blvd. and Franklin St.), the Field Museum (Lake Shore Dr. at E. Roosevelt Rd.), the Art Institute (Michigan Ave. at Adams St.), or the Water Tower (Michigan Ave. at Pearson St.). Tours cost $10 for adults, $6 for children, and leave daily 9:30–5.

BY BOAT➤ Boat tour schedules vary by season; be sure to call for exact times and fares.

Mercury Skyline Cruises (☎ 312/332–1353 for recorded information) has 90-minute river and lake cruises that leave from Wacker Drive at Michigan Avenue (the south side of the Michigan Ave. bridge). Departures May 1–Sept. 30 at 10, 11:30, 1:15, 3:15, and 7:30. Cost is $9 adults, $4.50 children under 12.

Half-hour boat trips on Lake Michigan are offered by **Shoreline Marine** (☎ 312/222–9328; cost: $6 adults, $3 children), daily between May 1 and October 1. Tours leave from the Shedd Aquarium during the day (11:15–5:15) and from Buckingham Fountain in the evening (7:15–11:15), between June and October.

From April to October, 90-minute guided tours traverse the Chicago River to south of the Sears Tower and through the locks; on Lake Michigan, they travel between the Adler Planetarium on the south and Oak Street Beach on the north. **Wendella Sightseeing Boats** (400 N. Michigan Ave., ☎ 312/337–1446) also offers an unscheduled, but fairly frequent one-hour tour on Lake Michigan only. There are also evening tours. All tours leave from lower Michigan Avenue at the foot of the Wrigley Building on the north side of the river.

The cost for 90-minute tours are $10 adults, $8 senior citizens, $5 children 11 and under; departures are at 10, 11:30, 1:15, 3, 4:30, and 7:30. The hour lake tour costs $7 adults, $3.50 children. two-hour evening tours: $11 adults, $5.50 children 11 and under; departure at 7:30.

WALKING TOURS

The **Chicago Architecture Foundation** (Tour Center, 224 S. Michigan Ave., ☎ 312/922–8687; cost: $5–$17 per person) has a Tour Center that leads the popular Lunchtime Loop Walking Tour, as well as tours of historic houses, on a daily or weekly schedule, depending on the season. The center offers other tours—Graceland Cemetery, Frank Lloyd Wright's Oak Park buildings, and bicycle tours of Lincoln Park—on an occasional, seasonal, or prescheduled basis. Departure times vary.

Friends of the Chicago River (407 S. Dearborn St., Chicago 60605, ☎ 312/939–0490) offers two-hour walking tours (cost: $5) along the river on occasional Saturday mornings. There are seven different tours; call in advance to find out which is being offered and where it starts. The organization also has maps of the routes available for a small donation.

SPECIAL-INTEREST TOURS

Besides the tours listed below, you can also

contact the following: **African American Heritage Tours** (☎ 312/443–9575); **Antique Coach** (☎ 312/735–9400), **Chicago Horse & Carriage Ltd.** (☎312/944–6773), and **Noble Horse** (☎ 312/266–7878) for horse-drawn carriage rides; or **Chicago by Air** (☎ 708/524–1172) for a bird's-eye view of the city.

The **Chicago Mercantile Exchange** (30 S. Wacker Dr., ☎ 312/930–8249) has two visitors' galleries, one or both of which offer views of the often frenetic trading floors, which are open 7:15–3:15. A presentation in the fourth-floor gallery explains the activity on the floor below.

On **Chicago Supernatural Ghost Tours** (Box 29054, Chicago 60629, ☎ 708/499–0300; cost $25 per person) you can visit famous murder sites, local Native American burial grounds, haunted pubs, and the scenes of various gangster rubouts, such as the St. Valentine's Day Massacre. Two five-hour tours operate on weekends and daily during October and November. Tours run noon–5 and 7–midnight.

The **Chicago Tribune** (777 W. Chicago Ave., ☎ 312/222–2116) offers free weekday tours of its Freedom Center production facility. Reservations must be made in advance of your visit.

The Chicago Office of Tourism (☎ 312/744–

2400) runs summertime **Loop Tour Trains.** In 1995, tours were on Saturday afternoons and tickets were free from the Chicago Cultural Center (77 E. Randolph St.).

Tour the **Pumping Station** (806 N. Michigan Ave., ☎ 312/467–7114; cost $5.75 adults, $4.50 children, students, and senior citizens) at the historic Water Tower and see *Here's Chicago!*, a multimedia show about the city. Shows are every 30 minutes, daily 10–4.

Untouchable Tours (Box 43185, Chicago 60643, ☎ 312/881–1195; cost: $20 adults, $15 children under 10) captures the excitement of jazz-age Chicago at old hoodlum haunts, brothels, gambling dens, and sites of gangland shootouts. Two-hour tours start at 10 AM Mon.–Sat., 11 on Sun.

STUDENTS

GROUPS

A major tour operator is **Contiki Holidays** (300 Plaza Alicante, Suite 900, Garden Grove, CA 92640, ☎ 714/740–0808 or 800/466–0610).

HOSTELING

Contact **Hostelling International–American Youth Hostels** (733 15th St. NW, Suite 840, Washington, DC 20005, ☎ 202/783–6161) in the United States, **Hostelling International–Canada** (205 Catherine St., Suite 400, Ottawa, Ontario K2P 1C3, ☎ 613/237–7884) in Canada, and

the **Youth Hostel Association of England and Wales** (Trevelyan House, 8 St. Stephen's Hill, St. Albans, Hertfordshire AL1 2DY, ☎ 01727/855215 and 01727/845047) in the United Kingdom. Membership ($25 in the U.S., C$26.75 in Canada, and £9 in the U.K.) gets you access to 5,000 hostels worldwide that charge $7–$20 nightly per person.

I.D. CARDS

To get discounts on transportation and admissions, get the **International Student Identity Card** (ISIC) if you're a bona fide student or the **International Youth Card** (IYC) if you're under 26. In the United States, the ISIC and IYC cards cost $16 each and include basic travel accident and illness coverage, plus a toll-free travel hot line. Apply through the Council on International Educational Exchange (*see* Organizations, *below*). Cards are available for $18 each in Canada from **Travel Cuts** (*see* Organizations, *below*) and in the United Kingdom for £5 each at student unions and student travel companies.

ORGANIZATIONS

A major contact is the **Council on International Educational Exchange** (CIEE, 205 E. 42nd St., 16th Floor, New York, NY 10017, ☎ 212/661–1450) with locations in Boston (729 Boylston St., 02116, ☎ 617/266–1926), Miami (9100 S. Dadeland Blvd., 33156, ☎ 305/670–9261), Los

Angeles (10904 Lindbrook Dr., 90024, ☎ 310/208–3551), 43 college towns nationwide, and the United Kingdom (28A Poland St., London W1V 3DB, ☎ 0171/437–7767). Twice a year, it publishes *Student Travels* magazine. The CIEE's Council Travel Service offers domestic air passes for bargain travel within the United States and is the exclusive U.S. agent for several student-discount cards.

Campus Connections (325 Chestnut St., Suite 1101, Philadelphia, PA 19106, ☎ 215/625–8585 or 800/428–3235) specializes in discounted accommodations and airfares for students. The **Educational Travel Centre** (438 N. Frances St., Madison, WI 53703, ☎ 608/256–5551) offers rail passes and low-cost airline tickets, mostly for flights departing from Chicago. Only for air travel contact **TMI Student Travel** (100 W. 33rd St., Suite 813, New York, NY 10001, ☎ 800/245–3672).

In Canada, also contact **Travel Cuts** (187 College St., Toronto, Ontario M5T 1P7, ☎ 416/979–2406 or 800/667–2887).

T

TAXIS

The principal taxi companies are **American United Cab Co.** (☎ 312/248–7600), **Flash Cab** (☎ 312/561–1444), **Yellow Cab Co.** (☎ 312/829–4222), and **Checker Cab Co.** (☎ 312/829–4222).

THE GOLD GUIDE / IMPORTANT CONTACTS

Among the companies selling tours and packages to Chicago, the following have a proven reputation, are nationally known, and offer plenty of options.

GROUP TOURS

For escorted deluxe tours to Chicago, contact **Maupintour** (Box 807, Lawrence KS 66044, ☎ 800/255–4266 or 913/843–1211) and **Tauck Tours** (11 Wilton Rd., Westport, CT 06880, ☎ 800/468–2825 or 203/226–6911). Another operator falling between deluxe and first-class is **Globus** (5301 South Federal Circle, Littleton, CO 80123, ☎ 800/221–0090 or 303/797–2800). For first-class and first-class superior, try **Collette Tours** (162 Middle St., Pawtucket, RI 02860, ☎ 800/832–4656 or 401/728–3805), and **Mayflower Tours** (1225 Warren Ave., Downers Grove, IL 60515, ☎ 708/960–3430 or 800/323–7604). For budget and tourist class programs, contact **Cosmos** (*see* Globus, *above*).

PACKAGES

Independent vacation packages are available from major tour operators and airlines. Contact **American Airlines Fly AAway Vacations** (☎ 800/321–2121), **Continental Airlines' Grand Destinations** (☎ 800/634–5555), **Delta Dream Vacations** (☎ 800/872–7786), **Certified Vacations** (Box 1525, Ft. Lauderdale, FL 33302, ☎ 305/522–1414 or 800/233–7260), **SuperCities** (617/621–9988 or 800/333–1234), **United Vacations** (☎ 800/328–6877), **Kingdom Tours** (300 Market St., Kingston, PA 18704, ☎ 717/283–4241 or 800/872–8857), and **USAir Vacations** (☎ 800/455–0123). **Funjet Vacations**, based in Milwaukee, Wisconsin, and **Gogo Tours**, based in Ramsey, New Jersey, sell Chicago packages only through travel agents.

FROM THE U.K.

Tour operators offering packages to Chicago include **British Airways Holidays** (Astral Towers, Betts Way, London Rd., Crawley, West Sussex RH10 2XA, ☎ 01293/518–022), **Kuoni Travel** (Kuoni House, Dorking, Surrey RH5 4AZ, ☎ 01306/742–222), **Americana Vacations Ltd.** (Morley House, 320 Regent St., London W1R 5AD, ☎ 0171/637–7853), and **Key to America** (1–3 Station Rd., Ashford, Middlesex TW15 2UW, ☎ 01784/248–777).

Independent travelers should contact **Trailfinders** (42–50 Earls Court Rd., London W8 7RG, ☎ 0171/937–5400 or 58 Deansgate, Manchester M3 2FF, ☎ 0161/839–6969). Travel agencies that offer cheap fares to Chicago include **Travel Cuts** (295a Regent St., London W1R 7YA, ☎ 0171/637–3161; *see* Students, *above*), and **Flightfile** (49 Tottenham Court Rd., London W1P 9RE, ☎ 0171/700–2722).

THEME TRIPS

HISTORIC HOMES➤ Historian-led tours of the private mansions along Chicago's elegant North Shore are available from **American Aristocracy** (1187 Wilmette Ave., Wilmette, IL 60091, ☎ 708/615–2251).

PERFORMING ARTS➤ **Dailey-Thorp Travel** (330 W. 58th St., New York, NY 10019, ☎ 212/307–1555; book through travel agents) specializes in classical music, opera, and ballet; its packages include tickets that are otherwise very hard to get.

SPORTS➤ For packages that include hotel accommodations, air transportation, and tickets to see the basketball Bulls, football Bears, and other local Chicago teams, contact **Dan Chavez's Sports Empire** (Box 6169, Lakewood, CA 90714, ☎ 310/809–6930 or 800/255–5258), **Sports Events** (15500 Wayzata Blvd., Suite 1028, Wayzata, MN 55391, ☎ 612/473–6500 or 800/473–6507), and **Sports Tours** (Box 84, Hatfield, MA 01038, ☎ 413/247–3155 or 800/722–7701).

ORGANIZATIONS

The **National Tour Association** (546 E. Main St., Lexington, KY 40508, ☎ 606/226–4444 or 800/755–8687) and **United States Tour**

Operators Association (USTOA, 211 E. 51st St., Suite 12B, New York, NY 10022, ☎ 212/750–7371) can provide lists of member operators and information on booking tours.

PUBLICATIONS

Consult the brochure **On Tour** or ask for a current list of member operators from the National Tour Association (*see above*). Also get a copy of the **"Worldwide Tour & Vacation Package Finder"** from the USTOA (*see above*) and the Better Business Bureau's **"Tips on Travel Packages"** (publication No. 24-195, $2; 4200 Wilson Blvd., Arlington, VA 22203).

TRAVEL AGENCIES

For names of reputable agencies in your area, contact the **American Society of Travel Agents** (1101 King St., Suite 200, Alexandria, VA 22314, ☎ 703/739–2782).

V

VISITOR

INFORMATION

For information on the city, contact the **Chicago Office of Tourism** (78 E. Washington St., Chicago, IL 60602, ☎ 312/744–2400 or 800/487–2446, TDD 312/744–2947, FAX 312/744–2359).

The **Chicago Office of Tourism's Welcome Center** is housed in the historic Water Tower, in the middle of the Magnificent Mile (806 N. Michigan Ave., ☎ 312/744–2400). The Office of Tourism has two other walk-in centers: the **Chicago Cultural Center** (78 E. Washington St.) and the **Pumping Station** (163 E. Pearson St.). The Cultural Center has a new facility called **'Round & About the Loop,** which has exhibits and information on the art, architecture, and history of the Loop, provides maps of the area, and rents audiocasette tours produced by the Landmarks Preservation Council of Illinois.

The **Mayor's Office of Special Events, General Information, and Activities** (121 N. La Salle St., Room 703, ☎ 312/744–3315) will tell you about city-sponsored events of interest.

The **State of Illinois Office of Tourism** (100 W. Randolph St.) maintains a **Tourism Hot Line** (☎ 312/814–4732).

Within minutes of your call to the **Chicago Convention and Tourism Bureau** (2301 S. Lake Shore Dr., Chicago, IL 60616, ☎ 312/567–8500, FAX 312/567–8533), their automated FaxBack Information Service (☎ 312/567–8528) can fax you with

information on events, sights, sports schedules, nightlife, and other tips.

If you plan to travel outside Chicago, contact the **Illinois Bureau of Tourism** (100 W. Randolph St., Suite 3-400, Chicago, IL 60601, ☎ 312/814–4732 or 800/223–0121) for a free packet about travel in Illinois.

In the U.K., also contact the **United States Travel and Tourism Administration** (Box 1EN, London W1A 1EN, ☎ 0171/495–4466). For a free USA pack, write the USTTA at Box 170, Ashford, Kent TN24 0ZX). Enclose stamps worth £1.50.

Chicago Mosaic, the city's server on the World Wide Web, can be accessed at http://www.ci.chi.il.us. It gives Internet users a virtual tour of the city, with information about architecture, neighborhoods, and museums. A calendar lists updoming festivals, exhibits, theater productions, and sporting events.

W

WEATHER

For current conditions and forecasts, plus the local time and helpful travel tips, call the **Weather Channel Connection** (☎ 900/932–8437; 95¢ per minute) from a touch-tone phone.

SMART TRAVEL TIPS A TO Z

Basic Information on Traveling in Chicago and Savvy Tips to Make Your Trip a Breeze

The more you travel, the more you know about how to make trips run like clockwork. To help make your travels hassle-free, Fodor's editors have rounded up dozens of tips from our contributors and travel experts all over the world, as well as basic information on visiting Chicago. For names of organizations to contact and publications that can give you more information, *see* Important Contacts A to Z, *above.*

A

ADDRESSES

Chicago's streets follow a grid pattern. Madison Street is the baseline for streets and avenues that run north–south; Michigan Avenue, for example, is North Michigan Avenue above Madison Street, South Michigan Avenue below it. Street-address numbers start at the baseline and climb in each direction, generally by 100 a block; thus the Fine Arts Building at 410 South Michigan Avenue is four blocks south of Madison Street. For streets that run east–west, State Street is the baseline; 18th Street, for example, is East 18th Street east of State Street and West 18th Street west of State Street. Street-address numbers start at the baseline and rise in each direction, east and west.

"The Loop" denotes the section of downtown that is roughly circled by the famous "El" train's elevated tracks, although the Loop's actual boundaries—Michigan Avenue on the east, Wacker Drive on the north and west, and Congress on the south—enclose a larger area than the tracks. The area immediately north of the Loop, from Wacker Drive to North Avenue, is known as the **Near North;** included are the Magnificent Mile and such neighborhoods as Streeterville, River North, and the Gold Coast. **Lincoln Park** is the neighborhood stretching north from North Avenue to Fullerton Avenue or Diversey Parkway. The northern neighborhoods are bounded on the west by the North Branch of the Chicago River. South of the Loop, the city is less clearly defined. The South Side neighborhoods you'll hear about most often are **Hyde Park and Kenwood,** which comprise the area south from 41st Street to 63rd Street, bounded on the west by Martin Luther King, Jr. Drive.

AIR TRAVEL

If time is an issue, **always look for nonstop flights,** which require no change of plane and make no stops. If possible, **avoid connecting flights,** which stop at least once and can involve a change of plane, although the flight number remains the same; if the first leg is late, the second waits.

CUTTING COSTS

The Sunday travel section of most newspapers is a good source of deals.

MAJOR AIRLINES➤ The least-expensive airfares from the major airlines are priced for round-trip travel and are subject to restrictions. You must usually **book in advance and buy the ticket within 24 hours** to get cheaper fares, and you may have to **stay over a Saturday night.** The lowest fare is subject to availability, and only a small percentage of the plane's total seats are sold at that price. It's good to **call a number of airlines, and when you are quoted a good price, book it on the spot**—the same fare on the same flight may not be available the next day. Airlines generally allow you to change your return date for a $25 to $50 fee, but most low-fare tickets are nonrefundable. However, if you don't use it, you can apply the cost toward the purchase price of a new ticket, again for a small charge.

CONSOLIDATORS➤ Consolidators, who buy tickets at reduced rates from scheduled airlines, sell them at prices below the lowest available from the airlines directly—usually without advance restrictions. Sometimes you can even get your money back if you need to return the ticket. Carefully **read the fine print** detailing penalties for changes and cancellations. If you doubt the reliability of a consolidator, **confirm your reservation with the airline.**

ALOFT

AIRLINE FOOD➤ If you hate airline food, **ask for special meals when booking.** These can be vegetarian, low-cholesterol, or kosher, for example; commonly prepared to order in smaller quantities than standard catered fare, they can be tastier.

SMOKING➤ Smoking is banned on all flights within the U.S. of less than six hours' duration and on all Canadian flights; the ban also applies to domestic segments of international flights aboard U.S. and foreign carriers. Delta has banned smoking system-wide.

AIRPORT TRANSFERS

BY PUBLIC TRANSIT

For cheap and convenient transfers to the North Side or Downtown, **take rapid transit to or from the airports.**

In O'Hare Airport, the Chicago Transit Authority station is in Terminal 4, in the underground concourse. Travel time to the city is 40–60 minutes. From the first stop in the Loop (Washington and Dearborn Sts.) you can take a taxi to your hotel or change to other transit lines.

At Midway Airport, a CTA line runs to the Loop. The stop at Adams Street and Wabash Avenue is the closest to the hotels on South Michigan Avenue; for others, the simplest strategy is to alight anywhere in the Loop and hail a cab.

BY BUS

When taking the coach to O'Hare to catch a departing flight, be sure to **allow at least 1½ hours.** If you're going from the South Side to Midway, **call 24 hours in advance.**

BY TAXI

Metered taxicab service is available at both O'Hare and Midway airports. Trips to and from O'Hare incur a $1 surcharge. Expect to pay about $30–$35 plus tip from O'Hare to Near North and Downtown locations, about $18 plus tip from Midway. Some cabs participate in a share-a-

ride program where each cab carries two or three individuals going from the airport to Downtown; the cost per person is substantially lower than the full rate.

BY RENTAL CAR

Leaving the airport, follow the signs to I–90 east, the Kennedy Expressway, which merges with I–94, the Edens Expressway. Take the eastbound exit at Ohio Street for Near North locations, the Washington or Madison Street exits for Downtown. After you exit, continue east about a mile to get to Michigan Avenue.

B

BUS TRAVEL

WITHIN CHICAGO

See Public Transportation, *below,* for information on CTA buses.

BUSINESS HOURS

Banks are generally open 8:30–3; a few open for a half day on Saturday and close on Wednesday. Many banks in the Loop and Near North stay open until 5 PM.

The main **U.S. Post Office** (433 W. Van Buren St., ☎ 312/765–4357) is open weekdays 7:30 AM–9 PM, Saturday 7:30–5, and is closed Sunday. The post office at O'Hare International Airport is open daily 24 hours.

Chicago City Hall (121 N. La Salle St., ☎ 312/744–5000) is open weekdays, closed on city holidays.

Most **department stores,** except those in

Water Tower Place, are open Monday–Saturday from 9:45 to 5:30 or 6, Thursday until 7. Sunday hours at Magnificent Mile department stores are usually noon–5. Loop department stores are open all week and occasionally hold blockbuster sales on Sunday (designated Super Sunday); the newspapers announce the specific dates. Lord & Taylor and Marshall Field's at Water Tower Place are open weekdays 10–9, Saturday 9–8 and Sunday 11–7.

C
CAMERAS, CAMCORDERS, AND COMPUTERS

LAPTOPS

Before you depart, **check your portable computer's battery,** because you may be asked at security to turn on the computer to prove that it is what it appears to be. At the airport, you may prefer to **request a manual inspection,** although security X-rays do not harm hard-disk or floppy-disk storage.

PHOTOGRAPHY

If your camera is new or if you haven't used it for a while, **shoot and develop a few rolls of film** before you leave. **Always store film in a cool, dry place**—never in the car's glove compartment or on the shelf under the rear window.

Every pass through an X-ray machine increases film's chance of clouding. To protect it, carry it in a clear plastic bag and **ask for hand in-** **spection at security.** Such requests are virtually always honored at U.S. airports. Don't depend on a lead-lined bag to protect film in checked luggage—the airline may increase the radiation to see what's inside.

VIDEO

Before your trip, **test your camcorder, invest in a skylight filter to protect the lens, and charge the batteries.** (Airport security personnel may ask you to turn on the camcorder to prove that it's what it appears to be).

Videotape is not damaged by X-rays, but it may be harmed by the magnetic field of a walk-through metal detector, so **ask that videotapes be handchecked.**

CHILDREN AND TRAVEL

BABY-SITTING

For recommended local sitters, **check with your hotel desk.**

DRIVING

If you are renting a car, **arrange for a car seat when you reserve.** Sometimes they're free.

FLYING

On domestic flights, children under 2 not occupying a seat travel free, and older children currently travel on the lowest applicable adult fare.

BAGGAGE➤ In general, the adult baggage allowance applies for children paying half or more of the adult fare.

SAFETY SEATS➤ According to the FAA, it's a good idea to **use safety seats aloft.** Airline policy varies. U.S. carriers allow FAA-approved models, but airlines usually require that you buy a ticket, even if your child would otherwise ride free, because the seats must be strapped into regular passenger seats.

FACILITIES➤ When making your reservation, **ask for children's meals or freestanding bassinets** if you need them; the latter are available only to those with seats at the bulkhead, where there's enough legroom. If you don't need a bassinet, **think twice before requesting bulkhead seats**—the only storage for in-flight necessities is in the inconveniently distant overhead bins.

LODGING

Most hotels allow children under a certain age to stay in their parents' room at no extra charge, while others charge them as extra adults; be sure to **ask about the cut-off age.**

CUSTOMS AND DUTIES

IN CHICAGO

Visitors aged 21 or over may import the following into the United States: 200 cigarettes or 50 cigars or 2 kilograms of tobacco; 1 U.S. liter of alcohol; gifts to the value of $100. Restricted items include meat products, seeds, plants, and fruits. Never carry illegal drugs.

BACK HOME

IN CANADA➤ Once per calendar year, when you've been out of Canada for at least seven days, you may bring in C$300 worth of goods duty-free. If you've been away less than seven days but more than 48 hours, the duty-free exemption drops to C$100 but can be claimed any number of times (as can a C$20 duty-free exemption for absences of 24 hours or more). You cannot combine the yearly and 48-hour exemptions, use the C$300 exemption only partially (to save the balance for a later trip), or pool exemptions with family members. Goods claimed under the C$300 exemption may follow you by mail; those claimed under the lesser exemptions must accompany you.

Alcohol and tobacco products may be included in the yearly and 48-hour exemptions but not in the 24-hour exemption. If you meet the age requirements of the province through which you reenter Canada, you may bring in, duty-free, 1.14 liters (40 imperial ounces) of wine or liquor or 24 12-ounce cans or bottles of beer or ale. If you are 16 or older, you may bring in, duty-free, 200 cigarettes, 50 cigars or cigarillos, and 400 tobacco sticks or 400 grams of manufactured tobacco. Alcohol and tobacco must accompany you on your return.

An unlimited number of gifts valued up to C$60

each may be mailed to Canada duty-free. These do not count as part of your exemption. Label the package "Unsolicited Gift—Value Under $60." Alcohol and tobacco are excluded.

IN THE U.K.➤ From countries outside the EU, including the United States, you may import duty-free 200 cigarettes, 100 cigarillos, 50 cigars or 250 grams of tobacco; 1 liter of spirits or 2 liters of fortified or sparkling wine; 2 liters of still table wine; 60 milliliters of perfume; 250 milliliters of toilet water; plus £136 worth of other goods, including gifts and souvenirs.

D

FOR TRAVELERS WITH DISABILITIES

When discussing accessibility with an operator or reservationist, **ask hard questions.** Are there any stairs, inside or out? Are there grab bars next to the toilet and in the shower/tub? How wide is the doorway to the room? To the bathroom? For the most extensive facilities, meeting the latest legal specifications, **opt for newer facilities,** which more often have been designed with access in mind. Older properties or ships must usually be retrofitted and may offer more limited facilities as a result. Be sure to **discuss your needs before booking.**

DISCOUNT CLUBS

Travel clubs offer members unsold space on airplanes, cruise

ships, and package tours at as much as 50% below regular prices. Membership may include a regular bulletin or access to a toll-free hot line giving details of available trips departing from three or four days to several months in the future. Most also offer 50% discounts off hotel rack rates. Before booking with a club, **make sure the hotel or other supplier isn't offering a better deal.**

DRIVING

Travelers coming from the east can take the Indiana Toll Road (I–80/90) westbound for about 30 miles to the Chicago Skyway (also a toll road), which runs into the Dan Ryan Expressway (I–90/94). Take the Dan Ryan north (westbound) just past the turnoff for I–290 to any of the Downtown eastbound exits (Monroe, Madison, Washington, Randolph, Lake) and drive east about a mile to reach Michigan Avenue. If you are heading to the Near North, take the Ohio Street exit eastbound and continue straight through local streets for about a mile to reach Michigan Avenue. Travelers coming from the south should take I–57 northbound to the Dan Ryan Expressway.

From the west, follow I–80 eastbound across Illinois to I–55, the major artery from the southwest. Continue east on I–55 to Lake Shore Drive. Those coming from areas due west of Chicago may prefer to pick up I–290 eastbound, which forks as it nears the city, heading to O'Hare in one direction (where it meets I–90) and to downtown Chicago in the other (where it ends).

From the north, take I–90 eastbound, which merges with I–94 south (eastbound) to form the Kennedy Expressway (I–90/94) about 10 miles north of Downtown. (I–90/94 is called the Kennedy Expressway north of I–290 and the Dan Ryan Expressway south of I–290).

WITHIN CHICAGO

Chicago's network of buses and rapid transit rail is extensive, and taxis and limousines are readily available (the latter often priced competitively with metered cabs), so **rent a car only to visit the outlying suburbs.** Chicago traffic is often heavy, on-street parking is nearly impossible to find, parking lots are expensive, congestion creates frustrating delays, and other drivers may be impatient with those who are unfamiliar with the city and its roads. There is extensive repair work underway on several of the city's major arteries, including Lake Shore Drive and the Kennedy Expressway (I–90/94), which causes a nightmare of snarled traffic during rush hours. In these circumstances, the visitor to Chicago may find a car to be a liability rather than an asset.

I
INSURANCE

Travel insurance can protect your investment, replace your luggage and its contents, or provide for medical coverage should you fall ill during your trip. Most tour operators, travel agents, and insurance agents sell specialized health-and-accident, flight, trip-cancellation, and luggage insurance as well as comprehensive policies with some or all of these features. Before you make any purchase, **review your existing health and homeowner's policies** to find out whether they cover expenses incurred while traveling.

BAGGAGE

Airline liability for your baggage is limited to $1,250 per person on domestic flights. On international flights, the airlines' liability is $9.07 per pound or $20 per kilogram for checked baggage (roughly $640 per 70-pound bag) and $400 per passenger for unchecked baggage. Insurance for losses exceeding the terms of your airline ticket can be bought directly from the airline at check-in for about $10 per $1,000 of coverage; note that it excludes a rather extensive list of items, shown on your airline ticket.

FLIGHT

You should **think twice before buying flight insurance.** Often purchased as a last-minute impulse at the airport, it

pays a lump sum when a plane crashes, either to a beneficiary if the insured dies or sometimes to a surviving passenger who loses eyesight or a limb. Supplementing the airlines' coverage described in the limits-of-liability paragraphs on your ticket, it's expensive and basically unnecessary. Charging an airline ticket to a major credit card often automatically entitles you to coverage and may also embrace travel by bus, train, and ship.

FOR U.K. TRAVELERS

According to the Association of British Insurers, a trade association representing 450 insurance companies, it's wise to **buy extra medical coverage when you visit the United States.** You can buy an annual travel-insurance policy valid for most vacations during the year in which it's purchased. If you go this route, make sure it covers you if you have a preexisting medical condition or are pregnant.

TRIP

Without insurance, you will lose all or most of your money if you must cancel your trip due to illness or any other reason. Especially if your airline ticket, cruise, or package tour is nonrefundable and cannot be changed, it's essential that you **buy trip-cancellation-and-interruption insurance.** When considering how much coverage you need, look for a policy that will cover the cost of your trip plus the nondiscounted price of a one-way airline ticket should you need to return home early. Read the fine print carefully, especially sections defining "family member" and "preexisting medical conditions." Also **consider default or bankruptcy insurance,** which protects you against a supplier's failure to deliver. However, such policies often do not cover default by a travel agency, tour operator, airline, or cruise line if you bought your tour and the coverage directly from the firm in question.

L
LODGING

APARTMENT AND VILLA RENTALS

If you want a home base that's roomy enough for a family and comes with cooking facilities, **consider a furnished rental.** It's generally cost-wise, too, although not always—some rentals are luxury properties (economical only when your party is large). Home-exchange directories do list rentals—often second homes owned by prospective house swappers—and some services search for a house or apartment for you (even a castle if that's your fancy) and handle the paperwork. Some send an illustrated catalogue and others send photographs of specific properties, sometimes at a charge; up-front registration fees may apply.

M
MONEY
AND EXPENSES

ATMS

Chances are that you can **use your bank card at ATMs** to withdraw money from an account and get cash advances on a credit-card account if your card has been programmed with a personal identification number, or PIN. Before leaving home, **check in on frequency limits** for withdrawals and cash advances.

On cash advances you are charged interest from the day you receive the money from ATMs as well as from tellers. Transaction fees for ATM withdrawals outside your home turf may be higher than for withdrawals at home.

TRAVELER'S CHECKS

Whether or not to buy traveler's checks depends on where you are headed; **take cash to rural areas and small towns, traveler's checks to cities.** The most widely recognized are American Express, Citicorp, Thomas Cook, and Visa, which are sold by major commercial banks for 1% to 3% of the checks' face value—it pays to shop around. American Express issues checks that can be counter-signed and used by you or your traveling companion. You can cash them in banks without paying a fee (which can be as much as 20%) and use them as readily as cash in many hotels, restaurants, and shops. Record the numbers of the checks, cross them off as you spend them, and keep this information separate from your checks.

WIRING MONEY

You don't have to be a cardholder to send or receive funds through MoneyGram℠ from American Express. Just go to a MoneyGram agent, located in retail and convenience stores and in American Express Travel Offices. Pay up to $1,000 with cash or a credit card, anything over that in cash. The money can be picked up within 10 minutes in cash or check at the nearest MoneyGram agent. There's no limit, and the recipient need only present photo identification. The cost, which includes a free long-distance phone call, runs from 3% to 10%, depending on the amount sent, the destination, and how you pay.

Money sent from the United States or Canada will be available for pickup at agent locations in 100 countries within 15 minutes. Once the money is in the system, it can be picked up at any one of 25,000 locations. Fees range from 4% to 10%, depending on the amount you send.

P.
PACKAGES
AND TOURS

A package or tour to Chicago can make your vacation less expensive and more convenient.

Firms that sell tours and packages purchase airline seats, hotel rooms, and rental cars in bulk and pass some of the savings on to you. In addition, the best operators have local representatives to help you out at your destination.

A GOOD DEAL?

The more your package or tour includes, the better you can predict the ultimate cost of your vacation. Make sure you know exactly what is included, and **beware of hidden costs.** Are taxes, tips, and service charges included? Transfers and baggage handling? Entertainment and excursions? These can add up.

Most packages and tours are rated deluxe, first-class superior, first class, tourist, and budget. The key difference is usually accommodations. If the package or tour you are considering is priced lower than in your wildest dreams, **be skeptical.** Also, **make sure your travel agent knows the hotels** and other services. Ask about location, room size, beds, and whether it has a pool, room service, or programs for children, if you care about these. Has your agent been there or sent others you can contact?

BUYER BEWARE

Each year consumers are stranded or lose their money when operators go out of business—even very large ones with excellent reputations. If you can't afford a loss, take the time to **check out the operator**—find out how long the company has been in business, and ask several agents about its reputation. Next, **don't book unless the firm has a consumer-protection program.** Members of the United States Tour Operators Association and the National Tour Association are required to set aside funds exclusively to cover your payments and travel arrangements in case of default. Nonmember operators may instead carry insurance; look for the details in the operator's brochure— and the name of an underwriter with a solid reputation. Note: When it comes to tour operators, **don't trust escrow accounts.** Although there are laws governing those of charter-flight operators, no governmental body prevents tour operators from raiding the till.

Next, **contact your local Better Business Bureau and the attorney general's office** in both your own state and the operator's; have any complaints been filed? Last, **pay with a major credit card.** Then you can cancel payment, provided that you can document your complaint. Always **consider trip-cancellation insurance** (*see* Insurance, *above*).

Big vs. Small➤ An operator that handles several hundred thousand travelers annually can use its purchasing power to give you a good price. Its high volume may also indicate financial stability. But some small companies provide more personalized service; because they tend to specialize, they may also be experts on an area.

USING AN AGENT

Travel agents are an excellent resource. In fact, large operators accept bookings only through travel agents. But it's good to **collect brochures from several agencies,** because some agents' suggestions may be skewed by promotional relationships with tour and package firms that reward them for volume sales. If you have a special interest, **find an agent with expertise in that area;** the American Society of Travel Agents can give you leads in the United States. (Don't rely solely on your agent, though; agents may be unaware of small niche operators, and some special-interest travel companies only sell direct).

SINGLE TRAVELERS

Prices are usually quoted per person, based on two sharing a room. If traveling solo, you may be required to pay the full double occupancy rate. Some operators eliminate this surcharge if you agree to be matched up with a roommate of the same sex, even if one is not found by departure time.

PACKING FOR CHICAGO

Pack light because porters and luggage

carts are hard to find. Be prepared for cold, snowy weather in the winter and hot, sticky weather in the summer. Jeans (shorts in summer) and T-shirts or sweaters and slacks are fine for sightseeing and informal dining. For many expensive restaurants, men will need jackets and ties, women dresses. **In winter pack boots** or a sturdy pair of shoes with nonslip soles for icy sidewalks, and a hat to protect your ears from the numbing winds that buffet Michigan Avenue. In summer, bring a swimsuit for Lake Michigan swimming or sunning.

Bring an extra pair of eyeglasses or contact lenses in your carry-on luggage, and if you have a health problem, **pack enough medication** to last the trip. In case your bags go astray, **don't put prescription drugs or valuables in luggage to be checked.**

LUGGAGE

Free airline baggage allowances depend on the airline, the route, and the class of your ticket; ask in advance. In general, on domestic flights you are entitled to check two bags—neither exceeding 62 inches, or 158 centimeters (length + width + height), or weighing more than 70 pounds (32 kilograms). A third piece may be brought aboard; its total dimensions are generally limited to less than 45 inches (114 centimeters), so it will fit easily under the seat in front of you or in the over-

head compartment. In the United States, the Federal Aviation Administration gives airlines broad latitude to limit carry-on allowances and tailor them to different aircraft and operational conditions. Charges for excess, oversize, or overweight pieces vary.

SAFEGUARDING YOUR LUGGAGE➤ Before leaving home, **itemize your bags' contents** and their worth, and label them with your name, address, and phone number. (If you use your home address, cover it so that potential thieves can't see it.) Inside your bag, **pack a copy of your itinerary.** At check-in, **make sure that your bag is correctly tagged** with the airport's three-letter destination code. If your bags arrive damaged or not at all, file a written report with the airline before leaving the airport.

PASSPORTS AND VISAS

CANADIANS

No passport is necessary to enter the United States.

U.K. CITIZENS

British citizens need a valid passport. If you are staying fewer than 90 days and traveling on a vacation, with a return or onward ticket, you will probably not need a visa. However, you will need to fill out the Visa Waiver Form, 1-94W, supplied by the airline.

While traveling, **keep one photocopy of the data page** separate

from your wallet and leave another copy with someone at home. If you lose your passport, promptly call the nearest embassy or consulate, and the local police; having the data page can speed replacement.

PUBLIC TRANSPORTATION

Most, but not all, rapid transit lines operate 24 hours; some stations are closed at night. (In general, late-night CTA travel is not recommended.) To transfer between the Loop's elevated ("El") lines and subway lines, or between rapid transit and bus service, you must use a transfer; be sure to **buy the transfer when you board the first conveyance.** Buses generally stop on every other corner northbound and southbound (on State Street they stop at every corner). Eastbound and westbound buses generally stop on every corner. Buses generally run either north or south from the Loop. Principal transfer points are on Michigan Avenue at the north side of Randolph Street for northbound buses, Adams and Wabash for westbound buses and the El, and State and Lake streets for southbound buses.

FARES

The CTA fare structure is as follows: The basic fare for rapid transit trains and buses is $1.50 weekdays; on weekends and holidays the fare is $1.25. **Use tokens for substantial** discounts; they can be used on both buses and trains. A roll of 10 costs $12.50. Tokens are sold at currency exchanges and Jewel and Dominick's supermarkets. Transfers, which must be bought when you board the bus or train, cost an extra 25¢; they can be used twice within a two-hour time period but not twice on the same route. Children ages 7–11 travel for between 75¢ and 85¢, depending on the hour. Children under 7 travel free. Several different weekly and monthly passes are available, but tokens are the most economical option for those staying in the city for only a short time.

R
RADIO STATIONS

Alternative Rock: Q101 101 FM, WXRT 93 FM; **Classical:** WFMT 98.7 FM; **Country:** WUSN 99.5 FM; **Jazz:** WNUA 95.5 FM; **National Public Radio:** WBEZ 91.5 FM; **News Stations:** WBBM 78 AM, WMAQ 67 AM; **Rock:** WCKG 105.9 FM; **R & B:** WGCI 107.5 FM; **Talk Radio & Local Sports:** WGN 72 AM.

RAIL TRAVEL

See Public Transportation, *above.*

RENTING A CAR

CUTTING COSTS

To get the best deal, **book through a travel agent and shop around.** When pricing cars, **ask where the rental lot is located.** Some off-airport locations offer lower rates—even though their lots are only minutes away from the terminal via complimentary shuttle. You may also want to **price local car-rental companies,** whose rates may be lower still, although service and maintenance standards may not be up to those of a national firm. Also **ask your travel agent about a company's customer-service record.** How has it responded to late plane arrivals and vehicle mishaps? Are there often lines at the rental counter, and, if you're traveling during a holiday period, does a confirmed reservation guarantee you a car?

INSURANCE

When you drive a rented car, you are generally responsible for any damage or personal injury that you cause as well as damage to the vehicle. Before you rent, **see what coverage you already have** by means of your personal auto-insurance policy and credit cards. For about $14 a day, rental companies sell insurance, known as a collision damage waiver (CDW), that eliminates your liability for damage to the car; it's always optional and should never be automatically added to your bill. California, New York, and Illinois have outlawed the sale of CDW altogether.

FOR U.K. CITIZENS

In the United States you must be 21 to rent a car; rates may be higher for those under 25. Extra costs cover child seats, compulsory for children under 5 (about $3 per day), and additional drivers (about $1.50 per day). To pick up your reserved car you will need the reservation voucher, a passport, a U.K. driver's license, and a travel policy covering each driver.

LOCAL INFORMATION

For information about getting around by car in Chicago and its suburbs, *see* Driving, *above.*

SURCHARGES

Before picking up the car in one city and leaving it in another, **ask about drop-off charges or one-way service fees,** which can be substantial. Note, too, that some rental agencies charge extra if you return the car before the time specified on your contract. To avoid a hefty refueling fee, **fill the tank just before you turn in the car.**

S
SENIOR-CITIZEN DISCOUNTS

To qualify for age-related discounts, **mention your senior-citizen status up front** when booking hotel reservations, not when checking out, and before you're seated in restaurants, not when paying your bill. Note that discounts may be limited to certain menus, days, or hours. When renting a car, **ask about promotional car-rental discounts**—they can net lower costs than your senior-citizen discount.

STUDENTS ON THE ROAD

To save money, **look into deals available through student-oriented travel agencies.** To qualify, you'll need to have a bona fide student I.D. card. Members of international student groups also are eligible. *See* Students *in* Important Contacts A to Z, *above.*

T

TAXIS

Chicago taxis are metered, with fares beginning at $1.50 for the first ⅕ mile and $1.20 for each additional mile. A charge of 50¢ is made for each additional passenger between the ages of 12 and 65, and a charge of 25¢ per bag may be levied when luggage is bulky. Taxi drivers expect a 15% tip.

TELEPHONES

LONG-DISTANCE

The long-distance services of AT&T, MCI, and Sprint make calling home relatively convenient and let you avoid hotel surcharges; typi-

cally, you dial an an 800 number in the United States.

W

WALKING

Chicago's **Pedway,** a pedestrianway system of skywalks and underground walkways, links more than 40 blocks in the central business district, connecting hotels, shops, office buildings, and apartments. Though it probably won't get you to everything you wish to visit, it can be a pleasant respite from crowded streets and unpleasant weather. Many entrances to the Pedway are marked, and maps are posted. You may also be able to get a map when you're in the Pedway.

WHEN TO GO

Chicago has activities and attractions to keep visitors busy at any time of year. Lake Michigan has a moderating effect on the city's weather, keeping it several degrees cooler in summer, a bit warmer in winter. Travelers whose principal concern is comfortable weather for touring

the city may prefer spring or fall, when moderate temperatures make it a pleasure to be out and about. Late fall in Chicago sees lavish Christmas decorations in the stores of the Magnificent Mile and the State Street Mall.

Summertime brings many opportunities for outdoor recreation, although temperatures will climb into the 90s in hot spells, and the humidity can be uncomfortably high.

Winters can see very raw weather and the occasional news-making blizzard, and temperatures in the teens are to be expected; come prepared for the cold. Yet mild winters, with temperatures in the 30s, are common, too. There are January sales to reward those who venture out, and many indoor venues allow you to look out on the cold in warm comfort.

CLIMATE

The following are the average daily maximum and minimum temperatures for Chicago.

Climate in Chicago

Jan.	32F	0C	May	65F	18C	Sept.	73F	23C
	18	− 8		50	10		58	14
Feb.	34F	1C	June	75F	24C	Oct.	61F	16C
	20	− 7		60	16		47	8
Mar.	43F	6C	July	81F	27C	Nov.	47F	8C
	29	− 2		66	19		34	1
Apr.	55F	13C	Aug.	79F	26C	Dec.	36F	2C
	40	4		65	18		23	− 5

1 Destination: Chicago

INTRODUCTION

A FEW YEARS AGO, the *Chicago Tribune* ran a piece in its Sunday magazine about what Chicago would be like without Lake Michigan. The artist's rendering showed a one-street town with a tumbleweed in the foreground. In many ways, Chicago *is* Lake Michigan. Whereas some cities radiate from a central hub, Chicago's heights squish clifflike to the lakeshore. On sunny summer weekends the whole city heads to the lakefront parks to swim (yes, you can swim in the lake, although the water could be cleaner), to sunbathe, to bicycle, to skate, to stroll, to jog, and just to soak up the atmosphere. Whatever the summer weather, it's always "cooler near the lake." In winter, many fleeting snowfalls come from the "lake effect," when cold clouds hit the warmer air above the water. The lake's moods range from glassy calm to roiling tempest, and the population reacts accordingly.

The city owes its origins to Lake Michigan. Chicago was born as a shipping center when it was discovered that a series of rivers and one portage could connect the lake with the Mississippi River. Any water traffic between the East Coast and the country's heartland had to pass through this damp, marshy land, christened Checagou, "place of the wild onion," by local Indians. In 1833 Chicago officially became a city. In 1836 ground was broken to turn the portage into a canal that was finally finished in 1848. The Illinois and Michigan Canal still links the Des Plaines and Illinois rivers.

People who like cities generally love Chicago. To urbanites, it has everything: architectural wonders old and new, gracious parks, cultural institutions that rival the world's finest, outstanding restaurants, classic and avant-garde theater, music from heavy metal to weary blues, nightlife, street life, urban grit, and urban sophistication. Because the city is not as large or as famous as New York, many Chicagoans suffer from "Second City" complex, a fear that out-of-towners won't appreciate their city's charms. But they're worrying needlessly, for the charms—from the stunning sweep of the skyline to the elegance of Michigan Avenue's shops to the tree-lined streets of the outlying neighborhoods—are hard to miss.

A number of events have left their mark on the city's history. The Great Fire of 1871 razed nearly every building between Roosevelt Road and Fullerton Avenue—a sizable chunk of the city, leaving behind a virtual blank canvas on which architects could design (*see* "The Builders of Chicago" *in* Chapter 9, Portraits). Such giants as Louis Sullivan and Daniel H. Burnham began experimenting with the steel frames that even today define the term "skyscraper." In these architects' wake came droves of carpenters, masons, and other laborers, who flocked here to build the new Chicago. Their arrival was nothing new to Chicago, which welcomed successive waves of Germans, Swedes, Poles, Irish, Jews, and Italians throughout the 19th and early 20th centuries.

Many of these immigrants came to work in the burgeoning industries here, and their eventual uprising against wretched labor conditions had a profound impact upon the city—and the country. When Upton Sinclair published his landmark novel *The Jungle,* describing the lives of Chicago's stockyard and meatpacking workers, the public outcry was so great that it led to the 1906 passage of the federal Pure Food and Drug Act. The Haymarket Riot of May 4, 1886, began as a demonstration by workers in sympathy with strikers at the McCormick Reaper plant and ended with a bomb explosion and a melee that killed four workers and seven policemen. The Haymarket became a rallying point for the world labor movement when eight "anarchists" were convicted of the bombing in a blatantly unjust trial, and four were executed. (Governor John P. Altgeld pardoned the others in 1893, committing political suicide in the process.)

THE LAWLESS ERA of Prohibition will forever be linked with Chicago in people's minds. Today's city hall would like people to forget the notorious criminals who subverted the police and courts and terrorized ordinary citizens here. The tourism council's "brief history" of the city breathes not a word about gangsters. But Al Capone and John Dillinger are more famous than Chicago luminaries Frank Lloyd Wright and Ludwig Mies van der Rohe (at least, they've had more movies made about them). According to a history of the city published in 1929, murders in Cook County rose from 190 in 1920 to 399 in 1928, and felony convictions fell almost 50%. And almost 24,000 felony charges were dropped or modified in 1923 alone, due primarily to "friendly" judges. If it didn't actually create the term "racketeer," Chicago played a key role in defining it.

Like so many American cities, Chicago saw its middle class flee to the suburbs during the postwar prosperity of the 1950s and the turbulence of the 1960s. Some neighborhoods turned from rich to poor, although many ethnic enclaves on the northwest and southwest sides remained relatively stable. But in the 1970s, young "urban pioneers" began to creep back to the city, picking up run-down properties for a song and renovating them into showplaces. Meanwhile, new groups of immigrants—Vietnamese, Thai, Cambodian, Hmong, Russian Jews—were finding their niches in the city. Today each of Chicago's dozens of neighborhoods has a distinct character: the wealthy socialite Gold Coast; "lakefront liberal" Lincoln Park and Lakeview; white-ethnic Bridgeport, Ukrainian Village, and Blue Island; black middle-class South Shore; integrated Hyde Park and Beverly; and battle-scarred ghettos such as North Lawndale and Austin. Black people and white people, divided as often by an economic abyss as by skin color, coexist with caution, although overt hatred has in many cases been replaced by the pragmatic need to get along in a city where neither group predominates. (Black and white each account for about 40% of Chicago's 2.6 million people.)

Nonetheless, factions abound. The North Side and the South Side are two different worlds. You're a White Sox fan or a Cubs fan, not both (unless one of the teams is down to the wire in a serious pennant race—a once-in-a-blue-moon event that sucks in even the nonfan). The conflicts in the city council, although currently muted, are legendary. Even in a city chronically strapped for cash, don't try to suggest closing an under-used public school or cutting service to a redundant El stop, except over the ward alderman's dead body.

It's true that Chicagoans can be contentious, territorial, and possessive. Although the city's official motto is "Urbs in Horto" (City in a Garden), its unofficial one is "Ubi est Meus?" (Where's Mine?). But to visitors, Chicagoans are as friendly and open as big-city dwellers can be. Perhaps the one thing that unites many of them is unparalleled civic chauvinism. Don't be shy about asking directions or questions; people will probably tell you more than you really want to know. You'll find the city straightforward and unpretentious: For every club imported from the coast where your outfit has to pass muster with the doorman, there are a hundred corner bars where you'll be welcome in anything from a tux to a T-shirt. To meet the real Chicago, try to get away from downtown a little and venture into the 'hoods, preferably with a local guide. (*See* Chapter 2, Exploring Chicago, for some of our favorites.) And if you get lost, just remember the one Chicago rule: The lake is east.

— Elizabeth Gardner

WHAT'S WHERE

The Chicago most visitors see first is the commercial and cultural heart of the city, the downtown and Near North areas that contain the world-famous architecture, the impressive skyline, the department stores, major hotels, and fine restaurants that together define a great American city. Yet there is another, equally interesting Chicago, vibrant with neighborhoods and their distinctive populations. Fodor's *Chicago '96*, through its walking tours and essays, examines the two Chicagos—the downtown and the neighborhoods—and tries to suggest the greater political and human entity that is the foremost city of the American Middle West.

The Loop

The heart of Chicago is the downtown area loosely bounded by elevated train lines, a.k.a. the Loop. Constantly evolving, the area in and around the tracks is stacked with handsome old landmark buildings and shimmering new ones. These are the centers of business and the mainstays of culture, new residential areas and renewed older districts.

Downtown South

In Downtown South, just south of the Loop, old forms take on new functions that merge with the life of the central city. Once thriving, this area decayed as its mainstay—the printing industry—moved out. Led by an aspiring restaurateur and ambitious investors, a gradual revival turned it into a thriving urban neighborhood enclave.

Hyde Park and Kenwood

Site of the World's Columbian Exposition of 1893, residence of the meatpacking barons Swift and Armour at the turn of the century, home of the University of Chicago, locale of five houses designed by Frank Lloyd Wright, and the nation's oldest stable racially integrated neighborhood, Hyde Park and the adjoining Kenwood are important historically, intellectually, and culturally. Turn-of-the-century mansions and workingmen's cottages are still there for the looking, along with museums, churches, and bookstores. All around are signs of the process of urban renewal and the changes it has wrought in the neighborhood.

South Lake Shore Drive

The best way to get from Hyde Park and Kenwood, which are south of downtown, back to the Loop is via South Lake Shore Drive. Chicago's skyline is awesome as it unfolds around every turn, and you'll also be able to pick out many individual skyscrapers from the panorama.

Near North

For many, Chicago highlife is the Near North, just across the river from the Loop. Glitzy shops along both sides of Michigan Avenue comprise what's known as the Magnificent Mile, and the side streets of Streeterville aren't lacking in riches either. To the east are the thriving, recently renovated Navy and North piers. In River North, rehabilitation has transformed an area of factories and warehouses into a neighborhood of upscale shopping strips and more than 50 art galleries.

Lincoln Park

The campuses of the old McCormick Seminary and De Paul University and the historic Biograph Theatre are included in our tour of Lincoln Park, a neighborhood that shares its name and part of its boundaries with the oldest park in Chicago's "emerald necklace," itself encompassing many wonders. Old Town Triangle, another section of the neighborhood, contains one of the oldest and most expensive streets in town.

North Clark Street

A ride up Clark Street, particularly the stretch of it north of Lincoln Park, is an urban tour through time and the waves of ethnic migration and replacement. Like north Milwaukee Avenue, which has gone from being Polish to Hispanic to Polish again as new immigrants have arrived, Clark Street is a microcosm of the city of Chicago and the continuing ebb and flow of its populations.

Argyle Street and Uptown

A walk on Argyle Street is one of the most complex experiences you can have in Chicago. You'll become totally immersed in the tastes and sounds of another culture; you'll see the classic immigrant pattern, the process of successful Americanization; and you'll appreciate the pushes and pulls at work as cities decay, are restored, and grow again. It is here that immigrant Vietnamese have created an economic miracle in one of Chicago's most depressed neighborhoods.

Devon Avenue

On Devon Avenue, in the city's far north side, immigrants from the Indian subcontinent live virtually side by side with Orthodox Jews newly arrived from Russia. This is an excellent area in which to find different customs and cultures in juxtaposition, and to sample their ethnic cuisines.

PLEASURES & PASTIMES

Architecture

The Chicago Fire of 1871, through its destruction, cleared a path for architectural experimentation. Architects flocked to rebuild the city, using new technology to develop the foundations of modern architecture. Louis Sullivan, William Holabird, John Wellborn Root, Frank Lloyd Wright, and Daniel Burnham are among the men whose creations influenced Chicago as well as cities around the world. They developed the skyscraper, and this type of structure fills the downtown skyline in hundreds of incarnations, from the crenelated Wrigley Building (Graham Anderson Probst and White) to the boxlike Federal Center and Plaza (Mies van der Rohe). Chicago and its environs also inspired Wright's low-lying Prairie School, exemplified in many Oak Park houses. The city still buzzes with new construction, though today's architects often favor the postmodern, as in Helmut Jahn's State of Illinois Center and the Harold Washington Public Library.

Blues

In the years following World War II, Chicago-style blues grew into its own musical form, flourishing in the 1950s, then fading in the 1960s with the advent of rock and roll. Today Chicago blues is coming back, although more strongly on the trendy North Side than on the South Side where it all began. Still, an evening at a blues club is a quintessential Chicago experience.

Eating

It takes a lot of energy to keep the "City of the Big Shoulders" going, and Chicago restaurants do the trick. Immigrants and their traditions give the dining scene variety and spice, their influence felt not just in ethnic storefront eateries but in bastions of haute cuisine. And then there's the all-American steak, to which there are many temples in town. During your visit, be sure to sample cuisine from all over the food spectrum: Polish sausage, Swedish pancakes, Thai curry, Greek *mezedes,* Japanese sashimi, Vietnamese noodle soup, and French cheeses are some of the delicious assortment of foods you can pile on your plate.

The Lake

Chicago wouldn't be the same without Lake Michigan. In fact, it might not even exist. But there it is, forming the city's eastern boundary, and providing residents with a constant source of conversation—the weather. It also provides much in the way of recreational opportunities, with more than 20 miles of trails (for walkers, skaters, and cyclists) and harbors and beaches. It's easy to appreciate the lake from nearby, but it's also a beautiful backdrop to the view from city skyscrapers.

Museums

The Art Institute, the Shedd Aquarium, the Field Museum, and the Museum of Science and Industry are some of the big names that attract the big crowds. They'll certainly satisfy many curiosities, whether it's Seurat, sharks, or stegosauruses, but smaller, more focused collections, of which there are many in Chicago, may give you a better chance to explore a particular interest. There's the Frank Lloyd Wright Home and Studio, for architecture buffs; the Bicycle Museum of America; the DuSable Museum, for African American history; the Terra Museum of American Art; the Spertus Museum of Judaica; and the International Museum of Surgical Sciences, to name a few.

Politics

The Windy City owes its designation not to the weather but to politics. Pick up a paper to read about the latest haranguing, or just look around. Lots of buildings are under construction or renovation—or not—thanks to long-fought political battles. You, too, can see the City Council in action, at the Chicago City Hall–Cook County Building.

FODOR'S CHOICE

No two people will agree on what makes a perfect vacation, but it's fun and helpful to know what others think. We hope you'll have a chance to experience some of our picks yourself while visiting Chicago. For detailed information about each entry, refer to the appropriate chapters in this guidebook.

Activities

★ **Strolling, biking, or rollerblading** along the lakefront, along with hundreds of other tourists and Chicagoans.

★ **Exploring the tomb of Unis-ankh,** at the Field Museum's "Inside Ancient Egypt."

★ **Singing "Take Me Out to the Ball Game"** during the seventh-inning stretch at Wrigley Field, regardless of who's winning.

★ **Viewing rain-forest animals** in a "thunderstorm" at the Brookfield Zoo.

Turn-of-the-Century Architecture

★ **Fisher Building.** Don't miss the cherubs as you enter this Gothic-style building.

★ **Monadnock Building.** One look at the thick base walls of this early skyscraper, and you'll see why the steel frame was such an innovation.

★ **Robie House.** A cantilevered roof, leaded glass windows, and the lack of a basement are typical of Frank Lloyd Wright's Prairie Style, of which this house is an excellent example.

★ **The Rookery.** It's exterior is imposing, but inside is an airy marble and gold leaf lobby.

Modern Architecture

★ **Northwestern Atrium Center.** Hordes of commuters rush through this train station–office tower every day; be sure to appreciate it outside and in.

★ **State of Illinois Center.** Love it or hate it, you're sure to find this red, white, and blue, postmodern, wedge-shaped structure intriguing. Take an elevator up to appreciate the atrium and its patterned floor.

★ **333 West Wacker Drive.** It's dark, shimmering glass curves along with the river, giving sense to the building's odd shape.

Special Moments

★ **Buckingham Fountain's evening light show,** held May 1–October 1.

★ **Gazing down upon the frenetic activity** on the trading floor from the fourth-floor visitor gallery at the Chicago Mercantile Exchange.

★ **Feeding time** at the coral reef of the John G. Shedd Aquarium, when sharks, eels, turtles, and the like get their lunch.

★ **The skylit sculpture court** at the Art Institute, some of the best sculptures you'll see indoors in Chicago.

★ **The winter orchid show** at the Chicago Botanic Garden, sure to brighten a blustery day.

Views

★ **Chicago River** from the Michigan Avenue Bridge, with the wedding-cake–like Wrigley building on one side, the Loop on the other.

★ **Chicago skyline from Olive Park,** where the lack of vehicular traffic makes you feel removed from the bustle.

★ **Chicago skyline from South Lake Shore Drive,** each curve providing a unique vista.

★ **The panorama of the city** from the top of the John Hancock Building—everything looks smaller from 96 stories up.

Restaurants

★ **Everest,** sure to be a peak experience for French food lovers. $$$$

★ **Park Avenue Cafe,** a newcomer, modeled on the Manhattan original, that serves imaginative American food. $$$$

★ **Spiaggia,** for luxury Italian dining and good views. $$$$

★ **Trio,** in Evanston, worth the trip for its wildly creative American dishes. $$$$

★ **Charlie Trotter's,** where the small dining room's only problem is that it won't ever accommodate all the people who'd like to try the experimental American cuisine. $$$–$$$$

★ **Yoshi's Café,** serving a tantalizing combination of French and Japanese. $$$–$$$$

★ **Arun's,** for delicious Thai food and upscale atmosphere. $$$

★ **Gibsons,** in Near North, arguably the convention crowd's favorite steak house. $$$

★ **Hubbard Street Grill,** classic American. $$$

★ **Vivere,** with its eye-catching decor and an interesting Italian menu. $$$

★ **Frontera Grill,** for cheery ambience, a constantly changing but always innovative and delicious Mexican menu, and the right price. $$

★ **Le Bouchon,** the best bistro in town. $$

★ **Heaven on Seven,** a coffee shop with remarkable Cajun and Creole specialties. $

★ **Lou Mitchell's,** homemade everything, and huge, delicious portions at this definitive luncheonette. $

Hotels

★ **The Four Seasons,** for Old World ambience where service is paramount. $$$$

★ **Omni Chicago Hotel,** comprising all suites, where you'll feel like you're staying at an English country manor. $$$$

★ **Omni Ambassador East,** elegant, gracious, and charming, and home to the Pump Room, restaurant of the rich and famous. $$$

★ **Belden-Stratford,** for Old Chicago feel and a peaceful location. $$

★ **Blackstone Hotel,** the choice of visiting presidents. You won't find every modern-day amenity here, but you won't be cramped or have to listen to Muzak either. $$

★ **The Raphael,** an intimate oasis near the John Hancock Building. $$

★ **City Suites Hotel,** a small, European-style hotel in Lakeview. $

★ **The Surf Hotel,** real character in the heart of Lincoln Park. $

FESTIVALS AND SEASONAL EVENTS

Chicagoans love celebrations. Spring and summer are the festival seasons, while celebrations move indoors for the winter. The following is a sampling of the many events in Chicago. For precise dates and details, contact the Chicago Office of Tourism (*see* Visitor Information *in* the Gold Guide's Important Contacts A to Z) or consult one of Chicago's local events calendars: *The Reader,* and *New City,* two free weekly newspapers distributed on Thursday in many stores in Hyde Park, the Loop, and the North Side; the "Friday" section of the Friday *Chicago Tribune;* and the "Weekender" section of the Friday *Chicago Sun-Times.*

WINTER

FEB.➤ **Black History Month** celebrations at the Museum of Science and Industry (57th St. and Lake Shore Dr., ☎ 312/684–1414), the DuSable Museum (740 E. 56th Pl., ☎ 312/947–0600), the Chicago Cultural Center (78 E. Washington St., ☎ 312/346–3278), the Field Museum (Roosevelt Rd. at Lake Shore Dr., ☎ 312/922–9410), the Art Institute of Chicago (Michigan Ave. at Adams St., ☎ 312/443–3600) and other Chicago cultural institutions include arts and crafts exhibitions and theater, music, and dance performances.

MID-FEB.–EARLY MAR.➤ **Azalea and Camellia Show** at Lincoln Park Conservatory (2400 N. Stockton Dr., ☎ 312/742–7736).

EARLY FEB.➤ **Chicago International Auto Show** previews the coming year's domestic and imported models (McCormick Pl., 2300 S. Lake Shore Dr., ☎ 708/954–0600).

LATE FEB.–MID-MAR.➤ **Medinah Shrine Circus** at Medinah Temple (600 N. Wabash Ave., ☎ 312/266–5000).

SPRING

MAR. 17➤ The Chicago River is dyed green and the center stripe of Dearborn Street is painted the color of the Irish for a **St. Patrick's Day parade** from Wacker Drive to Van Buren Street.

LATE MAR.–EARLY APR.➤ **Spring and Easter Flower Show** blooms at the Lincoln Park Conservatory.

MID-MAY➤ **International Art Exposition** at Navy Pier (600 E. Grand Ave., ☎ 312/791–6568) attracts more than 200,000 art aficionados.

MID-MAY➤ See masterpieces by Frank Lloyd Wright and other Prairie School architects on the **Wright Plus House Walk,** Oak Park (☎ 708/848–1978).

MAY 1–OCT. 1➤ **Buckingham Fountain,** in Grant Park, flows day and night. Colored lights nightly, 9–10, through October 1st.

SUMMER

EARLY JUNE➤ **Chicago Blues Festival** (☎ 312/744–3315) in Grant Park, a three-day, three-stage event featuring blues greats from Chicago and around the country.

EARLY JUNE➤ **57th Street Art Fair** (Ray School yard, 57th St., and Kimbark Ave.), one of the major juried art fairs in the Midwest, selects exhibitors from applicants from all over the country. Offerings include paintings, sculpture, jewelry, ceramics, and clothing and textiles (☎ 312/744–3315).

EARLY JUNE➤ **Old Town Art Fair** (Lincoln Park West and Orleans Sts., ☎ 312/337–1938), one of the top summer art fairs in quaint Old Town.

MID-JUNE➤ **Printer's Row Book Fair,** a two-day event in the historic Printer's Row District, is built around books and the printer's and binder's arts. Clowns, jugglers, and food vendors weave their way through displays from major and specialty booksellers and craftspeople demonstrating book-related arts (Dearborn St. between Harrison St. and Polk St., ☎ 312/987–9896).

MID-JUNE➤ The **Boulevard–Lakefront Bicycle Tour** (☎ 312/427–3325) brings 5,000 cyclists to the city's network of boulevards and parks for a 35-mile ride.

MID-JUNE➤ **Chicago Gospel Fest** brings its joyful sounds to Grant Park (☎ 312/744–5368).

LATE JUNE–MID-AUG.➤ **Grant Park Symphony Orchestra and Chorus** (☎ 312/742–7638) give four concerts weekly.

LATE JUNE–EARLY SEPT.➤ **The Ravina Festival** (☎ 312/728–4642) in Highland Park hosts a variety of classical and popular musical artists in a pastoral setting north of the city.

ALL SUMMER➤ **Noontime music and dance performances** are held outdoors weekdays at the Daley Plaza Civic Center (Washington St. between Dearborn and Clark Sts.) and at the First National Bank of Chicago Plaza (Dearborn St. at Madison St.).

JULY 3➤ Evening **fireworks** along the lakefront; bring a blanket and a portable radio to listen to the *1812 Overture* from Grant Park (☎ 312/744–3315).

EARLY JULY➤ **Taste of Chicago** (Columbus Dr. between Jackson and Randolph) feeds 4 million curious visitors with specialties from scores of Chicago restaurants.

LATE JULY➤ **Chicago to Mackinac Island Boat Race** originates at Belmont Harbor (Monroe St. Harbor, ☎ 312/861–7777).

LATE JULY–EARLY AUG.➤ The **Air and Water Show**

along the Near North lakefront at North Avenue features precision flying teams and antique and high-tech aircraft going through their paces.

LATE JULY–EARLY AUG.➤ **Newberry Library Book Fair** (60 W. Walton St., ☎ 312/943–9090) offers thousands of good, used books at low prices. The park across the street holds the Bughouse Square Debates the same weekend.

MID-AUG.➤ **Venetian Night** features fireworks and boats festooned with lights (Monroe St. Harbor, Grant Park, ☎ 312/744–3315).

LATE AUG.➤ **Chicago Triathlon** participants plunge in at Oak Street Beach for a 1-mile swim, followed by a 10-kilometer run and a 25-mile bike race on Lake Shore Drive.

LATE AUG.➤ **Chicago Jazz Festival,** is held at the Petrillo Music Shell in Grant Park.

LATE AUG.➤ **Viva Chicago,** a festival of Latin music, comes to Grant Park (☎ 312/744–8520).

AUTUMN

MID-SEPT.➤ **Festival of Illinois Film and Video Artists** (☎ 312/663–1600, ext. 434), a two-day visual arts display, has events at various theaters.

LATE SEPT.–EARLY OCT.➤ **Oktoberfest** brings out the best in beer and German specialties at the Berghoff Restaurant (17 W. Adams St., ☎ 312/427–3170) and Chicago area pubs.

MID-OCT.➤ The **Columbus Day Parade** follows Dearborn Street from Wacker Drive to Congress Street.

LATE OCT.➤ The **Chicago Marathon** (☎ 312/527–1105) starts at Daley Bicentennial Plaza and follows a course through the city.

LATE OCT.–EARLY NOV.➤ The **Chicago International Film Festival** brings new American and foreign films to the Music Box and Biograph theaters (☎ 312/644–3400).

SAT. BEFORE THANKSGIVING➤ The **Magnificent Mile Festival of Lights** kicks off the holiday season with a block-by-block illumination of hundreds of thousands of tiny white lights along Michigan Avenue and Oak Street.

THANKSGIVING WEEKEND➤ Friday marks the illumination of **Chicago's Christmas tree** in the Daley Center Plaza (Washington St. between Dearborn and Clark Sts.). The **Christmas parade,** with balloons, floats, and Santa travels down Michigan Avenue on Saturday.

LATE NOV.➤ **Chrysanthemum show** at Lincoln Park Conservatory.

LATE NOV.–DEC.➤ The **Christmas Around the World** display at the Museum of Science and Industry features trees decorated in the traditional styles of more than 40 countries.

LATE NOV.–DEC.➤ The Goodman Theatre (200 S. Columbus Dr., ☎ 312/ 443–3800) presents **A Christmas Carol,** and **The Nutcracker** is performed at the Arie Crown Theatre at McCormick Place (2300 S. Lake Shore Dr., ☎ 312/791–6000).

LATE DEC.–EARLY JAN.➤ **Christmas Flower Show** at Lincoln Park Conservatory.

2 Exploring Chicago

CHICAGO'S VARIETY IS DAZZLING. The canyons of the
Loop bustle with bankers, lawyers, traders, brokers,
politicians, and wheeler-dealers of all kinds, trans-
Updated by   acting their business in buildings that make architecture buffs swoon.
Julie Ann   Equally busy but sunnier is the Near North (near the Loop, that is),
Getzlaff   where the smart shops of Michigan Avenue give way to the headquarters
of myriad trade associations, advertising agencies, one of the nation's
leading teaching hospitals, and cathedrals of the Roman Catholic and
Episcopal churches.

Cultural life flourishes. The Shubert, Auditorium, and Goodman theaters, the Chicago bases for Broadway-scale shows, have been joined
by more than 40 small, neighborhood-based theaters where young actors polish their skills. The art galleries of Ontario and Superior streets
are alive and well, and there's a large new neighborhood of galleries
in resurgent River North. The Lyric Opera has extended its season into
February, offering eight productions annually that play to houses that
are, on average, 95% full; Chicago Opera Theatre augments the Lyric's
offerings with a spring season of smaller works. Chicago Symphony
subscriptions are a sellout; the Ravinia Festival and the Grant Park Concerts pack people in. Music lovers hungry for more turn to smaller performing groups: the Orpheus Band, Music of the Baroque, the Chicago
Brass Ensemble, Concertante di Chicago, and dozens more.

The city's skyline is one of the most exciting in the world. In the last
two decades the Sears Tower, the Amoco Building, the John Hancock
Building, the Stone Container Building (formerly the Associates Center), the NBC Building, Illinois Center, 333 West Wacker, the CNA Building, Lake Point Towers, and others have joined such legendary structures
as the Chicago Board of Trade, the Railway Exchange Building, and
the Wrigley Building.

Leave downtown and the lakefront, however, and you soon encounter
a city of neighborhoods: bungalows, two-flats, three-flats, and six-flats,
churches and shopping strips with signs in Polish, Spanish, Chinese,
Arabic, Hebrew, or Korean—symbols of an ethnic community life that
remains vibrant. The neighborhoods are the part of Chicago that a visitor rarely sees. Yet it is in the neighborhoods that one can encounter
the life of ordinary people, enjoy a great ethnic feast for a pittance,
and visit the museums and churches that house cultural artifacts reflecting the soul and spirit of the community. The hardscrabble Chicago
of emigrant enterprise may seem worlds away from Chicago the glitzy
megalopolis, but you can have no real understanding of the city without experiencing both.

Tour 1: The Loop

Numbers in the margin correspond to points of interest on the Tour
1: The Loop map.

Downtown Chicago, a.k.a the Loop, is a city lover's delight. It comprises the area south of the Chicago River, west of Lake Michigan, and
north of the Congress Parkway–Eisenhower Expressway. Downtown
Chicago's western boundary used to be the Chicago River, but the
boundary continues to push westward even as this book is written. Handsome new skyscrapers line every foot of South Wacker Drive east of
the river, and investors have sent construction crews across the bridges
in search of more land to fuel the expansion.

Exploring Chicago

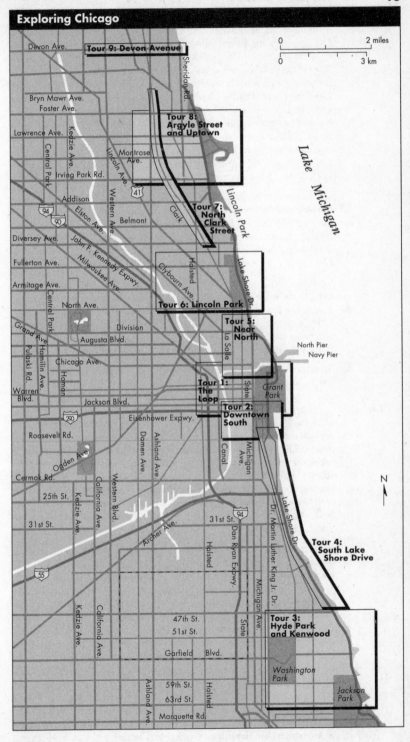

Devon Ave.

Bryn Mawr Ave.
Foster Ave.

Lawrence Ave.

Central Park

Kedzie Ave.

Lincoln Ave.

Western Ave.

Montrose Ave.

Irving Park Rd.

Addison

Belmont

41

94

90

Elston Ave.

Milwaukee Ave.

John F. Kennedy Expwy.

Diversey Ave.

Fullerton Ave.

Armitage Ave.

Central Park

Grand Ave.

Hamlin Ave.

Pulaski Rd.

North Ave.

Division

Augusta Blvd.

Homan

Warren Blvd.

Chicago Ave.

Jackson Blvd.

Eisenhower Expwy.

290

Roosevelt Rd.

Ogden Ave.

Cermak Rd.

25th St.

31st St.

Kedzie Ave.

California Ave.

Western Blvd.

Damen Ave.

Ashland Ave.

Archer Ave.

31st St.

94

Halsted

Dan Ryan Expwy.

Canal

Michigan Ave.

State

47th St.

51st St.

Garfield   Blvd.

Kedzie Ave.

California Ave.

Ashland Ave.

59th St.

63rd St.

Halsted

Marquette Rd.

55

Clark

Clybourn Ave.

Halsted

La Salle

State

Lincoln Park

Lake Shore Dr.

Sheridan Rd.

**Tour 8:
Argyle Street
and Uptown**

**Tour 7:
North
Clark
Street**

Tour 6: Lincoln Park

**Tour 5:
Near
North**

**Tour 1:
The
Loop**

**Tour 2:
Downtown
South**

Grant Park

North Pier

Navy Pier

Dr. Martin Luther King Jr. Dr.

Lake Shore Dr.

Michigan Ave.

**Tour 4:
South Lake
Shore Drive**

**Tour 3:
Hyde Park
and Kenwood**

Washington Park

Jackson Park

Lake Michigan

0   2 miles

0   3 km

N

We begin our tour on North Michigan Avenue at South Water Street. You can reach it from the north via Bus 3, 145, 146, 147, 151, or 157. Coming from the south, you can take Bus 3, 56, 145, 146, 147, 151, or 157; get off at Lake Street and walk one block north to South Water Street. If you arrive by car, you'll want to park it, for this tour is best done on foot. If possible, take this tour on a weekday; the lobbies of many of the office buildings discussed here are closed on weekends, and their interiors are some of the most interesting sights in the Loop. The tour will take at least a full day to complete; you may want to go as far as the Main Post Office (bullet 20 on the Loop map) on one day, and finish the tour on the next. If you decide to do this, you can catch Bus 151 from Union Station (bullet 19 on the Loop map) back to Michigan Avenue.

On the southwest corner of the intersection stands the elegant Art Deco
❶ **Carbide and Carbon Building** (230 N. Michigan Ave.). Designed by the Burnham Brothers in 1929, its sleek gold-and-black exterior is accented by curving, almost lacy brass work at the entrance. Inside, the lobby is splendid, with more burnished brass, glass ornamentation, and marble.

Continue south two blocks to Randolph Street. On the northwest corner, the office building with the distinctive angled, diamond-shape
❷ face is the **Stone Container Building,** formerly the Associates Center, (150 N. Michigan Ave.), the first building in Chicago to be wired for computer use; outlets in every office eliminate the need for costly cabling. An amusing sculpture sits in its small plaza.

❸ Two blocks east, the **Amoco Building** (200 E. Randolph St.), formerly the Standard Oil Building, was for a short time the largest marble-clad building in the world. Unfortunately, the thin slabs of marble, unable to withstand Chicago's harsh climate, began to warp and fall off soon after the building was completed. A two-year, $60-million project to replace the marble with light-colored granite was completed in 1992. The building looks as striking as it did before, but its massive presence is best viewed from a distance. The building sits on a handsome (if rather sterile) plaza, and Harry Bertoia's wind-chime sculpture in the reflecting pool makes interesting sounds when the wind blows. Next door is the **Prudential Building,** replaced in the late '60s as Chicago's tallest building by the John Hancock. Behind it rises a postmodern spire added in 1990.

Return west on Randolph Street to Michigan Avenue, walk south a
❹ block, and turn right onto East Washington Street, to the **Chicago Cultural Center** (78 E. Washington St., ☎ 312/744–6630 or 312/346–3278). When you've stepped inside the Romanesque-style entrance, notice the marble and the mosaic work before you climb the curving stairway to the third floor. There you'll find a splendid, back-lit Tiffany dome; Preston Bradley Hall, which houses the dome, is used for public events. Another Tiffany dome is on the second floor, and other parts of the building were modeled on Venetian and ancient Greek elements. More than an architectural marvel, however, the Cultural Center offers concerts and changing exhibitions. Civil War buffs will enjoy the artifacts on display in the Grand Army of the Republic Room. Here also is **'Round & About the Loop,** an information center that shows a seven-minute video about Chicago's downtown, and the new home of the **Museum of Broadcast Communications,** where you can see artifacts, audiotapes, and videotapes from the history of television and radio. There's a miniature TV studio where you can make a professional-quality video-

tape of yourself as a news anchor for $19.95 plus tax. ☎ 312/629–6000. *Free.* ⊙ *Mon.–Sat. 10–4:30, Sun. noon–5.*

❺ Turn right on leaving the Cultural Center from the Washington Street side, walk to Wabash Avenue, and enter **Marshall Field's & Co.** (111 N. State St.). This mammoth store boasts some 500 departments, and it's a great place for a snack or a meal; for the former, try the Crystal Palace ice cream parlor; for the latter, check out the grand Walnut Room or Hinky Dink Kenna's in the basement. Yet another spectacular Tiffany dome can be found on Field's southwest corner, near State and Washington streets. A recent multimillion-dollar renovation spruced up the entire store, though the synthetic look of the new atrium clashes drastically with the rest of the building's turn-of-the-century charm.

Exit Field's on State Street and turn right, heading north along the north end of the **State Street Mall.** Built a decade ago with federal funds, the mall was intended to revive the faltering State Street shopping strip by providing trees, sculptures, and outdoor cafés to encourage shoppers to visit the area and patronize the stores. Because of restrictions on the federal grant, however, the street could not be made a true pedestrian mall; it remained open to police cars, emergency vehicles, and buses, and has been a spectacular failure. The improvements and amenities were minimal: The new hexagonal gray concrete bricks are no more appealing than the original sidewalk, the few pieces of sculpture are undistinguished, and the outdoor cafés fail to thrive amid the exhaust fumes of the buses. The exodus of better stores to North Michigan Avenue and elsewhere has continued. However, the presence of department stores Field's and Carson's, and the hoards of business men and women, keep the Mall alive—at least on weekdays.

Cross Randolph Street. Half a block down, on your right, is the **Chicago Theatre** (175 N. State St.). Threatened with demolition in the mid-1980s, the 1921 Beaux Arts theater was saved through the efforts of a civic-minded consortium that bought the building and oversaw a multimillion-dollar restoration. It has had several managers who have been unable to make the theater a financial success. National tours of singers, mu-
❻ sicals, and variety acts are booked sporadically. Next door, the **Page Brothers Building** (177 N. State St.) is one of only two buildings in Chicago known to have a cast-iron front wall. Notice the delicate detail work on the horizontal and vertical bands between the windows. Notice also the very handsome building, directly across State Street, that houses WLS-TV, Chicago's ABC affiliate.

Turn back and head south along the State Street Mall. Across from Marshall Field's, on your right, notice the vacant lot across the street. Known as "Block 37," this lot was cleared a few years ago by developers and then abandoned when their deal fell through. Conscious that the space could become an eyesore, the city and several corporate sponsors have taken steps to use it for the civic good. In summer, it's used as an outdoor art gallery for the works of high school students, and in winter it's converted to "Skate on State," a small rink with free admission and skates available at a nominal charge.

❼ On the southwest corner of State and Washington streets is the **Reliance Building** (32 N. State St.). Designed by Daniel Burnham in 1890, it was innovative for its time owing to the use of glass and terra-cotta for its exterior. In 1985 the Mayor's Office decided to restore the building, and it is now undergoing a complete exterior renovation. The building should be restored to its original beauty by the first few months of 1996.

Tour 1: The Loop

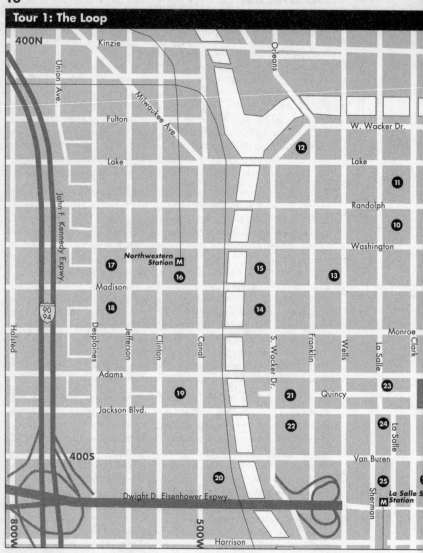

400N
Kinzie
Union Ave.
Milwaukee Ave.
Fulton
Orleans
W. Wacker Dr.
John F. Kennedy Expwy.
Lake
Lake
Randolph
Washington
12
11
10
Northwestern Station
17
16
15
13
Madison
Desplaines
Jefferson
Clinton
Canal
S. Wacker Dr.
Franklin
Wells
La Salle
Clark
Monroe
18
14
90 94
Halsted
Adams
Quincy
23
Jackson Blvd.
19
21
24
La Salle
22
4005
Van Buren
Sherman
25
20
La Salle St Station
Dwight D. Eisenhower Expwy.
800W
500W
Harrison

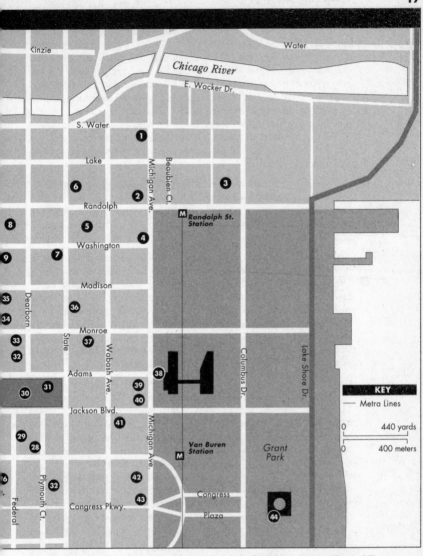

Kinzie

Water

Chicago River

E. Wacker Dr.

S. Water

1

Lake

6

3

Randolph

2

Michigan Ave.

Beaubien Ct.

M Randolph St.
Station

8

5

Washington

4

9

7

Madison

35

Dearborn

36

34

Monroe

State

33

37

Wabash Ave.

Columbus Dr.

Lake Shore Dr.

32

Adams

38

30

31

39

40

Jackson Blvd.

41

Michigan Ave.

29

28

Van Buren
Station

M

Grant
Park

6

Plymouth Ct.

32

42

Congress

Congress Pkwy.

43

Plaza

Federal

44

KEY

— Metra Lines

0   440 yards

0   400 meters

⑧ Heading west on Washington Street, we come to the **Daley Center**—named for late Mayor Richard J. Daley—where the Cook County court system is headquartered. The building is constructed of a steel known as Cor-Ten, which was developed as a medium that would weather naturally and attractively (and weathering has certainly improved its appearance). In the plaza is a sculpture by Picasso that is
★ made of the same material. Known simply as **"the Picasso,"** it provoked an outcry when it was installed in 1967. Speculation about what it is meant to represent (knowledgeable observers say it is the head of a woman; others have suggested it is a pregnant cow) has diminished but not ended. In summer the plaza hosts concerts, dance presentations, and a farmer's market.

⑨ Directly opposite the Daley Center is the **Chicago Temple** (77 W. Washington St.), a Methodist church whose beautiful spire is so tall that it is best seen at some distance; the bridge across the river at Dearborn Street is a good spot for viewing it. In the plaza is Joan Miró's sculpture *Chicago* (1981).

Walk a half block west on Washington to Clark Street and turn right (north). Right across from the Daley Center is the handsome, neoclassical
⑩ **Chicago City Hall–Cook County Building** (designed by Holabird and Roche in 1911), whose appearance is generally ignored by the citizens who rush in and out to do business with the city. Inside are spacious halls, high ceilings, plenty of marble, and lots of hot air, for this is where the Chicago City Council holds its infamous meetings. *121 N. La Salle St., ☎ 312/744–2725, free tour daily at 10. City council meetings are open to the public. Call 312/744–3081 for meeting times.*

Continue north on Clark for a block, and you'll reach the much-dis-
⑪ cussed **State of Illinois Center** (100 W. Randolph St.). Governor James Thompson, who selected the Helmut Jahn design for the building, hailed it in his dedication speech in 1985 as "the first building of the 21st century." Those who work there, and many other Chicagoans as well, have groaned in response, "I hope not." It is difficult to say more about the postmodern design of the building than to point out that it presents multiple shapes and faces. Narrow alternating vertical strips of mirrored and plain glass give the impression of taffeta streamers flying from a giant maypole. Many of its features, such as the practically dissolving keystone structures around the exterior, and the exposed escalator and elevator mechanics inside, were meant to break down barriers between the government and the people. And, like all good government buildings, it is capped by a dome. Some people love it and some do not; the structure's sky blue, white, and red exterior colors have elicited such adjectives as "garish" and "tacky." Its enormous interior atrium embraces a volume of 8 million cubic feet. The dramatically patterned circular floor at its base and the soaring vistas from the elevators and landings are impressive.

Guarding the entrance of the State of Illinois Center, on the northwest corner of Randolph and Clark streets, is *Monument to a Standing Beast,* a sculpture by Jean Dubuffet. Its curved shapes, in white with black traceries, set against the curving red, white, and blue of the center, add to the visual cacophony.

Now let's look at a building roughly contemporary to the State of Illinois Center that has had a very different public reception. Head west on Randolph Street, turn right on La Salle Street, left on Lake Street,
⑫ and walk two blocks to Franklin Street. The building at **333 West Wacker Drive,** designed by Kohn Pedersen Fox in 1983 and constructed on a

triangular plot, has forest-green marble columns, a spacious plaza, and a shimmering green glass skin. The unpromisingly irregular shape of the parcel on which it sits has been turned into an advantage, as the building's soft curve on the Wacker Drive side allows it to mimic and mirror the curve of the river. The structure is particularly lovely when viewed from the Orleans Street bridge over the Chicago River at sunset, when the river and surrounding buildings are reflected in the glass.

Walk three blocks south on Franklin to Madison Street and turn left. One block east, at Madison and Wells streets, is a 1983 Louise Nevelson sculpture—a vigorous, forceful construction of darkened steel incongruously titled **Dawn Shadows.**

Turn back and head west on Madison Street to Wacker Drive. Regard the pale grape-color buildings to your left; they are the twin towers of the **Chicago Mercantile Exchange** (10 and 30 S. Wacker Dr.). The visitor's gallery of the Merc, located on the 4th floor, is open weekdays from 7:30 AM to 3:15 PM and looks down on the frenetic activity on the trading floor. While it may look like utter chaos, the traders' shouts and frenzied hand movements are negotiations of the purchase and sale of billions in pork-belly futures (they have to do with the supermarket price of bacon), soybeans, currency rates, and other commodities on national and international markets.

TIME OUT   If you're hungry, stop into the **Wall Street Deli,** on the first floor of the building. It serves excellent soups (especially chicken gumbo), hot and cold sandwiches, and salads. If you really like your meal, you can purchase stock in the deli, as it is publicly traded on the stock market.

Upon exiting the Mercantile Exchange, cross Madison Street to view the **Civic Opera House** (20 N. Wacker Dr., ☎ 312/332–2244), where Chicago's Lyric Opera gives its performances. Built by the utilities magnate and manipulator Samuel Insull, the handsome Art Deco building is also an elegant older office building. The Civic Opera House is very grand indeed, with marble floors and pillars in the main hall, crystal chandeliers, and a marvelous sweeping staircase to the second floor. Lyric Opera performances are oversubscribed (subscriptions are willed to succeeding generations), so don't expect to just drop in on one of the productions (the season runs from late September through February). Nevertheless, if you stop by the corner of Madison Street and Wacker Drive early on the evening of a performance, you may find ticket holders with an extra ticket to sell. Right next door, on the north side of the Civic Opera House, is the equally ornate **Civic Theatre.**

Turn back onto Madison Street and continue west, crossing the Chicago River, to Canal Street and the smashing **Northwestern Atrium Center** (500 W. Madison St.), which replaced the old Northwestern Station and serves as one of several stations throughout the city for commuter trains to far-flung suburban areas. The building combines a boxlike office tower with glass half cylinders piled one atop the other at the lower levels. Broad contrasting horizontal bands of mirrored and smoked glass alternate up the building for a ribbon effect that is reminiscent of a similar theme—by the same architects—at the State of Illinois Center. Inside, the marble floors and exposed girders, painted a soft grayish blue, remind you of the grand old railroad stations in this country and in Europe. The girders seen against the rippling exterior glass make beautiful geometric patterns. The area over the entrance simulates a rose window in steel and clear glass. The gates to the tracks, elevated above street level to allow traffic to proceed east and west via underpasses, are reached by going up one level and heading to the north end of the building. Go up another flight for a grand view northward looking out over the tracks; at this level you'll also find the entrance to the building's office spaces.

⑰ Two blocks west is the **Social Security Building** (600 W. Madison St.), once a distant outpost in a dangerous neighborhood that was selected by the federal government because it was a low-rent district. Today the structure is one of several good-looking contemporary and renovated buildings in the area. Of interest here is pop-art sculptor Claes Oldenburg's *Batcolumn,* a gigantic baseball bat that failed to get critical acclaim when it was unveiled in 1977. Yet a 100-foot-high baseball bat is an amusing sight, and the current development west of the river will allow even more people the opportunity for a smile at this whimsical construction.

Directly across from the *Batcolumn* are the buildings that make up the
⑱ **Presidential Towers** residences. The easternmost and main building of the four is at 555 West Madison Street. Best seen from a distance, these attractive, if not architecturally distinguished, structures have lured some suburbanites back to the city and persuaded other young adults not to move away. An upscale supermarket, several fast-food restaurants, a drugstore, and other shops cater to the daily needs of the residents. The complex extends west to Des Plaines Street and south to Monroe Street, with the buildings aligned on a southwesterly diagonal.

Retrace your steps, walking east on Madison Street. Turn right onto
⑲ Canal Street and head south to the wonderful old (1917) **Union Station** (210 S. Canal St.). It's everything a train station should be, with a 10-story dome over the main waiting room, a skylight, columns, and gilded statues. Amtrak trains arrive and depart from here, as do suburban Metra trains.

⑳ Continue south on Canal if you'd like to see Chicago's **Main Post Office** (433 W. Van Buren St., ☎ 312/765–3802), the world's largest. Tours of this mammoth, highly automated facility are given weekdays at 10:30 AM or 12:30 PM. Call one week in advance; no children under nine admitted.

From the post office, return north along Canal Street and turn right
㉑ onto Jackson Boulevard. Cross the river and continue east to **Sears Tower** (233 S. Wacker Dr.). A Skidmore, Owings & Merrill design of 1974, Sears Tower has 110 stories and is almost 1,500 feet tall. Although this is the world's tallest building (until the Petronas towers in Kuala Lumpur, Malaysia, are completed), it certainly isn't the world's most livable one. Despite costly improvements to the Wacker Drive entrance (most of the street traffic is on the Franklin Street side) and the main-floor arcade area, the building doesn't really attract passersby.

Once inside, you'll probably be baffled by the dozens of escalators and elevators that stop on alternate floors (the elevators have double cars, one atop the other, so that when one car has stopped, say, at 22, the other is at 21). If you need to go to the upper reaches of the building (other than to go via direct express elevator to the 103rd-floor Skydeck), you'll find that you have to leave one elevator bank, walk down the hall and around a corner, and find another to complete your trip. There are rumors about new employees on the upper stories who spent their entire lunch hour trying to find a way out. In high winds the building sways noticeably at the upper levels and, most alarming, in 1988 there were two occasions on which windows were blown out. According to the architects and engineers, the odds against this happening even once were astronomical; imagine how red their faces must have been the second time it happened. When it did happen, the streets surrounding the building were littered with shards of glass, and papers were sucked out of offices that had lost their windows. On a clear day, however, the view from the Skydeck is unbeatable. (Check the visibility ratings at the security desk before you decide to ride up and take it in.) And don't miss the Calder mobile sculpture *The Universe* in the lobby on the Wacker Drive side. *Skydeck:* ☎ *312/875–9696.* ● *$6.50 adults, $3.25 children 5–17.* ☉ *Daily, Jan.–Feb. and Oct.–Dec. 9 AM–10 PM, Mar.–Sept. 9 AM–11 PM.*

㉒ Across Jackson Boulevard from the Sears Tower is **311 South Wacker Drive,** designed by Kohn Pedersen Fox and completed in 1990; this tower is the first of three intended for the site. The building's most distinctive feature is the "white castle" crown, which is blindingly lighted at night. During migration season so many birds killed themselves crashing into the illuminated tower that the building management was forced to tone down the lighting, though it wasn't turned off. The interior has a spectacular winter garden atrium entry with palm trees; it's the perfect spot for lunch in the colder months.

Continue east on Jackson Boulevard and turn left onto cavernous La
㉓ Salle Street. On the east side of the street is **The Rookery** (209 S. La Salle St.), an imposing red-stone building designed in 1886 by Burnham and Root. The Rookery was built partly of masonry and partly
★ of the more modern steel-frame construction. The magnificent **lobby** was remodeled in 1905 by Frank Lloyd Wright, and renovation has maintained his vision of airy marble and gold leaf. The result is a marvelous, lighthearted space that should not be missed.

Retrace your steps along La Salle Street to Jackson Boulevard, where
㉔ the street seems to disappear in front of the **Chicago Board of Trade** (141 W. Jackson Blvd., ☎ 312/435–3500). One of the few important Art Deco buildings in Chicago—the Civic Opera House and the Carbide and Carbon building are the others—it was designed in 1930 by the firm of Holabird and Root. At the top is a gilded statue of Ceres, the Roman goddess of agriculture, an apt overseer of the frenetic commodities trading that goes on within. The observation deck that over-
★ looks the trading floor is open to the public weekdays, 9–2. The **lobby** is well worth your attention.

Upon leaving the Board of Trade, walk east on Jackson Boulevard a half block, where La Salle Street continues. Turn right and head south, crossing Van Buren Street, to the striking 1985 building by Skidmore,
㉕ Owings & Merrill that is known as **One Financial Place** (440 S. La Salle St.). Both the exterior and interior are made of Italian red granite and marble, and among the building's interesting features is an arched section that straddles rushing traffic on the Congress Parkway/Eisenhower Expressway. The building's tenants include the Midwest Stock Exchange, whose visitor's gallery is open weekdays, 8:30–3, and the La Salle Club, which offers limited but elegant hotel accommodations and is the home of the superb Everest restaurant (*see* Chapter 5, Dining).

Walk back to Van Buren Street and turn right, heading east. Just past Clark Street, the odd, triangular, poured-concrete building looming up
㉖ on your right-hand side is the **Metropolitan Correctional Center** (71 W. Van Buren St.). A jail (rather than a penitentiary, where convicted criminals are sent), it holds people awaiting trial as well as those convicted and awaiting transfer. When erected in 1975, it brought an outcry from citizens who feared large-scale escapes by dangerous criminals. (Their

fears have not been realized.) The building was designed by the same Harry Weese who saved the Auditorium Theatre; with its long, slit windows (5 inches wide, so no bars are required), it looks like a modern reconstruction of a medieval fort, where slits in the walls permitted archers to shoot at approaching invaders.

Walk four blocks farther east on Van Buren Street to State Street and turn right. Taking up an entire block between Van Buren and Congress, the **Harold Washington Library Center** is a postmodern homage to classical-style public buildings. Chosen from six proposals submitted to a design competition, the granite and brick structure has some of the most spectacular terra-cotta work seen in Chicago since the 19th century: ears of corn, faces with puffed cheeks (representing the Windy City), and the logo of the Chicago Public Library are a few of the building's embellishments. In its final stages of construction, the building looked so much like the vintage skyscrapers around it that visitors mistook it for a renovation project. The library's interior is for the most part disappointingly cramped, and many Chicago residents point to problems with broken equipment and unshelved books as evidence that the city's investment in the library was more show than substance. The center's holdings include more than 2 million books and special collections on Chicago theater, Chicago blues, and the Civil War. For a special treat, check out the second-floor children's library, an 18,000-square-foot haven for the city's youngsters that includes a charming storytelling alcove. The primary architect was Thomas Beeby, of the Chicago firm Hammond Beeby Babka, who now heads the School of Architecture at Yale University. *400 S. State St., ☎ 312/747–4300. ✎ Free. ☉ Mon. 9–7; Tues., Thurs. 11–7; Wed., Fri., Sat. 9–5; Sun. noon–5. Tours daily; call for information.*

Retrace your steps back to Van Buren Street, walking west to Dearborn Street and the **Fisher Building** (343 S. Dearborn St.), designed by D.H. Burnham & Co. in 1896. This Gothic-style building, exquisitely ornamented in terra-cotta, is for some reason (perhaps because of favorable rents) the headquarters of dozens of arts and other not-for-profit organizations. Notice the beautifully carved cherubs frolicking over the glassed-in Van Buren Street entrance.

Across the street is the massive, darkly handsome **Monadnock Building** (54 W. Van Buren St.). The north half was built by Burnham and Root in 1891, the south half by Holabird and Roche in 1893. This is the tallest building ever constructed entirely of masonry. The problem with all-masonry buildings is that the higher they go, the thicker the base's walls must be to support the upper stories: The Monadnock's walls at the base are 6 feet thick. You can see why the introduction of the steel frame began a new era in construction. The building was recently and tastefully renovated inside (the original wrought-iron banisters, for example, have been retained) and cleaned outside, restoring it to its former magnificence from the rather dilapidated and slightly creepy hulk it had become. This is a popular office building for lawyers because of its proximity to the federal courts in the Kluczynski Building, which is next on our tour.

Continue north on Dearborn, crossing Jackson Boulevard. On the left-hand side of the street is The Kluczynski (219 S. Dearborn St.) and its twin federal building, the Dirksen (230 S. Dearborn St.). Both are part of the **Federal Center and Plaza.** Built in 1964, both buildings are classic examples of the trademark Mies van der Rohe glass-and-steel box. For the best view of both buildings, head one block east on Jackson to Dearborn Street and turn left. In the center's plaza, on the west side of Dearborn, is *Flamingo*. This wonderful Calder stabile—a sculpture that looks like a mobile—was dedicated on the same day in 1974 as Calder's *Universe* at the Sears Tower. It is said that Calder had a grand day, riding through Chicago in a brightly colored circus bandwagon accompanied by calliopes, heading from one dedication to the other.

③① Continue north on Dearborn to Adams Street and then jog a bit eastward to have a look at the westernmost building of the **Berghoff Restaurant** (17 W. Adams St.). Although at first glance it appears as though the front is masonry, it is in fact ornamental cast iron. The practice of using iron panels cast to imitate stone was common in the latter part of the 19th century (this building was constructed in 1872), but this building and the **Page Brothers Building** on State Street, built in the same year, are the only examples known to have survived. The iron front on the Berghoff building was discovered only a few years ago, and other such buildings may yet be extant, waiting to be found. If you're in need of refreshment, step inside for a hearty German meal or a pint or two of beer.

③② Walk back to Dearborn Street and turn right, heading north. The **Marquette Building** (140 S. Dearborn St.) of 1894, by Holabird and Roche, features an exterior terra-cotta bas-relief and interior reliefs and mosaics depicting scenes from early Chicago history.

③③ Walk the rest of the block north to Monroe Street; on the southwest corner is the **Xerox Building** (55 W. Monroe St.), designed in 1982 by the same firm (Murphy/Jahn) that would be responsible three years later for the State of Illinois Center. The building's wraparound aluminum-and-glass wall extends from the Monroe Street entrance around the corner onto Dearborn Street, communicating both vitality and beauty.

③④ Across Monroe Street is the famous **First National Bank Plaza,** which runs the length of the block from Dearborn to Clark streets. In summer, the plaza is the site of outdoor performances by musicians and dancers and a hangout for picnickers and sunbathers. In any season you can visit the Chagall mosaic *The Four Seasons* (1974) at the northeast end of the plaza, between Madison and Monroe streets on Dearborn Street. It is said that when Chagall arrived in Chicago to install the mosaic, he found it a more vigorous city than he had remembered, and he immediately modified the work to reflect the stronger and more vital elements he found around him. Not one of Chagall's greatest works, it is nevertheless a pretty, pleasing, sometimes lyrical piece.

From the Bank Plaza, glance across Dearborn to the turquoise-tinted **Inland Steel Building,** a 1957 homage to steel and glass by Skidmore, Owings & Merrill, and one of the first skyscrapers in the Loop. The supporting columns are outside the curtain wall, and there are none in the interior, so office spaces are completely open. All the elevators, stairs, and service areas are in the taller structure behind the building proper.

③⑤ Abutting the plaza that bears its name, at Dearborn and Madison streets, is the **First National Bank of Chicago.** Designed by Perkins and Will in 1973, this structure was a sensation when it was built because it slopes upward from its base in a shape that looks like an ornate letter *A*. Today it's just another good-looking downtown office building.

Now turn right onto Madison Street. Walk one block to State Street and turn right again. Halfway down the block, on the east side of the
③⑥ street, is **Carson Pirie Scott** (1 S. State St.), known to architecture stu-

dents as one of Louis Sullivan's outstanding works. The building illustrates the windowpane developed by the so-called "Chicago School" of architects: a large fixed central pane with smaller movable windows on each side. Notice also the fine exterior ornamentation at street level, ★ particularly the exquisite work over the **entrance** on the southeast corner of Madison and State streets. Dedicated shoppers may be less interested in the architecture of the building than in Carson Pirie Scott's contents; Chicago's "second" department store (always mentioned after Marshall Field's & Co.) is a bit tired looking inside, but it still carries a wide range of good-quality merchandise.

③⑦ The **Palmer House** (17 E. Monroe St., ☎ 312/726–7500), one of Chicago's grand old hotels, is one block south of Carson's, between State and Wabash; enter from Monroe Street, about halfway down the block. The ground-floor level is an arcade with patterned marble floors and antique lighting fixtures where you'll find upscale shops, restaurants, and service establishments. But it's the lobby—up one flight of stairs—that you must see: Richly carpeted, outfitted with fine furniture, and lavishly decorated (look at the ceiling murals), this room is one of the few remaining examples of the opulent elegance that was once de rigueur in Chicago's fine hotels.

From Palmer House, head east on Monroe Street and south on Michigan Avenue to Adams Street and the imposing entrance to the mar-
★ ③⑧ velous **Art Institute of Chicago.** You'll recognize the Art Institute by its guardian lions on each side of the entrance. (The lions have a special place in the hearts of Chicagoans, who outfitted them with Chicago Bears helmets when the Bears won the Super Bowl.) A map of the museum, available at the information desk, will help you find your way to the works or periods you want to visit. The Art Institute has outstanding collections of Medieval and Renaissance paintings as well as Impressionist and Postimpressionist works. Less well-known are its fine holdings in Asian art and its photography collection. Be sure to visit the Rubloff paperweight collection; a Chicago real-estate magnate donated these shimmering, multicolored functional objects. The Thorne Miniature Rooms show interior decoration in every historical style; they'll entrance anyone who's ever furnished a dollhouse or built a model. And don't miss the Stock Exchange room, a splendid reconstruction of the trading floor of the old Chicago Stock Exchange, which was demolished in 1972. The Daniel F. and Ada L. Rice Building has three floors of exhibition galleries, a large space for temporary exhibitions, and a skylighted central court dotted with sculpture and plantings.

If you have a youngster with you, make an early stop at the Children's Museum downstairs. Your child can choose from an assortment of 25 or so Gallery Games, some of which come with picture postcards. The delightful and informative games will keep kids from becoming hopelessly bored as you tramp through the galleries. The museum store has an outstanding collection of art books, calendars, merchandise related to current exhibits, and an attractive selection of gift items. *S. Michigan Ave. at Adams St.,* ☎ *312/443–3600.* ☛ *$6.50 adults, $3.25 senior citizens and children, free Tues.* ☉ *Weekdays 10:30–4:30 (Tues. until 8), Sat. 10–5, Sun. and holidays noon–5. Closed Thanksgiving and Dec. 25.*

TIME OUT   From Memorial Day to mid-September, an outdoor **café** in the **Art Institute's courtyard** is a charming spot for lunch. In inclement weather, there's the **Court Cafeteria,** which has snacks and family fare; **Restaurant on the Park** offers a more upscale menu.

㊳   **Orchestra Hall** (220 S. Michigan Ave., ☎ 312/435–6666), opposite the Art Institute, is the home of the internationally acclaimed Chicago Symphony Orchestra. Don't expect to find symphony tickets at the box office; subscription sales exhaust virtually all the available tickets. (You'll have better luck at hearing the symphony during the summer if you make the trek to Ravinia Park in the suburb of Highland Park. *See* Chapter 8, Excursions from Chicago) Sometimes it pays to stop by Orchestra Hall about an hour before a concert; there may be last-minute ticket returns at the box office, or there may be street-corner vendors. If you'd like to see the inside of Orchestra Hall, regardless of who's performing, buy a ticket to one of the recitals that are scheduled frequently, particularly on Sunday afternoon. For an incredible view, get a balcony ticket. The balconies are layered one atop the other in dramatic fashion, and because the seats are steeply banked, the view is splendid and the acoustics are excellent.

㊵ Next door is the Railway Exchange Building, better known as the **Santa Fe Building** (80 E. Jackson Blvd.; enter on Michigan Ave.) because of the large, rooftop "Santa Fe" sign that's now an integral part of Chicago's nighttime skyline. (The sign was put up early in the century by the Santa Fe Railroad, which had offices in the building.) Designed in 1904 by Daniel Burnham, who later had his office here, it underwent an extensive and very successful renovation a decade ago. The interior atrium is spectacular. The **Chicago Architecture Foundation (CAF) Shop and Tour Center** is here (☎ 312/922–3432 or 312/922–8687 for recorded information). CAF tours of the Loop originate at the center.

㊶ From the corner of Michigan Avenue and Jackson Boulevard, peer west to Wabash Avenue for a look at the rust-color **CNA Building.** On no one's list of landmarks, the structure is interesting principally because it leaves such a noticeable mark on the skyline. Chicagoans who thought the color was an undercoat of rustproofing paint that would be covered over by something more conventional were wrong.

㊷ Continuing south on Michigan Avenue, you'll reach the **Fine Arts Building** (410 S. Michigan Ave.). Notice first the handsome detailing on the exterior of the building; then step inside to see the marble and the woodwork in the lobby. The motto engraved in the marble as you enter says, "All passes—art alone endures." The building once housed artists and sculptors in its studios; today its principal tenants are professional musicians and those who cater to musicians' needs. A fine little music shop is hidden away on the ninth floor, and violin makers and other instrument repair shops are sprinkled about. The building has an interior courtyard, across which strains of piano music and soprano voices compete with tenors as they run through exercises and arias. The ground floor of the building, originally the Studebaker Theatre (the building was constructed to house the showrooms of the Studebaker Co., then makers of carriages), was converted into four cinemas in 1982, and the individual theaters have preserved much of the beautiful ornamentation of the original. The Fine Arts Theatres present an exceptional selection of foreign films, art films, and movies by independent directors.

㊸ Continue on Michigan Avenue to the Congress Parkway and **Roosevelt University,** a massive building that houses the remarkable **Auditorium Theatre** (430 S. Michigan Ave.). Built in 1889 by Dankmar Adler and Louis Sullivan, the hall seats 4,000 people and has unobstructed sight lines and near-perfect acoustics. It was allowed to fall into disrepair and even faced demolition in the 1950s and early 1960s, but determined supporters raised $3 million to provide for the restoration, which was undertaken by Harry Weese in 1967. The interior ornamentation, including arched rows of lights along the ceiling, is breathtaking. Though it's normally closed to the public unless there's a show or concert, ask for a tour of this elegant hall. Another beautiful, though less well-known, space is the library on the 10th floor of the building.

Finally, head east on Congress Parkway to Columbus Drive and the recently restored **Buckingham Fountain,** which is set in its own plaza. When dedicated in 1927, it was the world's largest decorative fountain. Given to Chicago by philanthropist Kate Sturges Buckingham in memory of her brother Clarence, it was patterned on one of the fountains at Versailles. Now it's perhaps better know for appearing in the opening credits of the Fox sitcom *Married . . . With Children.* The central jet can shoot up to 135 feet. You can see it in all its glory between May 1 and October 1, when it's elaborately illuminated at night.

Tour 2: Downtown South

Numbers in the margin correspond to points of interest on the Tour 2: Downtown South map.

The Downtown South area, bounded by Congress Parkway–Eisenhower Expressway on the north, Michigan Avenue on the east, Roosevelt Road on the south, and the Chicago River on the west, presents a striking and often fascinating contrast to the downtown area toured above. Once a thriving commercial area and the center of the printing trades in Chicago, it fell into disrepair as the printing industry moved south in search of lower costs. Sleazy bars, pawnbrokers, and pornographic shops filled the area behind what was then the Conrad Hilton Hotel, crowding each other on Wabash Avenue and State Street and on the side streets between. Homeless people found (and still find) a place to sleep at the Pacific Garden Mission (646 S. State St.). Declining business at the mammoth Hilton meant decreasing revenues; floors were closed off because they were too expensive to maintain, and the owners considered demolishing the building.

Then, about a decade ago, investors became interested in renovating the run-down-yet-sturdy loft and office buildings in the old printing district. With the first neighborhood rehab efforts just beginning, Michael Foley, a young Chicago restaurateur from an old Chicago restaurant family, opened a restaurant on the edge of the redevelopment area. The innovative cuisine at Printer's Row (*see* Chapter 5, Dining) attracted favorable notice, and the restaurant became a success. Soon other restaurants, shops, and businesses moved in, and today the Printer's Row district is a thriving urban neighborhood enclave.

At about the time that the first renovations were being undertaken in Printer's Row, a consortium of investors, aided by preferential interest rates from downtown banks, obtained a large parcel of land in the old railroad yards to the south and put up an expansive new development. This was Dearborn Park, affordable housing targeted at young middle-class families. Although its beginnings were rocky (the housing was attractive but there was no supermarket, no dry cleaner, and no public school nearby) Dearborn Park, too, became successful.

To the west, the architect and developer Bertrand Goldberg (of Marina City fame) acquired a sizable tract of land between Wells Street and the Chicago River. Driven by a vision of an innovative, self-contained city within a city, Goldberg erected the futuristic River City, the massed, almost cloudlike complex that seems to rise from the river at Polk Street. This development has been less commercially successful than Dearborn Park, yet the willingness of a developer to make an investment of this size in the area was an indication that the neighborhood south of downtown was here to stay.

Spurred by signs of revitalization all around, the owners of the Conrad Hilton scrapped their plans to abandon the hotel and instead mounted a renovation of tremendous proportion. Now one of the most beautifully appointed hotels in the city, the Chicago Hilton and Towers once again attracts the business it needs to fill its thousands of rooms.

We'll begin our tour of Downtown South at the corner of Balbo Drive and Michigan Avenue. You can drive here—traffic and parking conditions are far less congested in the Downtown South area than they are in the Loop—or you can take the Jeffery Express Bus 6 from the north (catch it at State and Lake streets) or from Hyde Park. This entire area tends to empty out on weekends and especially in the evenings, so it's best to visit in daytime hours during the work week. If you're touring alone, be sure to exercise caution—as you would in any big city.

★ ❶ East of the intersection of Balbo Drive and Michigan Avenue is the heart of beautiful **Grant Park.** On a hot summer night during the last week of August 1968, the park was filled with people protesting the Vietnam War and the Democratic presidential convention that was taking place at the Conrad Hilton Hotel down the street. Rioting broke out; heads were cracked, protesters were dragged away screaming, and Mayor Daley gave police the order to "shoot to kill." Later investigations into the events of that evening determined that a "police riot"—not the misbehavior of the protesters, who had been noisy but not physically abusive—was responsible for the violence that erupted. Those who remember those rage-filled days cannot visit this idyllic spot without recalling that time.

Today Grant Park is a lovely mix of gardens (especially above Monroe Street and around the fountain), tennis courts, softball diamonds, and a field surrounding the Petrillo band shell, at Columbus Drive and Monroe Street, where outdoor concerts are held. While it's not as heavily used as Lincoln or Jackson parks, Grant Park is home to several blockbuster events: the Grant Park Society Concerts held four times a week in the summer; notable blues, jazz, and gospel festivals; and the annual Taste of Chicago, a vast picnic featuring foods from more than 70 restaurants that precedes a fireworks show on July 3 (*see* Festivals and Seasonal Events *in* Chapter 1, Destination: Chicago).

❷ The **Blackstone Hotel** (636 S. Michigan Ave.), on the northwest corner of the intersection, is rich with history. Presidential candidates have been selected here, and many presidents have stayed here. Note the ornate little roofs that cap the first-floor windows. Inside, the elegant lobby has impressive chandeliers, sculptures, and handsome woodwork. Next door is the **Merle Reskin Theatre,** another vintage building, where Broadway-bound shows were once booked. The theater is now owned and run by De Paul University, which uses the venue to showcase the school's performances; De Paul also rents the stage to other local theater companies.

❸ Head north on Michigan Avenue to the **Spertus Museum of Judaica,** a small museum housed in Spertus College. The museum includes displays of ritual objects from Jewish life, including some lovely Medieval

Tour 2: Downtown South

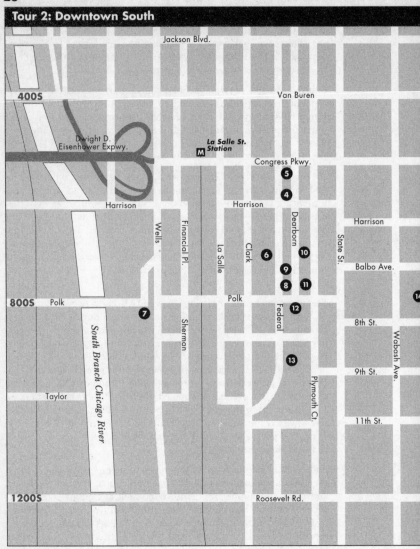

Blackstone Hotel, **2**

Chicago Hilton and Towers, **14**

Dearborn Park, **13**

Dearborn Station, **12**

Donohue Building, **11**

Franklin Building, **8**

Grace Place, **10**

Grant Park, **1**

Hyatt on Printer's Row, **5**

Printer's Row Restaurant, **4**

Printer's Square, **6**

River City, **7**

Sandmeyer's Bookstore, **9**

Spertus Museum of Judaica, **3**

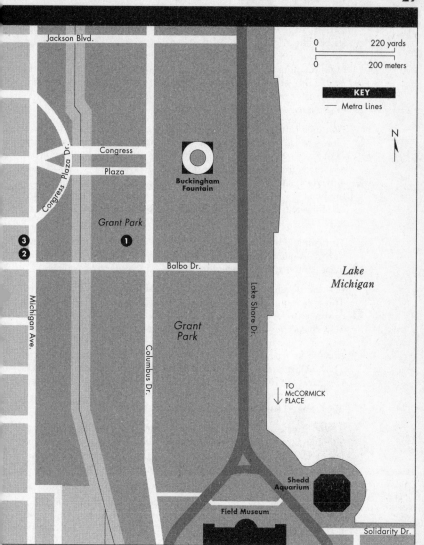

29

Jackson Blvd.

Congress Plaza Dr.

Congress
Plaza

Buckingham
Fountain

Grant Park

3
2
1

Balbo Dr.

Michigan Ave.

Columbus Dr.

*Grant
Park*

Lake Shore Dr.

0   220 yards
0   200 meters

KEY
— Metra Lines

N

*Lake
Michigan*

TO
McCORMICK
PLACE

Shedd
Aquarium

Field Museum

Solidarity Dr.

Jewish art; a Holocaust memorial; and a hands-on children's museum, the Artifacts Center. The museum regularly mounts exhibitions on topics broadly relevant to Judaism; for example, for a recent exhibit on the Sukkoth, a harvest festival, nine famous Chicago architects created interpretations of the traditional harvest booth. *618 S. Michigan Ave.,* ☎ *312/322–1747.* ☛ *$4 adults; $2 senior citizens, children, and students; $9 family rate; free Fri.* ☉ *Sun.–Thurs. 10–5, Fri. 10–3; children's museum Sun.–Thurs. 1–4:30.*

❹ Continue to the corner of Harrison Street, turn left, and walk three blocks to Dearborn Street. The pioneering **Printer's Row Restaurant** (550 S. Dearborn St.) is a wonderful place to stop for an elegant (but not inexpensive) lunch during the week. Nearby on Dearborn Street **❺** is the **Hyatt on Printer's Row** (500 S. Dearborn St.). Beautifully appointed, the hotel is in a group of renovated old buildings that have been interconnected. On the corner is the **Prairie Restaurant** (500 S. Dearborn St.).

❻ Turn left and walk west to Federal Street and turn left again. On your right as you head south is a massive beige-gray brick renovated apartment complex, **Printer's Square** (640–780 S. Federal St.).

❼ Continue south, turn west on Polk, and walk four blocks to Wells Street. This area is quite desolate, so be cautious. Turn left at Wells Street and continue to the entrance to **River City** (800 S. Wells St.). Apartments, all with curving exterior walls (making it a bit difficult to place square or rectangular furniture), ring the circumference of the building. Interior spaces are used for shops, walkways, and tenant storage closets. The building boasts a state-of-the-art health club. The west side of River City faces the river, providing a splendid view for apartment dwellers on that side, and 70 spaces for mooring boats are available. If you'd like to take a tour, speak to the guard.

Taylor Street, south of the River City entrance, will take you east to Sherman Street; turn left on Sherman Street, right on Polk Street, and left on Dearborn Street. If you're driving, this is a good place to park. We'll walk up the west side of Dearborn Street to the end of the block and return on the east side.

❽ The first building on your left is the grand old **Franklin Building** (720 S. Dearborn St.), originally "The Franklin Co.: Designing, Engraving, Electrotyping" and now condominium apartments. The decorative tile work on the facade leads up to the scene over the front door, *The First Impression;* representing a medieval event, it illustrates the first application of the printer's craft. Above the entryway is the motto "The Excellence of Every Art Must Consist in the Complete Accomplishment of Its Purpose."

❾ Next door, **Sandmeyer's Bookstore** (714 S. Dearborn St.) has an iron stairway set with glass bricks and a fine selection of books about Chicago.

In June this street is the locale of the Printer's Row Book Fair, a weekend event where dealers offer a wide variety of books and prints and where demonstrations of the papermaking and bookbinding crafts are given. Street performers and food vendors add to the festivity.

❿ Across the street is the rehabbed brick building **Grace Place** (637 S. Dearborn St.). This is not the newest condo on the block but a consortium of two churches: Grace Episcopal Church and Christ the King Lutheran Church. Each of the congregations is too small to support its own church building, so the two have joined together to share facilities.

① The **Donohue Building** (711 S. Dearborn St.), another grand renovated structure, houses a bar and several shops, including wine merchant **Wine Plus** and the distinguished **Prairie Ave. Bookshop** (707 S. Dearborn St.), which concentrates on new and out-of-print books about architecture, planning, and design. Take a look at the Donohue Building's main entrance; it is flanked by marble columns topped by ornately carved capitals, with tile work over the entrance set into a splendid granite arch. Note also the beautiful ironwork and woodwork in the doors and frames of the shops as you proceed south.

TIME OUT For a quick pick-me-up, stop at the **Deli on Dearborn** (723 S. Dearborn St.) or at the **Moonraker Restaurant and Tavern** (733 S. Dearborn St.). In summer, you can sit outside at either establishment, although the cool interior of the Moonraker may be more welcome after a tramp through the city streets.

② The recently restored **Dearborn Station** (47 W. Polk St.) at the foot of Dearborn Street, designed in Romanesque-Revival style in 1885 by the New York architect Cyrus L.W. Eidlitz, has a red-sandstone and red-brick facade ornamented with terra-cotta. The striking features inside the station are the brass fixtures set against the cream and white walls and woodwork and the white, rust, and jade marble floor. Since its opening in 1985, Dearborn Station has been successful in attracting office tenants, but less so in attracting retail tenants. ☉ *Mon.–Sat. 8:30 AM–7 PM.*

③ Walk east, turn right on Plymouth Court, and look south, where you can see **Dearborn Park.** A planned mix of high-rise, low-rise, and single-family units, some in redbrick and some in white, the development has a tidy look. The residents are enthusiastic about Dearborn Park, and they have developed a warm, supportive community.

Walk down Plymouth Court to 9th Street and turn left. Walk one block to State Street. Notice the attractive high-rise on the northeast corner. Built recently on a site that would have been unthinkable only a few years earlier, this building has reinforced the resurgent residential community of the area. Continue east another block to Wabash Avenue and turn left. At the corner of 8th Street and Wabash Avenue is the club of blues great Buddy Guy, the aptly named **Buddy Guy's Legends** (754 S. Wabash); you can stop in seven nights a week to hear some of the best play Chicago's signature sound (*see* Chapter 7, The Arts and Nightlife).

④ Walk east on 8th Street, across Wabash Avenue, to the **Chicago Hilton and Towers** (720 S. Michigan Ave.). Enter by the revolving doors, head a bit to your right and then straight, and stroll through the opulent lobby, tastefully done in shades of mauve and soft sea green. Notice the gilded horses that flank the main entrance on the inner wall and the sweeping stairway to your right, off the main entrance, that leads to the Grand Ballroom. Sneak a peek at the Grand Ballroom if possible; there isn't a more spectacular room in the city. On opening night at the opera, when a midnight supper and dance is held here, a brass quintet stationed at the top of this stairway plays fanfares as the guests arrive. Be sure not to miss the exquisite Thai hanging on the north wall of the lobby (directly behind and above the concierge's desk).

TIME OUT The Hilton has several options for dining and relaxing. **Buckingham's,** the hotel's fine-dining restaurant, specializes in steak and seafood dinners; **The Pavilion** offers light American dishes in a pretty setting that's perfect for people watching; and **Kitty O'Sheas** features Irish food, spirits, and musical entertainment.

When you're ready to leave, take the Jeffery Express Bus 6 to Hyde Park, which stops on Balbo Drive, directly across Michigan Avenue from the Hilton. Or you can catch any bus that stops on the northeast corner and then transfer to a Michigan Avenue bus at Randolph Street.

Tour 3: Hyde Park and Kenwood

Numbers in the margin correspond to points of interest on the Tour 3: Hyde Park and Kenwood map.

Although farmers and other settlers lived in Hyde Park in the early 1800s and Chicago's oldest Jewish congregation was founded here in 1847, the growth and development of the area really got under way as a result of two events: the World's Columbian Exposition of 1893 and the opening of the University of Chicago in 1892. The Columbian Exposition, whose influence on American public architecture was to prove far-reaching, brought about the creation of the Midway Plaisance and the construction of numerous buildings, of which the Museum of Science and Industry is the most famous survivor. The Midway Plaisance, surrounding the heart of the 1893 fair, still runs along the southern edge of the University of Chicago's original campus. Another legacy from the exposition was the civic moniker "The Windy City," used by *New York Sun* editor Charles Dana to ridicule Chicago's bid to host the exposition.

The University of Chicago was built through the largesse of John D. Rockefeller. Coeducational from the beginning, it was known for progressive education. The campus covers 184 acres, dominating the physical and cultural landscape of Hyde Park and South Kenwood. Much of the original campus was designed by Henry Ives Cobb, who was also responsible for the Newberry Library at the corner of Dearborn and Walton streets on the Near North Side. The university's stately gothic quadrangles recall the residential colleges in Cambridge, England, and the Ivy League schools of the East Coast. But the material is Indiana limestone, and the U. of C. retains a uniquely Midwestern quality.

The university boasts 61 Nobel laureates as graduates, resident researchers, or faculty members. Its schools of economics, law, business, and medicine are world famous. The University of Chicago Hospitals are leading teaching institutions. It was at U. of C. in 1990 that a baby received a successful transplant of a section of her mother's liver—the first operation of its kind. Perhaps the most world-altering event to take place at U. of C. (or anywhere else, for that matter) was the first self-sustaining nuclear chain reaction, created here in 1942 by Enrico Fermi and his team of physicists under an unused football stadium. Although the stadium is gone, there's a plaque on the spot now, near the Crerar Science Library.

In the 1890s the university embarked on a program to build housing for its faculty members, and the mansions that line Woodlawn Avenue are the result. Then the neighborhood began to attract well-to-do private individuals who commissioned noted architects to construct homes suitable to persons of great wealth. Many of their houses still stand in Kenwood.

With the coming of the Depression, followed by World War II, the neighborhood entered a period of decline. Grand homes fell into disrepair as the numbers of those with the resources to maintain them dwindled. Wartime housing shortages led to the conversion of stately houses into multifamily dwellings.

Alarmed by the decline of the neighborhood, concerned citizens formed the Hyde Park–Kenwood Community Conference. Aided by $29 million from the University of Chicago, which was anxious that it might not be able to retain—never mind recruit—faculty members, this group set about restoring the neighborhood. Prizes were offered to those who would buy and "deconvert" rooming houses, and the city was pressured to enforce the zoning laws.

The effort that was to have the most lasting effect on the neighborhood was urban renewal, one of the first such undertakings in the nation. Again with the backing and support of the University of Chicago, 55th Street from Lake Park Avenue to Cottage Grove Avenue was razed. Most of the buildings on Lake Park Avenue and on many streets abutting 55th Street and Lake Park Avenue were torn down as well. With them went the workshops of painters and artisans, the quarters of "little magazines" (some 20 chapters of James Joyce's *Ulysses* were first published at one of them), the Compass Theatre—where Mike Nichols and Elaine May got their start, the Second City comedy club (since relocated to Lincoln Park), and more than 40 bars where jazz and blues could be heard nightly. In their place came town houses designed by I.M. Pei and Harry Weese and a shopping mall designed by Keck and Keck. Cynics have described the process as one of "blacks and whites together, shoulder to shoulder—against the poor."

In the end, these efforts were successful beyond the wildest imaginings of their sponsors, but more than 20 years elapsed before the neighborhood regained its luster. As late as the early 1960s, the 18-room houses on Woodlawn Avenue that sell today for $600,000 could still be had for $35,000.

To reach the start of our Hyde Park tour if you're arriving by car, take Lake Shore Drive south to the 57th Street exit and turn left into the parking lot of the Museum of Science and Industry. Or you can take the Illinois Central Gulf (ICG) Railroad train from Randolph Street and Michigan Avenue; get off at the 55th Street stop and walk east through the underpass two blocks, then south two blocks.

❶ Our exploration of Hyde Park and Kenwood begins at the **Museum of Science and Industry,** built for the Columbian Exposition as a Palace of Fine Arts. Plan on at least half a day to explore this hands-on museum, where you can visit a U-505 submarine, descend into a coal mine, experience an auditory miracle in the whispering gallery, learn how telephones work, trace the history of computing and the development of computer hardware, explore spacecraft and the history of space exploration, visit "Main Street of Yesterday," learn how the body works, and much more. The Omnimax Theater shows science and space-related films on a giant five-story screen. Tickets to the Omnimax include museum admission. *5700 S. Lake Shore Dr.,* ☎ *312/684–1414.* ☛ *Museum: $6 adults, $2.50 children; Thurs. free. Omnimax (includes museum admission): $10 adults, $6 senior citizens, $5.50 children; discounts Thurs.* ☉ *Memorial Day–Labor Day, daily 9:30–5:30; Labor Day–Memorial Day, weekdays 9:30–4, weekends and holidays 9:30–5:30.*

Exiting the museum, cross 56th Street, and head west. Turn right under the viaduct and go north on Lake Park Avenue. Halfway down

Tour 3: Hyde Park and Kenwood

Bond Chapel, **15**

Chevrolet Building, **3**

Chicago Theological Seminary, **20**

Cobb Hall, **14**

Court Theatre, **10**

David and Alfred Smart Museum of Art, **9**

57th Street Books, **27**

First Unitarian Church, **18**

1400-1451 East 55th Street, **4**

Harper Court, **5**

Heller House, **6**

Hyde Park Historical Society, **2**

International House, **24**

John Crerar Science Library, **12**

Joseph Regenstein Library, **16**

Lutheran School of Theology, **8**

Mandel Hall, **17**

Midway Studios, **23**

Museum of Science and Industry, **1**

Nuclear Energy, **11**

O'Gara & Wilson Book Shop Ltd., **26**

Oriental Institute, **21**

Powell's Bookstore, **25**

Robie House, **19**

Rockefeller Memorial Chapel, **22**

St. Thomas the Apostle Church and School, **7**

University of Chicago Bookstore, **13**

② the block, you'll pass the **Hyde Park Historical Society** (5529 S. Lake Park Ave., ☎ 312/493–1893), a research library.

③ Just north stands the **Chevrolet Building** (5508 S. Lake Park Ave.), named for the car dealership that formerly occupied it. The beautiful terra-cotta border decorates an otherwise functional building, one of only two buildings in the area left standing when the neighborhood was razed and rebuilt.

Head west on 55th Street to one of the happy results of urban renewal, **④** **1400–1451 East 55th Street,** an apartment building designed by I.M. Pei, he of the Louvre's glass pyramid. He also designed the town houses that border it on the north, between Blackstone and Dorchester avenues. Turn right and head up Blackstone Avenue, passing a variety of housing between 55th and 51st streets. Although these houses command prices in the hundreds of thousands of dollars today, they were originally cottages for workers, conveniently located near the cable-car line that ran west on 55th Street.

Continue north on Blackstone Avenue to 53rd Street, Hyde Park's main **⑤** shopping strip. Across the street and a half block east is **Harper Court.** Another product of urban renewal, Harper Court was built to house craftspeople who were displaced from their workshops on Lake Park Avenue. Despite subsidized rents, it never caught on with the craftspeople, who moved elsewhere, while Harper Court evolved into a successful shopping center and community gathering place.

TIME OUT   Starbucks (1500 E. 53rd St.) serves an invigorating selection of coffees and pastries. Those who are very hungry might prefer the **Valois Cafeteria** (1518 E. 53rd St.) half a block away, where inexpensive meals are served all day.

Leaving the north exit of Harper Court, go west four blocks (the street dead-ends, but there's a pedestrian walkway between Kimbark and Kenwood Avenues to let you through) to Woodlawn Avenue and turn right. **⑥** The **Heller House** (5132 S. Woodlawn Ave.) was built by Frank Lloyd Wright in 1897; note the plaster naiads cavorting at the top. Now proceed south on Woodlawn Avenue to 55th Street. On the east side of **⑦** the street is **St. Thomas the Apostle Church and School** (5467 S. Woodlawn Ave.), built in 1922 and now a national landmark. Note its terra-cotta ornamentation. A more comprehensive view is available from Kimbark Avenue.

Turn right (west) onto 55th Street. This is the northern edge of the University of Chicago campus. A walking tour of the campus is offered daily (☎ 312/702–8374), but if you'd like to see things on your own, **⑧** continue west to University Avenue and the **Lutheran School of Theology** (1100 E. 55th St.). Built in 1968 by the firm of Perkins and Will, the massive structure seems almost to float from its foundation, lightened by the transparency of its smoked-glass exteriors. Across the street is **Pierce Hall** (5514 S. University Ave.), a student dormitory designed by Harry Weese.

Head south on University Avenue and turn right onto 56th Street. Walk **⑨** one block to Greenwood Avenue and the **David and Alfred Smart Museum of Art.** Founded in 1974 with a gift from the Smart Family Foundation, whose members David and Alfred founded *Esquire* magazine, the museum and an adjacent sculpture garden display the fine-arts holdings of the university. The 5,000-piece permanent collection is diverse and includes works by Old Masters; photographs by Walker Evans; furniture by Frank Lloyd Wright; sculptures by Degas, Matisse, Rodin, and Henry Moore; ancient Chinese bronzes; and modern Japanese ceramics. *5550 S. Greenwood Ave.,* ☎ *312/702–0200.* ☛ *Free.* ☉ *Tues.–Fri. 10–4, weekends noon–6.*

🔟 Continue west on 56th Street to Ellis Avenue and the **Court Theatre** (5535 S. Ellis Ave., ☎ 312/753–4472), a professional repertory company that specializes in revivals of the classics. An intimate theater, the Court offers unobstructed sight from every seat in the house. A flag flies atop the theater when a show is on.

Continue south on Ellis Avenue about half a block beyond 56th Street; ⑪ on your left is the Henry Moore sculpture *Nuclear Energy,* commemorating the first controlled nuclear chain reaction, which took place below ground roughly where the sculpture stands, in the locker room under the bleachers of what was then Stagg Field. Across 57th Street, ⑫ set into the small quadrangle on your right, is the **John Crerar Science Library** (5730 S. Ellis Ave., ☎ 312/702–7715). Inside the library is John David Mooney's splendid sculpture *Crystara,* composed of enormous Waterford crystal pieces made to order for this work, which was commissioned for the site.

⑬ Farther down the block is the **University of Chicago Bookstore,** which has, in addition to scholarly books, a large selection of general-interest books, an outstanding collection of cookbooks, and clothing, mugs, and other souvenirs. *970 E. 58th St.,* ☎ *312/702–8729.* ☉ *Mon.–Sat. 8:30–5.*

⑭ On the east side of Ellis Avenue just north of 58th Street is **Cobb Hall,** home of the Renaissance Society. The society was founded in 1915 to identify living artists whose work would be of lasting significance and influence. It was among the first hosts of works by Matisse, Picasso, Braque, Brancusi, and Miró. Come here to see what the next generation of great art may look like. *Cobb Hall 418, 5811 S. Ellis Ave.,* ☎ *312/702–8670.* ☛ *Free.* ☉ *Tues.–Fri. 10–4, weekends noon–4.*

North of Cobb Hall is the **University of Chicago Administration Building.** Between the two is a small passageway to the **quadrangle** of the university. Here is a typical college campus, green and grassy, with imposing neo-Gothic buildings all around. Tucked into the southwest corner between two other buildings is **Bond Chapel** (1025 E. 58th St.), a lovely Gothic-style chapel. The fanciful gargoyles outside belie the simple interior of dark wood, stained glass, and delicate ornamentation. The effect is one of intimacy and warmth.

Cross the quadrangle and head east to the circular drive. Bear left, then turn left at the intersecting road. Follow this path north, and you will pass a reflecting pool (Botany Pond) before you exit through the ⑯ wrought-iron gate. Directly ahead is the **Joseph Regenstein Library,** framed in the gate. The "Reg," the main library of the university, was designed by Skidmore, Owings, and Merrill and built in 1970.

Turn right on 57th Street and continue east. The massive building on ⑰ the southwest corner, **Mandel Hall** (1131 E. 57th St., ☎ 312/702–8068), is a gem of a concert hall that has been tastefully restored. Peek in, if you can, for a glimpse of gold leaf and soft greens against the dark wood of the theater. Professional musical organizations, including ensembles from the Chicago Symphony and such groups as Les Arts Florissants from France, perform in the 900-seat hall throughout the year. The building also houses the student union.

Continue east on 57th Street one block to Woodlawn Avenue. On the ⑱ northwest corner is the **First Unitarian Church** (5650 S. Woodlawn Ave.,

☎ 312/324–4100), whose graceful spire is visible throughout the area. Turn right on Woodlawn Avenue and head south, noting the stately brick mansions that line both sides of the street. To the north, the building at 5605 is on the National Register of Historic Places. Many of the buildings were built by the University of Chicago in the 1890s to provide housing for professors. Professors continue to live in several of them; others have been repurchased by the university for institutional use.

★ ⑲ Continue south on Woodlawn Avenue to Frank Lloyd Wright's **Robie House.** Built in 1909, Robie House exemplifies the Prairie style. Its cantilevered roof offers privacy while allowing in light. The house sits on a pedestal; Wright abhorred basements, thinking them unhealthful. You can tour Robie House and examine the interiors, including the built-in cupboards, the leaded-glass windows, and the spacious kitchen. Rescued by the university from the threat of demolition, the building now houses the university alumni office and is used for small official dinners and receptions. *5757 S. Woodlawn Ave.,* ☎ *312/702–8374.* ☛ *Free.* ⊙ *Tours daily at noon.*

⑳ Cross Woodlawn Avenue and continue west one block to the **Chicago Theological Seminary** (5757 S. University Ave.). Its basement accommodates the **Seminary Cooperative Bookstore** (☎ 312/752–4381), which includes an extensive selection of books in the humanities among its wide offerings. Defying the rules of marketing, this store—which does not advertise, is not visible from the street, and has no parking—has more sales per square foot than any other bookstore in Chicago. Upstairs in the chapel is the Reneker organ, donated by the widow of a university trustee. Free concerts are given Tuesday at noon on this exquisitely handcrafted replica of an 18th-century organ.

㉑ Across 58th Street is the **Oriental Institute,** which focuses on the history, art, and archaeology of the ancient Near East, including Assyria, Mesopotamia, Persia, Egypt, and Syro-Palestine. Permanent displays include statuary, small-scale amulets, mummies, limestone reliefs, gold jewelry, ivories, pottery, and bronzes from the 2nd millennium BC through the 13th century AD. *1155 E. 58th St.,* ☎ *312/702–9520 or 312/702–9521 for recorded information.* ☛ *Free.* ⊙ *Tues. and Thurs.–Sat. 10–4, Wed. 10–8:30, Sun. noon–4.*

㉒ Go down University Avenue one block to 59th Street. To your left, set back on a grassy expanse, is the neo-Gothic **Rockefeller Memorial Chapel** (5850 S. Woodlawn Ave.), designed by Bertram Goodhue and named in honor of the founder of the university. The interior has a stunning vaulted ceiling; hand-sewn banners decorate the walls. A university carillonneur gives regular performances on the carillon atop the chapel. Tours of the chapel are given by appointment (☎ 312/702–8374).

Continue south again, crossing 59th Street and entering the **Midway Plaisance.** Created for the World's Columbian Exposition, this green, hollowed-out strip of land was intended to replicate a Venetian canal. When the "canal" was filled with water, houses throughout the area were flooded as well, and the idea had to be abandoned. At the western end of the Plaisance, by Cottage Grove Avenue, you can see Lorado Taft's masterpiece *The Fountain of Time,* completed in 1922. Taft (1830–1926) was one of the most distinguished sculptors and teachers of his time. Like many, he got his start by creating pieces for the Columbian Exposition. One of these, the *Fountain of the Great Lakes,* is now at the Art Institute. Other works adorn Chicago's parks and public places, as well as those of other cities.

Heading west on 60th Street, you'll pass the **School of Social Service Administration** (969 E. 60th St.), an undistinguished example of the work of Mies van der Rohe.

㉓ One block farther, at 60th Street and Ingleside Avenue, is **Midway Studios,** the home and workplace of Lorado Taft. A National Historic Landmark since 1966, the building now houses the university's studio-art program and serves as an exhibit space for student works. *6016 S. Ingleside Ave.,* ☎ *312/753–4821.* ☛ *Free.* ⊙ *Weekdays 8:30–4.*

On 60th Street between Ellis and University avenues is the **Laird Bell Law Quadrangle** (1111 E. 60th St.). This attractive building, with fountains playing in front, is the work of Finnish architect Eero Saarinen. Two blocks farther east, between Kimbark Street and Kenwood Avenue, is the **New Graduate Residence Hall** (1307 E. 60th St.). This poured-concrete structure, elaborately ornamented, is reminiscent of the American embassy in New Delhi, India—architect Edward Durrell Stone designed both.

Cross the Midway again to 59th Street and continue east. The neo-
㉔ Gothic structure just past Dorchester Avenue is **International House** (1414 E. 59th St., ☎ 312/753–2270), where many foreign students live during their tenure at the university. It was designed in 1932 by the firm of Holabird and Roche. Continue east to Blackstone and turn left. **5806 South Blackstone Avenue,** a house designed in 1951 by Bertrand Goldberg of Marina City and River City fame, is an early example of the use of solar heating and natural cooling.

Continue north on Blackstone Avenue to 57th Street and turn right.
㉕ **Powell's Bookstore** (1501 E. 57th St., ☎ 312/955–7780) generally has a box of free books out front, and inside you'll find a tremendous selection of used and remaindered titles, especially art books, cookbooks, and mysteries. Walk west on 57th Street to Dorchester Avenue; on your left, at **5704 South Dorchester Avenue,** is an Italian-style villa constructed before the Chicago Fire. The two houses at **5642** and **5607 South Dorchester Avenue** also predate the fire.

On 57th Street, spanning the block between Kenwood Avenue and Kimbark Street, is the **Ray School** complex. One of the best public elementary schools in the city, Ray hosts the annual Hyde Park Art Fair, one of the oldest (since 1947) annual outdoor art fairs in the country.

TIME OUT This street has several spots where you can get a quick bite and rest your feet. **Medici Pan Pizza** (1327 E. 57th St.) has sandwiches and snacks as well as pizza, as does **Edwardo's** (1321 E. 57th St.). **Caffe Florian** (1450 E. 57th St.) serves pizza and Italian entrées as well as hearty sandwiches and salads, decadent desserts, and lots of java. Breakfast fare is your best bet at **Eddie's Collage** (1329 E. 57th St.), which specializes in mouthwatering cinnamon rolls.

㉖ Farther west is **O'Gara & Wilson Book Shop Ltd.** (1311 E. 57th St., ☎ 312/363–0993), which has another outstanding selection of used
㉗ books. Nearby is **57th Street Books** (1301 E. 57th St., ☎ 312/684–1300), a cooperatively owned bookstore that is sister to the Seminary Cooperative Bookstore on University Avenue and that specializes in current books of general interest. Copies of the *New York Times Book Review* and the *New York Review of Books* are always on a table to-

ward the rear, next to the coffeepot. An extensive children's section has its own room, where reading aloud to youngsters is encouraged.

To get back to the museum and our starting point, backtrack east on 57th Street, go under the viaduct, and cross Stony Island Avenue. The museum will be in front of you, and to the right are the lagoons of Jackson Park.

Tour 4: South Lake Shore Drive

The South Lake Shore Drive tour offers spectacular views of the downtown skyline; it serves as a bonus for those who have visited Hyde Park and Kenwood and are returning north via car or the Jeffery Express Bus 6 or (during the afternoon rush hour) the Hyde Park Express Bus 2. If you follow Tour 1 (*see above*) or Tour 5 (*see below*), you will visit some of the skyscrapers described here. This driving tour allows you to see these buildings from a distance and in relation to the surrounding skyline.

Enter Lake Shore Drive at 57th Street northbound, with the lake to your right. At 35th Street you will pass, on your left, the **Stephen Douglas Memorial.** Douglas was the U.S. Senator who debated the merits of slavery with Abraham Lincoln; you can see the monument, with Douglas at the top, from the drive, but you'd have to go inland to Lake Park Avenue to visit the lovely park and gardens there.

Directly ahead is the **Sears Tower** (233 S. Wacker Dr.), the world's tallest building until the Petronas towers in Kuala Lumpur, Malaysia, steal that title (they're scheduled for completion sometime in 1996). In case the perspective makes it appear unfamiliar, you can recognize it by the angular setbacks that narrow the building as it rises higher. To its left is the "white castle" top of **311 S. Wacker,** which is lighted at night (*see* Tour 1, *above*). Ahead and to your right is the low-rise, dark **McCormick Place Convention Hall** (2300 S. Lake Shore Dr.); to the left, the low-rise **McCormick Place North** is the latest addition to the complex, its completion having been delayed by almost a year because of political machinations and scandals, in true Chicago style.

The rust-color building to the east is the **CNA Building** (55 E. Jackson Blvd.). When it was newly constructed, Chicagoans believed that the color was that of a first coat of rustproofing paint. They were wrong. The **Stone Container Building** (150 N. Michigan Ave.), is the building with the more or less diamond shape, angled face at the top (*see* Tour 1, *above*).

The tall white building to the right of the Stone Container Building is the **Amoco Building** (200 E. Randolph St.), with its new granite exterior (*see* Tour 1, *above*). Next to the Amoco Building is the severe gray **Prudential Building,** with its postmodern annex rising behind it.

The building with the twin antennae, to the right of the Amoco Building, is the 98-story **John Hancock Center** (875 N. Michigan Ave., *see* Tour 5, *below*). Off to the right, seemingly out in the lake, are the sinuous curves of **Lake Point Towers** condominiums (505 N. Lake Shore Dr.).

Coming up on the left, the building with the massive columns on an ancient Grecian model is **Soldier Field** (425 E. McFetridge Dr.), the home of the Chicago Bears. There's some talk of constructing a new stadium on the near west side, but for at least the foreseeable future, Chicagoans will continue to share Lake Shore Drive with Bears fans on fall and winter Sunday afternoons.

To visit the three natural science museums on Chicago's nearby museum campus, turn right into the drive that's just past Meigs Field, drive to the end, and park. Or follow the signs to the left that lead to the Field Museum parking lot.

★ On your left as you turn onto the peninsula is the **John G. Shedd Aquarium.** The dazzling new **Oceanarium,** with four beluga whales, several Pacific dolphins, penguins, and a tide-pool environment is the big draw here. But don't miss the sharks, eels, turtles, and myriad smaller fish and other aquatic forms in the coral-reef exhibit. Hundreds of other watery "cages" display fish from around the world, some bizarre and many fantastically beautiful. *1200 S. Lake Shore Dr.,* ☎ *312/939–2438 or 312/939–2426.* ☛ *Both Aquarium and Oceanarium: $8 adults, $6 senior citizens and children 3–11; ½ price on Thurs.* ☉ *Weekdays 9– 5, weekends and holidays 9–6, last admission 5:15 on weekends.*

At the far end of the peninsula is the **Adler Planetarium,** featuring exhibits about the stars and planets and a popular program of Sky Shows. Past shows have included "The Space Telescope Story" and "Planetary Puzzles." *1300 S. Lake Shore Dr.,* ☎ *312/322–0304 (general information),* ☎ *312/322–0300 (information on current month's skies).* ☛ *Planetarium free; Sky Show $4 adults, $2 children 4–17.* ☉ *Mon.–Thurs. and weekends 9–5, Fri. 9–9.*

★ The **Field Museum** across Lake Shore Drive from the aquarium and accessible through a pedestrian underpass, is one of the country's great natural-history museums. From the reconstructed Pawnee earth lodge (completed with the assistance of the Pawnee tribe of Oklahoma) to the Mastaba tomb complex from ancient Egypt, the size and breadth of the museum's collections are staggering. The Mastaba complex alone includes a working canal, a living marsh where papyrus is grown, a shrine to the cat goddess Bastet, burial-ceremony artifacts, and 23 mummies. The museum's gem room contains more than 500 gemstones and jewels. Place for Wonder, a three-room exhibit for children, lets youngsters handle everything on display, including a ½-ton stuffed polar bear, shells, animal skins, clothing and toys from China, aromatic scent jars, and gourds. Music, dance, theater, and film performances are also scheduled.

A new, two-part permanent exhibit called Life Over Time was completely opened in 1995. "DNA to Dinosaurs" traces the evolution of life on earth from one-celled organisms to the great reptiles, and "Teeth, Tusks, and Tar Pits" moves from the dinosaurs' extinction to the evolution of humans. Besides dioramas, educational computer games, models, and interactive exercises, the exhibits feature more than 600 fossils—including gigantic, posed dinosaur skeletons. The new DinoStore sells a mind-boggling array of dinosaur-related merchandise. *Lake Shore Dr. at E. Roosevelt Rd.,* ☎ *312/922–9410.* ☛ *$16 families; $5 adults; $3 senior citizens, children, and students; free Wed. New exhibits: additional $2 adults, $1 senior citizens, children, and students.* ☉ *Daily 9–5.*

After you've had your fill of museums, retrieve your car and continue north. As you round the curve past the Shedd Aquarium, look to your right for a view of the harbor. Off to the left looms the handsome, massive complex of the **Chicago Hilton and Towers** (720 S. Michigan Ave.), and soon thereafter the **Buckingham Fountain** will appear immediately to your left. To the far right, at the north and east, you can just see the ornate towers of **Navy Pier** (*see* Tour 5, *below*).

Having reached the Loop, we've come to the end of the South
Shore Drive tour.

Tour 5: Near North

*Numbers in the margin correspond to points of interest on the Tour
5: Near North map.*

Some of the most beautiful and interesting sights in Chicago are within
a short walk of the multitude of hotels on the Near North Side. If business has brought you here, and you have a few hours to kill between
meetings, you can wander over to the lakefront and North and Navy
piers, browse the shops and museums of Michigan Avenue, or take a
turn around the galleries of River North. If you have a whole day to
spend, you can do all three comfortably. For more information on shopping Michigan Avenue, *see* Chapter 3, Shopping.

Magnificent Mile/Streeterville

The **Magnificent Mile,** a stretch of Michigan Avenue between the
Chicago River and Oak Street, got its name from the swanky shops
that line both sides of the street (*see* Chapter 3, Shopping) and from
its once-elegant low-rise profile, which used to contrast sharply with
the urban canyons of the Loop. Unfortunately, a parade of new high-
rises is making the Mag Mile more canyonlike each year, but you can
still see patches of what the entire street used to look like.

To the east of the Magnificent Mile is upscale **Streeterville,** which
began as a disreputable landfill presided over by notorious lowlife "Cap"
Streeter and his wife Maria. The couple set out from Milwaukee in the
1880s on a small steamboat bound for Honduras. When their boat was
stranded on a sandbar between Chicago Avenue and Oak Street,
Streeter claimed the "land" as his own, seceding from both the city of
Chicago and the state of Illinois. After building contractors were invited to dump their debris on his "property," the landfill soon mush-
roomed into 186 acres of saloons and shanties. Today this once-infamous
area is filled with high-rise apartment buildings and a smattering of
older structures, and has attracted young professionals who work
nearby. Where Cap Streeter's own shanty once sat is the John Hancock Center.

West of Streeterville, from Michigan Avenue to Dearborn Street, is a
peculiar stretch that mixes a few skyscrapers, lots of parking lots and
garages, a sprinkling of shops and restaurants, and some isolated examples of the stone town houses that once filled the neighborhood. Despite its lack of cohesion, the area is the seat of various types of power,
containing as it does two cathedrals and the headquarters of the American Medical Association, which is housed in a sterile high-rise at
Wabash and Grand avenues.

❶ Our tour starts at the north side of the **Michigan Avenue Bridge,** which
spans the Chicago River. The sculptures on the four pylons of the bridge
represent major Chicago events: its discovery by Marquette and Joliet,
its settlement by du Sable, the Fort Dearborn Massacre of 1812, and
the rebuilding of the city after the fire. The site of the fort is just across
the river, where 360 North Michigan Avenue now stands.

Around the bridge are several notable skyscrapers, old and new. On
❷ the west side of Michigan Avenue is the **Wrigley Building** (400 N. Michigan Ave., ☎ 312/923–8080), corporate home of the Wrigley chewing-
gum empire. It was built in the early 1920s by the architectural firm
of Graham Anderson Probst and White, the same firm that designed

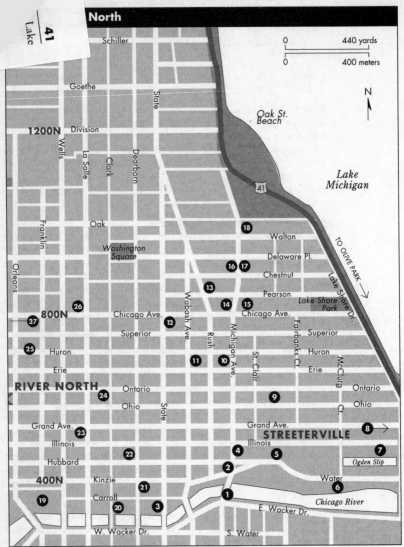

the Merchandise Mart (*see below*) and Union Station. The building is sheathed in terra-cotta that's remained remarkably white, considering the pollution around it. Its wedding-cake embellishments and clock tower make it an impossible structure to overlook. The building is brightly illuminated at night.

TIME OUT Behind and one level down from the Wrigley Building, at 430 North Michigan Avenue, is the (in)famous **Billy Goat Tavern,** the inspiration for *Saturday Night Live's* "cheezborger, cheezborger" skit and the hang-out of the best-known editorial columnist for the *Chicago Tribune,* Mike Royko. Grab a greasy but somehow satisfying hamburger (or cheese-burger) at this casual grill, or just wander in to absorb the comic under-tones.

3 Looking west on the river past the Wrigley Building, you'll see the twin "corncobs" of Bertrand Goldberg's **Marina City,** built in the late 1960s. Many architects love the complex, but engineers aren't so sure. If you get up close you can see patches in the concrete of the balconies. When it was first built, Marina City was popular with young professionals who worked in the area; today it's less sought after, although it does have the dubious distinction of housing the only bowling alley in downtown Chicago. Just to the east is Mies van der Rohe's boxlike IBM Building. Next to that is the headquarters of the *Chicago Sun-Times.*

4 Across Michigan Avenue is the crenelated **Tribune Tower** (435 N. Michigan Ave., ☎ 312/222–3232). In 1922 *Tribune* publisher Colonel Robert McCormick chose this Gothic design for the building that would house his paper, after rejecting a slew of functional modern de-signs. Embedded in the exterior wall of the tower are chunks of mate-rial taken from other famous buildings. Look for labeled blocks from Westminster Abbey, the Alamo, St. Peter's Basilica, the White House, and the Berlin Wall, among others; some of these bits and pieces were gifts to McCormick and others were "secured" by the Trib's foreign correspondents. On the ground floor, behind plate-glass windows, are the studios of WGN radio, part of the *Tribune* empire that also includes WGN-TV, cable-television stations, and the Chicago Cubs. (Modesty was not one of Colonel McCormick's prime traits: WGN stands for the *Trib's* self-bestowed nickname, World's Greatest Newspaper.)

5 Walk behind the Tribune Tower on Illinois Street and loop around to **NBC Tower** (200 E. Illinois St.). This 1989 limestone-and-granite edi-fice by Skidmore Owings and Merrill looks suspiciously like the 1930s-vintage Rockefeller Center complex in New York, another NBC home.

6 Head down the stairs at the base of St. Clair St. to the river. Continue east along the riverbank, past the Sheraton, to the **Centennial Foun-tain and Arc** (300 E. McClurg Ct.). This stepped fountain, which com-memorates the provision of clean water in and around the city, runs from May 1 to September 30 and shoots an awesome arc of water across the river for 10 minutes on the hour from 11 to 2 and 5 to midnight each day. On a sunny afternoon, you might see the hues of a rainbow in the arc.

7 From the fountain, head north on McClurg Court to Illinois Avenue and **North Pier** (435 E. Illinois St.). This fairly recent shopping and of-fice complex in a former shipping pier is a great place to bring kids. You'll find a number of interesting stores, including the City of Chicago Store, which offers unique souvenirs; a food court; several bars and restaurants; and a host of recreational games, from miniature golf to traditional arcade games to high-tech interactive games. Also located here is the **Bicycle Museum of America,** which through exhibits and a short video takes visitors through the chronological history of the bicycle. You can see bikes from every era, from the original designs of the 1800s to the high-tech models of today, and such novelty creations as the two-seater (side-by-side) "sociable" and the cycle mower. *North Pier,* ☎ *312/222–0500.* ☛ *$1, children under 5 free.* ☉ *Mon.–Thurs. 10–6, Fri.–Sat. 10–8, Sun. noon–5.*

❽ Farther east on Illinois, under Lake Shore Drive and across a park, is the new-and-improved **Navy Pier,** a wonderful place to enjoy the lake breezes and take in the skyline. Constructed in 1916 as a commercial-shipping pier, it was renamed in honor of the Navy in 1927 (the Army got Soldier Field). Several years of renovation was completed in 1995, and now the once-deserted pier contains shopping promenades; Navy Pier Gardens, an outdoor landscaped area that boasts fountains, a carousel, a giant 15-story Ferris wheel, and an enclosed ice-skating rink in addition to pretty gardens; the lakefront Skyline Stage (☎ 312/791–7437), a 1,500-seat, vaulted-roof theater; Crystal Gardens, one of the country's largest indoor botanical parks; an IMAX Theater; an outdoor beer garden; and myriad shops, restaurants, and bars. Navy Pier will continue to serve as the home port for a number of tour and dinner cruises. Prices are premium for these cruises, and the food's better on land, but the voyage can be pleasant on a hot summer night. Dinner cruise operators include *Spirit of Chicago* (☎ 312/836–7899) and *Odyssey II* (☎ 708/990–0800); the *Cap Streeter* offers 30-minute shoreline cruises that don't require reservations (☎ 312/222–9328).

The Chicago Children's Museum, formerly located in North Pier, is another welcome addition to Navy Pier. At 57,000 square feet, the museum has tripled its size and features many fascinating and educational hands-on exhibits, including: an early childhood exhibit with a kid-size neighborhood complete with a bakery, service station, and construction site; a hands-on art studio; science exhibits on subjects such as recycling and inventing; and an activity-filled exhibit that provides kids and adults with tools for addressing prejudice and discrimination. *Navy Pier,* ☎ *312/527–1000.* ☛ *$3.50 adults, $2.50 senior citizens and children; free Thurs. 5–8.* ☉ *Tues.–Sun. 10–4:30, Thurs. until 8.*

❾ As you leave Navy Pier, on either Illinois or Grand, you'll come back to McClurg Court. Take this to Ontario Street, turn left, and continue 1½ blocks, and you'll find the **Museum of Contemporary Art.** Started by a group of art patrons who felt the great Art Institute was unresponsive to modern work, this museum concentrates on 20th-century art, principally works created after 1940. Limited display space means that the collection of more than 4,000 works can be shown only in rotation; about six major exhibitions and 12 smaller ones are mounted each year. Because the museum closes in preparation for major exhibitions, be sure to call before planning a visit. The museum is planning to move in summer 1996 to larger quarters on the site of the old armory, on Chicago Avenue; if you're in Chicago after this period, be sure to call and check whether the museum has moved to its new site.*Before Summer 1996: 237 E. Ontario St.,* ☎ *312/280–5161. After Summer 1996: 234 E. Chicago Ave., ½ block east of Michigan Ave.* ☛ *Suggested donation: $5 adults; $2.50 senior citizens, students, and children under 16; free Tues.* ☉ *Tues.–Sat. 10–5, Sun. noon–5.*

If you see lots of people in white coats in the neighborhood, don't be surprised. Stretching east of Michigan Avenue from Ontario to Chicago avenues are various buildings belonging to one of the city's most prominent medical centers, **Northwestern Memorial Hospital.** The complex includes a veteran's hospital, a rehabilitation hospital, and a women's hospital, plus outpatient buildings. The downtown campus of Evanston's **Northwestern University,** including the law school and business school, is also in this area.

10 Continue west to Michigan Avenue, cross it, and turn right for the second museum in the Near North, the **Terra Museum of American Art.** Daniel Terra, Ambassador-at-Large for Cultural Affairs under Ronald Reagan, made his collection of American art available to Chicago in 1980; in 1987, it was moved here from Evanston. Subsequent acquisitions by the museum have added to this superb collection, which includes works by Whistler, Sargent, Winslow Homer, Cassatt, and three generations of Wyeths. *666 N. Michigan Ave.,* ☎ *312/664–3939.* ☞ *$4 adults, $2 senior citizens and students, children under 14 free; free Tues.* ☉ *Tues. noon–8, Wed.–Sat. 10–5, Sun. noon–5.*

11 Two blocks west of Michigan Avenue on Huron Street is the **St. James Cathedral** (65 E. Huron St., ☎ 312/787–7360). First built in 1856, the original St. James was largely destroyed by the Chicago Fire in 1871. The second structure, from 1875, is Chicago's oldest Episcopal church.

TIME OUT In sunny weather the plaza just east of St. James is a great place to eat a sandwich while you people-watch. For great fixings, try **L'Appetito** (Wabash Ave. and Huron St.), a take-out deli that has some of the best Italian sandwiches in Chicago.

12 Another block west and one block north is the Catholic stronghold, **Holy Name Cathedral** (735 N. State St., ☎ 312/787–8040). This yellow-stone Victorian cathedral, built between 1874 and 1875, is the principal church of the archdiocese of Chicago. Although the church is grand inside, the exterior is somewhat disappointing.

13 Go east on Chicago Avenue to Rush Street and turn left (north). At Pearson and Rush streets is **Quigley Seminary,** a 1918 Gothic-style structure. Its chapel is a little jewel, with perfect acoustics and a splendid rose window.

14 Continue east on Pearson Street to **Water Tower Park,** a Chicago icon. One of the few buildings to survive the fire of 1871, the 1869 **Water Tower** houses a 37-foot pipe that used to equalize water pressure for **15** the matching **Pumping Station** across the street. Today the pumping station and water tower house the **Chicago Office of Tourism** and the **visitor center,** respectively.

16 Two blocks north on the west side of Michigan Avenue is the **Fourth Presbyterian Church** (190 E. Delaware St., ☎ 312/787–4570). The courtyard of the church, a grassy spot adorned with simple statuary and bounded by a covered walkway, is an oasis amid Michigan Avenue's commercial bustle; many a weary shopper has found respite here. The granite church is a prime example of the Gothic Revival style popular at the turn of the century. Noontime organ concerts are given occasionally in the sanctuary; call for exact dates and times.

17 Across Michigan Avenue towers the 98-story **John Hancock Center,** which briefly held the title of world's tallest building when it was completed in 1969. The crisscross braces help keep the building from swaying in the high winds that come off the lake, although people who live in the apartments on the upper floors have learned not to keep anything fragile on a high shelf. On the 96th floor there's an observation deck for which you have to pay admission, or you can see the same view in a more festive setting by having an exorbitantly priced drink in the bar that adjoins the **Signature Room at the 95th** restaurant (*see* Chapter 5, Dining). A recent $25 million renovation of the Hancock added restaurants, shops, and year-round waterfalls to the public plaza, and increased parking capacity. ☎ 312/751–3681. ☛ *Observation deck: $4.75 adults, $3.25 senior citizens and students 5–17.* ☉ *Daily 9 AM–midnight.*

⓲ At the head of the Magnificent Mile is the **Drake Hotel** (140 E. Walton Pl.), one of the city's oldest and grandest; take a look at the marble-and-oak lobby, complete with a cherub-laden fountain. The lobby is one of the city's most popular spots for afternoon tea. Cross Oak Street in front of the Drake's main entrance and take the underground passage that leads to Oak Street Beach and the lakefront promenade. (Watch out for speeding bicyclists, skateboarders, and in-line skaters.)

River North

Bounded on the south and west by branches of the Chicago River, River North has eastern and northern boundaries that are harder to define than those of Streeterville and the Magnificent Mile. As in many neighborhoods, the limits have expanded as the area has grown more attractive; today they extend roughly to Oak Street on the north and Clark Street on the east. Richly served by waterways and by railroad tracks that run along its western edge, the neighborhood was settled by Irish immigrants in the mid-19th century. As the 20th century approached and streetcar lines came to Clark, La Salle, and Wells streets, the area developed into a vigorous commercial, industrial, and warehouse district.

But as economic conditions changed and factories moved away, the neighborhood fell into disuse and disrepair. Despite its location less than a mile from Michigan Avenue and the bustling downtown, River North became just another deteriorated urban area, a slide underscored by the depressed quality of life in the massive Cabrini Green public-housing project at the neighborhood's northern and western fringes.

As commerce moved away, artists and craftspeople moved into River North, attracted by low rents and the spacious abandoned storage areas and shop floors. Developers began buying up properties with an eye toward renovation. Today, although some buildings remain unrestored, and patches of the neighborhood retain their earlier character, the area has gone through a renaissance. Scores of art galleries, dozens of restaurants, and numerous trendy shops have opened here, bringing life and excitement to a newly beautiful neighborhood. Walking through River North, one is aware of the almost complete absence of contemporary construction; the handsome buildings are virtually all renovations of properties nearly a century old.

A typical River North building is a large, rectangular, solidly built structure made of Chicago redbrick, with high ceilings and hardwood floors. Even the buildings of the period that were intended to be strictly functional were often constructed with loving attention to the fine woodwork in doors and door frames, the decorative patterns set in the brickwork, the stone carvings and bas-reliefs, and the wrought-iron and handsome brass ornamentation.

⓳ Our tour begins on the plaza of the massive **Merchandise Mart,** on the river between Orleans and Wells streets. The Mart contains more square feet than any other building in the country except the Pentagon. Built by the architectural firm of Graham Anderson Probst and White in 1930, it's now owned by the Kennedys of political fame. Inside are wholesale showrooms for all sorts of merchandise, much of it related to interior decoration. You can view the showrooms either accompanied by an interior designer or on one of the Mart's tours. The first two floors of the Mart were converted into a retail shopping mall, with stores from many national chains, in late 1991. The anchor is a branch of the downtown department store Carson Pirie Scott. The somewhat macabre row of heads on the plaza is the Merchandise Mart Hall of Fame, installed at Joseph P. Kennedy's behest in 1953. The titans of retail portrayed here include Marshall Field, F.W. Woolworth, and Edward A. Filene. *13-156 The Merchandise Mart,* ☎ *312/527–7600. Showrooms open for tours only. Tours of the Mart,* ☎ *312/644–4664.* ☛ *1½-hour tours: $7 adults, $6 senior citizens and students; children under 16 not admitted on tours.* ☉ *Tours given weekdays at noon; closed major holidays.*

The nondescript building to the west is the **Apparel Center,** the Mart's equivalent for clothing.

From the plaza, walk north on Wells Street to Kinzie Street. Turn east on Kinzie Street, cross Clark Street, and look to your right to see two recent additions to Chicago's architectural scene. At the river's edge ❷⓿ is the **Quaker Oats Building,** a massive, glass-skin box designed by Skidmore, Owings & Merrill that was built to house the company's world headquarters after decades in the nearby Merchandise Mart. In the lobby there's an immense replica of the famous Quaker Oats box. This handsome office building dwarfs the Japanese **Hotel Nikko** (320 N. Dearborn St.) to the east. The hotel was built by a consortium headed by Japan Air Lines to provide both top-quality Japanese-style accommodations to Japanese businessmen and luxury Western-style facilities to traveling Americans (*see* Chapter 6, Lodging).

Before you turn left on Dearborn Street, notice the splendid ornamental ❷❶ brickwork of **33 West Kinzie Street,** a Dutch Renaissance–style building. Once a commercial building, it was twice renovated and is now the home of Harry Caray's restaurant, owned by the famed sportscaster (*see* Chapter 5, Dining).

❷❷ Proceed north to Hubbard Street, turn left, and pause at **Courthouse Place** (54 W. Hubbard St.), a splendid granite building that has been beautifully renovated; notice the bas-reliefs over the arched, pillared doorway. Inside, the restored lobby has black-and-white pictures of the original site. Continuing west you come to Clark Street, where two of Chicago's best restaurants, **Frontera Grill** and **Topolobampo,** stand. Owned by the same couple, both establishments focus on authentic Mexican cuisine, and both receive rave reviews. Topolobampo is the more formal (and more expensive) of the two, but you'll see people lined up to get into both restaurants when they open at 5, especially on weekends (*see* Chapter 5, Dining).

Go north on Clark Street to Grand Avenue. Turn left and continue one block west to La Salle Street. The funny, charming edifice on the south❷❸ west corner is the **Anti-Cruelty Society Building** (157 W. Grand Ave., ☎ 312/644–8338), designed by whimsical Chicago architect Stanley Tigerman. Next door is **Michael Jordan's Restaurant,** complete with an immense painting of the airborne one on its facade.

❷❹ Walk north on La Salle to Ontario Street and turn right. The **Rock and Roll McDonald's** at Clark Avenue and Ontario Street has a standard Micky D's menu (with slightly higher prices), 24-hour service, and a profusion of rock-and-roll artifacts, '50s and '60s kitsch, and just plain bizarre items to entertain you while you eat. Jukeboxes blast at all hours, and vintage '50s cars often crowd the parking lot on Saturday night. It's one of the highest-grossing McDonald's franchises in the world, so the company lets the operator decorate as he pleases. Even if you don't like the food, it's worth sticking your head in the door just to admire the '59 Corvette and the life-size Beatles statues positioned à la the *Abbey Road* album cover.

In case you haven't noticed, this once-desolate area has quickly become a tourist trap, with the **Hard Rock Cafe** (63 W. Ontario St.), **Planet Hollywood** (633 N. Wells St.), and Oprah Winfrey's **The Eccentric** and **The Big Bowl Café** (159 W. Erie St.) vying with Michael Jordan's Restaurant for tourist dollars. Even **Capone's Chicago** (605 N. Clark St.), a block of tongue-in-cheek '20s facades that houses a movie theater and souvenir store, has light snacks. Another popular spot for out-of-towners is **Ed Debevic's** (640 N. Wells St.), a '50s-style diner. If you are more interested in food than kitsch, Oprah's Big Bowl Café is where you'll get the most for your money.

Now double back and head west on Ontario Street. At Wells Street, turn right, and walk to Huron Street. Huron, Superior (one block north), and Hudson (a north–south street west of Orleans) streets form an area ㉕ known as **SuHu**—a word play on New York's SoHo, for this, too, is an arts district, home of more than 50 art galleries, showing every kind of work imaginable. Don't be shy about walking in and browsing; a gallery's business is to sell the works it displays, so most galleries welcome interested visitors and, time permitting, the staff will discuss the art they are showing. On Friday evening many galleries schedule openings of new shows and serve refreshments; you can sip jug wine as you stroll through the newly hung exhibit. Consider a gallery tour an informal, admission-free alternative to a museum visit. Although each gallery sets its own hours, most are open weekdays and Saturday 10–5 or 11–5 and are closed Sunday. For announcements of openings and other art-scene news, write for the *Chicago Gallery News,* 107 West Delaware Place, Chicago, IL 60610, or pick up a copy at the Pumping Station *(see above).*

Virtually every building on Superior Street between Orleans and Franklin streets houses at least one gallery. At 301 West Superior is **Eva Cohon** (☎ 312/664–3669), with contemporary American and Canadian painting. Colorful, large-scale Expressionist work is their primary concentration, but the focus is shifting toward more figurative pieces.

TIME OUT Nestled under the El tracks at Superior and Franklin streets is **Brett's Kitchen,** an excellent spot for a sandwich or an omelet during the week.

Go north on Franklin Street to Chicago Avenue. Two blocks east on ㉖ Chicago Avenue is the **Moody Bible Institute** (820 N. La Salle St., ☎ 312/329–4000), a massive contemporary brick structure. Other campus buildings spread out behind it to the north. Here students of various conservative Christian denominations study and prepare for religious careers.

Backtrack to Orleans Street. The bleak high-rises you see to the northwest are the southeastern edge of the infamous **Cabrini Green** public-housing project—so close to the affluence of River North but a world away. Cabrini Green is one of many war zones created in Chicago by public housing. Although some believe it's only a matter of time before the project is razed to accommodate developers of luxury properties who are eyeing the land, relocating the hundreds of people who live there is a political hot potato few want to face. Meanwhile the residents struggle to raise families amid squalor and disrepair, and gang violence claims several lives every year.

㉗ The **River North Concourse** (750 N. Orleans St. at Chicago Ave.) houses many galleries along with a collection of stores and businesses. The striking lobby is done in exposed brick and glass block.

To return by public transportation to Michigan Avenue in the Near North, take the eastbound Lincoln Bus 11 at the intersection of Chicago Avenue and La Salle Street. The bus travels Chicago Avenue to Michigan Avenue and turns south on Michigan Avenue. Or you can take the Chicago Bus 66, from the same stop, eastbound to Michigan Avenue and transfer to the Water Tower Express Bus 125 for points north between Chicago Avenue and Walton Street.

Tour 6: Lincoln Park

Numbers in the margin correspond to points of interest on the Tour 6: Lincoln Park map.

In the early years of the 19th century, the area bounded by North Avenue (1600 N.) on the south, Diversey Parkway (2800 N.) on the north, the lake on the east, and the Chicago River on the west was a sparsely settled community of truck farms and orchards that grew produce for the city of Chicago, 3 miles to the south. The original city burial ground was on the lakefront at North Avenue. The park that today extends from North Avenue to Hollywood Avenue (5700 N.) was established in 1864, after the city transferred about 20,000 bodies to Graceland and Rosehill cemeteries, then far north of the city limits (*see* Tour 7, *below*). Many of the dead were Confederate soldiers who perished at Camp Douglas, the Union's infamous prison camp on the lakefront several miles south. Called Lincoln Park after the then recently assassinated president, this swath of green became the city's first public playground. The neighborhood adjacent to the original park also became known as Lincoln Park (to the confusion of some visitors).

By the mid-1860s the area had become more populated. Germans predominated, and there were Irish and Scottish immigrants as well. The construction in 1860 of the Presbyterian Theological Seminary (later the McCormick Seminary, which moved to Hyde Park in 1977) brought modest residential construction. By the end of the century, immigrants from Eastern Europe—Poles, Slovaks, Serbs, Hungarians, Romanians, and some Italians as well—had swelled the population, and much of the housing stock in the western part of the neighborhood dates from this period.

Between the world wars, expensive new construction, particularly along the lakefront and the park, was undertaken in Lincoln Park. At the same time, however, the deteriorating, once elegant houses to the west were being subdivided into rooming houses—a process that was occurring at roughly the same period in Hyde Park, 10 miles to the south. Ethnic diversification and an increase in crime were also changing the face of the neighborhood. By 1930 a number of African American families had moved to the southwestern corner of Lincoln Park. Activity by the Black Hand terrorist organization, a Mafia-associated secret society, contributed to a climate of fear and heightened suspicion against the Italian community. The neighborhood was further rocked by the St. Valentine's Day Massacre in 1929 and the FBI shooting of John Dillinger at the Biograph Theatre in 1934, both of which took place on North Lincoln Avenue.

Following World War II, the ethnic groups that had been first to arrive in Lincoln Park had achieved some affluence and began to leave for the suburbs and northern parts of the city. A new wave of aspiring immigrants moved to take their place. These new residents—primarily poor Appalachians, Latin Americans, and African Americans—often lacked the resources to maintain their properties. By 1960 nearly a quarter of the housing stock in Lincoln Park was classified as substandard.

As housing prices fell, artists and others who appreciated the aesthetic value of the decaying buildings and were willing to work to restore them moved to the southeastern part of the area. The newcomers joined established residents in forming the Old Town Triangle Association; residents to the north, who had successfully resisted subdivision, formed the Mid-North Association. In 1954, neighborhood institutions, including De Paul University, the McCormick Seminary, four hospitals, a bank, and others dismayed by the decline of the area, formed the Lincoln Park Conservation Association. As the University of Chicago had done in Hyde Park, this association began exploring the possibilities of urban renewal as a means of rejuvenating the area.

As renewal plans progressed, African Americans and Latin Americans became incensed by what they perceived as an attempt to drive them out; sit-ins and demonstrations followed, but were ultimately unsuccessful. The original buildings along North Avenue were bulldozed and replaced with anonymous modern town-house developments, and many north–south streets were blocked off at North Avenue to create an enclosed community to the north. Since the 1960s the gentrification of Lincoln Park has moved steadily westward, spreading as far as Clybourn Avenue, formerly a light industrial strip.

Our tour is divided into three parts. First we'll explore De Paul University, which rules the center of the neighborhood, and visit the shops and restaurants of two nearby, upscale neighborhood arteries: North Lincoln Avenue—where the Biograph Theatre, site of John Dillinger's waterloo, still stands—and Halsted Street. The next section of the tour focuses on the Old Town Triangle, which accommodates a diverse population and has some of the oldest (and most expensive) streets in Chicago. Besides interesting architecture, the area also houses the Second City, one of the nation's most acclaimed comedy clubs. Finally we'll visit the lakefront and see several attractions in the city's oldest and most popular park.

De Paul and North Lincoln Avenue

Our tour starts at the De Paul University campus. The CTA is the best way to get here from the Loop and the Near North Side. Take the Howard A or B Train or the Ravenswood A or B Train to Fullerton Avenue. Sheffield Avenue will be the nearest north–south street. If you're driving, take Lake Shore Drive to Fullerton Avenue and drive west on Fullerton Avenue to Sheffield Avenue. Parking is scarce, especially evenings and weekends, so public transit or a cab is recommended.

The massive brick complex extending halfway down the block on the southwest corner of Fullerton and Sheffield avenues, now known as
❶ the **Sanctuary** (2358 N. Sheffield Ave.), was built in 1895 as the St. Augustine Home for the Aged.

Walk south on Sheffield Avenue and turn left onto Belden Avenue. Con-
❷ tinue east to the entrance to the **De Paul University** campus. Begun in 1898, the university today enrolls about 12,000 students, many of whom

commute from neighboring suburbs. De Paul has a large continuing-education program, and thousands of Chicago adults attend the many evening and weekend classes. This portion of the campus is the former **McCormick Seminary** grounds, where antislavery groups met during the Civil War and Chicagoans sought refuge from the Great Fire in 1871. Note the elegant New England–style church on your right as you enter. The small street inside the U on your left is Chalmers Place. The massive Queen Anne building on the north side has decorative shingles aligned in rows of different shapes; at the west end of the building is a great turret. Now enter the cul-de-sac, whose brick houses, more than 100 years old and once faculty residences at McCormick Seminary, are now privately owned. Note the semicircular brickwork around the windows. At the west end of the street is the Gothic seminary building. Continue south past the seminary, east on Chalmers Place, and south again to exit the university grounds where you entered on Belden Avenue.

Continue east on Belden Avenue and turn left onto Halsted Street. Walk north to the three-way intersection of Fullerton Avenue, Halsted Street, and Lincoln Avenue.

This section of Lincoln Avenue, which runs on a northwest–southeast diagonal, tells a good deal about the neighborhood. Upscale and trendy without being avant-garde, the strip caters to well-educated young and middle-age professionals, emphasizing recreation and leisure-time needs over more mundane requirements. In particular, there are a number of interesting shops catering to children. You'll be hard-pressed to find a drugstore or a shoemaker's shop on this strip: those conveniences have moved to Clark Street, several blocks east, or to Sheffield Avenue.

On the southeast side of the intersection, where Halsted Street and Lincoln Avenue come together at a point, is the huge **White Elephant Children's Memorial Resale Shop** (2380 N. Lincoln Ave., ☎ 312/281–3747), which carries every kind of used merchandise imaginable: furniture, clothing, kitchenware, china, books, and more.

Heading southwest down the street, on the same block, the buildings at **2312–2310 North Lincoln Avenue** were designed by Adler & Sullivan in the 1880s. At the corner of Lincoln and Belden, cross the street. The **John Barleycorn Memorial Pub** (658 W. Belden Ave., ☎ 312/348–8899) is one of Chicago's better-known pubs; classical music accompanies a continuous show of art slides, and ship models adorn the walls. Continuing the nautical theme, the brass-plated door on this 1890 building has not a window, but a porthole.

Head back up Lincoln, past the three-way intersection, to the **Biograph Theatre** (2433 N. Lincoln Ave., ☎ 312/348–4123). The theater is now on the National Register of Historic Places, since it was here that gangster John Dillinger met his end at the hands of the FBI in July 1934. The Biograph shows first-run movies with an emphasis on, as you might expect from the neighborhood, foreign and art films, not Jimmy Cagney flicks. Across the street is another movie theater, the **Threepenny Cinema** (2424 N. Lincoln Ave., ☎ 312/935–5744), which shows a combination of art films and second-run features.

Up the block from the Biograph is **Bookseller's Row** (2445 N. Lincoln Ave., ☎ 312/348–1170), one of several bookstores on the strip, where you'll find an impressive selection of used, out of print, and fine books, as well as a few new volumes. Several doors farther north, the **Children's Bookstore** (2465 N. Lincoln Ave., ☎ 312/248–2665) is the largest

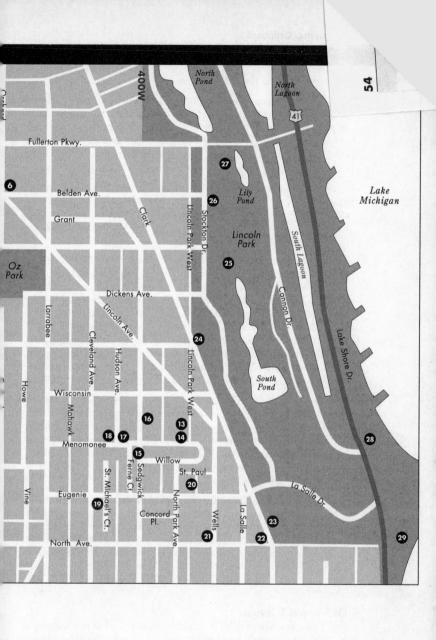

of its kind in the city; besides being unusually well organized and carrying both foreign-language and numerous nonfiction titles, the store hosts readings and storytelling hours.

10 Across Lincoln is the **Red Lion** (2446 N. Lincoln Ave., ☎ 312/348–2695), which advertises itself as "the only English pub in Chicago." Step inside to admire its red London phone booth, or pause for a pint of hard cider or ale. Just south of the Red Lion is **Lounge Ax** (2438 N. Lincoln Ave., ☎ 312/525–6620), one of the best spots in the city to see up-and-coming local and national alternative rock bands.

Return now to the intersection where the White Elephant stands, and head south on Halsted Street, one of the most vibrant, successful streets in Lincoln Park. Besides such chain outposts as The Gap, Gap Kids, and Banana Republic, you'll find a number of charming boutiques plus trendy diners and watering holes.

11 Two blocks down, past Webster Avenue, is **Saturday's Child** (2146 N. Halsted St., ☎ 312/525–8697), an intimate neighborhood toy store with its own play area for youngsters. As opposed to such chaotic emporia as Toys 'R' Us or F.A.O. Schwarz, this small shop emphasizes high-quality playthings that are interactive and educational. It has a good selection of handcrafted and imported toys—including Lego and Brio products—as well as cooperative board games, books, dolls, and arts-and-crafts supplies. A few doors away is a playground for a slightly older crowd: **Otis'** (2150 N. Halsted St., ☎ 312/348–1900), a popular bar, hosts bands Wednesday–Saturday at 9 PM.

12 **Nookies, too** (2114 N. Halsted St., ☎ 312/327–1400), one of the better known diners in this area, is a pleasant spot for an inexpensive meal of the burger or grilled cheese sort. It has a casual counter area in front, and is open a full 24 hours on both Friday and Saturday. On the same block is **Cafe Ba-Ba-Reeba!** (2024 N. Halsted St., ☎ 312/935–5000), which serves great tapas (Spanish appetizers) and a notorious sangria (*see* Chapter 5, Dining).

This ends our tour of Lincoln Avenue and Halsted Street. To continue with our tour of Old Town Triangle, you'll want to either retrieve your car or walk one block farther south on Halsted Street to Armitage Avenue and jump on the No. 73 bus, heading east. Get off where Armitage Avenue dead-ends into Clark Street and Lincoln Park, a trip of just over a half mile. A street called Lincoln Park West runs south from the Armitage and Clark intersection, and is the starting point for the Old Town tour.

Old Town Triangle
Old Town Triangle is filled with courts and lanes that run for only a block or so; to complicate matters, many of the streets have been made one-way in a pattern that can make it difficult to get from one place to another. (Urban planners commonly use this device in redeveloped areas to discourage the inflow of unwanted traffic.) Therefore, if you're driving, you may find it easier to park your car near the start of the tour and explore on foot. If you came by public transportation, you are rewarded by not having to find a place to park.

To reach Old Town Triangle, take Clark Street or Armitage Avenue to Lincoln Park West and walk south. (If you're on Lincoln Avenue, head south to Wisconsin Street, turn west, and proceed to Lincoln Park West.) Be sure to have a look at the elegant row of gracious old painted-brick buildings at **1850–1858 North Lincoln Avenue.**

The west side of Lincoln Park West, between Wisconsin and Menomonee, is a gold mine of historic residential architecture. The two marvelous frame houses at **1838 and 1836 North Lincoln Park West** were built for the Wacker family in the early 1870s. Frame houses are relatively uncommon in Lincoln Park, in part because of the restrictions on wood construction that went into effect following the Chicago Fire in 1871. (Some poorer areas in the southwest of Lincoln Park do have extensive frame construction; the regulations were not always strictly enforced.)

The smaller of the two buildings, 1836, was built just after the fire; it has narrow clapboards, bay windows, leaded glass, and decorative iron grillwork around the miniature widow's walk above the front entrance. Note also the decorative cutouts in the wood over the front door. The exterior painting has been done in contrasting brown, beige, and white to reveal the details of the woodwork. The larger house, painted gray and white, is a grand structure built to resemble a Swiss chalet. Notice the wider clapboards and detailed ornaments and traceries; other notable touches are the overhanging veranda, the twin attic windows, and the ornately carved supports under the veranda and eaves.

Just past the frame houses are five **Louis Sullivan row houses** (1826–1834 N. Lincoln Park). These brick, Queen Anne–style homes provide an unusual glimpse of the architect's early work (1885). His later projects were almost never residential. The love of geometric ornamentation that he eventually brought to such projects as the Carson Pirie Scott building is already visible here—notice the cornices and decorative window tops.

Continue south to the corner, turn west on Menomonee Street, and go two blocks to Sedgwick Street. On the southwest corner of the intersection is **Marge's Pub** (1758 N. Sedgwick St., ☎ 312/787–3900), the oldest commercial property in Lincoln Park and a good place to stop for a beer. The building, with its redbrick construction, decorated in stone around the windows, is a familiar style in older Lincoln Park buildings.

Turn right onto the **1800 North Sedgwick Street** block and proceed about halfway up the block. The materials used to build the houses on the right begin with handsome contemporary redbrick and move on to poured concrete, oddly colored brick, and gray wood. This strip may be the most expensive in Chicago. Each of the houses was custom-designed for its owner at an astronomical price by a different world-renowned architect. Such were the egos involved that the architects could agree on nothing—not style, not materials, not lot size, not even the height of the buildings. Although some of the structures might look good on another site, particularly if surrounded by some land, here they look like transplanted misfits, jammed in together, out of character with the neighborhood and with each other. Despite their monetary value, little about them is aesthetically pleasing.

If you're on foot, retrace your steps to Menomonee Street, turn right, and walk one block to Hudson Avenue. (If you're driving, continue north up Sedgwick Street, turn left at Wisconsin, and then left again at Hudson and head south a block; there are traffic barriers on Menomonee between Sedgwick Street and Hudson Avenue.) The Japanese-style building where the street curves is the **Midwest Buddhist Temple** (435 W. Menomonee St., ☎ 312/943–7801). Plain walls, landscaped gardens, and a pagoda-like roof strike an unusual but harmonious note in this largely brick neighborhood. In mid-June, Old Town

Triangle hosts the Old Town Art Fair, which claims to be the oldest juried art fair in the country, and the Midwest Buddhist Temple is one of the most popular food vendors at the fair.

18 Before you turn on Menomonee Street, regard the half-timber building at the corner, **1800 North Hudson Avenue,** a particularly handsome example of a style that's unusual for Lincoln Park.

19 Go west one block on Menomonee Street then south on Cleveland Avenue to Eugenie Street and **St. Michael's Church** (1633 N. Cleveland Ave., ☎ 312/642–2498). This massive, ornate Romanesque building was constructed on land donated in the 1850s by Michael Diversey (the early beer baron after whom Diversey Parkway was named) to provide a church where the area's German community could worship. The structure partially withstood the fire of 1871, and German residents of the neighborhood restored the interior of the church after the fire. Their work is a legacy of exquisite craftsmanship. Outside, notice the classical columns of different heights, the elaborate capitals, the many roofs with stonework at the top, and the elegant spire.

20 Walk east on Eugenie Street about five blocks and turn left onto **Crilly Court,** one of the oldest streets in Chicago. Built in the 1880s by developer Daniel Crilly, the court's town houses and apartment buildings were renovated 50 years later by one of Crilly's sons, who created beautiful private gardens behind the homes. The restoration was one of the first steps in the renewal and gentrification of Old Town Triangle in particular and Lincoln Park in general. Several years ago, the buildings were acquired by developers who converted them into condominiums. The existing tenants were given the option to buy, but most of them—some quite elderly—could not afford to and were forced to move.

21 When you come to St. Paul Avenue, turn east, proceed to Wells Street, and turn right. **Second City** (1616 N. Wells St., ☎ 312/337–3992) is 1½ blocks south, between Eugenie Street and North Avenue. This club, known for its improvisational comedy, was the training ground for such talents as Elaine May, Mike Nichols, Alan Arkin, Joan Rivers, John Belushi, Bill Murray, Shelley Long, and Rick Moranis. It eventually inspired several branch theaters—Toronto's Second City, which produced Dan Aykroyd, John Candy, and Gilda Radner, is probably the best known—as well as the hit TV show *SCTV*. Tickets run $5–$15, and shows are at 8:30 Monday–Thursday, 8 and 11 Friday–Saturday, and 8 Sunday. (*See* Chapter 7, The Arts and Nightlife.)

TIME OUT Topo Gigio (1437 N. Wells St., ☎ 312/751-8070), down the block from Second City, has a wide selection of wine and excellent traditional Italian cuisine. Their *bruschetta*—grilled Italian bread brushed with garlic and olive oil and crowned with tomato—is particularly recommended. In the summertime a lovely garden is open for dining.

Lincoln Park

With Old Town Triangle behind us, we enter Lincoln Park proper. For those who have followed the tour to this point, go south on Wells Street to North Avenue, turn left, and walk east to Clark Street. If you're just picking up the tour at this point, you can reach Lincoln Park by taking the Sheridan Road Bus 151 north from North Michigan Avenue. Get off at North Avenue. If you're driving, take Lake Shore Drive to the La Salle Street–North Avenue exit. Make a right turn onto Stockton Drive and look for metered parking. The area can be extremely congested, however, especially on weekends, so driving is not recommended.

The massive Romanesque structure on the west side of Clark Street is **(22) Moody Memorial Church** (1609 N. La Salle St., ☎ 312/943–0466), one of the largest Protestant churches in the nation. The nondenominational church, named after 19th-century evangelist Dwight L. Moody, is associated with the Moody Bible Institute (*see* Tour 5, *above*).

Across Clark is the southwestern entrance to the park. First pay a visit ★ **(23)** to the **Chicago Historical Society,** which stands at the northeast corner of North Avenue and Clark Street. The original stately brick Georgian structure was built in 1932, and if you walk around to the eastern side (facing the lake) you can see what it looked like at the time. On the Clark Street side, the original facade has been covered by a sparkling all-glass addition, which contains a café at its south end (the curved portion). In the café's north wall is a terra-cotta arch designed by Daniel Burnham more than 100 years ago. The historical society's permanent exhibits include the much-loved diorama room that portrays scenes from Chicago's history and has been a part of the lives of generations of Chicago children. Other highlights include collections of costumes and one of the park's several statues of Abraham Lincoln— the nose of which gleams from having been rubbed by countless visitors. In addition the society mounts temporary exhibitions; its Civil War installation, "A House Divided," will run for the next several years, and Civil War buffs shouldn't miss it. *1601 N. Clark St.,* ☎ *312/642– 4600.* ☛ *$3 adults, $2 senior citizens, $1 children; free Mon.* ☉ *Mon.–Sat. 9:30–4:30, Sun. noon–5.*

All of Chicago's parks, and **Lincoln Park** in particular, are dotted with sculptures—historical, literary, or just plain fanciful. East of the historical society is one of the most famous, a standing figure of Abraham Lincoln, completed in 1887 by the noted American sculptor Augustus Saint-Gaudens, whose portrayals of military heroes and presidents adorn almost every major city east of the Mississippi River. The sculptor used a mask of Lincoln's face and casts of his hands that were made before he became president.

Head north through the park, or walk along Clark Street, and you'll **(24)** see the imposing classical-style building that houses the **Chicago Academy of Sciences.** Despite its scholarly name, this is not an institution of higher learning but a museum specializing in the natural history of the Midwest. The permanent exhibits include dioramas showing the ecology of Chicago millions of years ago, before it was settled, and back-lit ceiling images of the night sky seen from Chicago. Special exhibits are mounted regularly. *2001 N. Clark St.,* ☎ *312/871–2668.* ☛ *$2 adults, $1 senior citizens and children, free Mon.* ☉ *Daily 10–5.*

Heading into the park and wandering north along the park's main **(25)** north–south artery, Stockton Drive, will bring you to the **Lincoln Park Zoo,** one of the finest small urban zoos in the country. (Look for the red barn, home of "Farm in the Zoo": The main entrance is just north of it.) Begun in 1868 with a pair of swans donated by New York's Central Park, the 35-acre zoo grew through donations of animals from wealthy Chicago residents and the purchase of a collection from the Barnum and Bailey Circus. Many of the big houses, such as the lion house and the elephant house, are built in the classical brick typical of 19th-century zoos. The older buildings are surrounded by newer outdoor habitats that try to re-create the animals' natural, wild surroundings. Outside the lion house there's a window that lets zoo visitors stand almost face to face with the tigers (if the giant cats are in the mood).

Lincoln Park Zoo is particularly noted for its Great Ape House; the 20 gorillas are considered the finest collection in the world. Because the park participates in breeding programs, there are usually several babies about. It's fascinating to spend an hour watching the members of each community interact. In addition to the reptile house, the large-mammal house (elephants, giraffes, black rhinos), the monkey house, the bird house, the small-mammal house, and a huge polar-bear pool with two bears, the zoo has several rare and endangered species, such as the Spectacle Bear (named for the eyeglasslike markings around its eyes). Several koalas live in a "koala condo" in the same building as the main gift shop. Youngsters will enjoy the children's zoo, the Farm in the Zoo (farm animals and a learning center with films and demonstrations), and the Kids' Corner Discovery Place, with hands-on activities. *2200 N. Cannon Dr.,* ☎ *312/742–7695.* ☛ *Free.* ۞ *Daily 9–5.*

The homely bronze figure at Stockton Drive opposite Dickens Street is Hans Christian Andersen, seated there since 1896. Beside him is the beautiful swan from his most famous story, "The Ugly Duckling."

㉖ Also near the zoo, at the western edge of the park, opposite Belden Avenue, is the **Shakespeare Garden,** featuring flowers and plants mentioned in the bard's works. The bronze statue of the great playwright was cast by William Ordway Partridge in 1894, after he had exhibited a plaster model of the work at the Columbian Exposition.

㉗ North of the zoo is the **Lincoln Park Conservatory,** which has a palm house, a fernery, a cactus house, and a show house in which displays are mounted: the azalea show in February, the Easter show in March or April, the chrysanthemum show in November, and the Christmas show in December. **Grandmother's Garden,** between Stockton Drive and Lincoln Park West, is a collection dating from 1893 of informal beds of perennials, including hibiscus and chrysanthemums. A large outdoor garden has flowering plants. *2400 N. Stockton Dr.,* ☎ *312/742–7736.* ☛ *Free.* ۞ *Daily 9–5, 10–5 during shows.*

In the conservatory garden is an uncommonly joyful fountain where bronze storks, fish, and small mer-boys cavort in the spraying water. The 1887 **Bates Fountain** was the collaborative effort of Saint-Gaudens and his assistant, Frederick MacMonnies.

㉘ At Fullerton turn right and walk under Lake Shore Drive to the lakefront. From here you can stroll in either direction for several miles. Toward the south end of the lake's waterfront, **North Avenue Beach** is likely to be thronged on summer weekends but sparsely populated at other times. To get back to the Near North Side, about 2 miles from here, walk south past North Avenue Beach and follow the lakefront promenade. Notice the blue-and-white beach house, its portholes and "smokestacks" mimicking an old ocean liner. At the south end of the **㉙** beach stop by the 1950s vintage **chess pavilion** to watch people of all ages engrossed in intellectual combat. Look for the carved reliefs along its base and the king and queen that flank it on either side.

If you don't feel like a walk on the beach, go west from Fullerton Avenue to Stockton Drive and catch Bus 151 southbound, which will take you back to Michigan Avenue. Buses 22 and 36 on Clark Street will also take you back to the Near North or the Loop.

Tour 7: North Clark Street

A car or bus ride up North Clark Street north of Lincoln Park provides an interesting view of how cities and their ethnic populations grow and change. Before the late 1960s the Clark Street area was solidly white and middle class. Andersonville, the Swedish community centered at Foster Avenue (5200 N.) and Clark Street, extended north half a mile and included residential buildings to the east and west as well as a vital shopping strip on Clark Street. Then, in the early 1970s, immigrants from Asia began to arrive. Chicago's first Thai restaurant opened at 5000 North Clark Street. (The Thai population has since become dispersed throughout the city without establishing a significant concentration here.) The Japanese community, which had shops and restaurants at the northern end of the North 3000s on Clark Street, became more firmly entrenched, joined by substantial Korean immigration. Korean settlement has since grown to the north and west, along north Lincoln Avenue. As the 1970s ended, the Asian immigrants were being joined by newcomers from the Middle East. In classic fashion, these groups have moved into the neighborhood as the old established group (the Swedish community) moved out to the suburbs. Today the shops on North Clark Street bear witness to the process of ethnic transition.

You can board the northbound Clark Street Bus 22 on Dearborn Street in the Loop or on Clark Street north of Walton Street. Or you can drive to Clark Street and North Avenue, where we'll begin our ride. North Avenue (1600 N.) is the southern boundary of the Lincoln Park neighborhood, which extends north to Diversey Avenue (2800 N.). The drive through Lincoln Park affords views of handsome renovated housing, housing in the process of being restored, upscale shops, and youthful joggers.

As you cross Belmont (3200 N.), you'll notice more and more ethnic restaurants and shops. You can get all of the ingredients for sushi at **Star Market** (3349 N. Clark St.), Chicago's largest Japanese grocery. Check out the mysterious condiments, unusual greens, and the exquisitely fresh (and astronomically expensive) fish to be used raw, thinly sliced, for sashimi. If you prefer to have your sushi prepared for you, try highly rated **Matsuya** (3469 N. Clark St.). For excellent Japanese noodle dishes, visit **Noodle Noodle** (3475 N. Clark St.), a cute storefront restaurant that's never empty.

Continuing north to the intersection with Addison Street, you'll find an abundance of bars and restaurants with the word "sport" somewhere in their names, all because of nearby **Wrigley Field,** home of the Chicago Cubs and, to many, the *ne plus ultra* baseball stadium. Although area residents and baseball purists lost their fight in 1988 against the installation of lights for night games, many Cubs games are still played in the afternoon. Just don't expect to see the home team win—the Cubs last appeared in the World Series in 1945, and it was 1908 when they last won.

At Clark Street and Irving Park Road (4000 N.), you'll find **Graceland Cemetery,** the final resting place of many 19th-century millionaires and other local luminaries. Architecture aficionados can pay their respects at the graves of Louis Sullivan and Ludwig Mies van der Rohe.

Foster Avenue is the old southern boundary of Andersonville. Around the corner on Foster Avenue, west of Clark Street, is the **Middle Eastern Bakery and Grocery** (1512 W. Foster Ave.). Here are falafel, meat pies, spinach pies, *baba ghannouj* (eggplant puree dip), oil-cured olives, grains, pita bread, and a seductive array of Middle Eastern sweets—flaky, honey-dipped, nut-filled delights. There's another Middle Eastern Bakery and Grocery branch on the 5200 North block, but it doesn't have as wide a selection of pastries. Also on the 5200 block, just north of Foster Avenue, the **Beirut Restaurant** serves *kifta* kebabs (grilled meatballs), baba ghannouj, *kibbee* (ground lamb with bulghur wheat), falafel, meat and spinach pies, and more. Across the street the original **Ann Sather** restaurant, with its white wood on redbrick storefront, specializes in Swedish cuisine and generally does a good business. South of Ann Sather, **Cousin's** offers steak sandwiches, Italian beef, burritos, and tacos; the specials of the day include potato stew with rice, *kheema* (ground beef) stew with rice, okra stew with rice, and other traditional dishes of the Middle East and the Indian subcontinent. Across the street on the same block the **Byblos I Bakery and Deli** offers Lebanese Middle Eastern bread and groceries. If you arrive at the right time, you'll see the window filled with pita breads still puffed.

Although new immigrants have changed the face of the neighborhood, the 5200 block still shows many signs of the earlier wave of Swedish settlers. Opposite the bakery, the **Swedish-American Museum Center** (5211 N. Clark St., ☎ 312/728–8111) has beautifully decorated papier-mâché roosters and horses, place mats, craft items, tablecloths, and candelabra in its gift store; it has changing art and cultural exhibits, too. North of the Byblos Bakery are several Scandinavian restaurants and food shops. The wares of **Nelson's Scandinavian Bakery** are classic European pastries: elephant ears and petit fours with chocolate, for example. The **Svea Restaurant** has polka-dot maroon tablecloths and mouthwatering breakfasts. **Erickson's Delicatessen** has glögg in bottles, crispbreads, Ramlösa, hollandaise sauce mix, homemade spiced herring, and imported cheese.

Just north of Erickson's the **Andersonville Artists Original Arts and Crafts Display** features the work of local artisans, which includes hand-painted china, small sculptures, and paintings. On the other side of the street, the shelves of **Wikstrom's Gourmet Foods** contain Wasa bread, Swedish pancake mix, coffee roll mix, lingonberries, dilled potatoes, and raspberry dessert. Just north of Wikstrom's is **G.M. Nordling Jeweler.** At **Reza's Restaurant** (5255 N. Clark St.) you can dine on outstanding Persian cuisine such as kebabs, *must* and *khiyar* (yogurt and cucumber), pomegranate juice, and charbroiled ground beef with Persian rice. The setting is very attractive, featuring white tablecloths and exposed brick walls, and the service is always good.

Phil House (5845 N. Clark St.) is a Philippine market that stocks fresh fish, taro root, fresh shrimp of all sizes, crayfish, langostinos, *longaniza* (Philippine sausage), and a huge selection of spring-roll skins. Chicago is home to a very large group of Philippine immigrants, but like the Thais (and unlike the Indians and the Koreans) they are not concentrated in a single area.

Tour 8: Argyle Street and Uptown

In many cities, *uptown* suggests an elite residential area, as opposed to *downtown,* the central business district. Something like that must have been in the mind of the Californian who bought Chicago's Uptown National Bank sight unseen a few years ago; ever since he got a look at his property and its neighborhood, he's been trying to sell it. In Chicago, Uptown—an area bounded by Irving Park Road (4000 N.) on the south, Foster Avenue (5200 N.) on the north, the lake on the east, and Clark Street and Ravenswood Avenue (1800 W.) on the west—is the home of the down-and-out: families on welfare, drug addicts, winos, and others of Chicago's most disadvantaged residents live here. The neighborhood is rough and the rents are low.

Given the characteristics of the neighborhood, numerous social-service agencies are located here. Because of that, and the low rents, Uptown is where Vietnamese immigrants were placed when they began arriving in Chicago in substantial numbers following the end of the Vietnam War. Hmong refugees from Laos likewise joined a polyglot community whose common bond, if any, was a shared destitution.

Yet the arrival of the Vietnamese groups brought interesting developments in Uptown. The first years were difficult: Although some of the families were educated and well-to-do in Vietnam, they came here with no money and no knowledge of English. The Hmong were further disadvantaged by having had no urban experience; these tribal mountain people were transplanted directly from remote, rather primitive villages into the heart of a modern urban slum. Nonetheless, like earlier immigrants who came to America, these people arrived with the determination to make new lives for themselves. They took any job that was offered, no matter how menial or how low the pay, and they worked two jobs when they could find them. From their meager earnings, they saved money. And they did two other important things: They sent their children to school and zealously oversaw their studies, and they formed self-help associations. Through the associations, they used pooled savings as rotating funds to set one, then another, up in business: grocery stores and bakeries to sell the foods that tasted like home, clothing shops and hairdressing salons to fill the needs of the community, and finally restaurants that attracted not only people from the old country who were beginning to have discretionary funds but also Americans of other ethnic backgrounds.

As their businesses prospered, they bought property. And the property they bought was the cheapest they could find, on the most depressed street in this crumbling neighborhood, Argyle Street (5000 N.). Today Argyle Street, a two-block strip between Broadway on the west and Sheridan Road on the east, is thriving. Its commercial buildings have been upgraded, thereby attracting the shops and restaurants of other Asian communities in Chicago, principally the Chinese and Thai. As "New Chinatown" or "Chinatown North," the area became so attractive that the old Chinatown merchant's association, representing the stores along Wentworth Street on the south side, considered relocating there en masse. Although that plan fell through, some stores moved on their own. The Argyle Street group has been so successful that there is now a rivalry between the two Chinatowns for customers in search of Asian goods and services.

If you've never been to Southeast Asia, a walk down Argyle Street is the next best thing. The neighborhood bustles with street traffic, and the stores are crowded with people buying fresh produce, baked goods, kitchen equipment, and 50-pound sacks of rice. Few signs are in English, though merchants know enough English to serve customers who don't speak their native language. Often older children and teenagers who learned English in school are pressed into service to help visitors. The tastes and smells of Southeast Asia are also in evidence on Argyle Street. Only here will you find, for example, the wonderful, vile-smelling durian fruit—an addiction for many, anathema to some—and other staples of Southeast Asian cuisine. Here, too, you will find many of the best Vietnamese restaurants in the city, including **Mekong** (4953 N. Broadway) and **Pho Xe Lua** (1021 W. Argyle St.), as well as Chinese restaurants serving noodles and barbecued duck and pork (which you might enjoy munching as you walk). At the **Chiu Quon Bakery** (1127 W. Argyle St.) you can purchase authentic Chinese pastries—everything from the appealing baby moon almond cookies to the more unusual thousand-year-old egg cake.

Today, fueled in part by the success of the Vietnamese and, more generally, the prosperity that success has brought, Uptown is changing. Renovators are buying once fine old properties and restoring them, and young middle-class folk, driven here by the high prices in such neighborhoods as Lincoln Park to the south, are beginning to move in. The area has become a political battleground between those who claim to represent the poor and downtrodden and those who believe that the undeniable social costs of rehabbing are less than the social costs of allowing the neighborhood to fall further and further into decay.

Tour 9: Devon Avenue

As immigration laws were made more lenient in the 1970s and 1980s, the number of immigrants arriving in Chicago increased substantially. In the 1970s, newcomers from the Indian subcontinent began to arrive, and in the 1980s they were followed by Asians from Thailand, Korea, the Philippines, and Vietnam, as well as large numbers from the Middle East, including Palestinians, Syrians, Lebanese, and Turks. The Soviet relaxation of restrictions on Jewish emigration shortly before the breakup of the Soviet Union turned many Jewish refuseniks into American residents.

Several of these diverse cultures mingle along a mile-long strip of Devon Avenue between Sacramento and Oakley streets, near the northern edge of the city. A stroll down the strip on any sunny Sunday afternoon or hot summer evening will allow you to appreciate the avenue's variety of cultures. At the eastern end is the hub of the Indian community, with stores catering to both Muslims and Hindus. As you walk west, you will see sari stores give way to Korean restaurants and Russian groceries. At the western end is an Orthodox Jewish neighborhood, dotted with kosher bakeries and butchers, and religious bookstores.

To get to Devon Avenue (6400 N.), take Lake Shore Drive north to Hollywood Avenue. Stay in one of the left lanes and go west on Hollywood Avenue to Ridge Avenue. Turn right on Ridge Avenue and head north for about a mile to Devon Avenue. Turn left on Devon Avenue, drive about 2 miles west to Oakley Street (2200 W.), and park your car. Your tour will take you down Devon Avenue as far as Sacramento Avenue (3000 W.).

Starting on the south side of Devon Avenue at Oakley Street, you'll see **Farm City Meats** (2255 W. Devon Ave.), purveyors of *Halal* meat, from animals slaughtered according to the provisions of Islamic law. The store sells baby goat meat, as well as a large selection of fish. As you walk west, you'll see many stores, such as **Video Palace** (2315 W. Devon Ave.), that sell or rent Indian and Pakistani movies and videotapes.

There are also at least a dozen stores that sell the colorful saris worn by Indian women, including the **Taj Sari Palace** (2553 W. Devon Ave.), **Sari Sapne** (2623 W. Devon Ave.), **Sagar Saris** (2627 W. Devon Ave.), and **ISP Indian Sari Palace** (2536 W. Devon Ave.).

Numerous grocery stores along your route sell Indian foods, condiments, and kitchenware; the exotic smells are enticing. Take a look at the **Middle East Trading Co.** (2505 W. Devon Ave.) and **Patel Brothers** (with 3 locations at 2542, 2600, and 2610 W. Devon Ave.).

For a quick snack, try the Indian food at **Chat and Chat** (6357 N. Claremont Ave., at the corner of Devon Ave.), or **Annapurna Fast Food Vegetarian Snacks and Sweets** (2608 W. Devon Ave.).

Several Indian restaurants along Devon Avenue are good choices for a meal, including **Viceroy of India** (2518 W. Devon Ave.), **Moti Mahal** (2525 W. Devon Ave.), and the vegetarian **Natraj** (2240 W. Devon Ave.). Try the tandoori chicken or fish, which is marinated and grilled, the *sagh paneer* (a creamy mixture of spinach and cheese), or the dal (a lentil puree soup).

Several stores specialize in Russian cuisine and are easily recognized by the signs in Cyrillic writing hanging outside. Among them are **Globus International Foods and Delicatessen** (2909 W. Devon Ave.), **Three Sisters Delicatessen** (2854 W. Devon Ave.), and **Kashtan Deli** (2740 W. Devon Ave.). Three Sisters has a large selection of *matrioshkas* (the popular Russian dolls that are stacked one inside another). At 2845 West Devon Avenue, you'll see the **Croatian Cultural Center.**

When you reach the western end of Devon Avenue, notice the many stores and restaurants catering to the orthodox Jewish community. The restaurants and bakeries are good bets for either a sit-down meal or a snack to eat while you walk. Watch for **Miller's Market** (2727 W. Devon Ave.), **Tel Aviv Kosher Bakery** (2944 W. Devon Ave.), **Kosher Karry** (2828 W. Devon Ave.), and **Levinson's Bakery** (2856 W. Devon Ave.). The **Good Morgan Kosher Fish Market** (2948 W. Devon Ave.) has lox and other smoked fish for sale.

Several stores along the way sell Hebrew books and sacramental items, including **Rosenblum's Hebrew Bookstore** (2910 W. Devon Ave.) and the **Chicago Hebrew Bookstore** (2942 W. Devon Ave.). Rosenblum's has a large selection of unusual cookbooks, including several on Yemeni and Sephardic cuisine.

Off the Beaten Track

Federal Reserve Bank (230 S. La Salle St., ☎ 312/322–5111) explains how checks are processed and how money travels; free tours are given daily 9–1. Call two weeks in advance for reservations. No children under 17 admitted. There's a public tour Tuesday at 1 that requires only one day's notice; it's also worth calling to see if you can squeeze into an already booked "private" tour that has fewer than the 20-person limit. A visitors center in the lobby has permanent exhibits of old bills, counterfeit money, and a million dollars in one-dollar bills (though to thwart would-be thieves, most of the stash is in dollar-size scraps of paper). ☉ *Weekdays 9–5.*

If you're at McCormick Place, take a walk on the promenade that runs between the convention center and the lake. You can watch small planes take off from and land at tiny Meigs Field and, in the summer, observe the sailboats as they bob in Burnham Harbor.

The **Trompe l'Oeil Building** (1207 W. Division St.) is on the northeast corner of La Salle and Division streets, but you should study its appearance from a block east, at Clark and Division streets, or approach it from the south for the full effect of its rose window, ornate arched doorway, stone steps, columns, and sculptures. As you move closer to the building, you'll discover that an ordinary high-rise has been elaborately painted to make it look like an entirely different work of architecture.

Olive Park juts out into Lake Michigan a block north of Lake Point Towers (505 N. Lake Shore Dr.); to find it, walk east on Grand Avenue, pass under Lake Shore Drive, and bear left. It has no roads, just paved walkways and lots of benches, trees, shrubs, and grass. The marvelous and unusual views of the city skyline from here, in addition to the absence of vehicular traffic, make it seem as though you're miles from the city, not just blocks from the busy Near North side.

Slightly northwest of Hyde Park, at the corner of Drexel Boulevard and 50th Street, is the headquarters of **Operation PUSH** (930 E. 50th St., ☎ 312/373–3366), Jesse Jackson's black self-help organization. You'll recognize the building, a former synagogue, by its splendid columns before you see its colorful cloth banner. Three blocks east and one block north you'll find **4995 South Woodlawn Avenue,** the home of the controversial black leader Louis Farrakhan, who has made it a headquarters of the Nation of Islam. The great house was built by Elijah Mohammed, the Nation's founder; its $3 million funding was rumored to have come from the Libyan despot Muammar Khadafi.

Nearby, at 49th Street and Kenwood Avenue, stand two early works by Frank Lloyd Wright, **Blossom House** (4858 S. Kenwood Ave.) and **MacArthur House** (4852 S. Kenwood Ave.), both built in 1892. Across from Blossom House is **Farmers' Field,** a park where animals grazed as recently as the 1920s. A few blocks away, at 49th Street and Ellis Avenue (4901 S. Ellis Ave.), is the 22-room Prairie Style **Julius Rosenwald Mansion** built by the Sears Roebuck executive in the early 1900s. After a stint as a home for boys, followed by years of disuse, the mansion was purchased by a family and extensively restored.

A treeless hill near Lincoln Park's **Montrose Harbor** draws kite-flying enthusiasts of all ages on sunny weekends. Take Lake Shore Drive north from the Loop about 5 miles, exit at Montrose, turn right into the park, and look for colorful stunt kites on your left. Windsurfers often practice at nearby **Montrose Beach.**

If you're interested in the social history of the late 19th century, there's no place that exemplifies the era better than the planned community of **Pullman** on the far south side. Built in 1880 by railcar tycoon George M. Pullman for the workers at his Palace Car Company, the town had its own hotel, hospital, library, shopping center, and bank. The styles of the homes reflect the status of their original occupants: Workers' homes are simple, those of skilled craftsmen slightly fancier, and executive housing more elaborate still. The town was the site of the famous Pullman strike of 1894 and also its partial cause, because the company cut wages without reducing the rents for workers in company-owned housing. The factory is closed now, but the houses are occupied and the community is thriving. To get to Pullman, take I–94 (Dan Ryan Expy.) south, exit at 111th Street, and turn right. For more information, call the Historic Pullman Foundation (☎ 312/785–8181).

CHICAGO WITH CHILDREN

Among the outstanding activities Chicago has in store for family groups are several museums that provide hours of fascination for youngsters, where dozens of exhibits not only don't forbid you to touch them but actually require that you interact with them.

Adler Planetarium (*see* Tour 4, *above*). The Sky Shows enthrall young and old.

Art Institute of Chicago (*see* Tour 1, *above*). Kids can choose from more than 20 Gallery Games that are as fun as they are educational at the downstairs Children's Museum.

Brookfield Zoo (*see* Chapter 8, Excursions from Chicago). Here are elephants, dolphins, a rain forest, and enough animals to keep you busy all day.

Chicago Academy of Sciences (*see* Tour 6, *above*) has many exhibits that will fascinate children.

Chicago Children's Museum (*see* Tour 5, *above*). Designed specifically for very young children, this museum at Navy Pier has many things to see and touch.

Children's Bookstore (*see* Tour 6, *above*). Browsing is encouraged among a superb collection of carefully selected books for children; story hours for children under six are scheduled several times a week.

Field Museum (*see* Tour 4, *above*). Three rooms are filled with the touchy-feely stuff that small folk love, and many of the regular exhibits have considerable appeal for children.

57th Street Books (*see* Tour 3, *above*). In addition to the excellent selection of children's books, the store has a play and reading area where youngsters can browse or grownups can read to them.

Harold Washington Library Center (*see* Tour 1, *above*) offers a variety of children's activities, including story time for preschoolers, film programs, theater and music performances, and tours.

John G. Shedd Aquarium (*see* Tour 4, *above*). The display of sea creatures is guaranteed to captivate every visitor, regardless of age.

Lincoln Park Zoo (*see* Tour 6, *above*). The Children's Zoo, the "Farm in the Zoo," and the Kids' Corner Discovery Place are the special attractions prepared just for youngsters.

Museum of Science and Industry (*see* Tour 3, *above*). Children and parents may find themselves competing here to see who gets to use the instruments or take part in the activities first.

Navy Pier (*see* Tour 5, *above*). A 15-story Ferris wheel, a colorful carousel, the Chicago Children's Museum, an outdoor skating rink, and a park make the new Navy Pier paradise for kids.

North Pier (*see* Tour 5, *above*). With splashy decor, miniature golf, a fast-food court, gimmicky sit-down restaurants, and every kind of video game imaginable (including interactive games), North Pier is very popular with kids and teens.

SIGHTSEEING CHECKLISTS

Galleries

Chicago has more art galleries than any American city but New York. Most galleries are open weekdays and Saturday 10–5 or 11–5 and at other times by appointment. The largest concentrations of galleries are in the River North area and on Superior and Ontario streets east of

Michigan Avenue. The Near North tour in this chapter points out many of the buildings that house galleries. Because the galleries and their shows change frequently, the prospective visitor should consult the *Chicago Gallery News* for a full current listing.

Historical Buildings and Sites

This list of Chicago's principal buildings and sites includes both attractions that were covered in the preceding tours and additional attractions that are described here for the first time.

Amoco Building (Tour 1)

Art Institute of Chicago (Tour 1)

Auditorium Theatre (Tour 1)

Biograph Theatre (Tour 6)

Blackstone Hotel (Tour 2)

Buckingham Fountain (Tour 1)

Carbide and Carbon Building (Tour 1)

Carson Pirie Scott (Tour 1)

Chevrolet Building (Tour 3)

Chicago Academy of Sciences (Tour 6)

Chicago Board of Trade (Tour 1)

Chicago City Hall–Cook County Building (Tour 1)

Chicago Cultural Center (Tour 1)

Chicago Hilton and Towers (Tour 2)

Chicago Historical Society (Tour 6)

Chicago Mercantile Exchange (Tour 1)

Chicago Temple (Tour 1)

Chicago Theatre (Tour 1)

Chicago Theological Seminary (Tour 3)

Civic Opera House (Tour 1)

Clarke House. Chicago's oldest building, Clarke House was constructed in 1836 in Greek Revival style. Period furniture enlivens the interior. Part of the Prairie Avenue Historical District. *1800 S. Prairie Ave.,* ☏ *312/922–8687.* ☛ *$8, includes tour of Clarke House and Glessner House.* ☉ *Fri.–Sun.*

Crilly Court (Tour 6)

Daley Center (Tour 1)

Dearborn Park (Tour 2)

Dearborn Station (Tour 2)

Donohue Building (Tour 2)

Drake Hotel (Tour 5)

Federal Center and Plaza (Tour 1)

Fine Arts Building (Tour 1)

First National Bank of Chicago (Tour 1)

Fisher Building (Tour 1)

Franklin Building (Tour 2)

Glessner House. The only surviving building in Chicago by the architect H.H. Richardson, Glessner House was designed in 1886. Part of the Prairie Avenue Historic District. *1801 S. Prairie Ave.,* ☏ *312/922–8687.* ☛ *$8, includes tour of Glessner House and Clarke House.* ☉ *Fri.–Sun.*

Heller House (Tour 3)

Hull House. The columned, redbrick, turn-of-the-century Hull House seems out of place on its site, surrounded by the massive and modern buildings of the University of Illinois campus. Here Jane Addams wrought social work miracles in a neighborhood that was then a slum. Here, too, Benny Goodman learned to play the clarinet. *800 S. Hal-*

sted St., ☎ *312/413–5353.* ☛ *Free.* ☺ *Weekdays 10–4, Sun. noon–5. Closed Sat. and most holidays.*

Illinois Institute of Technology (31st–35th Sts. on S. State St., ☎ 312/567–3000). The campus was designed principally by Mies van der Rohe, with participation by Friedman, Alschuler, and Sincere; Holabird and Roche; and Pace Associates. Built between 1942 and 1958, the structures have the characteristic box shape that is Mies's trademark. Unlike most of his work, these are low-rise buildings. Crown Hall (3360 S. State St.) is the jewel of the collection; the other buildings have a certain sameness and sterility.

International House (Tour 3)

John Hancock Center (Tour 5)

Joseph Regenstein Library (Tour 3)

Julius Rosenwald Mansion (Off the Beaten Track)

Laird Bell Law Quadrangle (Tour 3)

Lutheran School of Theology (Tour 3)

Main Post Office (Tour 1)

Marquette Building (Tour 1)

McCormick Seminary (Tour 6)

Merle Reskin Theatre (Tour 2)

Metropolitan Correctional Center (Tour 1)

Midway Plaisance (Tour 3)

Monadnock Building (Tour 1)

Moody Bible Institute (Tour 5)

Museum of Science and Industry (Tour 3)

Northwestern Atrium Center (Tour 1)

One Financial Place (Tour 1)

Orchestra Hall (Tour 1)

Oriental Institute (Tour 3)

Page Brothers Building (Tour 1)

Palmer House (Tour 1)

Promontory Apartments (5530 S. South Shore Dr.). The building, designed by Mies van der Rohe in 1949, was named for Promontory Point, which juts out into the lake just east of here.

Quaker Oats Building (Tour 5)

Railway Exchange Building (Tour 1)

Reliance Building (Tour 1)

River City (Tour 2)

Robie House (Tour 3)

Rockefeller Memorial Chapel (Tour 3)

The Rookery (Tour 1)

The Sanctuary (Tour 6)

Sears Tower (Tour 1)

State of Illinois Center (Tour 1)

Stone Container Building (Tour 1)

333 West Wacker Drive (Tour 1)

Tribune Tower (Tour 5)

Union Station (Tour 1)

University of Illinois at Chicago (705 S. Halsted St., ☎ 312/996–7000). Designed by Walter Netsch, of Skidmore, Owings & Merrill, the university buildings seem to surge and weave toward one another.

Water Tower (Tour 5)

Windermere House (1642 E. 56th St.). This was designed in 1920 by Rapp and Rapp, known generally for their movie palaces. Notice the grand gatehouse in front of the sweeping semicircular carriage path at the entrance; notice also the heroic scale of the building, with its ornate carvings.

Museums

Adler Planetarium (Tour 4)

American Police Center and Museum. The museum's exhibits are concerned with police work and relationships between the police and the public. Safety, crime and punishment, and drugs and alcohol are among the subjects. One exhibit shows how the police communication system works; another details the history of the Haymarket Riot. A memorial gallery is dedicated to policemen who have lost their lives in the line of duty. *1717 S. State St.,* ☎ *312/431–0005.* ☛ *$3 adults, $2 senior citizens, $1.50 children 6–11.* ☉ *Weekdays 8:30–4.*

Art Institute of Chicago (Tour 1)

Balzekas Museum of Lithuanian Culture. The little-known Balzekas Museum offers a taste of 1,000 years of Lithuanian history and culture on its three floors. You'll find exhibits on rural Lithuania; concentration camps; rare maps, stamps, and coins; textiles; and amber. The library can be used for research. *6500 S. Pulaski Rd.,* ☎ *312/582–6500.* ☛ *$4 adults, $3 senior citizens and students, $1 children under 12; free Mon.* ☉ *Daily 10–4 (Fri. until 8).*

Chicago Academy of Sciences (Tour 6)

Chicago Children's Museum (Tour 5)

Chicago Cultural Center (Tour 1)

Chicago Historical Society (Tour 6)

Czechoslovakian Society of America Heritage Museum and Archives. The collections of the Czechoslovakian Society include crystal, marble, dolls, musical instruments, china, ornamented eggs, vases, paintings, and statues. A library is part of the museum. *2701 S. Harlem Ave., Berwyn,* ☎ *708/795–5800.* ☛ *Free.* ☉ *Weekdays 10–noon and 1–4.*

David and Alfred Smart Museum of Art (Tour 3)

DuSable Museum of African American History. A 10-foot mural in the auditorium of the museum, hand-carved by Robert Witt Ames, depicts black history from Africa to the 1960s. Another gallery features great history makers: Martin Luther King, Jr., Rosa Parks, Paul Robeson, Sojourner Truth, and others. Special exhibits change frequently; a recent one on the cultural history of Haiti included paintings, papier-mâché crafts, flags, and other cultural artifacts. *740 E. 56th Pl.,* ☎ *312/947–0600.* ☛ *$3 adults, $2 senior citizens and students, $1 children 6–13; free Thurs.* ☉ *Weekdays 10–5, Sat. 10–4, Sun. noon–4.*

Field Museum (Tour 4)

International Museum of Surgical Sciences. The surgical sciences museum has medical artifacts from around the world. *1524 N. Lake Shore Dr.,* ☎ *312/642–6502.* ☛ *Free.* ☉ *Tues.–Sat. 10–4, Sun. 11–5.*

John G. Shedd Aquarium (Tour 4)

Mexican Fine Arts Center Museum. The exhibits of the work of contemporary Mexican artists change every two to three months. *1852 W. 19th St.,* ☎ *312/738–1503.* ☛ *Free.* ☉ *Tues.–Sun. 10–5.*

Museum of Broadcast Communications (Tour 1)

Museum of Contemporary Art (Tour 5)

Museum of Holography. Holograms are three-dimensional images produced by lasers. If you have never seen a hologram, consider this museum a must stop; the images seem to leap out at you from their frames. The exhibits of holographic art from around the world include computer-generated holograms, moving holograms, pulsed portraits of people, and color holograms. Two or three special exhibits are

mounted annually. *1134 W. Washington Blvd.,* ☎ *312/226–1007.* ☛
$2.50. ◯ *Wed.–Sun. 12:30–5.*

Museum of Science and Industry (Tour 3)

Newberry Library. This venerable research institution houses superb
book and document collections in many areas and mounts exhibits in
a small gallery space. *60 W. Walton Dr.,* ☎ *312/943–9090.* ☛ *Free.
Closed Sun.*

Oriental Institute (Tour 3)

Polish Museum of America. Dedicated to collecting materials on the
history of the Polish people in America, the Polish Museum has an eclectic collection that includes an art gallery, an exhibit on the Shakespearean
actress Modjeska, one on the American Revolutionary War hero
Tadeusz Koscziusko, and another on the pianist and composer Ignaczi
Paderewski. The latter has the last piano on which he performed and
the chair he carried everywhere and without which he could not perform. The Stations of the Cross from the first Polish church in America (which was in Texas) are on display. A library is available. *984 N.
Milwaukee Ave.,* ☎ *312/384–3352.* ☛ *$2 adults, $1 senior citizens
and students.* ◯ *Daily 11–4.*

Spertus Museum of Judaica (Tour 2)

Swedish-American Museum Association of Chicago. Permanent exhibits here include a history of Swedish immigrant travel to the United
States and a survey of the textile arts and industry in Sweden. Special
exhibits, often on loan from other museums, come every six weeks.
5211 N. Clark St., ☎ *312/728–8111.* ☛ *$2 adults, $1 senior citizens
and students, 50¢ children.* ◯ *Tues.–Fri. 11–4, weekends 11–3.*

Terra Museum of American Art (Tour 5)

Ukrainian Institute of Modern Art. Located in the heart of Ukrainian
Village on the west side, this museum focuses on contemporary paint-
ings and sculpture by artists of Ukrainian descent. *2320 W. Chicago
Ave.,* ☎ *312/227–5522.* ☛ *Free.* ◯ *Tues.–Sun. noon–4.*

Churches, Temples, and Mosques

For many decades the immigrants who settled in Chicago came principally from Ireland, Germany, Italy, and the Catholic countries of Eastern Europe. They struggled to build temples to their faith in their new
neighborhoods, and churches where the faithful could be uplifted and
carried away from the often grinding struggles of their daily lives. As
new waves of immigrants arrived, the churches became places where
the ethnic community gathered to reinforce its cultural and artistic traditions as well as its faith. In this sense, it has been observed that the
history of Chicago's churches is the history of the city.

Today many of the exquisite churches and the historical repositories
they represent are threatened; indeed, the churches may have fulfilled
their function and outlived it, for the communities they were meant to
serve are gone. It is rumored that as many as 25 old neighborhood ethnic churches may be demolished over the next 10 years. Ironically, while
churches in the ethnic neighborhoods languish, others—the Fourth Presbyterian Church on Michigan Avenue's Magnificent Mile, for example—whose congregations are well able to support them, are threatened
because of the tremendous underlying value of the property on which
they stand.

Many of Chicago's most beautiful churches may not be around much
longer, and the wise visitor will take the opportunity to see these trea-
sures while it is still possible. Always remember to call ahead before
planning to visit a church; economic constraints have forced many

churches to restrict the hours during which they are open to the public.

Baha'i House of Worship (Chapter 8, Excursions from Chicago)
Bond Chapel (Tour 3)
Fourth Presbyterian Church (Tour 5)
Holy Name Cathedral (Tour 5)
Holy Trinity Cathedral (1121 N. Leavitt Ave., ☎ 312/486–6064). This Russian Orthodox church was designed by Louis Sullivan. It is said that Czar Nicholas of Russia contributed $4,000 to the construction. The interior, elaborately detailed and filled with icons, contains no pews; worshipers stand during the services.
Lake Shore Drive Synagogue (70 E. Elm St., ☎ 312/337–6811). Located in gentile Lincoln Park, this is arguably the most magnificent synagogue in the city. Built in the late 1800s, the interior is decorated with ornate stained glass.
Midwest Buddhist Temple (Tour 6)
Moody Memorial Church (Tour 6)
Nativity of the Blessed Virgin Mary Ukrainian Catholic Church (4952 S. Paulina St., ☎ 708/361–8876). Note the Byzantine domes. The interior is richly ornamented with murals, icons, chandeliers, and stained glass.
Old St. Patrick Church (700 W. Adams St., ☎ 312/782–6171). This is the oldest church in Chicago; built in 1852–1856, it withstood the Chicago Fire. Located just west of the west Loop redevelopment area and the huge Presidential Towers high-rise development, Old St. Patrick's is in the happy (and unusual) situation of finding its membership increasing. The towers, one Romanesque and one Byzantine, are symbolic of West and East.
Our Lady of Mt. Carmel Church (690 W. Belmont Ave., ☎ 312/525–0453). Mother church for the north side Catholic parishes, Mt. Carmel is a serene oasis in the midst of urban cacophony.
Rockefeller Memorial Chapel (Tour 3)
St. Alphonsus Redemptorist Church (1429 W. Wellington Ave., ☎ 312/525–0709). Having originally served a German neighborhood, the Gothic St. Alphonsus is now in the heart of the redeveloping Lincoln Park. The beautiful interior has a vaulted ceiling and stained glass.
St. Basil Church (5443 S. Honore St., ☎ 312/925–6311). Originally an Irish church, St. Basil's congregation tried unsuccessfully to stave off the white flight that hit this west side neighborhood in the 1960s.
St. Clement's Church (642 W. Deming Pl., ☎ 312/281–0371). Combining both Roman and Byzantine elements in its design, St. Clement's has beautiful mosaics and lavish stained glass.
St. Gabriel Church (4522 S. Wallace St., ☎ 312/268–9595). Situated in the heart of the Irish Bridgeport neighborhood, St. Gabriel was designed more than 100 years ago by Daniel Burnham and John Root. Unlike many of Chicago's neighborhoods, Bridgeport has remained the Irish community it was 100 years ago, despite expansionist pressures from Latin American Pilsen to the northwest and Chinatown to the northeast.
St. James Cathedral (Tour 5)
St. Michael's Church (Tour 6)
St. Michael's Italian Roman Catholic Church (2325 W. 24th Pl., ☎ 312/847–2727). The beautifully ornate St. Michael's is now in a Latin American parish in the neighborhood of Pilsen.
St. Nicholas Ukrainian Catholic Cathedral (2238 W. Rice St., ☎ 312/276–4537). The Byzantine St. Nicholas is in the heart of Ukrainian Village, an ethnic enclave.

St. Thomas the Apostle (Tour 3)

Second Presbyterian Church (1936 S. Michigan Ave., ☎ 312/225–4951). Located in a black neighborhood just south of Downtown South, this handsome Victorian church endured years of struggles to stay afloat. The church has lovely stained glass, and oak is used lavishly throughout the interior.

Unity Temple (Chapter 8, Excursions from Chicago)

Parks and Gardens

Thanks to the Lakefront Protection Ordinance, most of Chicago's more than 20 miles of lakefront is parkland or beach reserved for public use. Visitors to the city tend to concentrate on the lakefront, even though the Chicago Park District maintains hundreds of parks in neighborhoods throughout the city.

Chicago Botanic Garden (Chapter 8, Excursions from Chicago)

Garfield Park Conservatory, perhaps the largest in the world, keeps more than 5 acres of plants and flowers indoors in near-tropical conditions throughout the year. Here are a palm house, a fern house, an aeroid house (which includes such plants as dieffenbachia and anthericum), and others. By car, take I–290 (Eisenhower Expressway) to Independence Boulevard. Turn right onto Independence Boulevard and go north to Lake Street. Turn right on Lake Street and left at the first traffic light. *300 N. Central Park Blvd.,* ☎ *312/746–5100.* ☛ *Free.* ⊙ *Daily 9–5, with extended hrs during shows.*

Grant Park (Tour 2)

Jackson Park, just south of the Museum of Science and Industry, features an island known as Wooded Island and a Japanese garden with authentic Japanese statuary.

Lincoln Park (Tour 6)

Morton Arboretum (Chapter 8, Excursions from Chicago)

Zoos

Brookfield Zoo (Chapter 8, Excursions from Chicago)

Lincoln Park Zoo (Tour 6)

3 Shopping

CHICAGO IS a shopper's smorgasbord, serving up something for every taste and budget. You can select from a host of possibilities, ranging from tony Updated by purveyors of clothing and jewelry to bargain-packed discount outlets. Julie Ann Major credit cards are generally welcome, as are traveler's checks. An Getzlaff 8.75% state and county sales tax is added to all purchases except groceries and prescription drugs. Many stores, particularly those on north Michigan Avenue and the north side, are open on Sunday; call ahead for Sunday hours.

The Reader, a free weekly paper available in stores and restaurants in the downtown, Near North, Lincoln Park, and Hyde Park areas, carries ads for smaller shops. Sales at the large department stores are advertised in the *Chicago Tribune* and the *Chicago Sun-Times.*

The following pages offer a general overview of Chicago's more popular shopping areas and list some specialty stores where certain items can be found. If you're looking for something in particular, check the Yellow Pages classified phone directory, but if you have no concrete shopping goals, simply choose a major shopping district and browse to your heart's content.

Two maps accompany this chapter: Shopping Downtown and Shopping Near North. Most of the stores and malls mentioned in the chapter appear on these maps; however, some shops and districts that are away from the city's two main shopping areas are not included on the maps. Most of these stores are in Chicago's popular north side; a few are on the south side. All can be easily reached via car, taxi, or public transportation.

Major Shopping Districts

The Loop

This area—named for the elevated train track that encircles it—is the heart of Chicago business and finance. The city's two largest department stores, Marshall Field's & Co. and Carson Pirie Scott, anchor the Loop's State Street–Wabash Avenue area, which has declined since the years when it was known as "State Street, that great street." Nonetheless, Field's and Carson's are still kept company by some interesting shops, including the Body Shop (3 N. State St.) for ecosensitive lotions and potions; Crate & Barrel (101 N. Wabash), the city's best spot for housewares and home furnishings; the Gap (133 N. Wabash Ave.); and Filene's Basement and T.J. Maxx for great clothing bargains (1 N. State St.). Most stores in the Loop are closed on Sunday except during the Christmas season.

The Magnificent Mile

Chicago's most glamorous shopping district stretches along Michigan Avenue from the Chicago River (400 N.) to Oak Street (1000 N.). The street is lined with some of the most exclusive names in retailing: Tiffany & Co. (715 N.), Neiman-Marcus (737 N.), Plaza Escada (840 N.), Chanel (940 N.), and the Polo Store (960 N.), to name just a few. Also look on the Mag Mile for such specialty stores as Crate & Barrel (646 N.), Sony (663 N.), Niketown (669 N.), Borders (830 N.), and F.A.O. Schwarz (840 N.), as well as art galleries and numerous boutiques offering clothing, shoes, jewelry, and accessories.

Michigan Avenue Malls

Aside from dozens of designer shops, Michigan Avenue has three "vertical malls." **Water Tower Place** (835 N. Michigan Ave.) contains branches of Lord & Taylor and Marshall Field's, as well as seven floors of specialty stores. Branches of national chains, such as the Gap, Banana Republic, the Limited, Casual Corner, and Benetton are all represented; the Ritz-Carlton Hotel sits atop the entire complex. The **900 North Michigan Avenue** complex houses the Chicago branches of Bloomingdale's and Henri Bendel, along with dozens of smaller boutiques and specialty stores, such as J. Crew, Cashmere Cashmere, and Gucci. Generally, the merchandise found here is more sophisticated, and more expensive, than that found in Water Tower Place. 900 North also has a hotel on top—the lavish Four Seasons. The restaurants and movie theaters found in both malls are a good option for entertainment during inclement weather. The third mall, **Chicago Place** (700 N. Michigan Ave.), has Saks Fifth Avenue, women's clothiers Ann Taylor and Talbots, kitchenware purveyor Williams-Sonoma, the sleek furniture store Room & Board, and a food court on the top floor.

Merchandise Mart

At this Kennedy-owned marketplace, between Wells and North Orleans streets just north of the Chicago River, there's a restaurant, a food court, a branch of Carson Pirie Scott, and well-known stores such as Crabtree & Evelyn, Episode, H_2O Plus, the Coach Store, and the Gap.

Oak Street

Oak Street, between Michigan Avenue and Rush Street, is the location of the incomparably fashionable Barneys (25 E. Oak St.), Ultimo (114 E. Oak St.), and other stores that sell designer clothing and European imports. Designers with Oak Street addresses include Jil Sander (48 E. Oak St.), Gianni Versace (101 E. Oak St.), Sonia Rykiel (106 E. Oak St.), and Giorgio Armani (113 E. Oak St.).

North Pier

This development on the lake, at 435 East Illinois Street, has some fascinating small shops, including a seashell store, a nautical gifts shop, a hologram showroom, and the City of Chicago Store, which carries some of the city's most original souvenirs. There is also a food court, five restaurants, and a nightclub.

River North

Contained by the Chicago River on the south and west, Clark Street on the east, and Oak Street on the north, River North is home to a profusion of art galleries, furnishing stores, and boutiques. The *Chicago Gallery News,* available from the Tourist Information Center at the Water Tower (Michigan Ave. and Pearson St.), provides an up-to-date listing of current art gallery exhibits.

Clybourn Corridor

Once a run-down industrial area, Clybourn Corridor now has a number of small boutiques and discount and outlet stores. Most of the shops along the "corridor" are on **Clybourn Avenue** between Halsted Street (2000 N.) and Fullerton Avenue (2400 N.), including Lands' End Outlet (2121 N.) and Wear In Good Health (2204 N.). However, you'll also find shops farther north on Clybourn, on North Avenue, and on the side streets off Clybourn. Because this area is so spread out, it's best explored by car.

Lincoln Park and Lakeview

The upscale residential neighborhoods of Lincoln Park and, to the north, Lakeview offer several worthwhile shopping strips. **Clark Street** between Armitage Avenue (2000 N.) and Addison Street (3600 N.) is home to myriad clothing boutiques and specialty stores. **Halsted Street** between Armitage and Fullerton (2400 N.) features chain stores the Gap and Banana Republic, as well as boutiques and gift shops. Farther north on Halsted, between Belmont Avenue (3200 N.) and Addison Street, there are more gift shops and boutiques as well as a smattering of vintage clothing and antiques stores. **Broadway** between Diversey Avenue and Addison Street also offers a variety of shops. The **Century Mall,** in a former movie palace at Clark Street, Broadway, and Diversey Parkway, houses a variety of national outlets including Cignal, the Limited, the Limited Express, and Victoria's Secret. To reach this neighborhood, take the Clark Street Bus 22 at Dearborn Street or the Broadway Bus 36 at State Street north.

Ethnic Enclaves

Chicago is famed for its ethnic neighborhoods, which give visitors the chance to shop the globe without actually leaving the city. Here are three popular areas: **Chinatown** has a dozen or so shops along a four-block stretch of Wentworth Avenue south of Cermack Road. The range of Far Eastern imports ranges from jade to ginseng root to junk. The **northside Lincoln Square neighborhood,** a stretch of Lincoln Avenue between Leland and Lawrence avenues, offers German delis, imported toys, and European-made health and beauty products. And many non–U.S. visitors make the trek to a cluster of dingy but well-stocked electronics stores in an **Indian neighborhood** on the city's far north side (Devon Ave. between Western and Washtenaw Aves.) to buy electronic appliances that run on 220-volt currency. Because the United States has no value-added tax—as of yet—it's often cheaper for international visitors to buy here than at home.

Department Stores

Barneys New York (25 E. Oak St., ☎ 312/587–1700) is a smaller version of the Manhattan store that's a paean to high style in men's and women's fashions.

Bloomingdale's (900 N. Michigan Ave., ☎ 312/440–4460). Unlike both its Michigan Avenue neighbors and its New York City sibling, this branch of Bloomie's, built in a clean, airy style that is part Prairie School and part postmodern, gives you plenty of elbow room to sift through its selection of designer labels.

Carson Pirie Scott (1 S. State St., ☎ 312/641–7000). Though this venerable Chicago emporium is looking a bit tired, it still carries a full line of clothing, housewares, accessories, cosmetics, and more. The building itself, the work of famed Chicago architect Louis Sullivan, is protected by landmark status. It's worth visiting just to see the northwest door at the corner of State and Madison streets; the iron scrollwork here shows Sullivan's work at its most ornate.

Lord & Taylor (Water Tower Place, 835 N. Michigan Ave., ☎ 312/787–7400) carries upscale clothing for men and women, plus shoes and accessories.

Marshall Field's & Co. (111 N. State St., at the corner of Randolph St., ☎ 312/781–1000 and Water Tower Place, 835 N. Michigan Ave., ☎ 335–7700). Though there are branches at several other locations in

Shopping Downtown

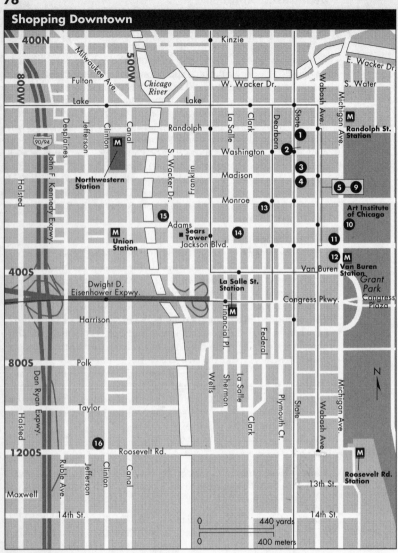

The Art Institute
of Chicago's
Museum Shop, **10**

Brooks Brothers, **14**

Carl Fischer, **9**

Carson Pirie Scott, **4**

Central Camera, **8**

Chernin's, **16**

Chicago Architecture
Foundation's Shop
and Tour Center, **11**

Crate & Barrel, **6**

Eddie Bauer, **5**

Filene's Basement, **3**

Jos. A. Bank, **2**

Marshall Field's
& Co., **1**

Rand McNally, **15**

Rose Records, **7**

Savvy Traveller, **12**

The Sharper
Image, **13**

Chicago and its suburbs, the State Street Field's is the granddaddy of them all. Founder Marshall Field's catchphrase was "Give the lady what she wants!" and, for many years, both ladies and gentlemen have been able to find everything they want—from furs to riding boots to padded hangers—on one of Field's nine floors. After a period of decline, Field's completed a $110-million renovation that restored the building to its original, glamorous splendor. A bargain basement was replaced with "Down Under," a series of small boutiques that sell clothing, luggage, picture frames, gourmet food, wine, and Field's famous Frango mints, which many consider to be Chicago's greatest edible souvenirs. You'll find restaurants on the seventh floor and in the basement. Architecture buffs will admire the Tiffany glass dome that tops the store's southwest atrium. Usually closed Sunday, Field's State Street store holds a monthly "Super Sunday" affair featuring superdeep discounts. Call for exact dates.

Neiman-Marcus (737 N. Michigan Ave., ☎ 312/642–5900). Neiman's prices may be steep, but browsing at this branch of the famous Dallas store is great fun. Be sure to take a look at the graceful four-story wooden sculpture that rises between the escalators.

Saks Fifth Avenue (700 N. Michigan Ave., ☎ 312/944–6500) is a smaller and less elaborate cousin to the original New York store. It offers the same upscale men's and women's clothing.

Specialty Stores

Books

GENERAL INTEREST

Borders (830 N. Michigan Ave., ☎ 312/573–0564). Special events, discount programs, a café overlooking Michigan Avenue, and a CD-listening area go along with 140,000 book titles, 60,000 music titles, 8,000 video titles, and 2,000 CD-ROM titles here.

57th Street Books (1301 E. 57th St., ☎ 312/684–1300). Wooden floors, brick walls, and books from the popular to the esoteric distinguish this Hyde Park institution. It's an excellent place to while away the hours on a rainy Sunday afternoon.

Rizzoli (Water Tower Place, 835 N. Michigan Ave., ☎ 312/642–3500). Art, design, and architecture titles are the store's specialty, although it also carries fiction, literature, domestic and foreign magazines, and gifts.

Stuart Brent (670 N. Michigan Ave., ☎ 312/337–6357). A Chicago literary landmark, Stuart Brent stocks an extensive and tasteful, if sometimes quirky, collection of hardcover and paperback books, as well as a good selection of music and art books. The walls are covered with photographs of well-known authors posing with owner Mr. Brent, who has been prominent in the Chicago literary scene for years.

Waterstone's Booksellers (840 N. Michigan Ave., ☎ 312/587–8080). This branch of the renowned British chain has more than 100,000 titles, an entire floor of fiction, and a small café.

SPECIALTY

Europa Books (832 N. State St., ☎ 312/335–9677 and 3229 N. Clark St., ☎ 312/404–7313). Step into this tiny but well-stocked bookstore and immediately you feel as though you're in Paris. Or, at the very least, not in Chicago. The latest copies of *Match* and *Le Monde* can be found here, as well as other foreign-language newspapers and books. There's also a small but decent selection of English volumes and travel books.

People Like Us Books (1115 W. Belmont Ave., ☎ 312/248–6363). Here you'll find a wide selection of books and periodicals on topics of gay and lesbian interest.

Rand McNally (150 S. Wacker Dr., ☎ 312/332–2009 and 444 N. Michigan Ave., ☎ 312/321–1751). Maps for everywhere from Manhattan to the moon, as well as travel books and globes, are available in abundance here.

Savvy Traveller (310 S. Michigan Ave., ☎ 312/913–9800). Aside from a full range of travel books and videos, the Savvy Traveller also carries odds and ends that can come in handy on the road.

The Stars Our Destination (1021 W. Belmont Ave., ☎ 312/871–2722). Science-fiction fans will find a large selection of their favorites, along with horror and fantasy books and the latest news on local sci-fi happenings.

Women & Children First (5233 N. Clark St., ☎ 312/769–9299). Dedicated to carrying books for and about women, this one-of-a-kind bookstore carries fiction and nonfiction, periodicals, journals, and small-press publications. The children's section has a great selection of books, all politically correct.

<u>USED</u>

Abraham Lincoln Bookstore (357 W. Chicago Ave., ☎ 312/944–3085). Civil War buffs will want to visit this shop, which specializes in Lincolniana and Civil War books.

Powell's (1501 E. 57th St., ☎ 312/955–7780; 828 S. Wabash Ave., ☎ 312/341–0748; and 2850 N. Lincoln Ave., ☎ 312/248–1444). Powell's bookstores have some of the largest and most diverse selections of used books in town.

Cameras and Electronic Equipment

Central Camera (230 S. Wabash Ave., ☎ 312/427–5580). This store, stocked to the rafters with cameras and darkroom equipment, is a Loop institution.

Helix (310 S. Racine St., ☎ 312/421–6000). Off the beaten track in a neighborhood west of the Loop, this warehouse store sells and rents all manner of camera and darkroom paraphernalia at competitive prices. A good selection of used equipment is also available. Helix has two smaller branches in the Loop, at 70 West Madison Street (☎ 312/444–9373) and 233 North Michigan Avenue (☎ 312/565–5901).

Wolf Camera and Video (750 N. Rush St., ☎ 312/943–5531). A block west of Michigan Avenue, there's a great array of film and cameras, and one-hour film processing is available.

Catalogue Stores/Factory Outlets

Crate & Barrel (800 W. North Ave., ☎ 312/787–4775). Chicagoans make frequent pilgrimages to this small but well-stocked outlet store for sensational deals on stylish kitchenware, furniture, and home accessories.

Filene's Basement (830 N. Michigan Ave., ☎ 312/482–8918 and 1 N. State St., ☎ 312/553–1055) has steep discounts on men's and women's clothing and accessories. Like shopping at any off-price store, sometimes you leave with a bundle of designer items, and sometimes you leave empty-handed.

Gap Factory Outlet (2778 N. Milwaukee Ave., ☎ 312/252–0594) is the place to go for all things Gap and Banana Republic—at amazing discounts.

Land's End Outlet (2121 N. Clybourn Ave., ☎ 312/281–0900). This Wisconsin mail-order firm sells casual and business wear, luggage, housewares, and outdoor gear. The quality of the stock may be inconsistent, but the savings can be considerable.

Sony (663 N. Michigan Ave., ☎ 312/943–3334) sells electronics in a rarefied atmosphere of almost hushed elegance.

Spiegel (1105 W. 35th St., ☎ 312/254–0091), the famous mail-order establishment, operates a warehouse store on the city's south side. It has an ever-changing inventory of clothing, appliances, and housewares, and can offer fabulous bargains to the sharp-eyed, flexible shopper. Don't expect elegant surroundings or helpful salespeople, and do check your merchandise thoroughly before you take it home.

Clothing

The major department stores are good sources of mainstream sportswear, and the smaller boutiques of 900 North Michigan Avenue, Water Tower Place, River North, Oak Street, and Lincoln Park can provide you with more unique designer clothing.

BUSINESS CLOTHING

Brooks Brothers (209 S. La Salle St., ☎ 312/263–0100 and 713 N. Michigan Ave., ☎ 312/915–0060) specializes in finely crafted, traditional clothing and accessories for men and women.

Jos. A. Bank (25 E. Washington St., ☎ 312/782–4432), which is its own manufacturer, offers high-quality business attire for about 10%–15% less than you'll find elsewhere.

Mark Shale (919 N. Michigan Ave., ☎ 312/440–0720) offers three floors of conservative yet stylish, competitively priced attire for both men and women.

MEN'S AND WOMEN'S

J. Crew (900 N. Michigan Ave., ☎ 312/751–2739). Bleached wood floors and clean lines make a perfect setting for the classic yet modern men's and women's clothing sold here. The store also sells shoes, accessories, and a small but beautiful selection of women's businesswear.

Ultimo (114 E. Oak St., ☎ 312/787–0906), a softly lit, plush temple of high fashion, is packed with the clothing and accessories of the world's most famous designers. Ultimo can be the ultimate shopping experience—if you can afford it.

Urban Outfitters (935 E. Walton St., ☎ 312/640–1919 and 2352 N. Clark St., ☎ 312/549–1711). This industrial-looking store offers funky clothing, shoes, belts, jewelry, and bags for the terminally hip. There's also an eclectic selection of home accessories.

MEN'S

Bigsby & Kruthers (1750 N. Clark St., ☎ 312/440–1750) offers business and casual clothing, designer labels, accessories, and shoes for the well-heeled man.

Eddie Bauer (123 N. Wabash Ave., ☎ 312/263–6005 and Water Tower Place, 835 N. Michigan Ave., ☎ 312/337–4353). Conservative, casual, and sporty best describe the clothing and accessories sold here. The Wabash store also carries camping gear and sporting equipment.

WOMEN'S

Ann Taylor (103 E. Oak St., ☎ 312/943–5411 and Chicago Place, 700 N. Michigan Ave., ☎ 312/335–0117) sells a selection of classic, up-scale women's wear, shoes, and accessories.

Henri Bendel (900 N. Michigan Ave., ☎ 312/642–0140) offers high-price, high-style women's clothing and accessories in a sumptuous set-ting.

Tashiro (3309 N. Clark St., ☎ 312/248–1487). Polished wood floors, Oriental carpets, and beautiful and unique clothing and accessories make this boutique a Chicago favorite. Home furnishings and accessories are sold on the top floor.

VINTAGE

Flashy Trash (3524 N. Halsted St., ☎ 312/327–6900). Come on in to browse through several generations of styles at bargain prices.

Hollywood Mirror (812 N. Belmont St., ☎ 312/404–4510). Unlike its upstairs neighbor, Ragstock, this store offers a carefully chosen—and more expensive—selection of vintage clothing and shoes.

Hubba-Hubba (3338 N. Clark St., ☎ 312/477–1414) offers a nice se-lection of vintage clothing and accessories for men and women. It's a great place to browse or buy.

Ragstock (812 N. Belmont St., ☎ 312/868–9263) carries a huge se-lection of used clothing at rock-bottom prices. If you're willing to dig through the duds, you just might find something spectacular.

Food

The Chalet (40 E. Delaware Pl., ☎ 312/787–8555). This branch is one of a chain that has several locations in the Near North and at points farther north. All have a large selection of wines, beers, cheeses, cof-fee, and other gourmet items.

Gene's Sausage Shop & Deli (5328 W. Belmont Ave., ☎ 312/777–6322). Over 40 varieties of homemade sausages are stuffed, smoked, and sold here, along with such European deli foods as blintzes, pierogies, stuffed cabbage rolls, mushroom dumplings, and three daily soups. The shop, featured on Frugal Gourmet Jeff Smith's cooking show, also stocks imported chocolates, wine, and other specialty foods.

Nuts on Clark (3830 N. Clark St., ☎ 312/549–6622). This ware-house, just a few blocks from Wrigley Field, displays bins full of nuts, as well as an assortment of candies, spices, jams and jellies, coffee, tea, mustards, and more.

Treasure Island (75 W. Elm St., ☎ 312/440–1144; 680 N. Lake Shore Dr., ☎ 312/664–0400; 1639 N. Wells St., ☎ 312/642–1105; 2121 N. Clybourn Ave., ☎ 312/880–8880; and 3460 N. Broadway, ☎ 312/327–3880). This combination supermarket–gourmet store is a Chicago in-stitution. It's ideal for buying the makings for a gourmet picnic or an elegant, edible house gift.

Gifts

Water Tower Place, the 900 North Michigan Avenue complex, Michi-gan Avenue, and the larger department stores are likely places to find gifts and toys. For artsy gifts with a twist, try the River North, Lin-coln Park, or Halsted Street art galleries and boutiques.

Hammacher Schlemmer (Tribune Tower, 435 N. Michigan Ave., ☎ 312/527–9100) offers upscale gadgets and unusual gifts—it's a great place to browse or buy.

Sharper Image (55 W. Monroe St., ☎ 312/263–4535 and Water Tower Place, 835 N. Michigan Ave., ☎ 312/335–1600) sells everything from the practical to the whimsical, often at high prices.

Tiffany & Co. (715 N. Michigan Ave., ☎ 312/944–7500). This is the spot for impeccably correct crystal, silver, and jewelry.

Kitchenware

Crate & Barrel (646 N. Michigan Ave., ☎ 312/787–5900 and 101 N. Wabash Ave., ☎ 312/372–0100). A sleek, modern white building with floor-to-ceiling curved windows overlooking Michigan Avenue is the perfect setting for Crate & Barrel's chic and affordable cookware, glassware, home accessories, and furniture.

Williams-Sonoma (17 E. Chestnut St., ☎ 312/642–1593 and Chicago Place, 700 N. Michigan Ave., ☎ 312/787–8991). The selection of kitchenware and cookbooks is excellent.

Music

Carl Fischer (312 S. Wabash Ave., ☎ 312/427–6652). This venerable store carries the largest selection of piano, vocal, choral, and band sheet music in Chicago.

Jazz Record Mart (11 W. Grand Ave., ☎ 312/222–1467). One of Chicago's largest collections of records, in addition to compact discs and tapes, is stocked in this specialty store. Jazz and blues fanciers will find the rare and the obscure here.

Reckless Records (3157 N. Broadway, ☎ 312/404–5080). This is one of the city's leading alternative and secondhand record stores.

Rose Records (214 S. Wabash Ave., ☎ 312/987–9044). This store has three floors of records, tapes, and compact discs, with an exceptionally large selection of movie and Broadway musical soundtracks. One entire floor is devoted to "cut-outs," budget labels, and other bargains.

Tower Records/Videos/Books (2301 N. Clark St., ☎ 312/477–5994). Abandon hope, all ye (music fans) who enter here. Tower's selection of 150,000 titles is a surefire way to torpedo a vacation budget. Open until midnight.

Wax Trax (1653 N. Damen Ave., ☎ 312/862–2121). Chicago's only record store that is also a record label relocated to the city's hip Wicker Park/Bucktown neighborhood a few years ago. The store continues to carry underground and alternative music (mostly CDs),plus clothing, accessories, and magazines.

Shoes

There are a great many shoe stores along Michigan Avenue, including several in Water Tower Place, 900 North Michigan Avenue, and Chicago Place. All of the department stores and stores such as Ann Taylor and The Gap also carry shoes.

Alternatives (2506-1/2 N. Clark St., ☎ 312/281–4801 and 942 N. Rush St., ☎ 312/266–1545) private label men's and women's shoes are all Italian-made. The designs might be under- or overstated, but never dull.

Brown's Shoe Shop (Water Tower Place, 835 N. Michigan Ave., ☎ 312/944–1111) has an expensive selection of shoes in styles that range from conservative to racy.

Chernin's (2665 N. Halsted St., ☎ 312/404–0005 and 606 W. Roosevelt Rd., ☎ 312/922–4545) is a great place to find bargains on men's, women's, and children's shoes.

Florsheim (622 N. Michigan Ave., ☎ 312/787–0779) offers business and casual shoes for men.

Hanig's (660 N. Michigan Ave., ☎ 312/642–5330) carries a variety of shoes for men and women.

Joan & David (717 N. Michigan Ave., ☎ 312/482–8585) offers high style, high-price designs for women and men.

Lori's Discount Designer Shoes (808 W. Armitage Ave., ☎ 312/281–5655). Located in Lincoln Park, this store sells women's designer shoes cheaper than department stores.

Souvenirs

Accent Chicago (Water Tower Place, 835 N. Michigan Ave., ☎ 312/944–1354) is stocked with gifts and Chicago memorabilia.

Art Institute of Chicago's Museum Shop (111 S. Michigan Ave. at Adams St., ☎ 312/443–3535). There's no charge to enter the enormous gift shop, which has an extensive collection of museum reproductions in the form of posters, books, and more.

Chicago Architecture Foundation's Shop and Tour Center (224 S. Michigan Ave., ☎ 312/922–3432). A large selection of books, posters, T-shirts, toys, mugs, and other souvenirs with architectural themes can be found here.

City of Chicago Store (North Pier, 401 E. Illinois St., ☎ 312/467–1111) carries merchandise from 35 of the city's cultural institutions and organizations, including the Art Institute and the Lincoln Park Zoo. There's also an eclectic collection of restored artifacts, such as traffic lights, ballot boxes, parking meters, and manhole covers, culled from 12 city departments.

Hello Chicago (Chicago Place, 700 N. Michigan Ave., ☎ 312/787–0838) is another good spot for Chicago souvenirs.

Sporting Goods

Erehwon Mountain Outfitters (644 N. Orleans St., ☎ 312/337–6400) can inspire even the most seasoned couch potato to explore the great outdoors with its upscale outdoor sports equipment, clothing, and accessories.

Niketown (669 N. Michigan Ave., ☎ 312/642–6363) glorifies athletic shoes and the people who wear them in a store-as-entertainment setting.

Sportmart (620 N. La Salle, ☎ 312/337–6151; 3134 N. Clark St., ☎ 312/871–8500; and 440 N. Orleans St., ☎ 312/222–0900). These large emporia, one in Lakeview and two in River North, offer low prices and good selections as long as you're not looking for uncommon sizes.

Sports Authority (630 N. Rush St., ☎ 312/266–6608) has 40,000 square feet of sporting goods, including equipment, apparel, and footwear.

Toys

F.A.O. Schwarz (840 N. Michigan Ave., ☎ 312/587–5000) is a fantasy toy emporium that's only a little smaller than the chain's New York flagship.

Saturday's Child (2146 N. Halsted St., ☎ 312/525–8697) specializes in educational and creative toys for children.

4 Sports, Fitness, Beaches

Participant Sports and Fitness

Bicycling

Chicago's lakefront bicycle path extends about 20 miles, offering a variety of scenic views. The prospect of the harbor, created with landfill several years ago when Lake Shore Drive's notorious S-curve between Monroe Street and Wacker Drive was straightened, is lovely. Be careful: A few blocks to the north, Grand Avenue is one of a few places along the route where the path crosses a city street (two others are parallel to Lake Shore Drive in the downtown area). Rent a bike for the day as you enter Lincoln Park at Fullerton Avenue or from the **Bike Shop** (1034 W. Belmont Ave., ☎ 312/868–6800). **Turin Bicycles** (435 E. Illinois St., ☎ 312/923–0100) at North Pier also rents bikes by the hour or the day. **Bike Chicago** (☎ 312/944–2337 or 800/915–2453, locations at Oak St. Beach, Lincoln Park Zoo, Buckingham Fountain, and Navy Pier) will deliver a bike to your hotel. It runs two two-hour lakefront tours daily, weather permitting. There are many other scenic routes downtown and in the Chicago area. For information, contact the **Chicagoland Bicycle Federation** (343 S. Dearborn St., Room 1017, Chicago, IL 60604, ☎ 312/427–3325).

Boating

The lakefront harbors are packed with boats, but if you're not familiar with Great Lakes sailing, it's best to leave the navigating to an experienced skipper. Sailboat lessons and rentals are available from the **Chicago Sailing Club** (Belmont Harbor, ☎ 312/871–7245) or **Sailboats Inc.** (400 E. Randolph St., ☎ 800/826–7010). Plenty of folks stand ready to charter boats if you're interested in fishing for coho or chinook salmon, trout, or perch. Call the **Chicago Sportfishing Association** (Burnham Harbor, ☎ 312/922–1100).

For a more placid water outing, try the paddleboats at Lincoln Park Lagoon. Rentals are located at the lagoon just north of "Farm in the Zoo."

Golf

The Chicago Park District (☎ 312/245–0909) maintains six golf courses—five with nine holes and one (Jackson Park) with 18—as well as two driving ranges, one in Jackson Park and one at Lake Shore Drive and Diversey Avenue (where there is a miniature 18-hole course). The Jackson Park facilities are two and three blocks east of Stony Island Avenue at 63rd Street.

Suburban Chicago abounds with public golf courses—more than 125 of them, with greens fees ranging from $10 to nearly $100. Most accept reservations up to a week in advance; some require a credit-card deposit. The following are a few of the more highly rated ones. **Cantigny** (27 W. 270 Mack Rd., Wheaton, ☎ 708/668–8463) won *Golf Digest's* 1989 "Best New Public Course of the Year" award. A wealth of mature trees await you on each of the 27 holes. **Cog Hill Golf and Country Club** (12294 Archer Ave., Lemont, ☎ 708/257–5872), with four 18-hole courses, hosts the PGA tour's Western Open in early July. **Kemper Lakes** (Old McHenry Rd., Long Grove, ☎ 708/320–3450) is one of the region's most expensive courses ($100 with mandatory cart rental included) and is the only local public course to have hosted a major PGA championship. **Village Links of Glen Ellyn** (485 Winchell Way, Glen Ellyn, ☎ 708/469–8180) has 27 holes and a driving range.

Health Clubs

No Chicago health clubs offer short-term memberships, but some have agreements with hotels that give guests access to their facilities. Check with your hotel.

Ice-Skating

During the winter months there is ice-skating at the **Daley Bicentennial Plaza** (☎ 312/294–4790), Randolph Street at Lake Shore Drive. A small fee is charged, and skate rentals are available.

Free ice-skating is available at **Block 37 Ice Rink** (☎ 312/744–3315), on State Street between Washington and Randolph streets.

In-Line Skating

In-line skating has become a popular lakefront pastime in recent years. You can rent blades from **LondoMondo Motionwear** (1100 N. Dearborn St., ☎ 312/751–2794) or Bike Chicago (*see* Bicycling, *above*). There's also a rental stand during peak times (roughly Memorial Day through Labor Day, and later if the weather's nice) near the North Avenue beach house, though hours there are unpredictable. On the lakefront, keep to the right and watch your back for bicyclists. Stretches of bumpy pavement make wrist guards, helmets, and knee pads a good idea. Skating is also allowed on Daley Bicentennial Plaza.

Jogging

The lakefront path accommodates joggers, bicyclists, and skaters, so you'll need to be attentive. You can pick up the path at Oak Street Beach (across from the Drake Hotel), at Grand Avenue underneath Lake Shore Drive, or by going through Grant Park on Monroe Street or Jackson Boulevard until you reach the lakefront.

On the lakefront path, joggers should stay north of McCormick Place; muggers sometimes lurk in the comparatively empty stretch between the convention center and Hyde Park. Loop streets are a little spooky after dark and too crowded during the day for useful running. In the Near North, joggers will want to stay east of Orleans Street.

Various groups also hold organized races nearly every weekend. Call the **Chicago-Area Runners Association** (☎ 312/666–9836) for schedules.

Swimming

Lake Michigan provides wonderful swimming opportunities between Memorial Day and Labor Day, particularly toward the end of the summer, when the lake has warmed up (*see* Beaches, *below*).

Tennis

The Chicago Park District maintains hundreds of tennis courts, most of which can be used free of charge. The facility at the **Daley Bicentennial Plaza,** Randolph Street at Lake Shore Drive, is the closest to downtown and Near North hotels; it's a lighted facility that can be used at night. There is a modest hourly fee, and reservations are advised (☎ 312/294–4790). The **Grant Park** tennis courts, at 9th Street and Columbus Drive (between Michigan Ave. and Lake Shore Dr.), are also lighted, and there is a modest fee. Public indoor tennis courts are available on the north side at the **McFetridge Sports Center** (3843 N. California Ave., ☎ 312/478–0210).

Spectator Sports

Chicago's loyal sports fans turn out regularly, year after year, to watch what have not been the winningest teams in professional sports (with the exception, at times, of the Chicago Bulls). The Cubs won two division championships in the 1980s, and the White Sox won one most recently in 1993, but it's been a while since either has captured a league title.

Baseball

The **Chicago Cubs** (National League) play at Wrigley Field (1060 W. Addison St., ☎ 312/404–2827); the baseball season begins early in April and ends the first weekend in October. Wrigley Field is reached by the Howard Street El line; take the B Train to Addison Street. Wrigley Field has had lights since 1988, when it became the last major-league ballpark in the nation to be lighted for night games. But the Cubs still play most of their home games during the day, and the bleachers are a great place to get a tan while listening to Chicagoans taunt the visiting outfielders. The grandstand offers a more sedate atmosphere. Most games start at 1:20 PM, but call for exact starting times.

The **Chicago White Sox** (American League) play at Comiskey Park (333 W. 35th St., ☎ 312/924–1000). Games usually start at 7 PM. Take an A or B Dan Ryan El Train to 35th Street.

Basketball

The **Chicago Bulls** play at the new United Center (1901 W. Madison St., ☎ 312/455–4000 for ticket information); the basketball season extends from November to May, and games usually start at 7:30 PM. Avoid leaving the game early or wandering around this neighborhood at night.

Football

The **Chicago Bears** play at Soldier Field (425 E. McFetridge Dr., ☎ 708/615–2327) from August (preseason) through January (postseason, if they're lucky). While subscription sales generally account for all tickets, you can sometimes go to the stadium shortly before game time and buy tickets from a subscriber who has extras. To reach Soldier Field, take the Jeffery Express Bus 6 to Roosevelt Road and Lake Shore Drive and follow the crowd. The stadium is just south of the Field Museum of Natural History.

Hockey

The **Chicago Blackhawks** play at the United Center (1901 W. Madison St., ☎ 312/455–7000) from October to April. Games usually start at 7:30 PM. Again, avoid leaving the game early or wandering around the neighborhood at night.

Horse Racing

The **Hawthorne Race Course** (3501 S. Laramie Ave., Stickney, ☎ 708/780–3700), just beyond the Chicago city limits in Cicero, features flat-track and harness racing. **Arlington International Race Course** (N. Wilke Rd. at W. Euclid Ave., Arlington Heights, ☎ 708/255–4300) has flat-track racing May–October. **Sportsman's Park** (3301 S. Laramie Ave., Cicero, ☎ 708/652–2812) hosts flat-track racing and harness racing. **Maywood Park** (8600 W. North Ave., Maywood, ☎ 708/343–4800) has harness racing February–May and October–December.

Beaches

Chicago has about 20 miles of lakefront, most of it sand or rock beach. Beaches are open to the public daily 9 AM–9:30 PM, Memorial Day–Labor Day, and many beaches have changing facilities. The **Chicago Park District** (☎ 312/747–0832) provides lifeguard protection during daylight hours throughout the swimming season. The water is too cold for swimming at other times of the year.

Along the lakefront you'll see plenty of broken-rock breakwaters that warn "no swimming or diving." Although natives frequently ignore these signs, you should heed them: The boulders below the water are slippery with seaweed and may hide sharp, rusty scraps of metal, and the water beyond is very deep. It can be dangerous even if you know the territory.

North Avenue Beach (1600–2400 N.) is heavily used; the crowd tends to be more family oriented than at Oak Street Beach. There are bathrooms, changing facilities, and showers. The southern end of this beach features lively volleyball action during the summer and fall.

Oak Street Beach (600–1600 N.) is probably Chicago's most popular, particularly in the 1000 North area, where the shoreline curves. You can expect it to be mobbed with trendy singles and people-watchers on any warm day in summer. There are bathrooms here, but for official changing facilities you'll have to make the walk to the North Avenue Beach bathhouse. The concrete breakwater that makes up the southern part of Oak Street Beach is a popular promenade on hot summer nights. You can walk along the water all the way to Grand Avenue, where you'll find both Navy Pier and Olive Park.

South Shore Country Club Beach (7100 S.), Chicago's newest and one of the nicest beaches, is quite pretty and not overcrowded. There are bathrooms, changing facilities, and showers. Enter through the South Shore Country Club grounds at 71st Street and South Shore Drive; you may see the police training their horses in the entry area.

Other Chicago beaches (all of which have changing facilities) on Lake Shore Drive are:

Foster Beach (5200 N.)
Jackson Beach, Central (5700–5900 S.)
Leone/Loyola Beach (6700–7800 N.)
Montrose Beach (4400 N.)
12th Street Beach (1200 S. at 900 E., just south of the planetarium)
31st Street Beach (3100 S.)

5 Dining

HOWEVER YOU JUDGE a city's restaurant scene—by ethnic diversity, breadth and depth of high-quality establishments, or nationally prominent chefs—Chicago ranks as one of the nation's finest restaurant towns. Here you'll find innovative hot spots, lovingly maintained traditional establishments, and everything in between.

By Phil Vettel

Chicago's more than 7,000 restaurants range from those ranked among the best in the country—and priced accordingly—to simple, storefront ethnic eateries and old-fashioned, unpretentious pubs offering good food at modest prices. Our listing includes what we recommend as the best within each price range.

We've divided the restaurants of Chicago into four areas, each with its own dining map that locates the restaurants: (1) Greater Downtown, (2) South, (3) Near North, and (4) Lincoln Park and North. Several noteworthy suburban restaurants appear at the end, with no map; other good places to eat outside the city are listed in Chapter 8, Excursions. Within each area, the restaurants are grouped first by type of cuisine, and then by price range. Unless we mention otherwise, restaurants serve lunch and dinner daily and neat, casual attire is acceptable dress.

Restaurant price categories are based on the average cost of a dinner that includes appetizer, entrée, salad, and dessert. Prices are for one person, food alone, not including alcoholic beverages, tax, and tip.

CATEGORY	COST*
$$$$	over $45
$$$	$30–$45
$$	$18–$30
$	under $18

*per person, excluding drinks, service, and sales tax (8.5%)

As a rule, you should tip 15% in restaurants in the inexpensive ($) and moderate ($$) price categories. The Chicago meal tax is 8.5%, and you can double that amount for a 17% tip when you feel generous and don't want to do higher math. Expensive ($$$) and very expensive ($$$$) restaurants have more service personnel per table, who must divide the tip, so it's appropriate to leave 20%, depending on the quality of the service. An especially helpful wine steward should be acknowledged with $2 or $3.

Finally, it's wise to call ahead; many restaurants require reservations, and at others, no reservation means a long wait for a table. Ordinarily, reservations can be made a day or two in advance, or even on the afternoon of the same day, but securing a table at the more popular restaurants may take planning, especially on weekend evenings. Some of the trendiest restaurants don't accept reservations; at such places, a wait of an hour or more on weekends is common.

Greater Downtown

American

$$$ **Buckingham's.** A reliable menu of well-prepared steaks and seafood plus proximity to downtown theater and music events (and complimentary self-parking) make Buckingham's a destination to consider. The dining room is elegant and classic, the service warm and attentive. ✗ *Chicago Hilton and Towers, 720 S. Michigan Ave.,* ☎ *312/922–4400. Reservations advised. AE, D, DC, MC, V. No lunch.*

Dining

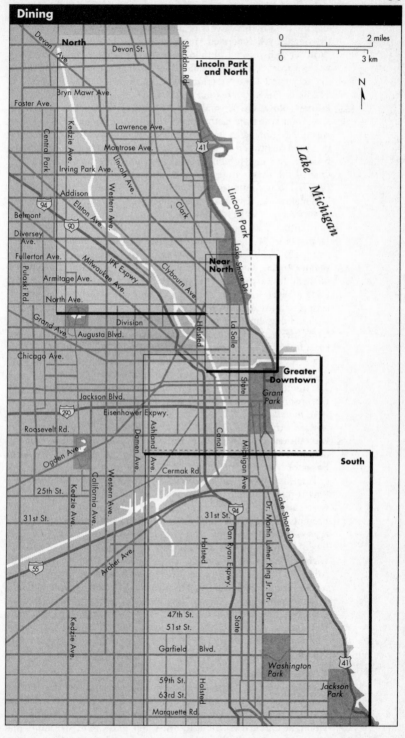

$$$ **Prairie.** The interior is inspired by the work of Frank Lloyd Wright, and the food by the flavors of the Midwestern states. The result is a thoroughly well-conceived American regional restaurant. Homey corn chowder and roasted buffalo with shallot sauce have strong Midwestern accents, as do regional fish specialties such as coho salmon and the acclaimed Lake Superior whitefish. ✕ *500 S. Dearborn St.,* ☎ *312/663–1143. Reservations advised. AE, D, DC, MC, V.*

$$$ **Printer's Row.** Owner and chef Michael Foley opened this stylish
★ restaurant when the historic, then-dilapidated Printer's Row district was just beginning to show signs of a renaissance. His is now the established institution in what has become a very attractive neighborhood of renovated loft buildings and gracious older apartment houses. One of the most interesting and satisfying restaurants in Chicago, Printer's Row continues to unveil fresh and intriguing regional American menus. Game meats and seafood receive uncommonly good treatment. Not only is the food consistently among Chicago's best, it is also substantially less expensive than at comparable restaurants. ✕ *550 S. Dearborn St.,* ☎ *312/461–0780. Reservations advised, required on weekends. AE, D, DC, MC, V. Closed Sun. No lunch Sat.*

$$ **Walnut Room.** Wood archways and beams and Oriental screens complement this carpeted, Victorian-style dining room at Marshall Field's. Long a haven for weary shoppers and business lunchers, this is a relaxing, unhurried spot—except at Christmas, when the room is mobbed with holiday shoppers vying for tables near the enormous Christmas tree. Offerings include beef tenderloin tips Stroganoff, chicken pot pie, roast free-range chicken, scallop and vegetable fettuccine, and a fresh fish of the day, broiled to order, along with an extensive salad and sandwich selection. Desserts include puddings, pies, and ice cream sundaes. The traditional tea served at 3 PM boasts Field's own Scotch scones with Devonshire clotted cream and jam. Complete bar service is available. ✕ *Marshall Field's, 111 N. State St.,* ☎ *312/781–1000. Reservations advised. AE, MC, V. Closed Sun. and holidays. No dinner.*

$ **Lou Mitchell's.** Be prepared to stand in line, but be assured that this
★ definitive luncheonette is worth the wait. Management even hands out boxes of Milk Duds (a very Chicago confection) to the women and girls in line. When you are seated, you're likely to find yourself at a long communal table—smaller tables may require a longer wait. The waitresses have a rough-and-hearty style that gets everyone served promptly, if brusquely. But what food! Fourteen omelets, made from eggs so fresh they remind you how eggs should taste, and cooked in lots of butter; pancakes, French toast, and Belgian waffles; plus sandwiches, salads, and a few hot plates for lunch. People flock to Lou Mitchell's because the ingredients are top quality and everything is homemade—the Greek bread, the raisin toast, the orange marmalade, the pies, the pound cake, the pudding with cream, everything. The food is so good that people routinely, and with only a little embarrassment, stuff themselves. The breakfast menu is served all day long. ✕ *565 W. Jackson Blvd.,* ☎ *312/939–3111. No reservations. No credit cards. No dinner.*

Cajun–Creole

$ **Heaven on Seven.** Officially known as the Garland Building Restau-
★ rant, this seventh-floor coffee shop, open daily for breakfast and lunch and for dinner on Friday nights only (often with live entertainment), would be unremarkable but for the Cajun and Creole specialties that augment the standard menu of egg dishes and sandwiches. Order a shrimp étouffée and marvel at the authentic cuisine served in these simple, incongruous surroundings. At peak lunchtimes, the line snakes out

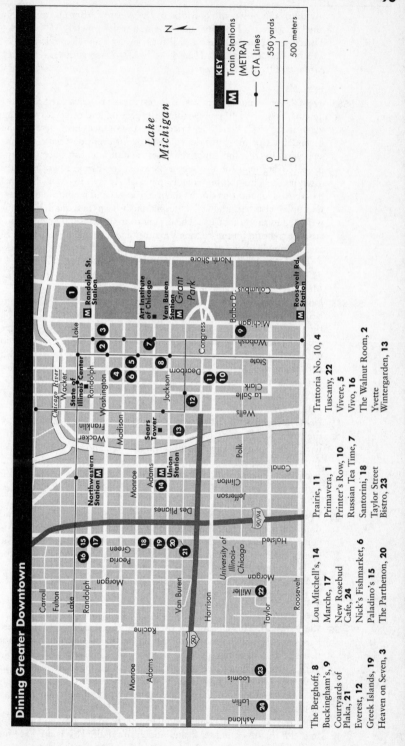

the door and down the corridor to the elevator. (But customers eat quickly, so even a long line often means a wait of merely 15 minutes.) The closest thing to liquor you'll find here is a nonalcoholic beer. ✗ *111 N. Wabash Ave.,* ☏ *312/263–6443. No reservations. No credit cards. BYOB at Fri. dinner.*

French

$$$$ **Everest.** As its name suggests, this restaurant reaches extraordinary
★   heights. First, it is 40 stories above the ground and offers a sweeping view of the city's west side. Price-wise, the dinner check here can be formidable (for most people, this is a major-event destination). Cuisine-wise, Everest hits highs that most restaurants can't begin to approach. Chef Jean Joho is one of the most creative in town; he takes often-ignored, humble ingredients (particularly favoring foods from his native Alsace) and transforms them into regal and memorable dishes. Examples: risotto with black trumpet mushrooms and quail, pheasant wrapped in savoy cabbage. The dining room is pleasingly neutral, focusing attention on the kitchen's exquisitely arranged plates; oversize tables provide plenty of room, and service is discreet and very professional. The wine list has tremendous depth. ✗ *440 S. La Salle St.,* ☏ *312/663–8920. Reservations required. Jacket required. AE, D, DC, MC, V. Closed Sun. No lunch or Mon. dinner.*

$$–$$$ **Marche.** This restaurant caught on almost instantly with the see-and-be-seen crowd; its continued popularity almost overshadows the thoughtfulness of chef-partner Michael Kornick's bistro food. Soups are hearty and satisfy the soul; classics such as duck confit are executed with precision. What is undoubtedly Chicago's largest dessert menu is teeming with perfectly executed choices, and the open kitchen lets you see it all happen—if you can take your eyes off the clientele. ✗ *833 W. Randolph St.,* ☏ *312/226–8399. Reservations strongly advised. AE, D, DC, MC, V.*

$$ **Taylor Street Bistro.** In the heart of Italian-restaurant row sits one of
★   the city's best French bistros. The steak au poivre (with peppercorn, wine, brandy, and cream sauce) is sensational, and the grilled salmon and roast grouper are marvelous. You'll even find the occasional pizza and pasta—sort of an homage to the locals. The atmosphere is relaxed and friendly. ✗ *1400 W. Taylor St.,* ☏ *312/829–2828. Reservations advised. MC, V.*

$$ **Yvette Wintergarden.** Only a few places in town allow you to dine and dance under one roof; this is one of the best. The large dance floor is complemented by nightly live music, from Latin Beat to Top 40. The menu, offering a classic bistro selection, is quite good, though the daily fish specials are often a better bet than, say, duck confit. ✗ *311 S. Wacker Dr.,* ☏ *312/408–1244. Reservations advised. AE, DC, MC, V. Closed Sun. No lunch Sat.*

German

$$ **The Berghoff.** This Chicago institution has been serving its signature beer since the end of Prohibition; in fact, the Berghoff holds city liquor license No. 1. The oak-paneled interiors are handsome and evoke an authentic, old Chicago feel. You can expect to wait for a table, but your meal will proceed rapidly once you're seated. (For even quicker service, grab a sandwich, a snort, and some elbow room among the businessmen at the standing-only bar.) A menu of German classics (Wiener schnitzel, sauerbraten) is augmented by American favorites and, in keeping with the times, lighter dishes and even salads. This is no place for coffee and conversation, and some find the restaurant's operation too efficient by half, but the food is competently prepared and occasionally excellent, portions are good, and the price is right. If you like hearty

No matter where you go, travel is easier when you know the code.^{SM}

dial 1 8 0 0 C A L L A T T®

Dial 1 800 CALL ATT and you'll always get through from any phone with any card* and you'll always get AT&T's best deal.** It's the one number to remember when calling away from home.

*Other long distance company calling cards excluded.
**Additional discounts available.

AT&T
Your True Choice

fare, washed down with excellent beer, you'll love this place. ✕ *17 W. Adams St.,* ☎ *312/427–3170. Reservations accepted for 6 or more. AE, DC, MC, V.*

Greek

\$\$ Courtyards of Plaka. With its salmon-colored walls, red-tile floors, aquamarine bar, white-clothed tables, and live music, Courtyards of Plaka is one of the most sophisticated Greek restaurants in Chicago. Friendly servers work hard to make sure everyone has a good time. Appetizers include the ubiquitous *saganaki* (fried cheese, flamed tableside), *melitzanosalata* (a puree of lightly spiced eggplant to be spread on Greek bread), and *taramosalata* (fish roe salad). Also available, though it doesn't appear on the menu, is *skordalia* (garlic-flavored mashed potatoes). ✕ *340 S. Halsted St.,* ☎ *312/263–0767. Reservations accepted. AE, D, DC, MC, V.*

\$\$ Greek Islands. This large, colorful, and noisily cheerful restaurant is in the heart of Greektown. The food is good, and the service fast. This restaurant draws lots of large parties, probably because the waiters know how to make things comfortable and fun for groups. ✕ *200 S. Halsted St.,* ☎ *312/782–9855. No reservations weekends. AE, D, DC, MC, V.*

\$\$ Santorini. Don't come to this spacious and friendly spot expecting a typical touristy Greek restaurant; instead, come for the impeccably fresh and well-prepared seafood. Be sure to try the charcoal-grilled octopus appetizer and the whole sea bass or red snapper (your waiter will tell you which is best that day), boned tableside. A large open hearth gives the dining room a romantic glow. ✕ *138 S. Halsted St.,* ☎ *312/829–8820. No reservations weekends. AE, MC, V.*

\$ The Parthenon. This 27-year-old restaurant is where saganaki, the flaming Greek cheese dish, was invented. It also claims to be the first restaurant in America to serve gyros, which are still made on the premises. Besides the abundance of history, the Parthenon is notable for its festive atmosphere, happy customers, and hearty, inexpensive food. Last year's remodeling greatly enhanced its visual appeal. ✕ *314 S. Halsted St.,* ☎ *312/726–2407. Reservations accepted. AE, D, DC, MC, V.*

Italian

\$\$\$ Primavera. Known best for its singing waiters (very talented, trained professionals—they get time off for touring), who do a great "Happy Birthday" chorus, this hotel restaurant can hit some culinary high notes, too. The something-for-everyone menu has plenty of pastas, and the veal chop is excellent; the restaurant also boasts the best (and largest) cappuccino in town. ✕ *Fairmont Hotel, 200 N. Columbus Dr.,* ☎ *312/565–6655. Reservations advised. AE, D, DC, MC, V.*

\$\$\$ Trattoria No. 10. Quarry-tile floors, theatrical lighting, and a burnt-orange, red, and ocher color scheme combine to give this below-street-level dining room the charm and warmth of an outdoor café. One of the signature dishes at this eclectic Italian restaurant is ravioli with exotic fillings of lobster or mushrooms. The pastas are fresh, and the interesting antipasti include sea scallops with orange-fennel relish and *rotolo di mozzarella* (homemade mozzarella cheese rolled around layers of pesto and prosciutto). The steaks, chops, and fish dishes are good but are not standouts on the menu. For dessert, try the *tiramisù* (espresso-soaked ladyfingers topped with mascarpone cheese) or the triple-chocolate cannoli. ✕ *10 N. Dearborn St.,* ☎ *312/984–1718. Reservations advised. AE, MC, V. Closed Sun. No lunch weekends.*

$$$ **Vivere.** This eye-catching dining room is worth a visit for looks alone:
★ A mesmerizing array of swirls, cones, and bright colors guarantees an interesting view from every seat in the house. The menu is pretty interesting, too, offering such traditional dishes as flawless veal scaloppine and well-executed pastas to such nouvelle spins as an eggplant-and-chocolate dessert, and nearly everything works beautifully. The restaurant also has one of the city's great wine lists. ✕ *71 W. Monroe St.,* ☎ *312/332–7005. Reservations advised. AE, DC, MC, V. Closed Sun. No lunch Sat.*

$$ **New Rosebud Cafe.** This extremely popular restaurant specializes in good old-fashioned, Southern Italian cuisine. One of the best red sauces in town can be found here, and the roasted peppers, homemade sausage, and exquisitely prepared pastas are not to be missed. The wait for a table can stretch to an hour or more, despite confirmed reservations, but those with patience—and tolerance for the extreme noise level—will find that the meal more than compensates. ✕ *1500 W. Taylor St.,* ☎ *312/942–1117. Reservations advised. AE, DC, MC, V. Closed Sun. No lunch Sat.*

$$ **Paladino's.** Spacious, high-ceilinged, and pretense-free, with easy access to the United Center (for Bulls and Blackhawks games, among other events) and Loop-area theaters, this Italian spot has a burgeoning pregame and pre-theater audience. Old-fashioned pizzas (plus a few "gourmet" types), bountiful pastas, and familiar Italian dishes dominate the menu, though there's room for more inventive fare. Carryout and delivery are available. ✕ *832 W. Randolph St.,* ☎ *312/455–1400. Reservations accepted. AE, D, DC, MC, V.*

$$ **Tuscany.** As the name suggests, this restaurant focuses on hearty flavors and simple preparations. The rotisserie-grilled chicken is especially good, as are the thin-crust pizzas. The Taylor Street neighborhood, just southwest of the Loop, is a popular destination at lunchtime. ✕ *1014 W. Taylor St.,* ☎ *312/829–1990. Reservations advised. AE, MC, V.*

$$ **Vivo.** Well off the beaten path, but still a leading see-and-be-seen restaurant, Vivo is the darling of the high-fashion set. The people-watching (okay, gawking) is fascinating. Striking visuals and attentive service (the waiters themselves are rather stylishly turned out) are more memorable than the rather unadventurous menu, which, though certainly contemporary Italian, offers no real surprises. But the antipasti assortment is a fine starter, and the kitchen does a good job with grilled portobello mushrooms and thin-sliced veal chop. ✕ *838 W. Randolph St.,* ☎ *312/733–3379. Reservations strongly advised. AE, D, DC, MC, V. No lunch weekends.*

Russian

$$–$$$ **Russian Tea Time.** In the heart of the Loop, steps from the Art Institute and Orchestra Hall, sits this delightful, dramatic gem. Mahogany trim, decorative samovars, and balalaika music create the perfect backdrop for a wide-ranging menu of authentic dishes from Russia and neighboring republics (the owners hail from Uzbekistan). Highlights include Ukrainian borscht, *blinis* (small, savory pancakes) with caviar and salmon, *shashlik* (lamb kebabs), and *golubtes* (stuffed cabbage with chicken and rice). Among 22 dessert offerings are homemade strudel and farmer's cheese blintzes. ✕ *63 E. Adams St.,* ☎ *312/360–0000. Reservations advised. AE, D, DC, MC, V.*

Seafood

$$$$ **Nick's Fishmarket.** A dark, sumptuous room filled with leather and wood, Nick's caters to the high-powered business set as well as to romantic couples. Anyone, in fact, who appreciates overwhelmingly attentive service (and is willing to pay accordingly) will enjoy this restaurant, where tuxedoed waiters greet you like a valued regular even if it's your first visit. Nick's is best known for its wide assortment of fresh seafood, particularly for its Pacific catches; the menu also includes some Italian specialties and lighter seafood-pasta pairings. Massive steaks are always available, too. Nick's Fishmarket in Rosemont (10275 W. Higgins Rd.), near O'Hare airport, is a virtual carbon copy of the downtown location. ✗ *1 First National Plaza,* ☎ *312/621–0200. Reservations advised. AE, D, DC, MC, V. Closed Sun. No lunch Sat.*

South

American

$$ Army & Lou's. Soul food at its finest is featured in this venerable South Side institution. The fried chicken here is arguably the city's best, the barbecued ribs rate highly, and don't overlook the roast turkey, collard and mustard greens, or the crunchy fried catfish. There's even a brief wine list. This home cooking is served up in a genteel setting: Waiters glide about in tuxedo shirts and bow ties, tables are dressed in white starched cloths, and African and Haitian art graces the walls. ✗ *420 E. 75th St.,* ☎ *312/483–3100. Reservations advised weekends. AE, MC, V. Closed Tues.*

$$ The Retreat. The South Pullman District is home to several wonderful mansions from the late 1800s, one of which houses this promising restaurant. Chef-owner John Meyer has restored this building to its original grandeur; the dining room has soaring 14-foot ceilings and lovely period decorative touches such as chandeliers, brass wall sconces, and carved wood trim. The cuisine, however, is a bit more modern: generally Southern, with mustard-fried catfish leading the way; other dishes, such as chicken-in-a-toque, display Meyer's classical training. Sunday brunch is extremely popular; don't come near the place without reservations. ✗ *605 E. 111th St.,* ☎ *312/568–6000. Reservations advised. MC, V. No dinner Sun.–Wed., no lunch Mon.*

$ Soul Queen. Come to Soul Queen for the food, not the ambience. Plentiful quantities of Southern-style entrées and down-home specials are available on a large buffet. Try channel catfish steaks served with Mississippi hush puppies, ham hocks with candied yams and fresh greens or peas, and stewed chicken with homemade dumplings, greens, and deep-dish apple pie. ✗ *9031 S. Stony Island Ave.,* ☎ *312/731–3366. No reservations. No credit cards. Closed some holidays.*

Cajun–Creole

$$ Maple Tree Inn. Owner Charlie Orr moved his venerable Cajun palace from the South Side to the nearby suburbs last year. The dining area is smaller now (total seating is less than 100), but the bar area is larger and cozier—essential for waiting patrons in this no-reservations spot. And the food remains worth traveling and waiting for: boldly seasoned jambalaya, spicy étouffées, and plenty of shell-on crawfish dominate the menu. Don't forget pecan pie for dessert. ✗ *13301 Old Western Ave., Blue Island,* ☎ *708/388–3461. No reservations. D, MC, V. Closed Mon. No lunch.*

Caribbean

$ Taste of Jamaica. If you've eaten indigenous food in the Caribbean, one look at this menu will activate your salivary glands. There are no appetizers. Instead, try one of the soups: pumpkin, pepper pot, conch, or tripe. Then move on to the curried goat, the oxtail and broad beans, the jerk chicken, or the brown-stewed fish. Entrées are served with rice, salad, and fried plantain. Side orders include rice and peas, yams, green-banana dumplings, fried plantain, patties (meat pies), codfish frit-

Dining South

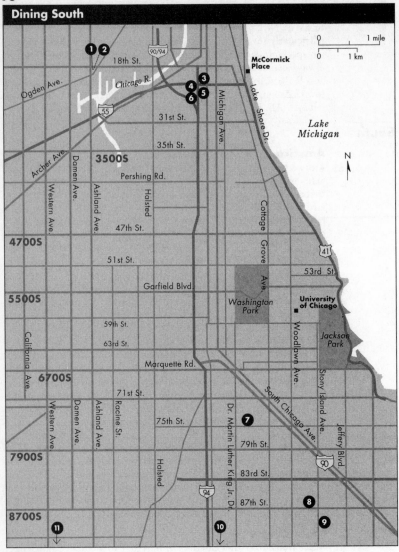

Army & Lou's, **7**
August Moon, **6**
Emperor's Choice, **3**
House of Fortune, **5**
Maple Tree Inn, **11**
Nuevo Leon, **1**
Playa Azul, **2**
The Retreat, **10**
Soul Queen, **9**
Taste of Jamaica, **8**
Three Happiness, **4**

ters, johnnycake (chewy deep-fried bread), and an astonishing variety of buns, flavored breads, and cakes (carrot, banana, dark wine rum fruitcake, coconut drops). Soursop and other juices, fruit nectars, frosties, lemonade and limeade, and tamarind–passion-fruit drink are available. ✕ *1448 E. 87th St.,* ☎ *312/978–6300. Reservations advised. No credit cards. BYOB. Closed holidays. No lunch.*

Chinese

$$ **Emperor's Choice.** This sophisticated but comfortable restaurant sets out to demonstrate that Chinese seafood specialties can go well beyond deep-fried prawns. It succeeds admirably; the seafood dishes are fresh and expertly prepared. A separate menu, including such dishes as rattlesnake soup and pork bellies, is for adventurous diners. ✕ *2238 S. Wentworth Ave.,* ☎ *312/225–8800. Reservations accepted. AE, D, MC, V.*

$–$$ **House of Fortune.** Elegant and spotless, this restaurant has a particularly large menu, offering more than 250 entrées, including such relatively uncommon items as tripe and sea cucumber. Not to worry; there are plenty of more familiar dishes. ✕ *2407 S. Wentworth Ave.,* ☎ *312/225–0880. Reservations accepted. AE, MC, V.*

$ **Three Happiness.** It's possible to eat lunch and dinner at Three Happiness, but folks in the know go for the Sunday dim sum brunch, served from 10 to 2. The crowd, in fact, begins to form at 9:30, and both floors of the spacious restaurant are full within minutes of opening. Try for a table near the door; that's closest to where the servers and their wheeled carts emerge from the kitchen. Each cart is laden with six or so individual orders of dim sum—bite-size morsels of noodle dough wrapped around various fillings of pork or shrimp, then steamed or fried; deep-fried taro root stuffed with pork; rice cake filled with barbecued pork and steamed in banana leaf; and countless other varieties. Each order typically contains three individual dim sum; when you go with a group, you can mix and match. Servers stop when you flag them down and tally your purchases on a "scorecard" at your table; you probably won't be able to keep track of what you've ordered or what it should cost, but don't worry, it's difficult to eat more than $10 worth before becoming stuffed. ✕ *2130 S. Wentworth Ave.,* ☎ *312/791–1229. Reservations accepted. AE, D, DC, MC, V.*

Indonesian

$$ **August Moon.** Although half the menu at this Chinatown restaurant is indeed Chinese, it's the Indonesian dishes that set the place apart. The rijsttafel dinner, an 18-course banquet ($35 per person, minimum four, advance notice requested) provides you with the widest possible variety—and quite a full stomach. If you're not in so expansive a mood, it's quite all right to sample just a dish or two (the shrimp in spicy gravy is a good choice). The kitchen is conservative on the heat, so speak up if you like things spicy. ✕ *225 W. 26th St.,* ☎ *312/842–2951. Reservations advised. MC, V. BYOB. Closed Mon.*

Mexican

$–$$ **Playa Azul.** You will find wonderful fresh oysters at both the original 18th Street location and the sister house at Broadway and Irving Park Road, along with a full selection of fish and seafood soups, salads, and entrées, including abalone, octopus, shrimp, crab, clams, and lobster. Red snapper *Veracruzaná* (deep-fried) or *al mojo de ajo* (in garlic sauce) are house specialties, both delectable. Grilled meat dishes and chilies rellenos are also available, and there are Mexican beers. ✕ *1514 W. 18th St.,* ☎ *312/421–2552. No reservations. No credit cards. Closed Sun.*

$ **Nuevo Leon.** A simple storefront houses this restaurant, a pleasant atmosphere for enjoying familiar or less familiar dishes that leave you satisfied. Appetizers include nachos, guacamole, quesos, and quesadillas with chili sauce. In addition to a large selection of enchiladas, tacos, tostadas, and tamales, you'll find less familiar items such as a rich and flavorful *menudo* (tripe soup), several beef soups, pork stew, chicken in mole sauce, tongue in sauce, and chopped steak simmered with tomatoes, jalapeño peppers, and onion (a house specialty). Not all servers are fluent in English, but cheerful goodwill prevails. ✕ *1515 W. 18th St.,* ☎ *312/421–1517. No reservations. No credit cards.*

Near North

American

$$$$ **Mrs. Park's Tavern.** At street level in the Doubletree Hotel is this handy
★ café, a cousin to Park Avenue Cafe upstairs. A smallish menu nevertheless includes some dandy offerings, often packaged intriguingly, such as the oyster assortment delivered in a wooden wine box. Serving breakfast, lunch, and dinner daily, the kitchen is open at least until 1 AM, a rarity in this posh neighborhood. ✕ *198 E. Delaware Pl.,* ☎ *312/280–8882. Reservations accepted. AE, D, DC, MC, V.*

$$$$ **Park Avenue Cafe.** A re-creation of Manhattan's famed Park Avenue
★ Café, this newcomer made an impressive debut in 1995. Imaginative American food, artistically presented, is remarkable for its complexity and quality. Salmon cured pastrami-style and a swordfish chop (a unique cut of swordfish) are two signature dishes from New York that are gaining new fans in Chicago. Desserts are even more eye-catching, highlighted by a park scene of all-edible ingredients. ✕ *198 E. Delaware Pl.,* ☎ *312/944–4414. Reservations advised. AE, D, DC, MC, V. No lunch.*

$$$$ **Seasons.** This hotel restaurant has become a stop on the gourmet circuit thanks to the creativity of executive chef Mark Baker. New England and Asian influences give the creations here—such as *papardelle* (long, broad noodles) with grilled Maine lobster and pesto-crusted rack of lamb—a distinct spark. The opulent dining room offers unmatched comfort and plenty of room to relax. Seasons also produces Chicago's best (and most expensive) Sunday brunch. ✕ *Four Seasons Hotel, 120 E. Delaware Pl.,* ☎ *312/280–8800. Reservations strongly advised. AE, D, DC, MC, V.*

$$$ **Cafe Gordon.** The former Cricket's has been reborn into this stylish American café, a casual cousin to the esteemed Gordon restaurant—though the café retains Gordon's signature sophistication and intimacy. As the name suggests, the food is relatively simple, though Gordon standbys such as artichoke fritters and flourless chocolate cake are prominent menu items. ✕ *Tremont Hotel, 100 E. Chestnut St.,* ☎ *312/280–2100. Reservations advised. AE, D, DC, MC, V.*

$$$ **Gordon.** For more than 18 years this has been one of the most inno-
★ vative restaurants in Chicago. Gordon's kitchen features a light, uncomplicated cooking style, revealed in such dishes as crispy shallot ravioli with sherry-vinegar jus. The four-course prix-fixe dinner is a very good value. Desserts are outstanding, ranging far beyond the usual chocoholics-only selection. Half-size portions are also available. The restaurant's decor is both sophisticated and whimsical: swag curtains held by tiebacks of plaster hands and subdued Oriental touches giving way to a mural of Rubenesque cavorters. On weekends there's dancing to a jazz trio. ✕ *500 N. Clark St.,* ☎ *312/467–9780. Reservations required. Jacket required. AE, DC, MC, V. Closed holidays. No lunch.*

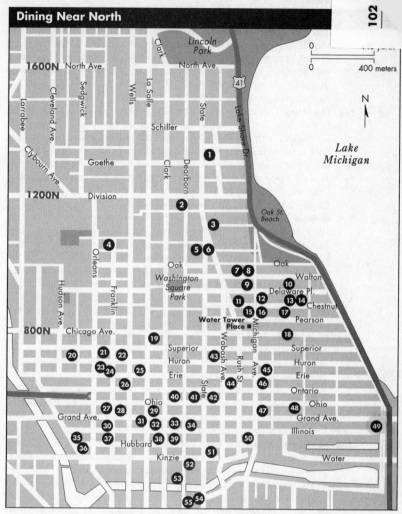

Avanzare, **45**

Benkay, **53**

Billy Goat Tavern, **50**

Bistro 110, **15**

Blackhawk Lodge, **43**

Cafe Gordon, **11**

Carmine's
Clamhouse **3**

Catch Thirty Five, **55**

Centro, **22**

Coco Pazzo, **37**

Costa D'Oro, **2**

Cuisines, **54**

The Dining Room, **17**

The Eccentric, **25**

Ed Debevic's, **26**

Eli's The Place for
Steak, **18**

Frontera Grill, **39**

Gene & Georgetti, **30**

Gibson's, **6**

Gordon, **32**

Grappa, **13**

Gypsy, **48**

Hard Rock Cafe, **40**

Harry Caray's, **52**

Hat Dance, **23**

Hatsuhana, **46**

Honda, **28**

House of Hunan, **47**

Hubbard
Street Grill, **35**

I Tre Merli, **24**

Kiki's Bistro, **4**

Klay Oven, **36**

La Locanda, **19**

Maggiano's
Little Italy, **29**

The Marc, **21**

Mare, **38**

Michael Jordan's
Restaurant, **31**

Mity Nice Grill, **16**

Morton's of
Chicago, **5**

Mrs. Park's
Tavern, **10**

Old Carolina
Crab House, **49**

Papagus, **41**

Park Avenue Cafe, **10**

Pizzeria Due, **44**

Pizzeria Uno, **42**

The Pump Room, **1**

Ruth's Chris Steak
House, **34**

The Saloon, **14**

Scoozi!, **20**

Seasons, **9**

Shaw's Crab
House, **51**

The Signature
Room, **12**

Spiaggia, **8**

T'ang Dynasty, **7**

Topolobampo, **39**

Tucci Benucch, **9**

Tuttaposto, **27**

Zinfandel, **33**

$$$ Hubbard Street Grill. David Schy shows a deft hand with seasonings
★ and a fine respect for classic American food with this well-conceived
restaurant, where grilled meats and fish are enlivened by various spicy
or sweet sauces, chutneys, and relishes. The ahi tuna burger justifies a
visit by itself. The interior is contemporary, comfortable, and casual,
free of trendy sensibilities. ✕ *351 W. Hubbard St.,* ☎ *312/222–0770.*
Reservations advised weekends. AE, D, DC, MC, V. No lunch Sat.–Sun.

$$$ The Marc. This restaurant fits right in with its gallery-district neigh-
bors; it occupies a loft space with exposed timbers and well-worn oak
floors, and with its white walls, Japanese line drawings, and cunning
presentations (in one, a basil leaf is set aflame before the dish is served),
it appeals to an arty crowd. There's serious culinary work on display
as well, along with such niceties as late hours, live jazz music, and a
knowing wine list. ✕ *311 W. Superior St.,* ☎ *312/642–3810. Reservations advised. AE, DC, MC, V. No lunch.*

$$$ Michael Jordan's Restaurant. A typical sports-theme restaurant with
adequate food, this restaurant succeeds because anything Michael Jor-
dan touches, particularly in Chicago, turns to gold. His Airness even
has a private dining room (glass-enclosed, with wood blinds) for his
rather frequent appearances here. The all-American menu is dominated
by meat offerings, and a massive bar area doubles as a memorabilia-
laden shrine to pro sports. Naturally, there's a large souvenir shop by
the front door. ✕ *500 La Salle St.,* ☎ *312/644–3865. Reservations
accepted for lunch. AE, D, DC, MC, V.*

$$$ Pump Room. Probably Chicago's most famous restaurant name among
out-of-towners, the Pump Room has in recent years augmented its tra-
ditional menu with dishes representing a fresh, new style of cooking.
The years-loyal clientele keeps coming back for the steaks and baked
Alaska, while a newer breed of customer enjoys such dishes as pine-
nut-breaded sole with flavored oils. Celebrity photos line the walls. ✕
Omni Ambassador East, 1301 N. State Pkwy., ☎ *312/266–0360.*
Reservations strongly advised. AE, D, MC, V.

$$$ Signature Room at the 95th. Formerly known simply as The 95th, this
restaurant has undergone a change in ownership and, to some extent,
in approach. The most welcome innovation is a bargain-priced buffet
served weekdays at lunch; at $6.95 it's one of the best deals in town.
Choose from roasts, prepared entrées, vegetable sides, a soup of the
day, and a full salad bar. Dinner is still a very formal and very expen-
sive affair, highlighted by superb service; unfortunately, the food can
be uneven. More reliable is the splendid (and quite expensive) Sunday
brunch. Whether you visit at day or night, the view from the 95th floor
is always breathtaking. ✕ *John Hancock Center, 875 N. Michigan Ave.,*
☎ *312/787–9596. Reservations advised for dinner. AE, D, DC, V. No
dinner Sun.*

$$–$$$ The Eccentric. Oprah Winfrey is a major partner in this aptly named
restaurant, where local artists' works hang throughout the dining
rooms and a wall mural depicts a highway map in which Chicago turns
into Paris, then London. The eclectic menu has standbys like prime rib
and Oprah's potatoes (laced with horseradish), but also includes dishes
with Southwestern and Asian influences, among them a marvelous gin-
ger catfish. Keep an eye out for Oprah herself; she does make ap-
pearances. ✕ *159 W. Erie St.,* ☎ *312/787–8390. Reservations accepted
for 6 or more. AE, D, DC, MC, V. No lunch weekends.*

$$ Blackhawk Lodge. Rustic, vacation-lodge decor sets this American re-
★ gional restaurant apart. Hickory-smoked cuisine is something of a
specialty, so the aromas coming from the kitchen are just about irre-
sistible. Besides the bacon, salmon, and smoky corn chowder, the ribs

are particularly good. ✗ *41 E. Superior St., ☎ 312/280–4080. Reservations accepted. AE, D, DC, MC, V.*

$$ **Gypsy.** Mediterranean influences abound in the decor and menu of this eclectic American restaurant. Potatoes and smoked salmon head the list of intriguing pizza toppings, and a roasted artichoke stuffed with Brie makes a great shared appetizer. Fresh, grilled fish dominate the daily specials. The terrific wine list offers dozens of wines by the glass, bottle, or 2-ounce taste, encouraging experimentation. The Sunday brunch is very good, too. ✗ *215 E. Ohio St., ☎ 312/644–9779. Reservations advised. AE, D, DC, MC, V.*

$$ **Hard Rock Cafe.** Street signs, musical instruments, and posters adorn this branch of the London-based Hard Rock Cafe chain. Music blares over the din of 275 diners (or is it 1,000?). Hamburgers, lime-barbe-cued chicken, and Texas-style barbecued ribs are among the house specialties, but does anyone come to the Hard Rock for the food? ✗ *63 W. Ontario St., ☎ 312/943–2252. Reservations accepted for lunch Mon.–Thurs.; at other times the wait can be substantial. AE, MC, V. Closed some holidays.*

$$ **Mity Nice Grill.** Nostalgic decor and menu are meant to evoke a kinder, gentler time period. Entrée offerings include pot roast and hot turkey, along with more contemporary noshes such as garlic-crusted white-fish, flat-bread pizza, and a heartening number of low-fat, low-choles-terol, and vegetarian options. ✗ *Water Tower Place, 835 N. Michigan Ave., ☎ 312/335–4745. Reservations accepted. AE, DC, MC, V.*

$$ **Zinfandel.** Classic regional American recipes are given a touch of '90s cooking sensibility in this ambitious restaurant. Burgoos, New England clambakes, and Pacific seafood all share space on this sea-to-shining-sea menu. Warm southwestern colors are enhanced by eclectic Amer-ican folk art; that, and the aromas from the kitchen, create a most homey atmosphere. ✗ *59 W. Grand Ave., ☎ 312/527–1818. Reservations ad-vised. AE, D, MC, V. Closed Sun.–Mon.*

$ **Billy Goat Tavern.** A favorite hangout for reporters, this counter-ser-vice bar and grill sits midway between the *Chicago Tribune* and *Chicago Sun-Times* and attracts veteran journalists from both papers. Don't come here if you're watching your cholesterol level: The famed "cheezborgers" are held together with grease. Do come for the atmo-sphere, a quick bite, and a cold one that won't set you back a day's pay. ✗ *430 N. Michigan Ave. (lower level), ☎ 312/222–1525. No reser-vations. No credit cards.*

$ **Ed Debevic's.** This tongue-in-cheek re-creation 1950s diner packs them in from morning till midnight. Gum-snapping waitresses in garish cos-tumes trade quips and snide remarks with customers, but it's all in fun and the employees never go overboard. The menu features eight dif-ferent hamburgers, a large sandwich selection, four chili preparations, five hot dogs, and a selection of "deluxe plates" including meat loaf, pot roast, and chicken potpie. Unlike a real 1950s diner, Ed's has a se-lection of cocktails, wines, and Ed Debevic's Beer. ✗ *640 N. Wells St., ☎ 312/664–1707. No reservations; wait may be substantial. No credit cards. Closed some holidays.*

Chinese

$$$ **T'ang Dynasty.** This lavishly appointed restaurant is not only the best-looking Chinese spot in the area, it also offers some of the best cook-ing. Along with the usual pot stickers, wonton soup, and hacked chicken are many innovative dishes—not always on the menu—that change at the chef's whim. ✗ *100 E. Walton St., ☎ 312/664–8688. Reservations advised. AE, DC, MC, V. No lunch Sun.*

$$–$$$ House of Hunan. The original Magnificent Mile Chinese restaurant, House of Hunan continues to please. The large, elegantly decorated dining area is appointed with porcelains and carvings. The enormous menu almost guarantees you'll find something to enjoy. Spicy hot dishes are plentiful, but so are mild ones. Pot stickers, scallop rolls, stuffed crab claws, drunken chicken, and jellyfish are highlights, along with shellfish, pork, duck, and *mu shu* (pancake-wrapped) specialties. ✕ *535 N. Michigan Ave.,* ☎ *312/329–9494. Reservations accepted. AE, D, DC, MC, V.*

French

$$$–$$$$ **Dining Room.** Gracious service and fine food in a beautiful setting make
★ this an outstanding restaurant. The Dining Room is decorated in a classic French style with walnut paneling, tapestry carpeting, and crystal chandeliers. Chef Sarah Stegner was named 1994 "Rising Star Chef of the Year" by the James Beard Society, and her kitchen turns out exemplary French cuisine with nouvelle accents. Daily specials complement the seasonal menu selections. ✕ *Ritz-Carlton Hotel, 160 E. Pearson St.,* ☎ *312/227–5866. Reservations required. Jacket and tie. AE, D, DC, MC, V. No lunch.*

$$$ **Bistro 110.** Like any good bistro, this place can be noisy and chaotic at times, but consider that a testimony to its popularity. Besides the lively bar scene, the real drawing card here is the food from the wood-burning oven. From chicken to seafood to steak frites, the kitchen consistently turns out excellent renditions of French classics. The Sunday jazz brunch is recommended. ✕ *110 E. Pearson St.,* ☎ *312/266–3110. Reservations advised for lunch and for 6 or more at dinner. AE, D, DC, MC, V.*

$$ **Kiki's Bistro.** Country French decor meets urban contemporary cook-
★ ing in this modern bistro. The kitchen seasons dishes aggressively and likes to experiment, but the food generally stays true to its roots. Grilled rabbit sausage with garlic and rosemary is a fine starter; for an entrée, try grouper served with an herb-scented fish bouillon and vegetable medley. And classics like steak frites are always reliable. ✕ *900 N. Franklin St.,* ☎ *312/335–5454. Reservations accepted. AE, MC, V. Closed Sun. No lunch Sat.*

Greek

$$ **Papagus.** Chicago's best Greek restaurant is a sprawling place, bright
★ and cheerful, rustic and comfortable. The menu focuses on *mezedes,* literally "small plates," appetizers resembling Spanish tapas. Servers proffer an assortment; you point to what you want and start grazing. There are additional appetizers on the menu, as well as substantial, hearty salads and fairly traditional entrées. Highlights include *tirosalata* (feta-cheese spread), sensational grilled octopus, and very good lamb chops. Desserts, so often a throwaway on Greek menus, are remarkably good here, especially the unusual dried-cherry-filled baklava. The all-Greek wine list includes some wonderful, inexpensive bottles; trust your waiter's recommendation. ✕ *Embassy Suites Hotel, 620 N. State St.,* ☎ *312/642–8450. Limited reservations accepted. AE, D, DC, MC, V.*

Indian

$$ **Klay Oven.** Quite possibly unlike any Indian restaurant you've ever seen,
★ Klay Oven is a bold experiment in applying fine dining standards to what is all too frequently represented as storefront food. The decor is lovely, the staff is extraordinarily well versed and communicative, and the food, at its best, can dazzle. Such offbeat treats as marinated prawns, mahimahi, rack of lamb, and pork ribs make their way onto

the menu here, and all succeed admirably. The prices are higher than you might expect but worth it. ✗ *414 N. Orleans St.,*☎ *312/527–3999. Reservations accepted. AE, DC, MC, V. No lunch weekends.*

Italian

$$$$ **Spiaggia.** Here, you'll find luxury-level Italian dining that is unsurpassed
★ in the city. The decor is elegant and modern, with marble-clad columns, stylish table appointments, and shades of pink and teal; a three-story bank of windows overlooks Michigan Avenue and Lake Michigan. The food, as opulent and complex as its surroundings, includes a veal chop coddled in a luscious vodka-cream sauce and several elaborate, filled pasta dishes. The dessert list is compact but delightful. The scholarly wine list is no place for bargain hunters, but there are some remarkable wines available. Note: A downscaled taste of Spiaggia's wonders is available next door at Cafe Spiaggia, a lower-priced, casual sidekick. ✗ *980 N. Michigan Ave.,* ☎ *312/280–2750. Reservations advised. Jacket required; no denim. AE, D, DC, MC, V.*

$$$ **Avanzare.** Sleek and urban-looking, Avanzare has long been a favorite of business travelers and those looking for a touch of sophistication with their Italian food. The menu offers a wide range of pastas, unusual salads, and entrées; try an appetizer of tuna carpaccio with avocado and sweet onions. The dozen regularly appearing pastas are carefully prepared, but the best pasta offerings come from the list of daily specials. In summer, there's a very popular sidewalk café. ✗ *161 E. Huron St.,* ☎ *312/337–8056. Reservations advised. AE, D, DC, MC, V. No lunch weekends.*

$$$ **Coco Pazzo.** The Chicago branch of a very successful Manhattan
★ restaurant, Coco Pazzo offers solid, mature, and professional service, and a kitchen that focuses on Tuscan cuisine—lusty, aggressively seasoned fare. Grilled game is a particular strength, as are the risotto dishes. ✗ *300 W. Hubbard St.,* ☎ *312/836–0900. Reservations advised. AE, DC, MC, V. Closed Sat. No lunch weekends.*

$$$ **Costa D'Oro.** Eye-catching and sophisticated, Costa D'Oro pulls in a
★ well-dressed clientele looking for contemporary cuisine with a fine-dining atmosphere. If you've got a killer outfit in the closet, this is the place to flaunt it. The menu is Italian, though with plenty of French influence, particularly in the saucing and presentation. Soups here are outstanding; order pastas in half portions to save room for such entrées as a sophisticated veal scaloppine. ✗ *1160 N. Dearborn St.,* ☎ *312/943–6880. Reservations advised. AE, DC, MC, V. Closed Sun. No lunch.*

$$$ **Grappa.** Spacious booths line the walls on the lower-level dining area;
★ the upper level offers a cozy fireplace in this very sophisticated, stylish Italian restaurant in the Streeterville area. Food is light and contemporary and occasionally rustic; highlights include baby octopus with a spicy tomato sauce, rabbit with pancetta and polenta, and grilled sea bass with tomato-porcini sauce. Service is particularly good, and there's a fine all-Italian wine list. ✗ *200 E. Chestnut St.,* ☎ *312/337–4500. Reservations strongly advised. AE, D, DC, MC, V. No lunch Sun.*

$$$ **I Tre Merli.** People-watching is fun at this beautiful-people hangout, although all that trendy black clothing gets to you after a while. Tables are preposterously small, the better to cram in the most customers, and you'll be cheek-to-jowl with the overflow bar crowd, too. Yet the simple, straightforward Italian food often rises above its surroundings, from a plate of perfectly grilled, balsamic-vinegar-splashed vegetables, to herbed-mousse ravioli with walnut-cream sauce. ✗ *316 W. Erie St.,* ☎ *312/266–3100. Reservations strongly advised. AE, DC, MC, V. Closed Sun.*

$$–$$$ Harry Caray's. Housed in a handsome brick building, Harry Caray's is one of few "celebrity" restaurants (Caray is a famed Chicago Cubs announcer) that actually has rather good food. Though the Italian-American menu offers no surprises, the pastas, fine chicken Vesuvio, and hefty steaks and chops make this a good spot for baseball fans who like to eat, and who don't take the dining experience too seriously. The restaurant's namesake stops by nearly every day the Cubs are in town. Holy cow! ✕ *33 W. Kinzie St.,* ☎ *312/465–9269. Reservations advised. AE, D, DC, MC, V.*

$$–$$$ La Locanda. If you love risotto, look no further. Every day La Locanda offers at least a dozen of the best risotti in town, along with imaginative pastas and excellent grilled calamari. The dining room is stylishly casual. ✕ *745 N. La Salle St.,* ☎ *312/335–9550. Reservations advised. AE, DC, MC, V. No lunch weekends.*

$$–$$$ Maggiano's Little Italy. Enormous portions of red-sauce Italian food star in a cleverly realized Little Italy setting. Order but two entrées for every three diners in your party, and you'll be as happy as the other cheerfully loud patrons in the wide-open dining room. This is the kind of Italian food we grew up with: brick-size lasagna, chicken Vesuvio, veal scaloppine. It's hearty rather than inspiring cuisine, but maybe it'll bring back a memory or two. ✕ *516 N. Clark St.,* ☎ *312/644–7700. Reservations strongly advised. AE, D, DC, MC, V. No lunch Sun.*

$$–$$$ Mare. As suggested by its name, this is an Italian restaurant that specializes in seafood. Some of the items are purely straightforward, while others, such as a creamy polenta topped with salt cod, are distinctly beyond the ordinary. The early crowd ranges from après-office to pretheater, but the mood gets more casual as the evening wears on. The decor is dramatic, with faux-stone walls, sheer fabrics draped from the ceiling, and cunning wall sconces that—surprise—look like fish. ✕ *400 N. Clark St.,* ☎ *312/245–9933. Reservations accepted. AE, DC, MC, V. No lunch weekends.*

$$ Scoozi!. You'll recognize Scoozi! by the gigantic tomato over the front door. This is a huge, noisy, trendy place popular with the young professional crowd. Booths flank the walls of a multilevel dining room, and wood beams and ceiling decorations complement the country Italian food. A large selection of antipasti, pizza, and pasta is augmented by a small selection of entrées. Steamed clams in garlic and white wine, steamed mussels in tomato sauce, and osso bucco appear on a generally attractive menu that invites grazing. Many offerings are available in small or large portions. ✕ *410 W. Huron St.,* ☎ *312/943–5900. Reservations strongly advised. AE, D, DC, MC, V. No lunch weekends.*

$$ Tucci Benucch. This cozy Italian country kitchen in the 900 North Michigan mall is a pleasant escape from the shopping hustle and bustle outside its doors. Thin-crust pizzas and pasta dishes feature unusual toppings, such as smoked chicken, red peppers, and Asiago cheese. The grilled eggplant, red pepper, and onion sandwich is rich and crusty. Leave room for dessert, because the gelato is worth a try. ✕ *900 N. Michigan Ave., 5th Floor,* ☎ *312/266–2500. No reservations. AE, D, DC, MC, V.*

$–$$ Centro. There's little chance you'll secure a reservation at this megahot restaurant, which draws trendies like moths to a flame. There's even less chance your reservation will be honored: VIPs arrive on a regular basis and force ordinary folk farther down the waiting list. Those who stick it out are rewarded with stupendously portioned pastas and a smattering of other traditional Italian dishes such as grilled pork chops with fennel and garlic. Prices are surprisingly reasonable. ✕ *710 N. Wells*

St., ☎ *312/988–7775. Limited reservations accepted. AE, D, DC, MC, V. Closed Sun. No lunch Sat.*

$ **Pizzeria Uno/Pizzeria Due.** This is where Chicago deep-dish pizza got its start. Uno has been remodeled to resemble its franchised cousins in other cities, but its pizzas retain their light crust and distinctive taste. Those not accustomed to pizza on a Chicago scale may want to skip the salad to save room. Pizzeria Due, a block away, has the same ownership and menu and slightly different hours. Some say Uno's pizza is better, but the product at both establishments is among the best in town. ✗ *Uno: 29 E. Ohio St.,* ☎ *312/321–1000. Due: 619 N. Wabash Ave.,* ☎ *312/943–2400. No reservations; phone-ahead orders accepted weekdays. AE, D, DC, MC, V.*

Japanese

$$$$ **Benkay.** Few Japanese restaurants offer such authentic Japanese high cuisine in such an elegant setting (or at such lofty prices). Choose among the serenely beautiful main dining room served by tuxedoed waiters, the 20-seat sushi room, one of six traditional tatami rooms (foot wells make them as comfortable for Americans as for Japanese) served by kimono-clad waitresses, a teppan-yaki room (in which chefs do their work inconspicuously, disdaining theatrics), and two private Western-style dining rooms. The restaurant's specialty is its *Kaiseki* menu—full-course dinners that include at least one item from each of the traditional Japanese styles of cooking. The sushi bar offers occasional all-you-can-eat specials—not inexpensive, but the value is good for food of this quality. ✗ *Hotel Nikko, 320 N. Dearborn St.,* ☎ *312/836–5490. Reservations required. Jacket and tie. AE, D, DC, MC, V. Closed Sun.–Mon.*

$$–$$$ **Hatsuhana.** A long, angled sushi bar and wood tables, white stucco walls, Japanese lanterns, and natural wood trim highlight the decor of this simple restaurant, which sushi and sashimi lovers have long esteemed as the best of its kind in Chicago. The printed menu lists numerous appetizers—broiled spinach in sesame-soy sauce, fried bean curd with sauce, steamed egg custard with shrimp, fish, and vegetables—and only a few entrée selections—but most of the customers come for the vinegared rice and raw fish delicacies. ✗ *160 E. Ontario St.,* ☎ *312/280–8287. Reservations advised. AE, DC, MC, V. Closed Sun. and holidays. No lunch Sat.*

$$–$$$ **Honda.** Owned and operated by a Tokyo restaurateur, Honda offers one of the most extensive Japanese menus in the city. Its sushi and sashimi are among the city's best, and it also features the country's first *kushi* bar, where morsels of meat, seafood, and vegetables are grilled or deep-fried. Diners have the option of sitting at the kushi bar or in one of Honda's several dining rooms; call a day in advance to reserve a traditional tatami room (foot wells under the low tables let you stretch your legs). The many authentic dishes include *chawan mushi* (steamed vegetables and fish in an egg custard). Sukiyaki is prepared at your table. ✗ *540 N. Wells,* ☎ *312/923–1010. Reservations accepted. AE, DC, MC, V. Closed Sun. No lunch Sat.*

Mediterranean

$$$ **Cuisines.** Chicago's first upscale Mediterranean restaurant successfully weds an informal cuisine to formal standards. Subdued elegance in the dining room makes this a very comfortable place to eat—the café by the main entrance offers tapas-style dining for those in a hurry. A particularly good paella highlights the main menu. Just steps away from the Chicago Theater, the restaurant is a handy pre- and post-theater destination. ✗ *Renaissance Chicago Hotel, 1 W. Wacker Dr.,* ☎

312/372–7200. *Reservations accepted. AE, D, DC, MC, V. No lunch weekends.*

$$ **Tuttaposto.** Chef-owner Tony Mantuano offers dishes from through-
★ out the Mediterranean in this casual but very serious restaurant. His
wood-roasted snapper is outstanding. The colorful decor is invigorat-
ing, and large windows revealing the rather gritty street scene outside
give the restaurant an energetic urban feel. Kids eat free 5–7 PM on
Sunday. ✗ *646 N. Franklin St.,* ☎ *312/943–6262. Reservations ad-
vised. AE, D, DC, MC, V. No lunch weekends.*

Mexican

$$$ **Topolobampo.** Located alongside Frontera Grill (*see below*),
★ Topolobampo shares Frontera's kitchen, address, and phone num-
ber—and its dedication to quality. Topolobampo is the more expensive room; it offers a more stately atmosphere, accepts reservations,
and, most importantly, affords the chef the opportunity to experiment
with more expensive ingredients. The ever-changing menu features
game, seasonal fruits and vegetables, and exotic preparations: Homemade tortillas with pumpkin-seed sauce and pheasant roasted in banana leaves are two examples. Good service and an interesting wine
list complete the scenario. ✗ *445 N. Clark St.,* ☎ *312/661–1434. Reservations advised. AE, D, DC, MC, V. Closed Sun.–Mon. No lunch Sat.*

$$ **Frontera Grill.** Chef-owner Rick Bayless (named 1995 Chef of the Year
★ by the James Beard Society) and his wife, Deann, literally wrote the
book (*Authentic Mexican*) on Mexican cuisine—and that's what you'll
find at this casual café, along with a tile floor, bright colors, and Mex-
ican folk art. The Baylesses learned about regional Mexican cuisine by
tramping across Mexico, and they return once a year (with their en-
tire staff) to further their research. The results are uncommonly deli-
cious, from charbroiled catfish, Yucatán style (with pickled red onions
and jicama salad), to garlicky skewered tenderloin, Aguascalientes
style (with poblano peppers, red onion, and bacon). The menu changes
frequently, and weekly specials are often the most tempting dishes. ✗
445 N. Clark St., ☎ *312/661–1434. Reservations accepted for 6 or
more; wait may be substantial. AE, D, DC, MC, V. Closed Sun.–Mon.*

$$ **Hat Dance.** The colorful sombreros hanging over the bar tell you that
you've come to the right place. The dazzling decor is made up of a dozen
or more shades of white, and the effect is almost palatial. The Mexican and Southwestern fare can be rather awe-inspiring, too, from duck
fajitas with pineapple-cantaloupe salad to pumpkinseed-crusted sea bass.
Dessert highlights include the white-chocolate taco, consisting of a cookie
shell with ice cream and fresh fruit sauces. ✗ *325 W. Huron St.,* ☎
*312/649–0066. Reservations advised. AE, D, DC, MC, V. No lunch
Sun.*

Seafood

$$$ **Carmine's Clamhouse.** This sprawling, Italian-accented seafood house
is a sister to Centro; it shares Centro's big-portion mentality, its high
popularity, and its tendency to overbook and be unable to honor reser-
vations on time. Choose a slow night and the restaurant can be de-
lightful, offering bounteous pastas, excellent grilled octopus and about
a dozen fresh catches daily; snapper *livornese* (in a tomato sauce) is a
treat when available. ✗ *1043 N. Rush St.,* ☎ *312/988–7676. Reser-
vations advised. AE, D, DC, MC, V. No lunch.*

$$$ **Catch Thirty Five.** Situated at street level in the Leo Burnett Building,
this restaurant specializes in Pacific fish, usually prepared with Asian
flair; Thai curries and ginger make frequent appearances. The multilevel dining room is wood paneled and handsome, and designed to afford a measure of privacy. An "ad wall" displays photographs from

well-known ad campaigns. ✗ *35 W. Wacker Dr.,* ☎ *312/346–3500. Reservations accepted. AE, DC, MC, V. No lunch weekends.*

$$–$$$ **Shaw's Crab House and Blue Crab Lounge.** This East Coast–style
★ restaurant features an oyster bar, in exposed brick and wood, and a wood-paneled, softly lit main dining room with loft ceilings. Though dressy in style, it remains a fairly noisy restaurant, but the fresh seafood is worth the din. Preparations tend toward the simple and the classic; appetizers include fried calamari, steamed blue mussels, and Maryland crab cakes. Crab, lobster, and shrimp offerings are standard on the menu, and there are always a half dozen varieties of fresh oysters available. Softshell crabs, stone crab claws, and King salmon are among the seasonal specialties the restaurant makes a point of featuring. ✗ *21 E. Hubbard St.,* ☎ *312/527–2722. Reservations advised for lunch. AE, D, DC, MC, V. Lounge closed Sun. No lunch weekends.*

$$ **Old Carolina Crab House.** This waterside restaurant, with fishing tackle and pictures of fishermen covering the walls, is rustic and charming, but sophisticated in its operation. Take a break from shopping in the North Pier boutiques for a laid-back lunch or dinner. Sunday brunch, especially in the room overlooking Ogden Slip and the lakefront skyline, is a great idea. ✗ *North Pier, 465 E. Illinois St.,* ☎ *312/321–8400. Reservations accepted. AE, MC, V. Closed Mon.*

Steak Houses

$$$ **Eli's The Place for Steak.** Clubby and inviting, in leather and warm wood, Eli's developed its outstanding reputation through an unflagging commitment to top-quality ingredients prepared precisely to customers' orders. Prime aged steaks are the specialty here, and among the best in Chicago. You'll also find superb, thickly cut veal chops and splendid calves' liver. For dessert, order Eli's renowned cheesecake, now sold nationally in countless varieties. ✗ *215 E. Chicago Ave.,* ☎ *312/642– 1393. Reservations required. Jacket required. AE, D, DC, MC, V. Closed holidays. No lunch weekends.*

$$$ **Gene & Georgetti.** A real guys' steak house, Gene & Georgetti is as far from trendy as you could get, and decor is nothing special. But for massive steaks, good chops, and the famed "garbage salad"—a kitchen sink creation of greens and vegetables and meats—you simply can't go wrong here. If you like rubbing elbows with the well-connected, you can do that, too, though service may be brusque if you're not connected yourself. ✗ *500 N. Franklin St.,* ☎ *312/527–3718. Reservations advised. AE, DC, MC, V. Closed Sun.*

$$$ **Gibsons.** On the site once occupied by the famous Mister Kelly's night-
★ club is now what is perhaps the convention crowd's favorite steak house. The reasons? Plenty of room, attractive decor, huge portions, and good service. You don't see chopped liver on many appetizer lists these days, but the version here is good. ✗ *1028 N. Rush St.,* ☎ *312/266– 8999. Reservations strongly advised. AE, DC, MC, V.*

$$$ **Morton's of Chicago.** This is Chicago's best steak house—and that's
★ no idle statement. Excellent service, classy ambience, and a very good wine list add to the principal attraction: beautiful, hefty steaks, cooked to perfection. It's no place for the budget conscious, but for steak lovers, it's a 16-ounce (or more) taste of heaven. ✗ *1050 N. State St.,* ☎ *312/266–4820. Reservations required. AE, D, DC, MC, V. No lunch.*

$$$ **Ruth's Chris Steak House.** The country's largest fine-dining steakhouse chain established this Chicago outpost in 1992. With excellent steaks and outstanding service, Ruth's Chris quickly demonstrated that it could compete with the best in this definitive steak town. As for the extras, the lobster is good, although expensive—largely because the smallest lobster in the tank is about 3 pounds—and there are more ap-

petizer and side-dish options here than at most steak houses. The wine list is good. ✗ *431 N. Dearborn St.,* ☎ *312/321–2725. Reservations advised. AE, D, DC, MC, V. Closed Sun.*

$$$ **Saloon.** This self-proclaimed "steakhouse for the '90s" is notable for its wide range of non-steak options, which include lots of seafood and pasta. But when there's a convention in town the restaurant is generally packed, and beef is king. The Kansas City strip (like the New York, only with the bone left in) and the massive porterhouse are the Saloon's top best steaks, and there's a double pork chop that's the city's best. The bright and cheery interior also is a reversal of steakhouse standards, but not many complain. ✗ *200 E. Chestnut St.,* ☎ *312/280–5454. Reservations advised. AE, D, DC, MC, V. No lunch Sun.*

Lincoln Park and North

Afghan

$$ **The Helmand.** Chicago's only Afghan restaurant is an inviting place, done in green plants, wall hangings, Persian rugs, and with candles on linen tablecloths. Anyone reasonably familiar with the cuisine of North India and the Middle East won't find The Helmand's menu terribly daunting; the food is richly seasoned but not spicy hot, pleasing for diners looking for something different but not ready for high adventure. Be sure to try the *aushak* (Afghan ravioli filled with leeks, served on yogurt, and topped with ground beef and mint) and the *mantwo* (pastry shell filled with onions and beef, served on yogurt, and topped with carrots, yellow split peas, and beef sauce). The *koufta challow* (lamb and beef meatballs with raisins, turmeric, green pepper, green peas, and fresh tomato sauce, served with rice) is delicious. Vegetable lovers will enjoy an order of *sabzi* (literally, vegetable—here, spinach sautéed with beef and spices), *bendi* (okra cooked to tenderness in a rich sauce), or *shornakhod* (a salad of potato, chickpeas, and scallions served with cilantro vinaigrette). This is satisfying food, graciously served. ✗ *3201 N. Halsted St.,* ☎ *312/935–2447. Reservations advised weekends. AE, DC, MC, V. Closed Sun. No lunch.*

American

$$$–$$$$ **Charlie Trotter's.** This tastefully renovated town house has only 20 closely
★ spaced tables, far too few to accommodate the people who would like to eat here. The owner and chef, Charlie Trotter, enjoys an international reputation for his light, experimental dishes. Menus, which change daily, have included such appetizers as antelope strudel with wild mushrooms and foie gras ravioli with mango and lemongrass sauce; and such entrées as mahimahi with leek and sorrel sauce and mushroom ravioli, a garlic-laced veal chop with wild mushrooms and an eggplant tartlet, and lasagna of sea scallops with squid-ink pasta and saffron sauce. Decor in the smoke-free dining room is unfussily elegant. Make reservations well in advance for this singular experience. ✗ *816 W. Armitage Ave.,* ☎ *312/248–6228. Reservations required. Jacket required. AE, DC, MC, V. Closed Sun.–Mon. No lunch.*

$$–$$$ **Star Top Café.** One of the most daring American eateries in Chicago is also one of the most reasonably priced. Star Top uses seasonings with what seems like wild abandon, but the combinations almost always work. If scallops with mint-Montrachet sauce seems too odd for you, try the sautéed sweetbreads and shrimp with Chinese mustard and rosemary or the grilled amberjack with black peppercorns and a mango glaze. Desserts are more traditional and also very good. The dining room is as eclectic as the menu, with Mylar-finish reptile-pattern tablecloths, turquoise-washed walls, and faux-stone wainscoting. You'll find wit and imagination and very little pretense here. ✗ *2748 N. Lincoln*

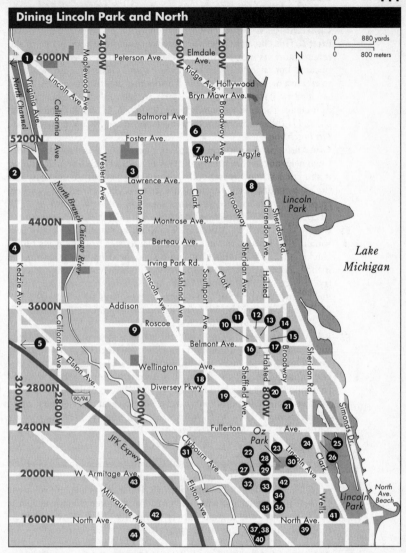

Dining Lincoln Park and North

Ave., ☎ *312/281–0997. Reservations strongly advised. AE, MC, V. Closed Mon. No lunch.*

$$ Brett's. This cute charmer in a gentrifying neighborhood is one of the few restaurants in town that bans smoking entirely. Decor is uncomplicated but cheerful, with soft lighting and classical music working to create a mellow environment. The menu is creative American, soups are a particular strength, and desserts are heavenly. Come here just to munch on the free homemade bread. ✗ *2011 W. Roscoe St.,* ☎ *312/248–0999. Reservations advised weekends. MC, V. Closed Mon. No lunch.*

$$ Café Absinthe. A funky, theatrical spot in the oh-so-fashionable Bucktown neighborhood, Café Absinthe is a trend-seeker's haven: It's noisy, it's full of stylishly dressed folks, there's a hot nightclub upstairs, and the menu is distinctly untraditional, from scallops in fennel bouillon to octopus with watercress-jicama salad. ✗ *1954 W. North Ave.,* ☎ *312/278–4488. Reservations advised. AE, DC, MC, V. No lunch.*

$$ Erwin. This charming American restaurant brims with the sunny per-
★ sonalities of owners Erwin and Cathy Drechsler. You'll always find a chicken dish, a vegetable tart, and a steak or chop on the menu, but it changes enough (monthly) to provide a whole new list of goodies to try. Service is friendly and capable, the wine list has some surprising inclusions, and there isn't an ounce of pretension anywhere. ✗ *2925 N. Halsted St.,* ☎ *312/528-7200. Reservations advised weekends. AE, D, DC, MC, V. Closed Mon. No lunch.*

$$ Relish. The important thing to remember here is to save room for dessert. It's wonderful, even if you find it awkward to order something called Very Chocolate Orgasm. (Bashful types can stick to the free-form ice-cream sandwich.) The wide-ranging American menu, strewn with international influences, offers plenty of pre-dessert temptations as well. Sunday brunch, in particular, can be very pleasant in this airy, open dining room. ✗ *2044 N. Halsted St.,* ☎ *312/868–9034. Reservations advised. AE, DC, MC, V. No lunch.*

Chinese

$$ Dee's. Servers at this yuppie-friendly Chinese restaurant in Lincoln Park are excellent and articulate—and, wonder of wonders, very knowledgeable about the ambitious wine list. The menu is a cut above most Chinese restaurants, including such treats as drunken chicken, eggplant in garlic sauce, and a good variety of noodle dishes. However, even the Szechuan dishes are tame spice-wise; if you like your food hot, be sure to mention that when you order. ✗ *1114 W. Armitage Ave.,* ☎ *312/477–1500. Reservations advised. AE, MC, V. No lunch. Takeout available.*

Ethiopian

$ Mama Desta's Red Sea. Dramatically different from European cooking, the stewlike dishes at Mama Desta's are intriguing combinations of herbs and spices with complex aromas and interesting textures. The food here is flavorful, earthy, and simple. Instead of silverware, diners use spongy, slightly sour flat bread to scoop up the chef's creations. ✗ *3216 N. Clark St.,* ☎ *312/935–7561. Reservations accepted. AE, DC, MC, V. No lunch Mon.*

French

$$$$ Ambria. In a spacious, Art Nouveau atmosphere, Ambria serves the
★ most contemporary of French food and light cuisine. The emphasis here is on using natural juices and vegetable reductions to create delectable food without excessive richness. Previous creations on the frequently changing menu have included cassoulet of crayfish, lobster gazpacho,

and lamb with couscous and ratatouille. The assortment of cheeses, sherbets, fruits, and pastries includes a hot soufflé. Ambria is a fine choice for those who want to dine graciously and well. ✕ *2300 N. Lincoln Park W,* ☎ *312/472–5959. Reservations required. AE, D, DC, MC, V. Closed Sun. and holidays. No lunch.*

$$$–$$$$ **Yoshi's Café.** This tiny, simply decorated restaurant, with its crisp
★ white linen tablecloths, is the establishment of Yoshi Katsumura, one of the best chefs in Chicago. His trademark is combining French and Japanese influences, and his menu tantalizes with elegant, original creations; all are skillfully prepared and exquisitely presented. Appetizers include pheasant pâté with duck liver mousse and lobster ravioli with champagne-caviar sauce; among the entrées are breast of chicken, sweetbreads, and shiitake mushrooms in a phyllo purse with red pepper coulis. The softshell crab tempura with tomato cilantro sauce is irresistible, as is a cream soup made with three types of mushrooms. Soups, a special salad, and desserts are made daily. ✕ *3257 N. Halsted St.,* ☎ *312/248–6160. Reservations required. AE, MC, V. Closed Mon. and holidays. No lunch.*

$$$ **Toulouse on the Park.** For years, Toulouse was a dark, moody Gold Coast fixture. Relocating to Lincoln Park helped it in a rebirth as an opulent, showy dining room, with a jazz cabaret next door (no cover charge for dinner guests) featuring top-notch talent. The menu is a notch or two above bistro in its ambitions, and the lavish surroundings are certainly more in keeping with fine dining—even though prices are considerably less. Service and food are uneven, maddeningly so at times, but when things are working right, Toulouse on the Park delivers a fine evening of dining and entertainment. ✕ *2140 N. Lincoln Park W,* ☎ *312/665–9071. Reservations strongly advised. AE, DC, MC, V. Closed Sun. No lunch.*

$$ **Le Bouchon.** A charming, 40-seat bistro in the Bucktown neighborhood,
★ Le Bouchon serves up French comfort food unmatched by any other bistro in town. Onion tart has been a signature dish of owner Jean-Claude Poilevey for years; other not-to-be-missed delights include hunter-style rabbit and salade Lyonnaise (mixed greens topped with a creamy vinaigrette and a poached egg). However hearty the previous courses, the fruit tarts are too good to skip. ✕ *1958 N. Damen Ave.,* ☎ *312/862–6600. Reservations strongly advised. AE, D, DC, MC, V. Closed Sun. No lunch.*

$$ **Un Grand Cafe.** This attractive bistro is the casual companion to the elegant Ambria at the same address. Steak frites, cassoulet, and roast chicken are specialties on a menu that reflects the simpler, earthier preparations of the French bistro style while drawing on fresh American produce. Though relaxed in ambience, the restaurant offers outstanding quality. ✕ *2300 N. Lincoln Park W,* ☎ *312/348–8886. Reservations advised. AE, D, DC, MC, V. No lunch.*

German

$$ **Golden Ox.** Dark wood, stained-glass windows, murals on themes from German mythology, a hand-carved bar of golden oak, cheerful waitresses in traditional costume, and strolling accordionists and zither players give this German restaurant—the last remnant of what was once a German neighborhood—an authentically ethnic flavor. White tablecloths laid with platters of pickles and relishes set the tone for leisurely, comfortable dining. The menu offers two dozen German specialties, including four veal preparations, two sausages, smoked pork loin, and several unusual items: roast goose with potato dumplings and red cabbage (Saturday and Sunday only), veal sweetbreads sautéed in butter with mushrooms, and hasenpfeffer (marinated rabbit in cream sauce, served with potato dumplings and red cabbage). This hearty, filling fare leaves you with a contented glow. ✗ *1578 N. Clybourn Ave.,* ☎ *312/664–0780. Reservations advised weekends. AE, D, DC, MC, V. No lunch Sun.*

$$ Zum Deutschen Eck. Here is a cozy German eatery where stained glass complements dark wood, and costumed waitresses create a warm, comfortable atmosphere. The fare includes the typically German homemade *suelze* (head cheese), herring salad, potato pancakes, Koenigsberger klops (German meatballs), and schnitzel *à la jaeger* (cutlet sautéed in red wine with green pepper, onion, fresh mushrooms, and red pepper sauce). Old favorites are also featured: sauerbraten, half roast duckling, Wiener schnitzel. Most entrées are served with whipped potato and sauerkraut; a few come with buttered noodles or spaetzle. ✗ *2924 N. Southport Ave.,* ☎ *312/525–8390. Reservations advised. AE, MC, V.*

Indian

$$ Raj Darbar. Raj occupies an important niche in Chicago's Indian dining scene: It is, perhaps, the ideal spot for novices. The menu covers the basics, and the knowledgeable, unintimidating, and mostly American wait staff serves above-average food. Begin with a traditional sampling of Indian appetizers, move on to the fine curried entrées, and don't fail to sample the soft, delicious Indian breads, such as paratha and nan. Though some dishes are spicy, none is particularly hot. Wine and a wide selection of beers, including three from India, are available at bargain prices. ✗ *2350 N. Clark St.,* ☎ *312/348–1010. Reservations advised weekends. AE, D, MC, V.*

International

$$ Bossa Nova. The menu includes everything from Jamaican jerk chicken to Vietnamese spring rolls—and lots in between—at this international tapas restaurant. There's live music on weekends (in keeping with the restaurant name, Latin music dominates), drawing a young crowd; you may see tables pushed aside to make room for dancers. ✗ *1960 N. Clybourn Ave.,* ☎ *312/248–4800. Reservations strongly advised. AE, D, DC, MC, V. Closed Sun. No lunch.*

Italian

$$–$$$ Adagio. Pretheater patrons looking for a quick bite and lingering diners waiting for the entertainment (singing by the owner himself) to kick in around 10 make this a hot spot. Straightforward, full-flavored Italian is the menu's forte, from spicy marinated artichokes to veal chop with wild-mushroom risotto. Chocolate Three, a chocolate sampler, is the signature dessert. ✗ *923 W. Weed St.,* ☎ *312/787–0400. Reservations advised. AE, DC, MC, V. No lunch.*

$$–$$$ Carlucci. This sophisticated urban Italian restaurant draws a see-and-be-seen crowd. The food is even better than the people-watching though, and the polished service ensures a terrific experience. It's one of the area's most consistent performers, and in summer months, the outdoor garden is a delightful place to dine. ✗ *2215 N. Halsted St.,* ☎ *312/281–1220. Reservations advised. AE, D, DC, MC, V. No lunch.*

$$–$$$ Trattoria Gianni. This Lincoln Park establishment successfully re-creates the homey atmosphere and skillful cooking common in Italian trattorias, though at a higher price. Appetizers are a standout: choose from among three antipasto plates, crunchy deep-fried squid, zucchini strips, or mussels. Imaginative and usually well-prepared pasta dishes include rigatoni *nocerina* (pasta tubes with cream, mushrooms, and sun-dried tomatoes), *farfalle contadina* (bow-tie macaroni with vegetables), and gnocchi *à la panna-pesto* (potato dumplings with cream-and-pesto sauce). Simple but satisfying entrées include grilled red snapper with herbs and olive oil, and the worthwhile charcoal-grilled Cornish game hen. If you can, save room for dessert. ✕ *1711 N. Halsted St.,* ☎ *312/266–1976. Reservations advised. MC, V. Closed Mon. No lunch weekends.*

$$ **Mia Francesca.** Why is this tiny restaurant so insanely popular? Principally because of chef-owner Scott Harris' very good, authentic Italian cooking. Its moderate prices, and the fact that the restaurant is pleasant and unpretentious, certainly don't hurt. Try the classic bruschetta, *quattro formaggi* (four cheese) pizza, or full-flavored pasta and chicken dishes. While you wait for one of the small, tightly spaced tables in the single dining room—and you will wait—you can have a drink at the bar. ✕ *3311 N. Clark St.,* ☎ *312/281–3310. No reservations; wait can be substantial. MC, V. No lunch.*

$$ **Sole Mio.** The warm ambience is created by dark wood teamed with white walls, wood-framed mirrors, and photographs of the Italian countryside. The main dining room is flanked by three smaller rooms, one for nonsmokers. The food, prepared by Dennis Terczak, is inspired by the cuisine of Northern and regional Italy and enhanced by an imaginative contemporary approach. The individual 8-inch pizzas are outstanding, even the familiar pizza *margherita* with mozzarella, fresh tomato sauce, basil, and sausage. Entrées include the adventurous— *misto alla griglia* is a mixed grill of lamb chop, quail, sausage, lentils, and escarole—and the tried-and-true—veal scallops, center-cut veal chop, and grilled T-bone steak with peppercorns. A fresh ocean fish, freshwater fish, and shellfish are available daily, and there are homemade desserts and ices. ✕ *917 W. Armitage Ave.,* ☎ *312/477–5858. Reservations advised. AE, DC, MC, V. No lunch weekends.*

$$ **Tra Via.** Adjacent to Victory Gardens Theatre (in fact, there's a connecting door), Tra Via has charms for the pre- and post-theater diner as well as the intermission-time imbiber. But you don't need a theater ticket to enjoy this place, though a little patience comes in handy on weekends. The standard-sounding contemporary Italian menu—grilled calamari, thin-crust pizzas, fresh fish—distinguishes itself thanks to skillful execution. Knowledgeable service is a plus. ✕ *2263 N. Lincoln Ave.,* ☎ *312/348–7200. Reservations for 6 or more. AE, D, DC, MC, V. No lunch.*

$$ **Un DiAmo.** A tiny storefront eatery that seats 45 in tight proximity, Un DiAmo works because of its communal atmosphere (cross-table conversations among complete strangers are common), its clever decor (cherubic angels smile down on guests from various vantage points), and its imaginative Italian cooking. It also helps that Second City, a comedy revue that's a popular tourist destination, is right across the street. ✕ *1617 N. Wells St.,* ☎ *312/337–8881. Reservations strongly advised. AE, MC, V. No lunch.*

$$ **Via Veneto.** This is a family-run restaurant with simple decor and sophisticated food. Pastas are excellent, and you'll find some daring versions among the daily specials. Desserts have improved enormously of late, and the wine list is thoughtful and thorough. Don't bother coming here on Saturday night, when the crowds are impossible. Friday is a better bet, midweek even better. There's a small parking lot in back, but street parking is never a problem in this extremely safe, residential neighborhood. ✕ *3449 W. Peterson Ave.,* ☎ *312/267–0888. Reservations advised weekends. AE, D, DC, MC, V. No lunch weekends.*

$$ **Vinci.** Paul LoDuca, who also owns Mare, created this very impressive, stylishly casual restaurant. Decor is all faux finishes and rustic touches; the menu offers robust regional Italian dishes such as grilled pork chops with fennel and garlic. Pizzas are creative; one combines Fontina cheese, roasted garlic, bitter greens, and tomato. The restaurant has quickly achieved popularity, especially among the pretheater crowd. ✕ *1732 N. Halsted St.,* ☎ *312/266–1199. Reservations strongly advised. AE, MC, V. Closed Mon.*

Japanese

$$ **Matsuya.** This small, storefront restaurant has a sushi bar, wood paneling, brown tile floor, and a floor-to-ceiling wood screen in front of the kitchen. Sushi and an extensive choice of appetizers dominate the menu: deep-fried spicy chicken wings, steamed spinach with sesame, whitefish with white smelt roe, seafood and vegetables on skewers, and dumplings with sauce are just a few. Tempura, fish, and meat teriyaki dishes, a few noodle dishes, and bowl-of-rice dishes (with toppings of your choice) round out the menu. ✕ *3469 N. Clark St.,* ☎ *312/248–2677. Reservations accepted for 4 or more. MC, V. Closed holidays. No lunch weekdays.*

Korean

$$ **Bando.** For a city awash in Asian (especially Thai) restaurants, Chicago
★ is not blessed with a great many Korean establishments. Bando, however, goes a long way toward compensating for this inequity, thanks to its consistently excellent food. First-timers will like the *pa-jun,* a pancake made with oysters and scallions, and *bul-go-ki* (barbecued beef); the more adventurous can attempt the *jun-gol,* a spicy seafood stew. In any case, helpful waiters are reliable guides through the exotic menu. ✕ *2200 W. Lawrence Ave.,* ☎ *312/728–7400. Reservations advised. AE, MC, V.*

Mediterranean

$$ **Jezebel.** Just steps away from the always-packed Mia Francesca (*see above*) is this quiet, solid restaurant that's rarely crowded, yet certainly deserves to be. Faux-finish aged walls and eggshell napery give the room a warm feeling. The food is simple—occasionally too simple—but there are treats for the adventurous diner. Baked shrimp in phyllo dough and sizzling calamari are highlights. Service is very attentive, probably because the owner is rarely out of the dining room. ✕ *3517 N. Clark St.,* ☎ *312/929–4000. Reservations accepted. AE, D, DC, MC, V.*

$$ **Piatti.** The tapas craze goes Mediterranean in this colorful little restaurant, where appetizer-sized nibbles are drawn from Italian, Greek, French, and Spanish cuisines. The interior courtyard is a wonderful place to dine on balmy evenings; otherwise, the inside, decorated with hundreds of hand-painted plates, is very comfortable. Try pear-Gorgonzola salad with sesame oil; garlicky mashed potatoes; and cioppino, among others. ✕ *215 W. North Ave.,* ☎ *312/266-2929. Reservations accepted. AE, DC, MC, V. No lunch.*

$–$$ **Clark Street Bistro.** This neighborhood charmer has reasonable prices, comfortable surroundings, and more than fair prices. And as a bonus, dishes are pretty as a picture when they arrive, whether it's a complex bouillabaisse or a simple saffron couscous with cilantro and cumin. ✕ *2600 N. Clark St.,* ☎ *312/525–9992. Reservations advised weekends. AE, D, DC, MC, V.*

Polish

$$–$$$ **Lutnia.** The menu here is Polish-Continental, but stick to the hearty, straightforward Polish creations unless you're dying for steak Diane or other similarly unremarkable Continental dishes. Start with an assortment of pierogi, and perhaps some hunter's stew, then try the terrific stuffed quail. Decor is upscale, and a pianist performs most nights. ✗ *5332 W. Belmont Ave.,* ☎ *312/282–5335. Reservations advised. AE, D, MC, V.*

$ **Busy Bee.** Busy Bee is among the best of the many unpretentious Polish restaurants found throughout Chicago. Two large storefronts have been converted to provide one area with a large U-shape counter and booths and a second, carpeted room furnished with well-spaced, cloth-covered tables. What makes this and other restaurants of its type special are the generous quantities of pleasing, stick-to-the-ribs food at very low prices. Pierogi (stuffed with your choice of meat, potato, and cheese, or potato and sauerkraut) are served with sour cream or applesauce. Homemade mushroom soup, barley soup, and *czarnina* (duck gravy soup) are among the daily specials. *Bigos* (hunter's stew), Polish sausages, boiled beef brisket, boiled short ribs, tripe stew, and roast duck are among the entrées. Plenty of standard American dishes are also available, satisfying finicky youngsters while parents enjoy ethnic specialties. Service can be somewhat slow. ✗ *1546 N. Damen Ave.,* ☎ *312/772–4433. Reservations accepted. No credit cards. Closed some holidays.*

Seafood

$$ **Bub City Crabshack and Bar-B-Q.** You can't help but have fun at this cavernous place, a re-creation of a Gulf Coast crab shack. Decor is playfully rustic—there's even a sink in the middle of the dining room—and the menu teems with sloppy treats, such as pick-'n'-lick shrimp, garlic blue crab, and barbecued ribs. The adjacent Club Bub (no cover charge) offers live country music most evenings. ✗ *901 W. Weed St.,* ☎ *312/266–1200. Reservations accepted. AE, D, DC, MC, V. No lunch weekends.*

Southwestern

$$ **Blue Mesa.** Although this casual, festive restaurant is noisy and a popular neighborhood joint, the food is taken quite seriously. In fact, the kitchen is downright sophisticated in its use of hot chilies. Cases in point: jalapeño grilled shrimp, blackened tuna with a sesame-*pasilla* (smoked pepper) beurre blanc, and the can't-miss fiery chocolate fritter sundae, topped with a chili-laced chocolate sauce. ✗ *1729 N. Halsted St.,* ☎ *312/944–5990. Reservations strongly advised weekends. AE, D, DC, MC, V.*

$$ **Santa Fe Tapas.** Southwestern flavors crash headlong into the tapas format here, with surprisingly nice results. The kitchen cares not a whit for authenticity, as the menu selection (spinach-Brie quesadillas, *queso fundido* with goat cheese) demonstrates. But if it's a bit yuppified, it's fun and not terribly expensive. ✗ *1962 N. Halsted St.,* ☎ *312/404–9168. Reservations accepted for 8 or more. AE, D, DC, MC, V. No lunch.*

Spanish

$$ **Cafe Ba-Ba-Reeba!.** Chicago's best-known purveyor of tapas cuisine, this large, open restaurant, with its prominent bar, is usually crowded with upscale young folk having a very good time. Choose among a large selection of cold and warm tapas, ranging from cannelloni stuffed with tuna, asparagus, and basil, served with tomato basil sauce and white wine vinaigrette, to veal with mushrooms, eggplant, tomato, and sherry sauce. A few soups and salads are available, as is a limited entrée menu that includes two paellas, baked salmon with mustard topping and vegetable vinaigrette, sautéed pork tenderloin with caramel orange sauce, and two seafood casseroles. There are several desserts for those who have the room. ✕ *2024 N. Halsted St.,* ☎ *312/935–5000. Limited reservations accepted; wait may be substantial. AE, DC, MC, V. No lunch Mon.*

Swedish

$ **Ann Sather.** The two branches of this large, light, airy Swedish restaurant emphasize home-style food and service. Both are popular for weekend breakfasts. Specialties include homemade cinnamon rolls, potato sausage, and chicken croquettes; a full sandwich menu is also offered. A Swedish sampler lets you try duck breast with lingonberry glaze, a Swedish meatball, a potato sausage, a dumpling, and sauerkraut. Very reasonable entrée prices include an appetizer (Swedish fruit soup and pickled herring are among them), two side dishes (choose from Swedish brown beans, homemade applesauce, mashed or boiled potatoes, pickled beets, and more), and dessert (homemade fruit or cream pies, puddings, cakes, and ice creams). Daily specials augment the standard menu. ✕ *5207 N. Clark St.,* ☎ *312/271–6677; 929 W. Belmont Ave.,* ☎ *312/348–2378. Reservations accepted for 10 or more. MC, V. Closed holidays.*

Thai

$$$ **Arun's.** Many think Arun's is the best of Chicago's more than 80 Thai
★ establishments. Influenced by both Chinese and Indian cuisines, Thai food nevertheless has its own characteristics. Lemongrass, *kha* (a type of ginger), lime juice and leaves, and basil figure heavily in the cuisine, as do sauces based on coconut milk. Some dishes are spicy hot; let your server know if you prefer dishes mild or very hot. Appetizers include the familiar pork satay (marinated, grilled pork strips served with peanut sauce and cucumber) and egg rolls as well as the less familiar *yum wunsen* (glass noodles with cooked shrimp and ground pork, spiced with scallion, cilantro, chili peppers, and lime). Shrimp or fish is a must: Try the garlic prawns, the whole fried red snapper, or the squid in hot pepper sauce with garlic and chili peppers. The extensive basic menu is supplemented by daily specials. The two-level dining room has lots of natural wood, complemented by Thai art and a small art gallery—a far cry from the typical storefront ethnic restaurant. ✕ *4156 N. Kedzie Ave.,* ☎ *312/539–1909. Reservations strongly advised. AE, D, DC, MC, V. Closed Mon. and holidays. No lunch.*

$–$$ **Thai Classic.** This attractive, spotless restaurant just a few blocks south of Wrigley Field features contemporary decor, good service, and meticulously prepared dishes. Bring your own beer or wine; there's a liquor store about a block away that's eager for your business (why else would it stock Singha beer?). ✕ *3332 N. Clark St.,* ☎ *312/404–2000. Reservations accepted weekends. AE, MC, V. No lunch Mon.*

$ **Thai Touch.** This former luncheonette has been transformed into a lovely, well-appointed dining room. Creatively prepared and beautifully presented Thai food makes this place worth seeking out, even though it's off the beaten restaurant track. All of the traditional Thai dishes are here—the curries are especially good—and presentation goes far beyond the norm. Occasional surprises, such as crab-in-a-basket, are worth trying as well. ✕ *3200 W. Lawrence Ave.,* ☎ *312/539–5700. Reservations accepted. MC, V.*

Vietnamese

$$ **Julie Mai's Le Bistro.** This Vietnamese restaurant with a menu that's part French occupies a former Italian restaurant in an old Scandinavian neighborhood. Only in America. The unchanged decor lets diners sit in secluded stuccoed alcoves while deciding among such choices as lemon beef salad, Vietnamese fisherman's soup, or shrimp le Bistro. A serious wine list and very helpful servers make decisions—and the whole experience—a pleasure. ✕ *5025 N. Clark St.,* ☎ *312/784–6000. Reservations accepted. AE, D, MC, V. No lunch Sun.–Mon.*

$–$$ **Pasteur.** This recently redecorated restaurant offers an extensive menu,
★ which includes appetizers of whole sautéed Dungeness crab, classic shrimp paste wrapped around sugarcane, and the house specialty—a deep-fried shrimp cake served with fresh salad and special sauce. Noodle lovers will be delighted with the selection: three rice noodle soups, five egg noodle soups, five fried rice noodle dishes, five soft rice noodle dishes, and three fried egg noodle dishes. Shrimp, poultry, beef, pork, and fish selections are available. ✕ *4759 N. Sheridan Rd.,* ☎ *312/271–6673. Reservations advised. AE, MC, V. Closed Mon. No lunch.*

Worth a Special Trip

American

$$$$ **Trio.** Three veteran restaurateurs—chef Rick Tramanto, pastry chef Gale
★ Gand, and proprietor-sommelier Henry Adaniya—have pooled their efforts to create this masterpiece of multi-influenced American cuisine. Dishes are wildly creative and visually stunning, and borne to the table on anything from a slab of granite to a sandwich of glass. Recent standouts include wild-mushroom cappuccino with a parmesan *tuile* (crisp wafer), apple-smoked fillet with wasabi mashed potatoes, and tea-smoked lobster with lemongrass. ✕ *1625 Hinman Ave., Evanston,* ☎ *708/733–8746. Reservations required. AE, D, DC, MC, V. No smoking. Closed Mon. No lunch.*

French

$$$$ **Carlos.** This restaurant continues to challenge Le Francais (*see below*)
★ for the title of best French restaurant in the area. Service is particularly good—owner Carlos Nieto (himself a Le Francais graduate) gets involved in the front-room operations—but even the lowest-ranking assistant has a firm grasp of the menu, can explain preparation methods, and can even offer informed wine recommendations. The contemporary French menu changes frequently and invariably offers an array of delights, such as squab ravioli with garlic sauce and rabbit tournedos with creamed leeks and truffles. Desserts are heavenly. The substantial wine list includes some magnificent vintages, although at eye-popping prices. ✕ *429 Temple, Highland Park,* ☎ *708/432–0770. Reservations required. Jacket and tie. AE, D, DC, MC, V. Closed Tues. No lunch.*

$$$$ **Le Francais.** The husband-wife team of Roland and Mary Beth Liccioni
★ has Le Francais, in many eyes Chicago's finest restaurant, running beautifully. Roland rules the kitchen, turning out Oriental-influenced contemporary French creations. His plates are visual masterpieces, and portions are substantial for cuisine this fine. Mary Beth is arguably the city's best pastry chef; her desserts are unparalleled and her chocolates—now available on a retail basis—are equally superb. A veteran wait staff inspires confidence and imparts conviviality; intimidation isn't part of the experience. Lunch at Le Francais is one of Chicago's great gastronomic events and substantially less expensive than dinner. ✕ *269 S. Milwaukee Ave., Wheeling,* ☎ *708/541–7470. Reservations required. AE, D, MC, V. Closed Sun. No lunch Sat., Mon.*

6 Lodging

AS THE NATION'S MOST POPULAR convention destination, Chicago can be a challenging place to find a room. Recent additions to downtown attractions—the Navy Pier complex, the nearby 9-hole golf course, and a barrage of glitzy restaurants and shops—are bound to lure even more travelers. Advance reservations are practically mandatory, except perhaps in the dead of winter.

Updated by
Steven K.
Amsterdam

When there's not a major show in town, virtually all hotels do something to try to woo customers, whether it's corporate rates, shopper's packages, senior citizen and auto club savings, honeymoon deals, or discounts to the clergy and military personnel. It never hurts to ask whether you're eligible for a discount.

When Not to Go

While Chicago's infamous frigid winters should be a consideration when planning your trip, also be aware that there are more than 1,000 conventions scheduled in the Chicago area for 1996. Unless you're fearless in the face of 25,000-plus representatives of a single industry, it's wise to check your travel dates with the **Chicago Convention and Tourism Bureau** (☎ 312/567–8500).

Choosing a Neighborhood

Hotels are clustered primarily at three locations: the Loop, the Near North Side, and the airport. They're listed below by location and then by price category within each location.

Business travelers may prefer Loop hotels because they're within walking distance to the financial district and government offices. Major cultural institutions are nearby as well: the Art Institute, the Symphony, the Lyric Opera, and the Fine Arts Theater. The Field Museum, Shedd Aquarium, and Adler Planetarium are just a short bus or cab ride away, and then there are the skyscrapers that put Chicago on the architectural map of the world. Loop hotels tend to be older and somewhat less expensive than those in the Near North. The main drawback to staying here is that the neighborhood gets deserted, even a little spooky, late at night. People traveling alone may prefer the brighter lights of North Michigan Avenue.

In addition to safety, dining and shopping are the big draws north of the river, where hotels line both sides of Michigan Avenue as well as area side streets. Association headquarters, art galleries, advertising agencies, and media companies are located here. Hotels range from high-tech to homey. A bit north of Michigan Avenue and close to Lincoln Park and the lakefront is the Gold Coast, a stately residential neighborhood where the hotels are quiet and dignified. Farther up, around Diversey Parkway, less expensive properties sit amid less touristy ethnic restaurants and the Midwest's finest—or, at least, most eclectic—array of clothing, book, and record stores (new, alternative, and used).

Even though prices are slightly lower, airport hotels are not a good deal for the typical Chicago tourist. The area around O'Hare is drab, depressing, and far from the center of action. The trip into town can take an hour or more during rush hour, bad weather, or periods of heavy construction on the Kennedy Expressway, all of which are likely at any given time.

Booking Your Room

When you make your reservation, be sure to get a reservation number and keep it with you for reference. Notify the hotel if you anticipate arriving later than 5 PM; many hotels will guarantee your reservation to your credit card and have a room waiting for you even if you arrive at 2 AM. Should you need to cancel your reservation, notify the hotel as soon as possible—and be sure to get a cancellation number. Otherwise, you may be responsible for at least one night's charge.

One alternative to reserving a room through a hotel is to contact a booking service. These agencies book excess rooms at major hotels, often at a significant discount. To reserve a room in any property in this chapter, you can contact **Fodor's new toll-free lodging reservations hot line** (☎ 1–800–FODORS–1 or 1–800–363–6771; 0800–89–1030 in Great Britain; 0014/800–12–8271 in Australia; 1800–55–9101 in Ireland). A discount hotel-reservation service that specializes in Chicago is **Hot Rooms** (☎ 312/468–7666 or 800/468–3500); the agency does not charge a fee.

Facilities

Most of the upscale hotels have business centers, or at least the capability to assist with faxing, copying, and word processing. Most also offer room service, as well as laundry and dry cleaning. Cable TV is the standard in Chicago hotels and often comes with free movie channels, or the option to pay to watch a particular film. A few hotels charge for using on-site health facilities. Guests at hotels that don't have their own health club may be allowed to use one nearby, usually for a daily fee ranging from $5 to $10. Ask if this is important to you.

Many hotels in the Chicago area have adapted some accommodations for people using wheelchairs or for guests with vision or hearing impairments. If you have a special need, call the hotel for specific information on what adaptations have been made.

Ratings

Hotel price categories in this chapter are based on the standard weekday rate for one room, double occupancy. These are the rack rates—the highest price at which the rooms are rented. As noted above, discounts are often available. But note that, unlike standard rates that are quoted *per room,* package rates are often quoted *per person, double occupancy.*

CATEGORY	COST*
$$$$	over $200
$$$	$150–$200
$$	$100–$150
$	under $100

All prices are for a standard double room, excluding service charges and the unpleasantly surprising 14.9% room tax.

O'Hare Airport

$$$ **Hotel Sofitel O'Hare.** Subtle Parisian touches—a boulangerie-patis-
★ serie, nightly turndown with a rose and a chocolate truffle, and a quietude that's hard to find near O'Hare—make Sofitel the best of the airport options. The staff is well informed and enthusiastic. Room decor is a reasonably successful copy of light country French, with blond-wood furniture and floral print fabrics. Overall, rooms are spacious and comfortable and have such thoughtful details as irons and boards, extra pillows and blankets, hair dryers, and telephones equipped for modems.

The compact health club includes a lap pool and a sundeck. The French theme carries through to the restaurant, the café, and the all-imports gift shop. ⊡ *5550 N. River Rd., Rosemont 60018,* ☎ *708/678–4488 or 800/233–5959,* FAX *708/678–4244. 304 rooms, 9 suites. 2 restaurants, bar, patisserie, minibars, no-smoking rooms, room service, indoor lap pool, exercise room, concierge, airport shuttle, parking. AE, D, DC, MC, V.*

$$$ **Hyatt Regency O'Hare.** This Hyatt's signature concrete atrium has all the personality of an office park, and the other public spaces and the staff only make the experience more impersonal. The contemporary, mauve-and-beige-tone rooms, which are large and have sitting areas, aren't particularly charming either. Even the rotating rooftop restaurant and the short walk to the convention center don't compensate. ⊡ *9300 W. Bryn Mawr Ave., Rosemont 60018,* ☎ *708/696–1234 or 800/233–1234,* FAX *708/698–0139. 1,100 rooms, 58 suites. 4 restaurants, no-smoking rooms, room service, indoor pool, exercise room, concierge, airport shuttle, parking (fee). AE, D, DC, MC, V.*

$$$ **Marriott Suites O'Hare Chicago.** This slightly generic all-suite hotel is decorated in deep-'80s style, with lots of mauve and gray-green tones. The suites are good sized: Double French doors open between the bedroom and a sitting room; included is a king-size bed, a writing desk, two TVs, two telephones, a refrigerator, and a bathroom with tub and separate shower stall. Amenities such as hair dryers, irons and boards, coffeemakers, free cable movies, and complimentary newspapers on weekdays make up in service what the establishment lacks in character. ⊡ *6155 N. River Rd., Rosemont 60018,* ☎ *708/696–4400 or 800/228–9290,* FAX *708/696–2122. 256 suites. Restaurant, bar, no-smoking suites, pool, hot tub, sauna, exercise room, concierge, airport shuttle, free parking. AE, D, DC, MC, V.*

$$$ **O'Hare Marriott Hotel.** On the outside, this 1960s white concrete structure is showing its age; inside the two low-rise buildings and one 12-story high-rise are tidy, quiet, and comfortable rooms. A 1994 renovation ensures that the standard floral-print fabrics and dark-wood furnishings are at least in good shape. Highlights are the five different restaurants, including one Japanese and one Chinese, and a superb (and complimentary) health club, with a whirlpool, a tanning booth, separate men's and women's saunas, massage, and a large, circular indoor-outdoor pool. ⊡ *8535 W. Higgins Rd., Chicago 60631,* ☎ *312/693–4444 or 800/228–9290,* FAX *312/714–4297. 681 rooms, 22 suites. 5 restaurants, no-smoking rooms, indoor-outdoor pool, outdoor pool, hot tub, massage, sauna, exercise room, concierge, airport shuttle, free parking. AE, D, DC, MC, V.*

$$$ **Radisson Suite O'Hare.** The public spaces of this handsome hotel are decorated in the unmistakable style of Frank Lloyd Wright. The two-room suites aren't—but they *are* large, functional, and bland. Living rooms have sofa beds as well as kitchen areas, each with wet bar, refrigerator, microwave, and dining table. Each suite also has two TVs and two telephones. Rooms open onto a bright interior courtyard-atrium, across which a colorful sculpture hangs. The health club includes a pool, a whirlpool, weight machines, and a sauna. The full breakfast and newspaper in the morning and cocktails in the evening are complimentary. ⊡ *5500 N. River Rd., Rosemont 60018,* ☎ *708/678–4000 or 800/333–3333,* FAX *708/928–7659. 296 suites. Restaurant, bar, kitchenettes, minibars, no-smoking rooms, indoor pool, hot tub, sauna, exercise room, concierge, airport shuttle, free parking. AE, D, DC, MC, V.*

$$$ **Westin O'Hare.** Faux-antique cherry wood, modern brass and glass, and framed botanical prints don't distinguish this concrete high-rise from the average airport hotel. Rooms are roomy, though, and redeem themselves with their sheer quirkiness; an old TV bolted to the bathroom sink keeps you tuned in at all times. ⚏ *6100 N. River Rd., Rosemont 60018,* ☎ *708/698–6000 or 800/228–3000,* ⅋ℵ *708/698–4591. 525 rooms, 31 suites. Restaurant, café, minibars, no-smoking rooms, room service, indoor lap pool, basketball, exercise room, racquetball, concierge, airport shuttle, free and fee parking. AE, D, DC, MC, V.*

$$ Holiday Inn O'Hare International. A little tired on the outside, this familiar 1960s hostelry has an atrium lobby built around an indoor pool—all under exposed white girders. You can absorb this weird lesson in postindustrial architecture while sipping cocktails, snug in your bamboo lounge chair. Rooms are done in the unexciting Holiday Inn Style, with pink-and-blue color schemes and plenty of space. Restaurants and a '50s-style bar provide at least visual entertainment. ⚏ *5440 N. River Rd., Rosemont 60018,* ☎ *708/671–6350 or 800/465–4329,* ⅋ℵ *708/671–5406. 507 rooms, 16 suites. 2 restaurants, bar, food court, minibars, no-smoking rooms, indoor and outdoor pools, exercise room, concierge, airport shuttle, free parking. AE, D, DC, MC, V.*

$$ O'Hare Hilton. This former airport dumping ground is now a pleasant haven for business travelers. The only hotel on airport property, the Hilton is extremely neat and convenient; day rates are available for travelers with short stopovers, and for some flights, you can check your bags at the hotel and walk to your gate unencumbered. A dramatic high-ceiling lobby eschews the usual institutional pastel hues in favor of a snappy red-and-black color scheme. The small rooms have that dreary changing-planes-in-Chicago feel, but they're suitably comfortable. A pool, a Jacuzzi, a sauna, tanning beds, and a golf center with driving range all make the stay between the terminals more comfortable. ⚏ *Box 66414, O'Hare International Airport, Rosemont 60666,* ☎ *312/686–8000 or 800/445–8667,* ⅋ℵ *312/601–2873. 858 rooms, 18 suites. Restaurant, bar, minibars, no-smoking rooms, room service, indoor pool, hot tub, sauna, driving range, exercise room, business services. AE, D, DC, MC, V.*

$ Comfort Inn O'Hare. For savings, this late-80s low rise packs a punch, offering a 24-hour airport shuttle; free coffee, juice, and doughnuts in the morning; and a spa with several exercise machines and a whirlpool. Teal-and-pink rooms are spotless and surprisingly quiet, considering the hotel's location at a busy intersection. An adjacent coffee shop provides room service. ⚏ *2175 E. Touhy Ave., Des Plaines 60018,* ☎ *708/635–1300 or 800/222–7666,* ⅋ℵ *708/635–7572. 148 rooms, 12 suites. Coffee shop, no-smoking rooms, hot tub, exercise room, dry cleaning, airport shuttle. AE, D, DC, MC, V.*

$ Travelodge Chicago O'Hare. The rooms in this '60s motel are freshly decorated, tidy, and incomparably cheap. For the budget business traveller who travels with a set of earplugs, this is the most sensible place to bed down near the airport. ⚏ *3003 Mannheim Rd., Des Plaines, 60018,* ☎ *708/296–5541 or 800/255–3050,* ⅋ℵ *708/803–1984. 95 rooms. Coffee shop, no-smoking rooms, airport shuttle, free parking. AE, D, DC, MC, V.*

Downtown

$$$$ The Fairmont. This 45-story pink granite tower in the sterile Illinois
★ Center complex, just blocks from the Loop, is a stand-out inside and out. Rooms are grand, with warm, neutral color schemes; plants; marble-top, dark-wood furniture; and plenty of space—extra-long beds are standard. The building's relative isolation gives it spectacular views (the lake, Grant Park, or downtown) and windows can be opened to catch the breeze. Neutrogena toiletries, plush robes, and nightly turndown

with chocolates make you feel well cared for, and th
drinking, and entertainment options should please
one. There's no health club, but guests get a disco
high-tech facility where Michael Jordan has bee
hoops. ☎ *200 N. Columbus Dr., Chicago 60601, ☎ 312/565–8000
or 800/527–4727,* FAX *312/856–1032. 692 rooms, including 66 suites.
2 restaurants, 1 bar, lobby lounge, in-room modem lines, minibars, no-
smoking rooms, room service, golf privileges, laundry service and dry
cleaning, concierge, business services, meeting rooms, parking (fee). AE,
D, DC, MC, V.*

$$$$ **Hyatt Regency.** A cozy hideaway it's not. The two-story greenhouse
lobby has trees, palms, and gushing fountains, but the lobby bar overlooks a hectic scene. Between the crashing water and the traffic from
the hotel's many meeting rooms, a dull roar permeates. Getting lost is
alarmingly easy in the labyrinth of halls and escalators that snake
through the two towers and connect thousands of rooms. The guest
rooms, just renovated with classic contemporary decor to the tune of
$21 million, do feature such conveniences as voice mail and built-in
hair dryers. Unless you're attending a meeting here, however, opt for
the nearby and less chaotic Fairmont or Swissôtel. As at the Fairmont,
guests here have access to the Athletic Club Illinois Center. ☎ *151 E.
Wacker Dr., Chicago 60601, ☎ 312/565–1234 or 800/233–1234,* FAX
*312/565–2966. 2,019 rooms, 150 suites. 4 restaurants, 5 lounges, mini-
bars, no-smoking rooms, room service, concierge, business services, parking. AE, D, DC, MC, V.*

$$$$ **Renaissance Chicago Hotel.** Behind the modern stone-and-glass exte-
★ rior is a tidy '90s interpretation of turn-of-the-century splendor. Lavish floral carpets, tapestry upholstery, crystal-beaded chandeliers, and
vaguely French provincial furniture create rich-looking public areas.
Bellhops dress in traditional waistcoats and pillbox hats. These classic pretensions combined with cheerful, unpretentious service distinguish this from other hotels along the south banks of the river. Most
rooms have sitting areas and rounded windows with spectacular river
views. Black marble and mahogany vanities in the bathroom add to
the grand old hotel effect. Amenities include robes, free shoe shines,
complimentary coffee, a newspaper each morning, and an especially
plush (if small) pool and health spa. This used to be called the Stouf-
fer Renaissance—there's been no change in management. ☎ *1 W.
Wacker Dr., Chicago 60601, ☎ 312/372–7200 or 800/468–3571,* FAX
*312/372–0093. 565 rooms, 40 suites. 2 restaurants, lobby bar, mini-
bars, no-smoking rooms, room service, indoor pool, hot tub, sauna,
exercise room, laundry service and dry cleaning, concierge, parking.
AE, D, DC, MC, V.*

$$$ **Chicago Hilton and Towers.** The Hilton, built in 1927, is a vast con-
vention hotel, with the largest exhibit space, the largest health club
(28,000 square feet), and the largest and grandest ballroom of any hotel
in the city, all leaving the visitor feeling a little like someone lost in an
endless, Vegas-style convention center. The lobby is a sea of green-and-
mauve marble with gilt and crystal galore. The first-floor concourse
buzzes with service possibilities—shops, ticket services, ATMs—you
may need a map to find your way. The dizzying eagerness to please
continues in the guest rooms, which are done in teals and purples with
cherry wood. Most doubles have two bathrooms. Kitty O'Shea's, the
hotel's Irish bar and restaurant, offers live entertainment. ☎ *720 S.
Michigan Ave., 60605, ☎ 312/922–4400 or 800/445–8667,* FAX
*312/922–5240. 1,543 rooms, 149 suites. 3 restaurants, 2 lounges, mini-
bars, no-smoking rooms, room service, pool, beauty salon, spa, exer-
cise room, concierge, business services, parking. AE, D, DC, MC, V.*

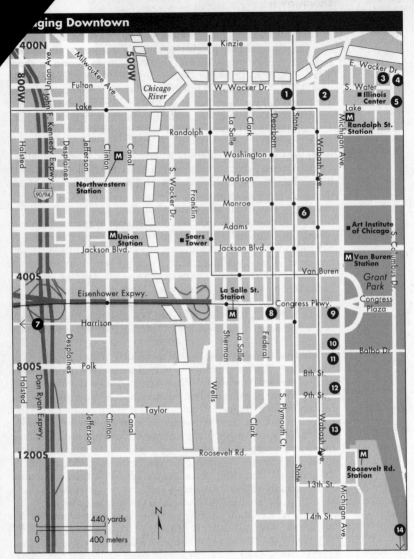

Blackstone Hotel, **10**

Chicago Hilton and
Towers, **11**

The Congress
Hotel, **9**

Essex Inn, **12**

The Fairmont, **5**

Grant Park Hotel, **13**

Hyatt on Printer's
Row, **8**

Hyatt Regency, **3**

Inn at University
Village, **7**

Oxford House, **2**

The Palmer House
Hilton, **6**

Ramada Inn
Lakeshore, **14**

The Renaissance
Chicago Hotel, **1**

Swissôtel, **4**

$$$ **Hyatt on Printer's Row.** A series of three older buildings forms this small European-style hotel. The rooms, with a sage-and-gray color scheme and black-lacquer furniture, are quiet retreats from the chaos of the Loop, just outside the window (the impressive and imposing Harold Washington Public Library is across the street). Bathroom amenities include hair dryers, phones, and TVs. Room sizes and shapes vary by building, but they're generally spacious, and many have 12-foot ceilings and large windows. Service is overtaxed but genial. The hotel restaurant, Prairie, serves top-notch New American cuisine. This Hyatt is an excellent alternative to the noisy Hilton and is only a few blocks from the city's financial center. ☎ *500 S. Dearborn St., Chicago 60605,* ☎ *312/986–1234 or 800/233–1234,* FAX *312/939–2468. 161 rooms, 4 suites. Restaurant, bar, minibars, no-smoking rooms, concierge, parking. AE, D, DC, MC, V.*

$$$ **Swissôtel.** A 1988 concrete-and-glass high-rise addition to the Wacker
★ Drive skyline, the Swissôtel's triangular, Harry Weese design ensures panoramic lake and river vistas. The hotel (successfully) affects European ambience with unobtrusive and well-polished service. Each of the spacious guest rooms has a superb city or lake view, a sitting area, two-line phones, its own doorbell, and a marble bathroom with separate tub and shower. The hotel has an agreement with the adjacent Illinois Center Golf Course and Driving Range, so guests can easily book tee times for the nine-hole course and 112-position driving range. A Sunday brunch is served in the 43rd floor penthouse. ☎ *323 E. Wacker Dr., 60601,* ☎ *312/565–0565 or 800/654–7262,* FAX *312/565–0540. 636 rooms, 32 suites (5 duplexes). Restaurant, bar, patisserie, minibars, no-smoking rooms, room service, indoor pool, golf privileges, exercise room, concierge, business services, parking. AE, D, DC, MC, V.*

$$ **Blackstone Hotel.** Built in 1910, the Blackstone's dark Second Empire
★ decor makes it look 60 years older. Appointments of a bygone era include chandeliers and marble statues in the lobby and original brass hardware that glows against warm mahogany doors, and a roaring fireplace in the winter. Bill Clinton is the only American president who hasn't stayed here since it was built. The passage of time has left a mark here or there, and some of the usual amenities are missing (though guests may use the business services and the health club across the street at the Hilton). Then again, rooms have high ceilings and big closets, and there's jazz instead of Muzak in the elevators. Jazz Showcase, one of the city's premier clubs, is just off the lobby. Developers occasionally threaten to refurbish the Blackstone, but most prefer to keep it—along with its reasonable prices—just as it is. ☎ *636 S. Michigan Ave., Chicago 60605,* ☎ *312/427–4300 or 800/622–6330,* FAX *312/427–4300. 305 rooms, 25 suites. Restaurant, lounge, no-smoking rooms, night club, theater, parking. AE, D, DC, MC, V.*

$$ **Congress Hotel.** The original building opened in 1893, and its public areas still retain touches of that ornate period. More recent additions have added little personality. An overflow hotel for the nearby Chicago Hilton and Towers, the Congress is favored by convention goers, tour groups, and airline crews. Rooms are clean, secure, and relatively inexpensive. Some are quite roomy, and those facing east, although pricier, have views of the lake and Grant Park. Except for these features and the hotel's location near McCormick Place and the museums, there's little reason to stay here. ☎ *520 S. Michigan Ave., 60605,* ☎ *312/427–3800 or 800/635–1666,* FAX *312/427–4840. 818 rooms, 60 suites. Restaurant, parking. AE, D, DC, MC, V.*

$$ **Grant Park Hotel.** While not exactly pretty, this Best Western is a good value for travelers attending functions at nearby McCormick Place. The mauve-and-gray rooms are plain, smallish, and have an antiseptic feel—still, they are functional. The south Loop location is near Printer's Row as well as the cluster of museums at the south end of Grant Park. ⌨ *1100 S. Michigan Ave., Chicago 60605,* ☎ *312/922–2900 or 800/528–1234,* ℻ *312/922–8812. 172 rooms, 13 suites. Restaurant, no-smoking rooms, pool, exercise room, parking. AE, D, DC, MC, V.*

$$ Inn at University Village. Two miles west of the Loop, this 1988 red-brick property attracts people visiting the University of Illinois or Rush Presbyterian St. Lukes Medical Center, which owns the hotel. Unless you fit one of those categories, this is a fairly isolated spot. As befits its hospital ownership, public areas are completely accessible to people using wheelchairs. The lobby's dark-wood antiques, reproductions, and velvet sofas and chairs give it a vague clubby feel. Guest rooms, however, have a more modern decor: blond-wood furnishings with black accents, ceramic pieces resembling fragments of Egyptian friezes overhanging the beds, and tabletops and bathroom sinks made of granite and marble. The restaurant specializes in "heart-healthy" cuisine and offers a Sunday jazz brunch that has a local following. Little Italy is a few blocks south on Taylor Street. ⌨ *625 S. Ashland Ave. (corner of Harrison St.), Chicago 60607,* ☎ *312/243–7200 or 800/622–5233,* ℻ *312/243–1289. 113 rooms (all no-smoking), 5 suites. Restaurant, exercise room, parking. AE, D, DC, MC, V.*

$$ Palmer House Hilton. Built in 1871 by Chicago merchant Potter Palmer,
★ this landmark hotel in the heart of the Loop has some of the city's most ornate and elegant public areas. The main lobby, up a floor from the marble, street-level shopping arcade, has 21 ceiling murals by Louis Rigal, lots of gilding, Victorian velvet, brocade furniture, crystal chandeliers, and a late-19th-century patina. Upstairs, rooms are less spectacular but still pleasant, with light peach florals and reproduction antique furniture. There are wildly different configurations, so be sure to request a larger room. The modern feel of the health club and pool show the management's dedication to keeping the property cared for and current. Like many big-meeting hotels, though, the Palmer House can get hectic, and service can be brusque. ⌨ *17 E. Monroe St., Chicago 60603,* ☎ *312/726–7500 or 800/445–8667,* ℻ *312/263–2556. 1,639 rooms, 88 suites. 5 restaurants, bar, minibars, no-smoking rooms, indoor pool, barbershop, exercise room, concierge, business services, parking. AE, D, DC, MC, V.*

$ Essex Inn. Two-thirds of the Essex's guests are in town for trade shows at McCormick Place, which is not a surprise given the hotel's South Michigan Avenue location. The motel-modern lobby is plain and rooms are shabby in places. Come here for basic facilities and amenities at a low price. ⌨ *800 S. Michigan Ave., Chicago 60605,* ☎ *312/939–2800 or 800/421–6909,* ℻ *312/939–1605. 255 rooms, 16 suites. Restaurant, lounge, minibars, pool, concierge, parking. AE, D, DC, MC, V.*

$ Oxford House. This is possibly the cleanest, cheapest, most centrally located property in the city. The paint job isn't that fresh, the furniture is mismatched, and the elevators are slow, but the rooms are large and have kitchen areas. The operative word here is budget. ⌨ *225 N. Wabash at Wacker Dr., Chicago 60601,* ☎ *312/346–6585,* ℻ *312/346–7742. 167 rooms. Restaurant, kitchenettes, no-smoking rooms, parking. AE, D, MC, V.*

$ Ramada Inn Lakeshore. The only reason to stay at this former Hilton, now seriously downgraded, is its proximity to Hyde Park and the University of Chicago. Despite attempts at renovation, the rooms are composed of haphazard hotel elements. The din of traffic on Lakeshore Drive is unavoidable in the rooms facing Lake Michigan. ⌨ *4900 S. Lakeshore Dr., Chicago 60615,* ☎ *312/288–5800,* ℻ *312/288–5745.*

184 rooms. Restaurant, no-smoking rooms, indoor pool, convention center, free parking. AE, D, MC, V.

Near North

$$$$ **The Drake.** Built in the style of an Italian Renaissance palace, and on the National Register of Historic Places since 1981, heads of state have been parading through this hotel since it opened in 1920. The public areas are maintained to impress: The oak-paneled lobby has a lavish red carpet, crystal chandeliers, a marble fountain, and a palm court where high tea is served. The average guest rooms, however, show that the property has been resting on its laurels; in condition and style, the reproduction antique furniture, marble bathrooms, striped wallpaper, and floral bedspreads are unexceptional and starting to look mismatched. Service is enthusiastic, if harried. Amenities still include flowers and fruit baskets on each floor, turndown service with a complimentary chocolate each evening, complimentary newspaper daily, and bathrobes in each room. ☎ *140 E. Walton Pl., Chicago 60611,* ☎ *312/787–2200 or 800/553–7256,* FAX *312/787–1431. 535 rooms, 65 suites. 3 restaurants, 2 lounges, minibars, no-smoking rooms, room service, barbershop, exercise room, laundry service and dry cleaning, concierge, business services, parking. AE, D, DC, MC, V.*

$$$$ **Four Seasons.** Visiting celebrities stay here for one reason: the pam-
★ pering. And the Four Seasons aims to treat every guest like a celebrity— service is paramount. The hotel sits atop the stores of 900 North Michigan, but it feels more like a grand English country house than an urban skyscraper. The lobby, which has the only wood-burning fireplace in a Chicago hotel, has cabinets stocked with antique Minton china and a marble fountain that was imported from Italy. Afternoon tea is served here daily. The Old World feeling continues in the elegant furnishings of the pastel-tone guest rooms, decorated with Italian marble, handcrafted woodwork, custom-woven rugs, and botanical prints. Plush bathrobes, multiple phones, hair dryers, unusually lavish bath supplies, and well-stocked minibars and snack stations are standard. ☎ *120 E. Delaware Pl., Chicago 60611,* ☎ *312/280–8800 or 800/332–3442,* FAX *312/280–9184. 343 rooms, 121 suites. 2 restaurants, bar, minibars, no-smoking rooms, room service, indoor pool, exercise room, concierge, business services, parking. AE, D, DC, MC, V.*

$$$$ **Hotel Inter-Continental Chicago.** The Inter-Continental is really two properties with the same management: the 1929 Inter-Continental Building (originally a men's club) and what was the Forum Hotel (adjacent to the north). The rooms and common areas of the latter are decorated in drab, contemporary style, but the 1929 Inter-Continental is a bit more upscale club style (and priced accordingly). Unique architectural features preserved in the southern wing—such as the mosaic swimming pool—earned the hotel National Landmark status. Banquet and meeting rooms have been so lovingly restored that the self-guided tour offered is worth the effort, if only to see the different examples of renaissance style in the rooms. The riverside location puts the Inter-Continental within easy walking distance of the Loop and Near North business districts. ☎ *505 N. Michigan Ave., Chicago 60611,* ☎ *312/944–4100 or 800/327–0200,* FAX *312/944–3050. 844 guest rooms, 42 suites. 2 restaurants, bar, minibars, no-smoking rooms, room service, indoor pool, exercise room, concierge, business services, parking. AE, D, DC, MC, V.*

$$$$ **Hotel Nikko.** Chicago jazziness is melded with Asian understatement at this quietly bustling property. Sitting in the expansive lobby of polished granite, black lacquer, and mahogany, you can enjoy a swing trio

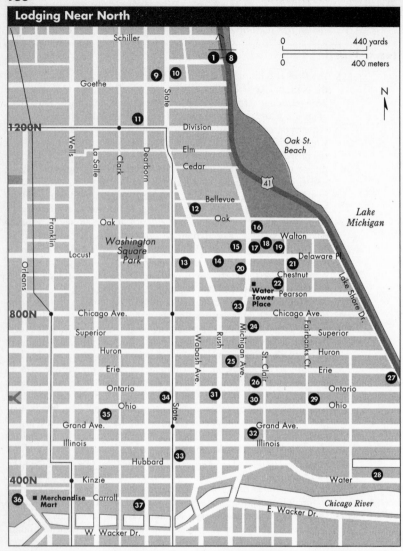

Ambassador West, **9**

The Barclay Chicago, **24**

Belden Stratford, **7**

City Suites Hotel, **4**

Claridge Hotel, **11**

Comfort Inn of Lincoln Park, **1**

Courtyard by Marriott, **33**

Days Inn Chicago Hotel Lincoln, **8**

Days Inn Lake Shore Drive, **27**

Days Inn Near North, **3**

The Drake, **16**

Embassy Suites, **34**

The Four Seasons, **15**

Guest Quarters Suite Hotel, **19**

Holiday Inn Chicago City Centre, **29**

Holiday Inn Mart Plaza, **36**

Hotel Inter-Continental Chicago, **32**

Hotel Nikko, **37**

Inn of Chicago, **30**

The Knickerbocker, **18**

Lenox House, **31**

Margarita—A European Inn, **2**

Motel 6 Chicago, **26**

Omni Ambassador East, **10**

Omni Chicago Hotel, **25**

Park Brompton Hotel, **6**

Park Hyatt, **23**

Raphael, **21**

The Ritz-Carlton, **22**

River North Hotel, **35**

Sheraton Chicago Hotel and Towers, **28**

The Surf Hotel, **5**

The Sutton Place Hotel, **12**

The Talbott, **13**

The Tremont, **20**

The Westin Hotel, **17**

The Whitehall Hotel, **14**

and a cocktail while still gazing out at a serene rock garden. The rooms, furnished in either contemporary or traditional Japanese style, have marble baths, bathrobes, dressing areas, and three phones; most rooms have views of the river or the city's northern sprawl. Besides a fully equipped business center and full-service health club (with gym clothes and sneakers to borrow), amenities include nightly turndown service and complimentary coffee and newspaper. Benkay, the hotel's Japanese restaurant, has received stellar reviews (*see* Chapter 5, Dining). The Sunday Jazz brunch at the Continental Celebrity Café draws such a wide and devoted audience that it is now broadcast live on the radio. ☎ *320 N. Dearborn St., Chicago 60610,* ☎ *312/744–1900 or 800/645–5687,* FAX *312/527–2650. 422 rooms, 4 suites. 2 restaurants, lounge, minibars, no-smoking rooms, room service, exercise room, laundry service and dry cleaning, concierge, business services, parking. AE, D, DC, MC, V.*

\$\$\$\$ **Omni Chicago Hotel.** Michigan Avenue's apparent obsession with En-
★ glish country manor ambience is most successful here; the suites are sparkling studies of hunter greens and cherry wood with rich coordinated floral patterns throughout. The well-equipped sitting room–desk area is separated from the bedroom by French doors. Each suite also includes turndown service, two TVs, two two-line phones, minibars, irons and boards, in-room movies, and hair dryers and robes in the bathrooms. The Omni's restaurant, Cielo, offers American-Italian cuisine. A fully equipped health club and pool are available to all guests free of charge, as is limousine service. ☎ *676 N. Michigan Ave., Chicago 60611,* ☎ *312/944–6664 or 800/843–6664,* FAX *312/266–3015. 347 suites. Restaurant, bar, no-smoking rooms, indoor pool, hot tub, exercise room, concierge. AE, D, DC, MC, V.*

\$\$\$\$ **Park Hyatt.** You'll pay a stiff tariff here, but the mostly corporate travelers are satisfied with this Hyatt. The contemporary-classic decor has striking Oriental touches, and the establishment is maintained as well as possible given the constant stream of traffic; even in the dead of winter, the Park Hyatt is abuzz. Coffee and tea in the lobby are standard, as are fax machines and multiple phones in each room; complimentary cookies, fruit, and bottled water daily; and bathrooms with robes, scales, phones, and TVs. Guests can have exercise equipment set up in their room or use a nearby health club. The lobby lounge has live music nightly, and the hotel's restaurant, La Tour, is one of the city's finest. A caveat: The building's mostly glass outer wall doesn't adequately drown out traffic sounds from Chicago Avenue. ☎ *800 N. Michigan Ave., Chicago 60611,* ☎ *312/280–2222 or 800/233–1234,* FAX *312/280–1963. 255 rooms, 40 suites. Restaurant, 2 lounges, minibars, no-smoking rooms, room service, concierge, parking. AE, D, DC, MC, V.*

\$\$\$\$ **Ritz-Carlton.** The Ritz-Carlton, which is run by Four Seasons–Regent
★ Hotels and Resorts and not the Ritz-Carlton chain, spends more than a quarter-million dollars annually on floral arrangements, and that's just to adorn common areas. The Ritz is perched on the 12th-floor above Water Tower Place, Michigan Avenue's most famous vertical shopping mall. Tea is served every afternoon in the two-story greenhouse lobby; a fountain makes a crashing backdrop—and a posh spot for one of the city's few late-night dinners. Upstairs there's more luxury: The spacious rooms are outfitted in a blend of European styles, with fine mahogany furniture, cherry Chippendale-style armoires, floral pattern wallpaper with border prints, and such comfy touches as wing chairs. Hair dryers, bathrobes, windows that open, multiple telephones, and lighted makeup mirrors are standard. ☎ *160 E. Pearson St., Chicago 60611,* ☎ *312/266–1000 or 800/691–6906,* FAX *312/266–1194. 431*

rooms, 82 suites. 3 restaurants, bar, minibars, no-smoking rooms, room service, indoor pool, spa, exercise room, laundry service and dry cleaning, concierge, parking. AE, D, DC, MC, V.

$$$$ **Sheraton Chicago Hotel and Towers.** Sheraton has achieved every convention hotel's dream—vastness that's manageable. The room colors are not particularly inspired (salmon, gray, etc.), but the hotel's lighthouse-like location on the edge of the river and the lake guarantees fabulous views. There are two lobby bars, one of which has a piano, and several restaurants. Service is efficient and cheerful. The Sheraton is close to Michigan Avenue, the North Pier complex on Illinois Street, and the Illinois Center office complex. 🏢 *Cityfront Plaza, 301 E. North Water St., Chicago 60611,* ☎ *312/464–1000 or 800/325– 3535,* ℻ *312/464–9140. 1,200 rooms, 51 suites. 2 restaurants, 2 bars, minibars, no-smoking rooms, room service, indoor pool, exercise room, laundry service and dry cleaning, concierge, business services, parking. AE, D, DC, MC, V.*

$$$$ **Sutton Place Hotel.** Formerly Le Meridien, this plain modern build-
★ ing, on one of the few truly quiet streets near North Michigan Avenue, still has its predecessor's pretensions and its charms: a small but well-appointed lobby, original Robert Mapplethorpe photos (lurid orchids and the like), and management with European affectations. Visiting musicians seem to favor the location, the service, and the style. Rooms are done in neat grays, blacks, and whites and come complete with entertainment centers—including VCRs, CD players with several compact discs, radios, and TVs. The bathrooms have terry-cloth robes, hair dryers, and a separate tub and shower. If you're a chocoholic, don't leave without a trip to the Saturday afternoon chocolate buffet in the hotel's French-style Brasserie Bellevue. And, if a step aerobic setup (available in your room on request) and the nearby health club won't be enough to work that off, the truly obsessed should stay in the Fitness Suite. 🏢 *21 E. Bellevue Pl., Chicago 60611,* ☎ *312/266–2100 or 800/543–4300,* ℻ *312/266–2141. 247 rooms, 41 suites. Restaurant, bar, minibars, no-smoking rooms, room service, laundry service and dry cleaning, concierge, business services, parking. AE, D, DC, MC, V.*

$$$$ **The Tremont.** This small, European-style hotel is one of several of its type tucked away near North Michigan Avenue. Renovations in 1994 brought a cheerful yellow to the design scheme and brightened the property immensely. Rooms are fitted with traditional Williamsburg-style decor and Baker furniture; some are quite small, so be sure to ask about size. The hotel pulls in mostly independent business types and is not at all family oriented. 🏢 *100 E. Chestnut St., Chicago 60611,* ☎ *312/751–1900 or 800 621–8133,* ℻ *312/280–1304. 127 rooms, 10 suites. Restaurant-bar, no-smoking rooms, room service, laundry service and dry cleaning, concierge, parking. AE, D, DC, MC, V.*

$$$ **Ambassador West.** This 1920s hotel's marble-and-oak lobby is loaded with antiques and reproductions, and the rooms retain some vintage flavor with faded pink furnishings and (the inevitable) fox-hunt prints on the walls. The rooms vary greatly in size, and renovations in 1995 brought a newer vintage look and a club floor to the hotel; be sure to ask about these when making reservations. The hotel sometimes acts as a home away from home for movie people shooting films in Chicago. For real action, however, head for the Pump Room across the street in the Omni Ambassador East. 🏢 *1300 N. State Pkwy., Chicago 60610,* ☎ *312/787–3700 or 800/300–WEST,* ℻ *312/640–2967. 220 rooms, 50 suites. Restaurant, bar, minibars, no-smoking rooms, beauty salon, exercise room, concierge, parking. AE, D, DC, MC, V.*

$$$ Barclay Chicago. A small, intimate lobby paneled in blond oak sets the tone for this hotel's traditional look, though some rooms and upstairs public areas are looking worn. It's an all-suite establishment, but some seem no more than slightly extended rooms. Many do, however, have kitchens. Phones in bathrooms are standard, as are built-in hair dryers. A complimentary breakfast buffet is offered to guests each morning, and shoe shines and exercise equipment are available upon request. One block off the Magnificent Mile, the Barclay caters to business travelers during the week and packs in shoppers on the weekend. ☎ *166 E. Superior St., Chicago 60611,* ☎ *312/787–6000 or 800/621–8004,* FAX *312/787–4331. 120 suites. Restaurant, 2 lounges, kitchenettes, minibars, no-smoking rooms, in-room VCRs, indoor pool, barbershop, laundry service, concierge, parking. AE, D, DC, MC, V.*

$$$ Claridge Hotel. Once a superb value, now just a nice spot for the night, this 1930s hotel offers peace and quiet. The Gold Coast location is convenient to the singles scene on nearby Division Street and other Near North nightlife. Public areas are tastefully decorated in dark wood and green marble; guest rooms tend toward mauves, grays, and other neutral colors. Rooms that don't get direct sunlight are livened up with deep jewel tones. Standard rooms are smallish; deluxe rooms are large enough to have a sitting area. In-room amenities aren't lavish, but almost any toiletry is available from the front desk. Continental breakfast, complimentary newspaper, and limited limousine service are included. ☎ *1244 N. Dearborn Pkwy., Chicago 60610,* ☎ *312/787–4980 or 800/245–1258,* FAX *312/266–0978. 168 rooms, 1 suite. Restaurant, bar, minibars, no-smoking rooms, room service, beauty salon, parking. AE, D, DC, MC, V.*

$$$ Embassy Suites. Built primarily for a '90s corporate audience, these fully equipped suites have been hugely successful thanks to their location and efficient management. Rooms are arranged around an 11-story atrium overlooking a plant-filled, multilevel courtyard, complete with decorative pool and fountain. That's where guests are served a complimentary full breakfast each morning and cocktails each evening during the manager's reception. Furniture in the salmon-tint and blond-wood-furnished rooms shows effects of the heavy traffic, however, and the staff seems taxed to capacity. Microwave ovens, minirefrigerators, phones, and coffeemakers are standard. There is a small fitness center, a lap pool, and a laundry room on the top floor. Papagus, a popular Greek-style restaurant, is just off the lobby, and Starbucks is next store. ☎ *600 N. State St., Chicago 60610,* ☎ *312/943–3800 or 800/362–2779,* FAX *312/943–7629. 358 suites. Restaurant-bar, minibars, no-smoking rooms, indoor pool, exercise room, laundry service and dry cleaning, concierge, parking. AE, D, DC, MC, V.*

$$$ Guest Quarters Suite Hotel. Like the other hotels flanking Michigan Avenue, it's a big weekend travel destination for shoppers. More unusual is its striking postmodern lobby, with a bow in the direction of Arts and Crafts. The two-room standard suite is snug, probably with no more floor space than one room at most comparably priced hotels, but families may prefer this setup because parents can have a bedroom to themselves while children sleep (free if under 19) on a living room sofa bed. Suites have wet bars, coffeemakers, TVs in both rooms, two phones, and good-size bathrooms, and many have views of the lake. ☎ *198 E. Delaware Pl., Chicago 60611,* ☎ *312/664–1100 or 800/424–2900,* FAX *312/664–9881. 345 suites. 2 restaurants, bar, no-smoking rooms, room service, indoor pool, exercise room, concierge, business services, parking. AE, D, DC, MC, V.*

$$$ Holiday Inn Chicago City Centre. With 1995 renovations (and new prices), this standout Holiday Inn aims to boost its status as a sports enthusiast's sanctuary. Selected by *Fitness* magazine as a choice hotel for fitness-minded business travelers, its visitors have free access to McClurg Court, one of the city's biggest health clubs, and Lake Michigan's jogging path is also nearby. Polished service and decor is expanding the clientele from teams and families to include energetic business travelers and a few sports celebrities. There are great city views from almost every room. ⊞ *300 E. Ohio St., Chicago 60611,* ☎ *312/787–6100 or 800/465–4329,* ℻ *312/787–6238. 500 rooms, 9 suites. Coffee shop, bar, no-smoking rooms, indoor pool, coin laundry, laundry service and dry cleaning, concierge, parking (fee). AE, D, DC, MC, V.*

$$$ The Knickerbocker. This 1927 hotel offers some of the nearby Drake's charm and tradition, but without the high rates and the hordes. You can't beat the hotel's location for Magnificent Mile shopping. Independently owned and operated, the Knickerbocker has undergone renovations. Guest rooms are now decorated in peach and gray tones, though the marble bathrooms are still small. The hotel has a casual eatery, the Walton Place Cafe, and one of the coziest hotel bars in the city, the Limehouse Pub. ⊞ *163 E. Walton Pl., Chicago 60611,* ☎ *312/751–8100 or 800/621–8140,* ℻ *312/751–0370. 254 rooms, 26 suites. 2 restaurants, no-smoking rooms, concierge, parking. AE, D, DC, MC, V.*

$$$ Omni Ambassador East. The renowned Pump Room restaurant, a fa-
★ vorite of the glitterati, put the Ambassador East on the map; elegance, charm, and gracious service keep it there. Tucked into the quiet residential Gold Coast, this small, 1920s hotel is a 10- to 15-minute cab ride from the Loop. For the distance, you get larger rooms and the scent of celebrity seclusion; it's popular with movie stars and literary figures. The lobby has an Old World elegance, with crystal chandeliers, marble floors, and curving banisters. Rooms vary in size, shape, and decor; some have reproductions of 19th-century American antiques; others have more of a 1950s feel. ⊞ *1301 N. State Pkwy., Chicago 60610,* ☎ *312/787–7200 or 800/842–6664,* ℻ *312/787–4760. 274 rooms, 52 suites. Restaurant, minibars, no-smoking rooms, room service, barbershop, concierge, parking. AE, D, DC, MC, V.*

$$$ The Talbott. There's a comforting quirkiness to finding a small, homelike hotel just off Magnificent Mile where the clerk is reading Nietzsche, and that's what the smart and friendly service here is about. Most of the rooms feature a full kitchen and dining area—a legacy from the 1927-vintage structure's earlier life as an apartment building—and all bathrooms include hair dryers. Neutrogena toiletries are a nice touch. The traditional decor of the guest rooms (hunter green) complements the twin parlors at the front of the hotel; they're filled with antique and reproduction club-style furnishings. Although there's no restaurant, the room-service menu is extensive. A Continental breakfast is complimentary. ⊞ *20 E. Delaware Pl., Chicago 60611,* ☎ *312/944–4970 or 800/621–8506,* ℻ *312/944–7241. 147 rooms, 28 suites. Bar, in-room safes, minibars, kitchenettes, parking. AE, DC, MC, V.*

$$$ Whitehall Hotel. Like many prestigious buildings from before the Crash of '29, the Whitehall has seen different incarnations. First an apartment building and then a hotel, it was taken over by Preferred Hotels and Resorts Worldwide in 1991, closed and gutted, and reopened in 1994. The resulting neat, if unextraordinary, establishment has English 18th-century decor with Asian accents and a staff that's eager to please. Despite such extemporaneous features as fax and PC capability in each room, there is an intimate feel. Special touches include turndown service, a morning newspaper, a terry bathrobe, and Crabtree & Evelyn niceties. ☎ *105 E. Delaware Pl., Chicago 60611, ☎ 312/944–6300, FAX 312/944-8552. 221 rooms. Restaurant, bar, no-smoking rooms, exercise room, concierge, parking. AE, D, DC, MC, V.*

$$ **Belden-Stratford.** A magnificent '20s facade overlooking the Lincoln
★ Park Conservatory fronts the ideal spot for the visitor who wants to get away from more touristed areas. With a permanent set of residents and a semipermanent set of monthly tenants, the management keeps several apartments available for shorter stays. The spacious, 9-foot-ceiling rooms speak of old Chicago; cherry-wood furnishings and deep blue bedspreads and accompaniments are low key and impeccably maintained. Completely equipped kitchens, a polished and elegant lobby, the restaurant Ambria (*see* Chapter 5, Dining) on the ground floor, and the location close to busy Clark Street add to the appeal. And the prices, even for one night, are a steal. ☎ *2300 Lincoln Park West, Chicago, 60614, ☎ 312/281–2900 or 800/800–8301, FAX 312/880–2039. 10 rooms/suites, depending on availability. 2 restaurants, deli, beauty salon, exercise room, parking. AE, D, MC, V.*

$$ **Courtyard by Marriott.** Marriott Hotels and Resorts launched the now familiar Courtyard concept after asking business travelers what they wanted in a hotel. The answers: soothing, large rooms that feature desks, well-lighted work areas, and voice mail on every phone. Although this Courtyard opened in 1992, it still looks new. A spacious marble-floored lobby opens onto a lounge with a bar, and the restaurant is a few steps away. If you feel like venturing out, you can bill dinner to your room from nearby Shaw's Crab House and Tucci Milan, two popular downtown eateries. And if you're staying in, you can occupy yourself with the exercise facility, the lap pool, the extensive pay-movie selection, and the Pizza Hut in the building. ☎ *30 E. Hubbard St., Chicago 60611, ☎ 312/329–2500 or 800/321–2211, FAX 312/329–0293. 334 rooms, 35 suites. Restaurant, bar, no-smoking rooms, indoor pool, exercise room, laundry service and dry cleaning, parking. AE, D, DC, MC, V.*

$$ **Days Inn Lake Shore Drive.** Lakefront access is the best thing about this concrete high-rise. Rooms, done in greens and jewel tones, are pleasant and sunny; they have either two double beds or one king-size bed. Half have lake views; the others look out on the city, and most aren't too badly blocked by surrounding skyscrapers. Amenities aren't lavish, but neither is the price high. The location is convenient to the North Pier complex, a small beach, and a Treasure Island supermarket. ☎ *644 N. Lake Shore Dr., Chicago 60611, ☎ 312/943–9200 or 800/541–3223, FAX 312/649–5580. 578 rooms, 6 suites. Restaurant, lounge, no-smoking rooms, pool, exercise room, car rental, parking. AE, D, DC, MC, V.*

$$ **Holiday Inn Mart Plaza.** Perched on the 14th floor, atop the Apparel Center and next to Merchandise Mart, this hotel is off the beaten track unless you have business in the neighborhood. The just-renovated forest green and peach rooms, ringed around a multistory atrium, are completely unremarkable. Free hors d'oeuvres are served in the lobby at night. There's no fitness center, but there is a nice indoor pool. The Shops at the Mart complex on the floors below the hotel holds an assortment of interesting stores, but you'd be better off venturing toward the River North Gallery district for more exciting goods. ☎ *350 N. Orleans St., Chicago 60654, ☎ 312/836–5000 or 800/465–4329, FAX 312/222–9508. 524 rooms, 18 suites. 2 restaurants, 2 lounges, no-smoking rooms, indoor pool, exercise room, laundry service and dry cleaning, parking. AE, D, DC, MC, V.*

$$ **Inn of Chicago.** The hotel dates back to 1927 and was recently taken over by Best Western. One block east of Michigan Avenue, it's a bargain for visitors who want to be near the Magnificent Mile. Rooms are spotless, if spartan, and if you don't feel pampered, you'll be comfortable. The lobby—often crowded with tour groups enjoying a good deal—has live piano music during cocktail hour. An extra $10 gets you a first-class upgrade, including drinks in the hotel lounge, breakfast in the restaurant, a morning newspaper, and a suite if available. ⌗ *162 E. Ohio St., Chicago 60611, ☎ 312/787–3100 or 800/528–1234, FAX 312/787–8236. 357 rooms, 26 suites. Restaurant-bar, no-smoking rooms, laundry service and dry cleaning. AE, D, DC, MC, V.*

$$ **Lenox House.** Most suites in this all-suite hotel are actually just one large room with a Murphy bed, a queen sleeper-sofa, and a wet-bar kitchenette. Still, you can sleep four people without difficulty, and the Water Tower–area location is convenient to shopping and nightlife. Though public areas verge on quaint, guest rooms are generic 1980s. Service is brisk but friendly. ⌗ *616 N. Rush St., Chicago 60611, ☎ 312/337–1000 or 800/445–3669, FAX 312/337–7217. 325 suites. Restaurant, bar, no-smoking rooms, concierge. AE, D, DC, MC, V.*

$$ **Raphael.** One of few buildings from the thick of the glittering 1920s
★   to retain honest charm as a 1990s hotel, this is on a side street near the John Hancock Building. Originally a dorm for Northwestern nursing students, it's small enough, quiet enough, and inexpensive enough to have a devoted following of Chicago regulars, who come for spacious, comfortable rooms and obliging yet unpretentious service. Most rooms are actually 1½- or 2-room suites with sitting areas; some have chaise longues for extra relaxation. The lobby and wide, floral-carpeted hallways have a late-19th-century feel. The restaurant is an intimate oasis. ⌗ *201 E. Delaware Pl., Chicago 60611, ☎ 312/943–5000 or 800/821–5343, FAX 312/943–9483. 172 rooms, 75 suites. Restaurant-bar, minibars, no-smoking rooms, room service, laundry service and dry cleaning, parking. AE, D, DC, MC, V.*

$$ **River North Hotel.** The past few years have seen the River North be-
★   come a thriving restaurant district with a mix of ethnic, celebrity-owned, and chain eateries. Right across from one of the busiest—Chicago's famous Rock 'n' Roll McDonald's—is this warehouse turned Best Western. Its undistinguished exterior is more than offset by surprisingly stylish, large, and reasonably priced guest rooms, with black, white, and gray Crate & Barrel furnishings to boot. The public spaces, which include a plain lobby, a large indoor pool, and a rooftop sundeck, are all busy but immaculate. ⌗ *125 W. Ohio St., Chicago 60610, ☎ 312/467–0800 or 800/727–0800, FAX 312/467–1665. 148 rooms, 26 suites. 115 no-smoking rooms. Restaurant-bar, no-smoking rooms, in-room VCRs, indoor pool, sauna, exercise room, recreation room, laundry service and dry cleaning, free parking. AE, D, DC, MC, V.*

$$ **Westin Hotel.** A renovation has brought new tubs and showers but not much more to this Magnificent Mile spot. With more than 700 rooms, it's basically a tourist warehouse, the lobby mall-like down to the Starbucks counter. Visiting pro-sports teams often stay here, but signs in the lobby ask you not to snap photos of the players. This Westin does offer more sports facilities than most hotels, but be warned: Gender-specific gym spaces leave women with less equipment. ⌗ *909 N. Michigan Ave., Chicago 60611, ☎ 312/943–7200 or 800/228–3000, FAX 312/943–9347. 740 rooms, 43 suites. Restaurant, bar, minibars, no-smoking rooms, room service, exercise room, laundry service and dry cleaning, concierge, business services, parking. AE, D, DC, MC, V.*

$ City Suites Hotel. The price is right and the location ideal at this small European-style hotel. It's in the Lakeview neighborhood, close to many of Chicago's most popular restaurants, bars, theaters, and boutiques. Wrigley Field is a leisurely walk away, and the El and several bus lines are right around the corner. Rooms and suites are cozy and feature chic black-and-white tile baths. Room service comes from Chicago's much-loved Ann Sather (*see* Chapter 5, Dining), a Swedish restaurant. ☎ *933 W. Belmont, Chicago 60657,* ☎ *312/404–3400,* FAX *312/404–3405. 45 rooms, 30 suites. Room service, parking (fee). AE, D, DC, MC, V.*

$ Comfort Inn of Lincoln Park. It's a motel. You park your car in a lot visible from your room, and the price is about what you'd expect for clean, no-frills lodging. The lobby is quaint, with wood-and-brass decor and a small sitting area. The residential Lincoln Park neighborhood is a bit far from the downtown hoopla, but it's packed with small shops and restaurants that are interesting in their own right, and it's close to Wrigley Field. Continental breakfast is included. ☎ *601 W. Diversey, Chicago 60614,* ☎ *312/348–2810 or 800/221–2222,* FAX *312/348–1912. 74 rooms, 3 suites. Parking. AE, D, DC, MC, V.*

$ Days Inn Chicago Hotel Lincoln. A renovated 1928 facade looking over central Lincoln Park has the appropriate faded grandeur and the expected practical feel of a Days Inn. With cramped rooms and unextraordinary furnishings, the perks here are location and quaint, if worn, charm. Ask for a lake view. ☎ *1816 N. Clark St., Chicago 60614,* ☎ *and* FAX *312/664–3045. 273 rooms. Restaurant, no-smoking rooms, laundry service and dry cleaning, parking. AE, D, DC, MC, V.*

$ Days Inn Near North. The heavy traffic that comes through this nondescript hotel might be off-putting, were it not for the central Lincoln Park location and the low price. The lobby is nicely decorated for a chain hotel, with floral carpets, a grandfather clock, and draped hallways, and the rooms are comfortable and well-maintained, with floral bedspreads and floral prints on the walls. All guests are entitled to complimentary coffee, sweet rolls, juice, yogurt, cereal, and bagels in the morning. ☎ *646 W. Diversey Pkwy., Chicago 60614,* ☎ *312/525–7010 or 800/329–7466,* FAX *312/525–6998. 137 rooms. No-smoking rooms. AE, D, DC, MC, V.*

$ Margarita—A European Inn. Because it's in Evanston, one town north of Chicago, the Margarita is a perfect choice if you need a break from the city or if you need to be near Northwestern University. The inn is within walking distance of the latter and is also close to Evanston's many shops, restaurants, and art galleries. A former women's boarding house (built 1915), this is smaller than most hotels but larger than a typical bed-and-breakfast. Sunlight streams in through several arched floor-to-ceiling windows in the parlor, showing off the antiques and houseplants. Guest rooms are models of reserve, in terms of decor and size. Continental breakfast is included. The nearby French-influenced Northern Italian restaurant, Va Pensiero, is one of the area's finest eateries. ☎ *1566 Oak Ave. (2 blocks from train/bus), Evanston 60201,* ☎ *708/869–2273,* FAX *708/869–2353. 10 rooms with bath, 39 rooms share bath. Restaurant, library, parking. AE, MC, V.*

$ Motel 6 Chicago. The renovations that turned the Richmont into a Motel 6 did not improve this low-budget establishment. There are new TVs, but gone are the restaurant and bar. Standard rooms can't hold much more than the usual complement of bed, dresser, and nightstand, so if you lean toward claustrophobia or plan to spend a lot of time in your room, spring for the "deluxe" accommodations—they're still a relative bargain. Continental breakfast and afternoon wine-tasting and hors d'oeuvres are complimentary. The really notable advantage here? Local calls are completely free. ⊡ *162 E. Ontario, Chicago 60611,* ☎ *312/787–3580 or 800/621–8055,* ꓝꓮꓫ *312/787–1299. 191 rooms, 26 suites. No-smoking rooms, coin laundry, parking. AE, D, DC, MC, V.*

$ Park Brompton Hotel. Modeled after an old English inn, and owned by the same people who run City Suites and the Surf Hotel, the Park Brompton is an intimate hotel with poster beds and tapestry furnishings in the rooms. The only drawback is the lack of amenities, but those who prefer ambience over a pool or a health club will be satisfied here. The hotel is in the Lakeview area, close to Wrigley Field, the lakefront, restaurants, bars, cafés, boutiques, and transportation to downtown. ⊡ *528 W. Brompton, Chicago 60657,* ☎ *312/404–3499,* ꓝꓮꓫ *312/404–3495. 31 rooms, 7 suites. AE, D, DC, MC, V.*

$ Surf Hotel. This hotel, which sits on a quiet tree-lined street in the heart of Lincoln Park, is short on amenities but overflowing with character. Built in the 1920s, the Surf has a small, elegant lobby with a regal fireplace and tall, arched windows. Guest rooms are large, quiet and handsomely appointed. It's close to the lakefront, the Lincoln Park Zoo, and countless restaurants, boutiques, theaters, and bars. ⊡ *555 W. Surf St., Chicago 60657,* ☎ *312/528–8400,* ꓝꓮꓫ *312/528–8483. 32 rooms, 2 suites. AE, D, MC, V.*

Bed-and-Breakfasts

Staying in someone's home lends a personal touch to your visit and is also a good way to see residential neighborhoods that you might not get to otherwise. You may also save some money. **Bed & Breakfast/Chicago** (Box 14088, Chicago 60614, ☎ 312/951–0085) is a clearinghouse for more than 50 options that range from a guest room in someone's home to a furnished apartment to a full-fledged inn. Most cost less than $100 a night and are concentrated in the Near North or Lincoln Park, though some are as far away as Indiana. Most require a two-night minimum, and weekly or monthly rates are available for some. Reservations can be made by phone (weekdays 9–5) or by mail. The office will send sample listings and a reservation form on request.

Hostels and Student Housing

If you're truly budget-conscious and don't need your own bathroom, frilly decor, or to be downtown, these three places may be of interest. They offer safe accommodation and access to interesting neighborhoods.

$ Arlington House. Choose either dormitory or double rooms in this "international hotel," which is also a senior-citizen facility, on a quiet street in Lincoln Park. Most hostelers stay in bunk rooms in the basement; it's dank, but how else can you have a kitchen and be close to north side restaurants and clubs and transportation to downtown for $16? Linens are available for rental. IYH and AYH cardholders get a discount. ⊡ *616 W. Arlington Pl., Chicago 60614,* ☎ *312/929–5380 or 800/HOSTEL–5. 75 dormitory beds, 20 double rooms. Coin laundry. DC, MC, V.*

$ Chicago International Hostel. These dormitory-style accommodations are near Loyola University in Rogers Park. One hitch—there's a curfew. Guests must be in by midnight on Sunday through Thursday and by 2 AM on weekends; in the summer, you can stay out until 2 AM every night. The nearest mass transit is the Loyola stop on the Howard Street elevated line. Linens are provided and there's a kitchen. IYH cardholders get a discount. ☎ *6318 N. Winthrop Ave., Chicago 60660,* ☏ *312/262–1011. 100 beds. Coin laundry. No credit cards.*

$ **International House.** Rooms on the faux-Cambridge style campus of the University of Chicago are spare but attractive singles. The baths are shared; towels and sheets are provided. Availability varies with the season, with fall the busiest time. ☎ *1414 E. 59th St., Chicago 60637,* ☏ *312/753–2280,* FAX *312/753–1227. 500 rooms. Exercise room, coin laundry. MC, V.*

7 The Arts and Nightlife

THE ARTS

Updated by
Mark Kollar

CHICAGO IS A SPLENDID CITY FOR THE ARTS. In addition to dozens of classical music organizations, including a world-class symphony orchestra and opera company, there are hundreds of clubs featuring jazz, rock, folk, and country music; some 50 theaters; an outstanding dance company; and movie theaters that show everything from first-run features to avant-garde films. For complete music and theater listings, check two free weeklies, *The Reader* and *New City;* the Friday and Sunday editions of the *Tribune* and *Sun-Times;* and the monthly *Chicago* magazine.

Ticket prices vary wildly depending on whether you're seeing a high-profile group or venturing into more obscure territory. Chicago Symphony tickets go from $16 to $65, Lyric Opera from $20 to more than $100 (if you can get them). Smaller choruses and orchestras charge from $10 to $25; watch the listings for free performances. Commercial theater ranges from $15 to $60; smaller experimental ensembles might charge $5, $10, or pay-what-you-can. One group lets you roll dice to determine your ticket price. Movie prices vary from $6.50 to $7.50 for first-run houses down to as low as $2 at some suburban second-run houses. Some commercial chains take credit cards.

Music

The Chicago Symphony is internationally renowned, and Chicago's Lyric Opera is one of the top three opera companies in America today. Season subscribers take virtually all the tickets to these performances, but subscribers who can't use their tickets sometimes return them to the box office. If you go to the opera house or Symphony Hall a half hour before performance time, you may find someone with an extra ticket to sell.

Orchestras

Chicago Sinfonietta (☎ 312/857–1062). This medium-size but highly polished orchestra plays classical, romantic, and contemporary pieces exactly as they were written by the composer. The Sinfonietta performs about 15 times a year at various locations and is in residence at Rosary College in the suburb of River Forest.

Chicago Symphony (220 S. Michigan Ave., ☎ 312/435–6666). The season at Symphony Hall extends from September through May, with music director Daniel Barenboim conducting. In summer, you can see and hear the Chicago Symphony at Ravinia Park in suburban Highland Park, a 25-mile train trip from Chicago. The park is lovely, and lawn seats are always available even when (rarely) those in the Shed and the smaller Murray Theatre are sold out. Performances usually feature one or more notable soloists. For program, ticket, and travel information, ☎ 312/728–4642.

Grant Park Symphony Orchestra (☎ 312/742–7638). Sponsored by the Chicago Park District, the Grant Park Symphony gives free concerts during the summer at the James C. Petrillo Music Shell in Grant Park, between Columbus and Lake Shore drives at Jackson Boulevard. Performances usually are on Wednesday, Friday, Saturday, and Sunday evenings. The weekly *Reader* or a daily newspaper will have program details and performance times.

Concert Halls

Mandel Hall (1131 E. 57th St., ☎ 312/702–8068). Guest orchestras and performers are scheduled regularly at this hall on the University of Chicago campus.

Orchestra Hall (220 S. Michigan Ave., ☎ 312/435–8122). A variety of concerts and recitals are performed during the year.

Smaller halls in the Loop/Near North area include **Curtiss Hall** in the Fine Arts Building (410 S. Michigan Ave., ☎ 312/939–3380), **Fullerton Auditorium** in the Art Institute (Michigan Ave. at Adams St., ☎ 312/443–3600), the **Newberry Library** (60 W. Walton Ave., ☎ 312/943–9090), and the **Three Arts Club** (1300 N. Dearborn Pkwy., ☎ 312/944–6250).

Choral and Chamber Groups

Apollo Chorus of Chicago (☎ 708/960–2251), formed in 1872, is one of the oldest oratorical societies in the country. Apollo performs Handel's *Messiah* every December and other chorale classics throughout the year.

Chicago Baroque Ensemble (1216 W. Sherwin Ave., ☎ 312/274–2528). This unique group of six musicians plays throughout the city on such period instruments as the harpsichord, viola da gamba, and baroque cello. The ensemble also includes vocal soloists.

Chicago Children's Choir (☎ 312/849–8300). One of the country's premier children's choirs, its members are drawn from a broad spectrum of racial, ethnic, and economic groups. Performances are given each year during the Christmas season and in early June; other concerts are scheduled periodically.

His Majestie's Clerkes (410 S. Michigan Ave., ☎ 312/461–0723). The group, which takes its name from a Renaissance term for professional chorale, was founded 12 years ago and does mostly sacred and a cappella music in churches throughout the city. Season runs October through May.

Music of the Baroque (☎ 312/551–1415), the granddaddy of independent ensembles in Chicago, is a nationally known, highly polished professional chorus and orchestra concentrating on the works—particularly the choral works—of the Baroque period. It schedules eight concerts a year, with performances at various locations.

Oriana Singers (☎ 312/262–4558) is an outstanding a cappella sextet with an eclectic classical repertoire.

William Ferris Chorale (☎ 312/527–9898). This distinguished choral ensemble focuses on 20th-century music and gives concerts throughout the year.

Opera

Chicago Opera Theatre (2936 N. Southport Ave., ☎ 312/292–7521). The Chicago Opera specializes in English-language productions of smaller works. Its 1995 season included *The Magic Flute*.

Lyric Opera of Chicago (20 N. Wacker Dr., ☎ 312/332–2244). The season at the Civic Opera House runs from September through February. Performances are almost always sold out and the Lyric Opera does not offer standing-room tickets.

Light Opera

Light Opera Works (☎ 708/869–6300). Gilbert and Sullivan operettas and other light operas are performed during a June–December season.

Theater

While road-show productions of Broadway hits do come to Chicago, the theater scene's true vigor springs from the multitude of small ensembles that have made a home here. They range from the critically acclaimed Steppenwolf and the Goodman Theatre to fringe groups that specialize in experimental work.

Many smaller companies perform in tiny or makeshift theaters, where admission prices are moderate to quite inexpensive. You can save money on seats at **Hot Tix** (108 N. State St.), where unsold tickets are available at usually half price (plus a small service charge) on the day of performance; you don't know what's available until that day, and you have to pay cash. The main Hot Tix booth is open Monday noon–6, Tuesday–Friday 10–6, and Saturday 10–5; tickets for Sunday performances are sold on Saturday. When the temperature is below freezing, Hot Tix gives theatergoers a break and allows them to call 312/977–1755 to reserve tickets. At other times, calling that number activates a recorded message about shows available that day. Hot Tix also has outlets at various suburban locations.

Theater groups from throughout the world perform at the International Theatre Festival (☎ 708/329–0333), held every other year in the spring. The 1996 festival is expected to run from late May to early June.

Commercial Theater

Most of the houses listed here are hired by independent producers for commercial (and sometimes nonprofit) productions; they have no resident producer or company.

Apollo Theater (2540 N. Lincoln Ave., ☎ 312/348–3000) houses local versions of Broadway and off-Broadway plays—generally solid but not highly imaginative productions.

Auditorium Theater (50 E. Congress Pkwy., ☎ 312/922–2110). Acoustics and sight lines are excellent in this Louis Sullivan architectural masterpiece. You're likely to see touring productions of such Broadway hits as *Crazy for You.*

Briar St. Theater (3133 N. Halsted St., ☎ 312/348–4000). Local productions of hit Broadway plays often find their way to this modest space in Lakeview.

Candlelight Dinner Playhouse (5620 S. Harlem Ave., Summit, ☎ 708/496–3000). Just over the city line in Summit, the Candlelight usually offers superb productions of classic Broadway musicals. The food is edible, and the dinner-theater package is a good deal, or you can just go for the show. The **Forum,** a smaller theater, shares the location.

Chicago Theater (175 N. State St., ☎ 312/443–1130). This former movie palace and vaudeville house was gaudily but lovingly restored in 1986 and ran into financial trouble shortly thereafter. It's now open sporadically for national tours of musicals and other performances.

Drury Lane (100 Drury La., Oakbrook Terr., ☎ 708/530–0111). Musicals and other Broadway productions are usually well produced at this dinner theater that caters mostly to suburbanites.

Ivanhoe (750 W. Wellington St., ☎ 312/975–7171). This theater,which has a medieval half-timbered exterior, performs musicals and Broadway shows with varying degrees of success.

Mayfair Theater (Blackstone Hotel, 636 S. Michigan Ave., ☎ 312/786–9120). The audience-participation mystery *Shear Madness* has been playing here since 1982 and shows no signs of closing.

Merle Reskin–Blackstone Theater (60 E. Balbo Dr., ☎ 312/362–8455). This grand and ornate space is owned by De Paul University and used for productions by its theater school.

Organic Theatre (3319 N. Clark St., ☎ 312/327–5588). Once a theater company in its own right, the Organic is now largely just another performance space that features stage productions, improvisation, and music.

Royal George Theater Center (1641 N. Halsted St., ☎ 312/988–9000). A new building, the Royal George has one large, gracious theater, one smaller studio theater, a cabaret space, and a restaurant.

Shubert Theater (22 W. Monroe St., ☎ 312/977–1700). A grand 19th-century-style theater, the Shubert is a remnant of the Loop's once-thriving theater district.

Performing Groups

Chicago's reputation as a theatrical powerhouse was born from its small not-for-profit theater companies that produce everything from Shakespeare to Stephen Sondheim. The groups listed below do consistently interesting work, and a few have gained national attention. Some, such as Steppenwolf and the Remains Theater Company, are ensemble troupes; others, notably the Goodman, the Court, and the Body Politic, are production companies that use different casts for each show. Be open-minded when you're choosing a show; even a group you've never heard of may be harboring one or two underpaid geniuses. *The Reader* carries complete theater listings and reviews of the more avant-garde shows.

Bailiwick (1229 W. Belmont Ave., ☎ 312/883–1090) presents new and classical material. Its Pride Performance series, every spring, features plays by gays and lesbians.

Body Politic (2261 N. Lincoln Ave., ☎ 312/348–7901). This venerable production company offers a variety of performances written by both local and national playwrights.

Court Theater (5535 S. Ellis Ave., ☎ 312/753–4472). On the University of Chicago campus, the Court revives classic plays with varying success.

Goodman Theater (200 S. Columbus Dr., ☎ 312/443–3800). One of the oldest and best theaters in Chicago, the Goodman is known for its polished performances of contemporary works starring well-known actors. Situated behind the Art Institute, the space also includes the Studio Theater, where new works and one-act plays are staged.

Neo-Futurists (5153 N. Ashland Ave., ☎ 312/275–5255). Performing in a space above a funeral home, this group's long-running cult hit *Too Much Light Makes the Baby Go Blind* is a series of 30 two-minute plays whose order is chosen by the audience. In keeping with the spirit of randomness, the admission price is sometimes set by the roll of the dice.

Pegasus Players (1145 W. Wilson Ave., ☎ 312/271–2638). Pegasus tackles interesting and difficult works, usually producing at least one Stephen Sondheim musical each season. The spacious theater is at the city's Truman College.

Remains Theater (863 N. Dearborn St., ☎ 312/335–9800). Remains specializes in original scripts by American writers, featuring gritty acting in the Steppenwolf tradition (*see below*). Cofounder William Petersen turns up in the movies now and then.

Shakespeare Repertory (820 N. Orleans St., ☎ 312/642–2273). This extremely talented group is almost single-handedly keeping the Bard's flame alive in the Chicago area.

Steppenwolf (1650 N. Halsted St., ☎ 312/335–1650). The nationally known Steppenwolf company brings a dark, brooding, method-acting style to its consistently successful productions. Illustrious alumni include John Malkovich, Joan Allen, and Laurie Metcalf. Its Broadway production of John Steinbeck's *The Grapes of Wrath* won a Tony award in 1990 for best play.

Theatre Building (1225 W. Belmont Ave., ☎ 312/327–5252). This rehabbed warehouse provides a permanent home for small companies of local renown.

Touchstone Theater (2851 N. Halsted St., ☎ 312/404–4700). This company took over the Steppenwolf company's former space in Lakeview and specializes in 20th-century works.

Victory Gardens (2257 N. Lincoln Ave., ☎ 312/871–3000). Known for its workshops and premiere performances, this production company features local playwrights.

Dance

Though there are fewer organized dance troupes in Chicago than one might expect in a city so renowned for music and theater, there are several companies that perform regularly. The most popular dance performance spaces are the Civic Opera House (20 N. Wacker Dr.) and the Shubert Theater (22 W. Monroe St.).

Ballet Chicago (185 N. Wabash Ave, ☎ 312/251–8838) is the city's only resident classical ballet troupe and has received critical acclaim for its work.

Chicago's most notable success story in dance is the **Hubbard Street Dance Chicago** (☎ 312/663–0853), whose contemporary, jazzy vitality has made it extremely popular. Another company worth seeing is the **Joseph Holmes Chicago Dance Theater** (410 S. Michigan Ave., ☎ 312/986–1941).

Film

Many cinemas in the Near North offer first-run Hollywood movies on multiple screens, including **Chestnut Station** (830 N. Clark St., ☎ 312/337–7301), **Water Tower Theater** (845 N. Michigan Ave., ☎ 312/649–5790), **900 N. Michigan Theater** (☎ 312/787–1988), and **McClurg Court** (330 E. Ohio St., ☎ 312/642–0723).

The **Esquire** (58 E. Oak St., ☎ 312/280–0101), an Art Deco landmark on the Gold Coast, underwent a renovation that preserved its facade but divided it into four theaters. They show first-run movies.

A north-side first-run movie house of some historical interest is the **Biograph Theatre** (2433 N. Lincoln Ave., ☎ 312/348–4123); gangster John Dillinger was shot in front of it by FBI agents in 1934. If you ask around, you may be able to find a local who can show you the bullet marks in the side of the building.

The most convenient first-run movie theater for those staying in the south Loop is **Burnham Plaza** (826 S. Wabash Ave., ☎ 312/922–1090).

For something a bit different, try the **Fine Arts Theatre** (418 S. Michigan Ave., ☎ 312/939–3700), whose four screens show independent, foreign, and avant-garde films.

Facets Multimedia (1517 W. Fullerton Ave., ☎ 312/281–9075) presents a variety of rare and exotic films and is home to many an ethnic film festival; call and see whether a particular day's fare appeals to you.

Film Center of the Art Institute (Columbus Dr. at Jackson Blvd., ☎ 312/443–3737) specializes in unusual current films and revivals of rare classics. The program here changes almost daily, and filmmakers sometimes give lectures at the Film Center.

Music Box Theatre (3733 N. Southport Ave., ☎ 312/871–6604) is a small and richly decorated restored 1920s movie palace. Programs change nightly, except for special runs; the theater shows a mix of classics and outstanding recent films, emphasizing independent filmmakers. The theater organ is played during intermission at special events and as an accompaniment to silent films. If you love old theaters and old movies, don't miss a trip here.

NIGHTLIFE

Chicago comes alive at night, with something for everyone, from loud and loose to sophisticated and sedate. *The Reader* and *New City* (available Thursday and Friday in Lincoln Park and Hyde Park) are your best guides to the entertainment scene. The *Chicago Tribune* and the *Chicago Sun-Times* on Friday are good sources of information on current shows and starting times. Shows usually begin at 9 PM; cover charges generally range from $3 to $10, depending on the day of the week; Friday and Saturday nights are the most expensive. There's a free concert hot line (☎ 312/666–6667).

If you want to find "Rush Street," the famous Chicago bar scene, don't bother looking on Rush Street itself. Most of the nightlife is now on Division Street between Clark and State streets, having been pushed north by office and apartment development. Among the better-known singles bars are **Butch McGuire's** (20 W. Division St.), **The Lodge** (21 W. Division St.), and **Mother's** (26 W. Division St.), featured in the motion picture *...About Last Night*. This area is particularly festive on warm weekend nights, when the street adopts a carnival-like atmosphere. The crowd here is mostly out-of-towners.

You can find a similar atmosphere in the establishments at the North Pier development (455 E. Illinois St.), notably the **Baja Beach Club** and **Dick's Last Resort**. North Pier is the center of a growing nightlife scene just north of the Loop and east of Michigan Avenue.

The list of blues and jazz clubs includes several South Side locations, and visitors to Chicago should be cautious about transportation here late at night, because some of these neighborhoods are dangerous. Drive your own car or take a previously reserved cab or limo, and avoid public transportation. Some clubs provide guarded parking lots or can arrange cab service for visitors. Parking in North Side neighborhoods, particularly Lincoln Park and Lakeview, can be scarce on weekends. If you're visiting nightspots in these areas, consider leaving your car behind and taking cabs or public transportation.

Music

Blues

In the years following World War II, Chicago-style blues grew into its own musical form, flourishing in the 1950s, then fading in the 1960s with the advent of rock and roll. Today Chicago blues is coming back, although more strongly on the trendy North Side than on the South Side where it all began.

Blue Chicago (736 N. Clark St., ☎ 312/642–6261) and **Blue Chicago on Clark** (536 N. Clark St., ☎ 312/661–0100). One cover gets you into two clubs, and they're practically neighbors now that the original has moved from North State Street to River North. Both have good sound systems and attract a cosmopolitan, heterogeneous crowd. Cover varies. Minimum.

B.L.U.E.S. (2519 N. Halsted St., ☎ 312/528–1012). The best of Chicago's own musicians play here and attract a large, friendly crowd to this Lincoln Park venue.

B.L.U.E.S. Etcetera (1124 W. Belmont Ave., ☎ 312/525–8989). A spacious and comfortable change from overcrowded spots.

Buddy Guy's Legends (754 S. Wabash Ave., ☎ 312/427–0333). One of Chicago's own blues legends is part-owner and often sits in at this converted double storefront in the south Loop. It's spacious, with good sound, good sight lines, pool tables, and weekday sets that start at 8:30 PM. Cover charge varies.

Kingston Mines (2548 N. Halsted St., ☎ 312/477–4646). One of the North Side's oldest spots, the Mines attracts large numbers of blues lovers and cruising singles, the first because of its continuous live weekend entertainment on two stages, the second because of its late closing (4 AM Fri., 5 AM Sat.).

Lilly's (2513 N. Lincoln Ave., ☎ 312/525–2422). Lilly's is a tiny, warm, and friendly spot near the DePaul University campus.

New Checkerboard Lounge (423 E. 43rd St., ☎ 312/624–3240). Although the neighborhood is rough, this remains one of the great old South Side clubs. The music by name performers is usually worth the trip.

Rosa's Lounge (3420 W. Armitage St., ☎ 312/342–0452). Expect good music at this homey spot in a Latin American and Polish neighborhood. No cover Monday.

Jazz

Andy's Lounge (11 E. Hubbard St., ☎ 312/642–6805). Once just a big old friendly neighborhood bar in the shadow of the IBM Building, Andy's has become one of Chicago's best spots for serious jazz. The jazz at noon during the workweek is a boon for music lovers who aren't night owls. No cover at noon.

Bop Shop (1807 W. Division St., ☎ 312/235–3232). Small groups play in an intimate setting at this Wicker Park club. Cover charge varies.

The Bulls (1916 N. Lincoln Park W, ☎ 312/337–3000). This small club showcases the best of local groups in the Old Town neighborhood.

Cotton Club (1710 S. Michigan Ave., ☎ 312/341–9787). This spot at the far end of the south Loop is a favorite of upscale young black professionals. There's open mike every Monday.

Dick's Last Resort (435 E. Illinois St., ☎ 312/836–7870). This crowded, raucous North Pier fixture has hot Dixieland jazz most nights.

Gold Star Sardine Bar (680 N. Lake Shore Dr., ☎ 312/664–4215). Housed in a splendid renovated building in Streeterville that once was the Chicago Furniture Mart, this tiny spot books top names that attract a trendy clientele. Patricia Barber, a local favorite, performs here every Tuesday.

Green Mill (4802 N. Broadway, ☎ 312/878–5552). This Chicago institution, off the beaten track in untrendy Uptown, has been around most of this century and has been skillfully renovated to look as if it's never been redecorated. The entertainment ranges from good to outstanding, and the club can get crowded on weekends. On Sunday evening, the Uptown Poetry Slam, a competitive poetry reading, takes center stage.

Jazz Showcase (636 S. Michigan Ave., ☎ 312/427–4300). Nationally known acts perform in the once elegant but decaying setting of the Blackstone Hotel. A no-smoking policy is strictly enforced. Closed Monday.

Milt Trenier's Lounge (610 N. Fairbanks Ct., ☎ 312/266–6226). Cabaret acts augmented by Milt, who plays with his jazz quintet on weekends, draw people to this Streeterville location.

Pops for Champagne (2934 N. Sheffield Ave., ☎ 312/472–1000). Despite the incongruous name, this is a good spot for serious jazz fans. Pops sports a popular champagne bar and serves tasty appetizers and desserts.

Rock

Cabaret Metro (3730 N. Clark St., ☎ 312/549–0203). The Metro presents a wide range of artists, from the nationally known to the cream of the local crop, and a wide range of rock styles. People come for a specific show, so the crowd will vary according to the attraction. The cover varies too.

Cubby Bear (1059 W. Addison St., ☎ 312/327–1662). A variety of acts plays this scruffy but roomy Uptown venue across the street from Wrigley Field. The music usually starts around 10 PM. During baseball season, the Cubby Bear opens in the afternoon to give Cub fans another place to drown their sorrows.

Elbo Room (2871 N. Lincoln Ave., ☎ 312/549–5549). This multilevel space in an elbow-shaped building has good food, a popular pool table, and a wide range of talented, live bands.

Lounge Ax (2438 N. Lincoln Ave., ☎ 312/525–6620). A mix of local rock, folk, country, and reggae acts is presented here nightly at this DePaul University joint. Cover varies.

Wild Hare (3530 N. Clark St., ☎ 312/327–4273). Local groups perform reggae; a Caribbean decor adds to the atmosphere. Shows are at 10 PM. Cover varies.

Folk and Ethnic

Abbey Pub (3420 W. Grace, ☎ 312/478–4408). Irish music by Irish performers is the fare at this neighborhood establishment. Cover varies.

Cafe Continental (5515 N. Lincoln Ave., ☎ 312/878–7077). Up in the German Lincoln Square neighborhood, this club's regular acts include the Maxwell Street Klezmer Band. Closed Monday and Tuesday. Minimum.

Deni's Den (2941 N. Clark St., ☎ 312/348–8888). This large, attractive Lincoln Park restaurant features Greek performers. Until 4 AM Friday, 5 AM Saturday.

Kitty O'Shea's (720 S. Michigan Ave., ☎ 312/922–4400). This handsome room in the Chicago Hilton and Towers re-creates an Irish pub, complete with Irish music and food by Irish chefs.

No Exit (6970 N. Glenwood Ave., ☎ 312/743–3355). Folk, jazz, poetry readings, and comedy sketches are offered in a comfortable coffeehouse setting reminiscent of the late 1960s. Backgammon and chess sets are available.

Old Town School of Folk Music (909 W. Armitage Ave., ☎ 312/525–7793). Chicago's only folk music school, Old Town offers outstanding folk performances.

Tania's (2659 N. Milwaukee Ave., ☎ 312/235–7120). This Cuban restaurant becomes a nightclub with salsa bands on weekends.

Country
There isn't much country music in Chicago, but you might try one of these places:

Carol's Pub (4659 N. Clark St., ☎ 312/334–2402).
Clearwater Saloon (3937 N. Lincoln Ave., ☎ 312/549–5599).
Lakeview Lounge (5110 N. Broadway, ☎ 312/769–0994).
Whiskey River (1997 N. Clybourn Ave., ☎ 312/528–3400).

For country music with food, try **Bub City Crabshack and Barbecue** (901 W. Weed St., ☎ 312/266–1200).

Eclectic
Clubs in this category don't limit themselves to a single type of music. If you have strong feelings about what you'd like to hear, call ahead to find out what's playing.

Beat Kitchen (2100 W. Belmont Ave., ☎ 312/281–4444). A good sound system and varied local acts make this small club in Bucktown popular. Cover.

Biddy Mulligan's (7644 N. Sheridan Rd., ☎ 312/761–6532). The neighborhood ambience attracts a nice mix of customers. Biddy's started out as a blues bar but has branched out into rock and reggae, so there's no telling what you'll find here.

Fitzgerald's (6615 W. Roosevelt Rd., Berwyn, ☎ 708/788–2118). Though a bit out of the way, Fitzgerald's draws crowds from all over the city and suburbs with a mix of folk, jazz, and blues and a homey summer-cabin ambience. Cover.

The Hothouse (1565 N. Milwaukee Ave., ☎ 312/235–2334). An arty crowd flocks to this cavernous room in Wicker Park to hear everything from heavy metal to Brazilian samba, with the occasional evening of performance-art thrown in.

Park West (322 W. Armitage Ave., ☎ 312/929–5959). Shows here tend to be name acts, glossily performed; expect high cover, high drink prices, and high attitude. The hall itself is large, with good sight lines and acoustics.

The Vic (3145 N. Sheffield Ave., ☎ 312/472–0366). This former movie palace advertises "all ages" shows, heavy on rock and R&B. Some nights feature "brew and view"—current movies with beer.

Dance Clubs

Asi Es Colombia (3910 N. Lincoln Ave., ☎ 312/348–7444). Good salsa bands attract good dancers. Open weekends only.

Drink (541 W. Fulton St., ☎ 312/441-0818). Chicago futures traders hang out at this trendy spot in the meatpacking district. The music is good, loud, and fun.

Excalibur (632 N. Dearborn St., ☎ 312/266–1944). This River North brownstone hides a super-disco with multiple dance floors and bars, a games room, and a restaurant. Popular with young adults, it attracts a large suburban crowd on weekends. Open Friday until 4 AM, and Saturday till 5 AM. Cover and minimum.

Gordon (500 N. Clark St., ☎ 312/467–9780). Principally a fine restaurant, Gordon has dancing and a very good jazz combo on Saturday.

Neo (2350 N. Clark St., ☎ 312/528–2622). Neo is loud but not way out. Open until 4 AM Friday, 5 AM Saturday.

Riviera Night Club (4746 N. Racine St., ☎ 312/275–6800). Laser beams and name bands are the attractions at this cavernous former movie palace. Open until 1 AM Friday, 2 AM Saturday.

Piano Bars

Coq d'Or at the Drake Hotel (140 E. Walton St., ☎ 312/787–2200). Chicago legend Buddy Charles holds court here Tuesday to Saturday nights.

Four Seasons (120 E. Delaware Pl., ☎ 312/280–8800). Enjoy drinks or dessert to the sounds of jazz here. A trio performs Friday and Saturday nights.

Jaxx at the Park Hyatt (800 N. Michigan Ave., ☎ 312/280–2222). Jaxx is an intimate, elegant spot.

Pump Room (Omni Ambassador East Hotel, 1301 N. State Pkwy., ☎ 312/266–0360). You can still dance cheek-to-cheek at this longtime celebrity hangout. Jacket required.

Zebra Lounge (1220 N. State St., ☎ 312/642–5140). A small, funky hangout that attracts a good crowd of regulars. Music goes until 2 AM most nights, and till 3 AM on Saturday. Minimum.

Sports Bar

Sluggers (3540 N. Clark St., ☎ 312/248–0055). Across from Wrigley Field, this roomy, comfortable bar is packed after Cub games, and the players themselves make occasional personal appearances. Check out the fast- and slow-pitch batting cages on the second floor.

Coffeehouses

During the past few years, cafés have sprung up throughout the lakefront to accommodate those who wish to hang out and talk without necessarily drinking alcohol. Most offer the full gamut of coffees and teas, as well as gooey desserts. Some have small menus of real food too. Yuppie to arty to the seemingly ubiquitous Starbucks, there's a coffeehouse for every taste. Here are a few of the more offbeat ones:

Café Voltaire (3231 N. Clark St., ☎ 312/528–3136). With exposed brick and a vegetarian menu in addition to the usual coffee and desserts, this place caters to artists and entertains everyone else. A space downstairs doubles as a theater.

Coffee Chicago (828 N. State St., ☎ 312/335–0625; 2922 N. Clark St., ☎ 312/327–3228; 3323 N. Clark St., ☎ 312/477–3323; 1561 N. Wells St., ☎ 312/787–1211). A chain, but it doesn't look like one. All four locations are quiet and congenial, decorated in tasteful Laura Ashley prints. Scones and tortes are especially good.

Kopi, a Traveler's Cafe (5317 N. Clark St., ☎ 312/989–5674). The first café in Andersonville, it has a selection of travel books and artifacts from foreign lands, artfully painted tables, and outrageous cakes.

Third Coast Café (29 E. Delaware Pl., ☎ 312/664–7225; 1260 N. Dearborn St., ☎ 312/649–0730). The Delaware location has indoor and outdoor seating; the one in Dearborn is cavernous and open late. You can spend the day sipping and talking in either.

Comedy Clubs

Improvisation has long had a home and a successful following in Chicago; stand-up comedy has fared less well. Up-and-coming local talent has brightened the scene in recent years.

All Jokes Aside (1000 S. Wabash Ave., ☎ 312/922–0577). This is the only stand-up outpost in the south Loop.

ComedySportz (504 N. Wells St., ☎ 312/549–8080). Specializing in "competitive improv" (two teams vie for the favor of the audience), this troupe has had many homes over the past several years, but now seems more or less firmly situated. Cover and minimum.

Improvisation Institute (2319 W. Belmont Ave., ☎ 312/929–2323). The resident improv group is very good, particularly when they do the Finnegans Wake skit. Cover.

Improvisations (504 N. Wells St., ☎ 312/782–6387). When you tire of the comedy here, you can munch dim sum in the attached restaurant. Cover and minimum.

Second City (1616 N. Wells St., ☎ 312/337–3992). An institution for more than 30 years, Second City has spawned some of the hottest comedians around. Yet in recent years the once bitingly funny, loony improvisation has given way to a less imaginative and more raunchy style. There are two stages, the Main and the ETC, for Extra-Tasty Comedy. Cover.

Zanies (1548 N. Wells St., ☎ 312/337–4027). Perhaps Chicago's best stand-up comedy spot, Zanies books outstanding national talent. Cover and minimum.

Gay and Lesbian Bars

Chicago's gay nightlife scene is diverse; its bars appeal to mixed crowds and tastes. Most are on North Halsted Street (3200 N. and above), an area called "Boys Town." Bars generally stay open until 2 AM weekends, but a few keep the lights on until 5 AM Sunday. The *Windy City Times* and *Gay Chicago Magazine* list nightspots, events, and gay and lesbian resources.

Baton Show Lounge (436 N. Clark St., ☎ 312/644–5269). This popular drag show caters mostly to curious out-of-towners. Even so, it's a fun spot and some of the regular performers, such as Chili Pepper, have become Chicago cult figures.

Berlin (954 W. Belmont Ave., ☎ 312/348–4975). This video bar is hot with the fast-lane set from the futures exchanges. Wednesdays are a big night: The last one of every month is "Disco Wednesday," and the first and third ones are predominately lesbian.

Big Chicks (5024 N. Sheridan Rd., ☎ 312/728–5511). The bar sponsors several men's and women's sports teams, making it a favorite with alternative jocks. Though the crowd is mixed, it's gays who are catered to. The great jukebox and the fun-loving staff are the payoff for the hike to get here.

Charlie's (3726 N. Broadway, ☎ 312/871–8887). You can dance nightly to achy-breaky tunes at this country-and-western bar. It's mostly a suburban boots-and-denim crowd on weekends, but even hard-core urbanites rate it high on their cruising lists.

The Closet (3325 N. Broadway, ☎ 312/477–8533). A small neighborhood bar, locals call it a "friendly joint." Don't miss the infamous "Bloody Sundays," for what are hailed as the best Bloody Marys in town. Mixed crowd.

Gentry (712 N. Rush St., ☎ 312/664–1033). This piano bar draws the "coat-and-tie" set. Regulars sing along to show tunes. Two separate bars—one video, one intimate—provide meeting spots to dish. One of the few gay bars in either Near North or downtown.

Little Jim's (3501 N. Halsted St., ☎ 312/871–6116). Another neighborhood bar with a good mix of regulars. Video screens show films of varying repute. Wednesday is bingo night.

Paris Dance (1122 W. Montrose Ave., ☎ 312/769–0602). This spirited, lesbian dance club plays Top-40 music but also features disco and salsa nights. The place rocks on weekends.

Roscoe's Tavern and Cafe (3356 N. Halsted St., ☎ 312/281–3355). This crowded yuppie bar has great dance music, outdoor patios, and a late-night café famed for its desserts.

Vortex (3631 N. Halsted St., ☎ 312/975–6622). A pulsating disco of bulked-up men, the live entertainment here has included Marky Mark, Ru Paul, and gaggles of go-go boys.

8 Excursions from Chicago

THE WESTERN SUBURBS

Updated by
Mark Kollar

CHICAGO'S WESTERN SUBURBS, particularly those near the city, are quite different from the sumptuous enclaves of the North Shore. Gracious villages that date from the 1800s mingle with more modest developments from the postwar housing boom. Our tour of the western suburbs includes a visit to Oak Park, one of the most interesting neighborhoods of residential architecture in the United States. A little farther west is the planned community of Riverside, designed by Frederick Law Olmsted and Calvert Vaux, who laid out New York's Central Park. Riverside's neighbor, Brookfield, has one of the country's foremost zoos. We'll also stop at two nature preserves, one a restored prairie, the other a spectacular arboretum. Finally, we'll visit Wheaton and the estate of one of Chicago's most influential citizens earlier in the century, *Tribune* publisher Robert McCormick.

Exploring

Numbers in the margin correspond to points of interest on the Northeastern Illinois map.

Oak Park

① Ernest Hemingway once called **Oak Park**—his birthplace and childhood home from 1899 to 1917—a town of "broad lawns and narrow minds." The ethnic and political leanings of this village have diversified since Hemingway played on its streets, however, due in part to the past decade's influx of young professionals fleeing the city with their children in search of safer streets, better public schools, and easy access to the Loop.

Founded in the 1850s, just west of the Chicago border, Oak Park is not only one of Chicago's oldest suburbs, but also a living museum of American architectural thought. It has the world's largest collection of Prairie School buildings, an architectural style created by Frank Lloyd Wright to reflect the expanses of the Great Plains. Constructed from materials indigenous to the region, Prairie School houses hug the earth with their emphatic horizontal lines; inside, open spaces flow into each other, rather than being divided into individual rooms.

To get to the heart of Oak Park, take the Eisenhower Expressway (I–290) west to Harlem Avenue and exit to the left. Turn right at the top of the ramp, head north on Harlem Avenue to Lake Street, turn right, and proceed to Forest Avenue.

On the southeast corner of Forest and Chicago avenues you'll see the **Frank Lloyd Wright Home and Studio.** In 1889, the 22-year-old Wright began building his own Shingle Style home, financed by a $5,000 loan from his then-employer and mentor, Louis Sullivan. Over the next 20 years, Wright expanded his business as well as his original modest cottage, establishing his own firm in 1894 and adding a studio in 1898.

In 1909 Wright left his wife and six children for the wife of a client; the focus of his career changed, too, as he spread his innovative designs across the United States and abroad. Sold by Wright in 1925, his home and studio were turned into apartments that eventually fell into disrepair. In 1974, a group of local citizens calling itself the Frank Lloyd

Wright Home and Studio Foundation, together with the National Trust for Historic Preservation, embarked on a 13-year, $2.2 million restoration that returned the building to its 1909 appearance.

Wright's home, made of brick and dark shingles, is filled with natural wood furnishings and earth-tone spaces; Wright's determination to create an integrated environment prompted him to design the furniture as well. The leaded windows have colored art glass designs, and several rooms feature skylights or other indirect lighting. A spacious playroom on the second floor is built to a child's scale. The studio is made up of four spaces—an office, a large reception room, an octagonal library, and an octagonal drafting room that uses a chain harness system rather than traditional beams to support its balcony, roof, and walls. *951 Chicago Ave.,* ☎ *708/848–1976.* ☞ *$6 adults, $4 senior citizens and children under 18.* ☉ *Tours weekdays at 11, 1, and 3, and continuously on weekends 11–4. Reservations required for groups of 10 or more.*

The Ginkgo Tree Bookshop, at the home and studio, carries architecture-related books and gifts and has tour information. Pick up a map (or, on weekends, a guided tour) to guide you to several other examples of Wright's work that are within easy walking or driving distance. Except for the Unity Temple, though, these are all private homes, so you'll have to be content with what you can view from the outside. One block west on Chicago Avenue takes you past **1019, 1027,** and **1031 Chicago Avenue.** Turn left on Marion Street and then left again on Superior Street to reach **1030 Superior Street.** Continue down Superior Street, turn right onto Forest Avenue, and take a look at **333, 318, 313, 238,** and **210 Forest Avenue.** Head left for a detour to **6 Elizabeth Court.** Follow Forest Avenue a few blocks south to Lake Street and turn left.

On the corner of Lake Street and Kenilworth Avenue is **Unity Temple** (875 Lake St., ☎ 708/383–8873), built for a Unitarian congregation in 1905. The stark, concrete building consists of two spaces, a sanctuary and a parish house, connected by the low-ceilinged main entrance. The cubical sanctuary is lit by high windows of stained glass. Wright would no doubt be delighted to find his original furniture still in use here.

Hemingway fans may want to head back up Forest Avenue to Chicago Avenue. One block east and two blocks north brings you to **Ernest Hemingway's boyhood home** (600 N. Kenilworth). This gray stucco house is privately owned and not open to the public. You can, however, visit **Ernest Hemingway's birthplace** at 339 North Oak Park Avenue, just two blocks south and two blocks east of his boyhood home. The **Ernest Hemingway Museum** is down the street at No. 200. Call (☎ 708/848–2222) for hours and fees for both.

Maps, tour information, and tickets for tours of other historic buildings in the River Forest/Oak Park area (including those by Prairie School architects E. E. Roberts and George Maher) are available through the **Oak Park Visitors Center** (158 N. Forest Ave., ☎ 708/848–1500).

Riverside/Brookfield Area

❷ The planned community of **Riverside** is the next stop. The village was founded in the 1860s, when the beautiful Des Plaines River setting inspired a group of Eastern businesspeople to finance the development of a resort-style suburb. They hired Frederick Law Olmsted and Calvert Vaux, designers of New York City's Central Park and a large percentage of memorable land on the East Coast, to create their "village in a park." The name is apt, since Olmsted and Vaux gave Riverside five large parks and 41 smaller ones. Housing construction continued through the 19th century and the first quarter of the 20th.

Today, Riverside is an affluent suburb whose 9,000 residents are passionate about their town, designated a National Historic Landmark in 1970. The village declined federal aid intended to help repave a road because intersections would have had to be converted to safer (but less aesthetically pleasing) 90-degree angles. The **Frederick Law Olmsted Society** (☎ 708/447–1158) offers occasional walking and biking tours and crusades against unwelcome modernization.

To get to Riverside, return to Harlem Avenue and drive south to the Eisenhower Expressway, taking it west to 1st Avenue. Go south on 1st (also called Golfview and Forbes at various points) past 31st Street. (To get to the Brookfield Zoo, *see below,* turn right on 31st. St.) Turn left onto Forest Avenue and right onto Longcommon Road. (Notice the Swiss Gothic water tower.) Turn right just beyond the train station onto Barrypoint Road and right onto Bloomingbank Road. As you curve around, the river is on your right and stunning Victorian houses are on your left. At the stop sign, turn left onto Scottswood Road.

At 300 Scottswood is one of Frank Lloyd Wright's finest works, the **Avery Coonley House.** Built in 1908 as the centerpiece of a large estate, the house has a raised ground floor, with most of the principal rooms on the second floor. The house is privately owned, so you can view it only from the outside. The original complex included a garage and formal gardens, but the lot was subdivided for other buildings.

As you drive through Riverside (or park your car for a walk), notice the curving streets and generous parklands, in contrast to the strict rectangles of Oak Park.

Return to 31st Street and go directly west until you see signs ❸ for the **Brookfield Zoo.** (To reach the zoo from Chicago by train, take the Burlington Northern train from Union Station to Hollywood Avenue, also known as the zoo stop; it's a walk of about a half mile from the station to the zoo.) You can easily spend an entire day here. Established in 1934, the zoo has more than 2,000 animals, inhabiting naturalistic settings that give visitors the sense of being in the wild rather than in a zoo environment. One exhibit, simulating a tropical rain forest, comprises the world's largest indoor zoo of mixed species. Monkeys, otters, birds, and other rain-forest fauna cavort in a carefully constructed setting of rocks, trees, shrubs, pools, and waterfalls. Thunderstorms occur at random intervals, although visitors on the walkways are sheltered from the rain. In the Aquatic Bird House visitors can test their "flying strength" by "flapping their wings" on a machine that simultaneously measures wing action and speed and decides what kind of bird you are, based on how you flap. A 5-acre Habitat Africa has a water hole and rock formations characteristic of the African savanna. Here, visitors can see tiny animals such as klipspringer antelope, which are only 22 inches tall, and rock hyraxes, which resemble prairie dogs. The daily dolphin shows, a highlight of the zoo, are a favorite even among jaded adults, and the show area accommodates 2,000 spectators. Seals and sea lions inhabit a rocky seascape exhibit that simulates a Pacific Northwest environment, and there's a splendid underwater viewing gallery. From late spring through early fall the "motorized safari" tram will carry you around the grounds; in wintertime the heated *Snowball Express* does the job. *8400 W. 31st St.,*

WISCONSIN ↑ TO MILWAUKEE

0 ———— 10 miles
0 ———— 15 km

N

Channel Lake
Loon Lake
Grass Lake
12
Old Mill Creek
Zion
13
13 Illinois Beach State Park
Wadsworth
Pistakee Lake
Fox Lake
Lake Villa
Druce Lake
Gurnee
14
Waukegan
McHenry
Volo
45
North Chicago
Ivanhoe
Lake Bluff
Wauconda
Libertyville
21
Lake Michigan
Mundelein
94
41
Lake Forest
Lake Zurich
43
12 Ft. Sheridan
11 Highwood
Barrington Hills
12
Buffalo Grove
Deerfield
10 Willits House
Carpentersville
14
Northbrook
94
9 Glencoe
Dundee
Arlington Heights
Winnetka
Schaumburg
Kenilworth
Elgin
90
Mt. Prospect
Glenview
8 Baha'i House of Worship
20
72
Des Plaines
Morton Grove
41
7 Evanston
Roselle
290
Chicago-O'Hare International Airport
Skokie
Eisenhower Expwy.
Park Ridge
14
West Chicago
64
355
Villa Park
Franklin Park
294
CHICAGO
38
Lombard
Elmhurst
River Forest
1 Oak Park
Cantigny
6
Glen Ellyn
Hillside
Eisenhower Expwy.
Wheaton
38
Wolf Road Prairie
290
Berwyn
Warrenville
Morton Arboretum
5
53
Oak Brook
4
3 2 Riverside
Cicero
88
34
Brookfield Zoo
55
41
Hyde Park
Lisle
Downers Grove
Chicago Midway Airport
Aurora
Naperville
Darien
Bedford Park
94
Chicago Skyway
53
55
83
Burbank
12
Evergreen Park
90
59
45
294
57
TO INDIANA DUNES
Des Plaines R.
171
Orland Park
43
Riverdale
94
Plainfield
Lockport
Calumet City
INDIANA
Marley
80
Homewood
Lansing
394
Joliet
52
30
Chicago Heights
57
Park Forest

Brookfield, ☎ *708/485–0263 or 312/242–2630.* ☛ *$4 adults, $1.50 senior citizens and children 3–11; ½ price Tues. and Thurs. Parking: $4. Children's zoo: $1 adults, 50¢ senior citizens and children 3–11; free Nov.–Feb. Dolphin shows: $2 adults, $1.50 senior citizens and children 3–11. Motorized safari: $2 adults, $1 senior citizens and children 3–11. Rental strollers and wheelchairs available. Snowball Express free.* ☉ *Memorial Day–Labor Day, daily 9:30–5:30; Labor Day–Memorial Day, daily 10–4:30. Weekends Labor Day–Nov. 10–4:30.*

Before the Midwest was plowed and planted to feed the nation, tall-grass prairie stretched from Illinois to the Rocky Mountains. To see what the state of Illinois looked like until the 1800s, stop off at **Wolf Road Prairie.** This 80-acre black-soil prairie has been painstakingly restored by volunteers to its original array of tall grasses, wildflowers, and other characteristic plants. Birds and other wildlife are especially active at dawn and twilight. From Brookfield Zoo drive west about 10 miles on 31st Street to Wolf Road. Park on the north side of 31st Street just west of Wolf Road.

Lisle

To reach the next stop go north on Wolf Road to I–290, and almost immediately get on I–88 (the East–West Tollway), going west (toll: 40¢). Take it to Route 53 north and go about ½ mile to the **Morton Arboretum.** Established by salt magnate Joy Morton in 1922, it consists of 1,500 acres of woody plants, woodlands, and outdoor gardens. The complex also includes a library and a gift shop, a restaurant that serves lunch, and a coffee shop. It's possible to drive through, but you really should get out and walk some of the 25 miles of trails. Most are short and take 15–30 minutes to complete; some are designed around themes, such as conifers or plants from around the world. A love of trees ran in the Morton family: Joy's father, J. Sterling Morton, originated Arbor Day. In the spring, the flowering trees are spectacular. Tours and special programs are scheduled most Sunday afternoons. *Rte. 53, Lisle,* ☎ *708/968–0074.* ☛ *$6 per car, walk-ins free.* ☉ *Daily 7–7.*

Wheaton

For the last stop, take Route 53 south to Warrenville Road, turn right, and follow it for about 10 miles. Turn right onto Winfield Road and go about 4 miles to the entrance of **Cantigny,** the former estate of Col. Robert McCormick, editor and publisher of the *Chicago Tribune* from 1925 to 1955. (Don't turn in at the "Cantigny Golf" sign unless you wish to play golf; *see* Golfing *in* Chapter 4, Sports, Fitness, Beaches.) Splendid formal gardens, a restored 1870s mansion, and a tank park are a few of the attractions here. McCormick's will left his 500-acre estate to be maintained as a public park. The estate is named after the village of Cantigny, France, which McCormick helped capture in World War I as a member of the U.S. army's first division. There's a museum devoted to the history of the first division from 1917 to Desert Storm. The tank park contains tanks from World War II, the Korean War, and the Vietnam War. Children are encouraged to play on the tanks, which are surrounded by soft wood chips. The first and second floors of the Georgian-style mansion are open to the public and are furnished with antiques and artwork collected by Colonel McCormick's two wives. There's also a beautiful wooded picnic area. *1 S. 151 Winfield Rd.,* ☎ *708/668–5161.* ☛ *Free; parking $5 per car.* ☉ *Park: daily 9–6. Mansion: Tues.–Sun. 10–3:15. Museum: Tues.–Sun. 10–4. Sites remain open 1 hr later Memorial Day–Labor Day.*

To get back to Chicago, take Winfield Road south to Butterfield Road and turn left. At Naperville Road, turn right to return to I–88, which merges with I–290 and takes you back to the Loop.

Dining

Note: Berwyn is directly south of Oak Park. Hillside and Oak Brook are west of Brookfield. For price categories, *see* Chapter 5, Dining.

Berwyn

$$ Capri. This old-fashioned Italian dining room has a loyal local following that comes for the steamed mussels in white or red sauce, pastas, and desserts. ✕ *3126 Oak Park Ave.,* ☎ *708/484–6313. Reservations advised. AE, MC, V.*

$ Salerno's. People from nearby towns make pilgrimages here expressly for the purpose of eating the thick-crust pizza, which ranges in size from "baby" to extra large. The pastas are good, too, as is the veal marsala. ✕ *6633 W. 16th St.,* ☎ *708/484–3400. Reservations advised. AE, DC, MC, V.*

Hillside

$$ La Perla. A wide-ranging Mediterranean menu offers dishes from France, Spain, Italy, Greece, and Morocco. Fresh fish and seafood entrées change daily, and there are plenty of pastas and pizzas, as well. The white-painted, colorfully tiled interior is in keeping with the cuisine. The lounge has music (piano jazz, flamenco, and blues) Monday through Saturday. ✕ *2135 S. Wolf Rd. at 22nd St.,* ☎ *708/449–1070. Reservations advised. AE, MC, V.*

Oak Brook

$$ Zarrosta Grill. An eclectic menu, a wood-burning pizza oven, and a rotisserie set this pleasant spot apart from most restaurants you find in shopping-mall and office-park territory. Try the roasted chicken and California-style pizzas on focaccia bread. ✕ *118 Oak Brook Center Professional Bldg., Cermak Rd. and Rte. 83,* ☎ *708/990–0177. Reservations advised. AE, DC, MC, V.*

Oak Park

$$ Philander's. This hotel dining room has the feel of a classy tavern, and its reliable fish and seafood have recently been supplemented with nonfish items. One of Oak Park's few fine-dining spots, Philander's usually has a crowd. ✕ *Carleton Hotel, 1120 Pleasant St.,* ☎ *708/848–4250. Reservations advised. AE, D, DC, MC, V. Closed Sun. No lunch.*

$ Robinson's No. 1 Ribs. Meaty ribs, barbecued chicken wings, baked beans, and coleslaw are the stars at this eat-in/take-out storefront. ✕ *940 W. Madison St.,* ☎ *708/383–8452. No reservations. AE, MC, V.*

Western Suburbs Essentials

Getting There

BY CAR

This excursion is best done by car. The main arteries serving the western suburbs are the Eisenhower Expressway (I–290), which goes west from the Loop; the Tri-State Tollway (I–94/294), which circles the region from north to south; and newly built I–355, which connects I–290 with I–55, the road from Chicago to St. Louis.

BY TRAIN

Commuter. You can take **Metra** commuter trains (☎ 312/322–6777) to individual attractions. The Metra Chicago and Northwestern Line departs from **Northwestern Station** (165 N. Canal St.) and stops in Oak

Park and Wheaton. The Burlington Northern line (☎ 312/836–7000) departs from **Union Station** (210 S. Canal St.) and stops at Riverside, Brookfield, and Lisle.

El Train. The Lake Street line of the **Chicago Transit Authority's** El train goes to Oak Park, but it's not recommended because of the high number of crimes reported on it. The Congress line also stops in Oak Park, but several miles south of the historic district.

Guided Tours

The **Chicago Architecture Foundation** (*see* Visitor Information, *below*) has tours of Oak Park and occasional tours of other western suburbs, and the **Oak Park Visitors Center** (*see* Visitor Information, *below*) has self-guided tours of Oak Park and adjacent River Forest, as well as information on guided tours.

Visitor Information

The **Chicago Office of Tourism** (78 E. Washington St., ☎ 312/744–2400) has some information on major attractions in the western suburbs, as does the **Illinois Bureau of Tourism** (100 W. Randolph St., ☎ 312/814–4732). Also check with the **Chicago Architecture Foundation** (☎ 312/922–3432) and the **Oak Park Visitors Center** (☎ 708/848–1500).

SHERIDAN ROAD AND THE NORTH SHORE

The shore of Lake Michigan north of Chicago has well-to-do old towns with gracious houses, on lots ever larger and more heavily wooded the farther you travel north. The first stop here is polyglot Evanston, which sits on the northern border of Chicago and is the home of Northwestern University. First settled in 1826, Evanston is also the headquarters of the Women's Christian Temperance Union. Even today it's tough to find a drink here.

Hollywood films have helped make the North Shore synonymous with the upper middle class through such hit films as *Home Alone* (filmed in Winnetka), *Ordinary People* (Lake Forest), and *Risky Business* (Glencoe). The farthest suburbs on our tour, Lake Forest and Lake Bluff, were first settled in the 1830s and grew to prominence as summer settlements for wealthy Chicagoans.

Beyond the borders of suburbia is Illinois Beach State Park, where you can see a somewhat wilder version of Lake Michigan's shore. A detour west brings you to Gurnee, home of a huge theme park and an equally huge shopping mall.

The drive up Sheridan Road, in most spots a stone's throw from the lakefront, is pleasant in itself, even if you don't stop. It's particularly scenic in spring, when the trees flower profusely, and in the fall, when their foliage is downright gaudy.

Exploring

Numbers in the margin correspond to points of interest on the Northeastern Illinois map.

Take Lake Shore Drive north to its end, at Hollywood Avenue, and turn right onto Sheridan Road. Follow it through a zone of 1960s highrises, past Mundelein College, and into Rogers Park, home of Loyola University. A few blocks north of Loyola, the road runs along the lake, and there's a cemetery on the left. Beyond the cemetery is the Evanston town limit.

Although Sheridan Road goes all the way to the Wisconsin border, it twists and turns and occasionally disappears. Don't lose hope; just look for small signs indicating where it went. When in doubt, keep heading north, and stay near the lake.

Evanston

As you wind through the Victorian, Prairie Style, and Queen Anne–style houses of **Evanston,** look for Greenwood Street, one block north of Dempster. Turn right and proceed to 225 Greenwood Street, where you'll enter the grounds of the **Evanston Historical Society,** housed in the châteaulike former home of Nobel prize winner Charles Gates Dawes, vice president under Calvin Coolidge. The 28-room mansion has been restored to its 1920s appearance and has vaulted ceilings, stained-glass windows, and period furniture. The historical society also maintains a costume collection and research facilities on the premises. *225 Greenwood St.,* ☎ *708/475–3410.* ☛ *$5 adults, $3 senior citizens and students.* ☉ *Tues.–Sat. 1–5.*

At the junction of Sheridan Road and Clark Street is the southern edge of **Northwestern University.** Founded in 1855, Northwestern has 7,400 undergraduates and 4,300 graduate students at its Evanston campus, which stretches along the lakefront for 1 mile. Its schools of business, journalism, law, and medicine are nationally known, and its school of speech has graduated many leading actors. Its football team is a perennial underdog in the Big Ten midwestern conference, in which Northwestern is the only private school.

The visitor center is in the Tudor Revival mansion at the corner of Sheridan Road and Clark Street; here you can pick up a map of the campus. The undergraduate-admissions office is directly west at Sheridan Road and Hinman. Stop here for a complete tour of the campus (*see* Guided Tours, *above*).

To reach the Mary and Leigh Block Gallery, a university-owned fine-arts museum that hosts traveling exhibits, go north on Sheridan Road until it jogs left at the southern edge of the Northwestern campus. Instead of following it, turn right and look for the arts complex on your left. The gallery shows a variety of exhibits: European Impressionist and American Realist paintings, photography, decorative arts, and modern sculpture. The adjacent sculpture garden has large-scale sculptures by Henry Moore, Joan Miró, and Arnoldo Pomodoro. *1967 S. Campus Dr.,* ☎ *708/491–4000.* ☛ *Free.* ☉ *Tues.–Wed. noon–5, Thurs.–Sun. noon–8. Gallery closes periodically to install new exhibits.*

The irregularly shaped white building across the way is the **Pick-Staiger Concert Hall,** with a 1,003-seat auditorium that regularly presents performances by internationally known artists, as well as Northwestern faculty and students, and is acclaimed for its acoustics.

Leaving the arts complex, continue on Sheridan Road as it travels west and then north. On the right side of Sheridan Road, between Garrett Place and Haven Street, is the **Shakespeare Garden.** Set back from the street and enclosed by 6-foot hedges, this tranquil refuge is planted with 70 flowers, herbs, and trees mentioned in Shakespeare's plays. Park on the side streets west of Sheridan Road.

Although it looks placid enough most of the time, Lake Michigan has enough fog, violent storms, and sandbars to make navigation treacherous. **Grosse Point Lighthouse** was built in 1873 to help guide ships into the port of Chicago. The lighthouse was decommissioned in 1935, but the Evanston Historical Society has restored it and offers guided tours of the interior on weekend afternoons from June through September. The surrounding park is open year-round and has a nature center and a community arts center. *2535 Sheridan Rd.,* ☎ *708/328–6961.* ☛ *Lighthouse: $2 adults, $1 children.*

Wilmette

8 Continue up Sheridan Road into Wilmette. The **Baha'i House of Worship,** at Sheridan Road and Linden Avenue, is a sublime nine-sided building that incorporates a wealth of architectural styles and symbols from the world's religions. The temple is the U.S. center of the Baha'i faith, which celebrates the unity of all religions. The symmetry and harmony of the building are paralleled in the formal gardens that surround it. Begun in 1920, the temple wasn't finished until 1953. Ask at the visitor center for a guide to show you around. To reach the temple by public transportation, take the Evanston shuttle from Howard Street to the end of the line at Linden Avenue and walk two blocks east. *100 Linden Ave., Wilmette,* ☎ *708/853–2300.*

Glencoe

Pass through the tiny (population 2,708), wealthy community of Kenilworth, marked by gray pillars at its entrance, and the equally lovely but less haughty village of Winnetka. The road curves sharply back
9 and forth through the ravine that separates Winnetka from **Glencoe,** so drive carefully and watch for daredevils in sports cars.

At Lake Cook Road, turn left and drive west past Green Bay Road to the **Chicago Botanic Garden.** It covers 300 acres and has 15 gardens, among them a traditional rose garden, a three-island Japanese garden, a waterfall garden, a sensory garden for the visually impaired, an aquatic garden, a learning garden for the disabled, and a 3.8-acre fruit-and-vegetable garden whose yields are donated to area soup kitchens. Ten greenhouses provide flowers all winter long. Special events and shows are scheduled most weekends, many sponsored by local plant societies. Major shows are the winter orchid show, August bonsai show, daffodil show, cactus-and-succulent show, and Japan Festival in May. To reach the gardens by public transportation take the Evanston shuttle to Davis Street; transfer there for the Nortran Bus 214, which stops at the garden. *Lake Cook Rd., Glencoe,* ☎ *708/835–5440.* ☛ *$4 per car.* ☉ *Daily 8 AM–sunset. Closed Dec. 25.*

Backtrack on Lake Cook Road to Sheridan Road and turn left. You'll pass the main entrance to **Ravinia Park,** important to remember if you'll be returning here later. Summer visitors might want to combine a North Shore excursion with an evening trip to the Ravinia Music Festival for an outdoor concert (*see* Chapter 7, The Arts and Nightlife). You can pack a picnic and blanket and sit on the lawn for about the cost of a movie. (Seats are also available in the pavilion for a significantly higher price.) Picnic fixings can be bought at several spots along the way, including **Plaza del Lago,** a shopping center on Sheridan Road on the border between Wilmette and Kenilworth, and the grocery stores in Highwood. There are also restaurants and snack bars on the park grounds. Concerts usually start at 8; plan to arrive at the park no later than 6:30 to allow time for parking, hiking from the parking lot to the lawn, and getting settled.

Highland Park

10 At 1445 Sheridan Road in Highland Park is the **Willits House,** a 1902 building designed by Frank Lloyd Wright, which has a cruciform plan built around a large fireplace in the center. Wright and other Prairie School architects used this technique frequently. The house is now privately owned.

Highwood

The next village north, a working-class ethnic community, is an anomaly
11 on the North Shore. **Highwood** was incorporated in 1887, and its fortunes have been entwined with those of the adjacent army post, Ft. Sheridan, which was opened in the same year to maintain an army presence near Chicago in the wake of the labor unrest surrounding the Haymarket Riot. In the early days Highwood was the only place nearby where soldiers could get a drink, because most of the North Shore suburbs were dry.

A large Italian population has helped make Highwood the restaurant row of the North Shore, although for some reason several of its most famous spots are French (*see* Dining, *below*).

TIME OUT Many of Highwood's restaurants are open only for dinner, but you can grab a bite throughout the day at **Mexico Lindo** (830 Sheridan Rd.), **Virginia's Restaurant** (415 Sheridan Rd.), or **Rainbows Bar and Grill** (432 Sheridan Rd.). There are more dining spots on Green Bay Road, a block west of Sheridan Road and across the train tracks. For Italian-style picnic fare try **Bacio Foods** (424 Sheridan Rd.).

As you continue north, you'll see on your right the distinctive yellow
12 buildings of **Ft. Sheridan.** Designed by the noted Chicago firm of Holabird and Roche, the 54 buildings were constructed of brick that was manufactured on the building site from indigenous clay. The fort has been closed, but it's worth turning in at the main gate and asking the military police officer on duty if you can drive around.

The next town north is tony Lake Forest, where you'll pass the beautifully landscaped campuses of Lake Forest and Barat colleges, as well as many sumptuous mansions set far back on heavily wooded lots. Beyond Lake Forest is Lake Bluff, Chicago's northernmost suburb, which began life during the 19th century as a summer resort and Methodist camp-meeting ground.

Zion

About 10 miles north of Lake Bluff, beyond the town of Waukegan and the industrial waterfront of North Chicago, is Zion and the en-
13 trance to **Illinois Beach State Park,** where you can swim if you're willing to brave the cold water. This beach is less developed than those in Chicago, although you can see signs of industry along the lake in both directions. You'll also see the dune plants that covered the lakefront until the 19th century. The nature preserve at the south end of the park has areas of marsh and forest. The northern section of the park was used as a prisoner-of-war camp during the Civil War and provided a site for army basic training in both world wars. *Sheridan and Wadsworth Rds.,* ☏ *708/662–4811.* ☺ *Daily.*

At this point, to return to Chicago, you can backtrack on Sheridan Road or take I–94 for a quicker ride back to the city. To get to I–94, head west on Wadsworth Road for 3 miles from the park's main entrance to Route 131 (Green Bay Rd.). Turn left and go south 4 miles to Route

132 (Grand Ave.), and turn right. Head almost 4 miles west to the junction with I–94.

Gurnee

⑭ At the intersection of Route 132 and I–94 is **Gurnee,** which has two attractions you probably won't have the energy to visit after a day exploring Sheridan Road—but you may want to return another day.

Six Flags Great America has 132 rides, but it specializes in roller coasters. Turn upside-down on the Shock Wave and the Iron Wolf, or go for major ups and downs on the classic wooden American Eagle and Viper. Warner Brothers characters—Bugs Bunny, Daffy Duck, Sylvester the Cat—prowl the grounds. It's best to arrive early in the morning or late in the day. If the midday crowds wear you out, you can have your hand stamped for free readmission later and go somewhere else for a while. Hours and prices vary, and sometimes the park is closed for private events, so call ahead. Look for discount coupons in flyers at hotels and tourist offices. *I–94 at Rte. 132 (Grand Ave.),* ☎ *708/249–1776.* ☛ *$29.50 ages 11–59, $24.50 children under 11, $14.75 adults over 59.* ☉ *May–Sept., daily 10–10; weekends only early spring and late fall; closed winter.*

Shoppers may prefer **Gurnee Mills,** across I–94 from Six Flags. This massive mall combines factory outlets, discount stores, and regular-price stores. There are also several food courts. *6170 W. Grand Ave. at I–94 and Rte. 132,* ☎ *800/937–7467.* ☉ *Mon.–Sat. 10–9, Sun. 11–6.*

To get back to Chicago, enter I–94 south/east and follow the signs. For the Near North Side, exit at Ohio Street; for the Loop, take any of the eastbound exits between Washington Street and Congress Parkway.

Dining

For price categories, *see* Chapter 5, Dining.

Evanston

$$$ **Oceanique.** As its name suggests, this storefront place specializes in fish. Grilled dishes such as Scottish salmon and striped bass stand out, but there are also excellent pasta dishes, soups, and sinful chocolate desserts. ✕ *505 Main St.,* ☎ *708/864–3435. Reservations advised. AE, D, DC, MC, V. Closed Sun. No lunch.*

$ **Dave's Italian Kitchen.** A traditional hangout for Northwestern students, Dave's has a collegiate atmosphere that may bring on nostalgia even among nonalumni. Dishes are large, inexpensive, and successfully lure the clientele away from dorm food. Stick with the reliable pizzas (deep-dish and thin-crust) and pastas. ✕ *906 Church St.,* ☎ *708/864–6000. No reservations; expect to wait on weekends. D, MC, V. No lunch.*

Highwood

$$ **Froggy's French Cafe.** This comfortable bistro is known for sumptuous six-course, prix-fixe dinners and lunches, excellent cassoulet and other hearty dishes, and a huge wine list. Expect to wait at peak hours. ✕ *306 N. Green Bay Rd.,* ☎ *708/433–7080. Reservations accepted for 6 or more. D, DC, MC, V. Closed Sun.*

$ **Bistro in Highwood.** The former Alouette has been renovated into a more comfortable and cheaper bistro-style restaurant with butcher block furniture and green-and-white checked tablecloths. The menu is varied and tasty with French-based fare, including fish and poultry dishes. ✕ *440 N. Green Bay Rd.,* ☎ *708/433–5600. Reservations advised. AE, D, DC, MC, V.*

Wilmette

$$ **Betise.** This bistro in Wilmette's Plaza del Lago shopping center offers a pastiche of dishes from southern France and Italy, most of them emphasizing tomatoes, potatoes, fish, and roasted chicken. Cobblestone floors and off-white walls add to the Riviera atmosphere. ✕ *1515 Sheridan Rd., ☎ 708/853–1711. Reservations advised. AE, D, DC, MC, V.*

$ **Walker Bros. Original Pancake House.** This traditional breakfast-all-day spot has fluffy omelets, several varieties of pancakes, and fresh-ground coffee served with whipping cream. ✕ *153 Green Bay Rd., ☎ 708/251–6000. MC, V.*

Sheridan Road and the North Shore Essentials

Getting There

BY CAR

This excursion is designed as a driving tour, although you can take a commuter train to individual attractions (*see below*). The route follows Sheridan Road along the lakeshore. The other major artery serving the North Shore is the Edens Expressway (I–94).

BY TRAIN

Commuter. The **Metra Chicago/Northwestern line** (☎ 312/322–6777) departs from the Northwestern station at 165 North Canal Street and stops in Evanston (Davis St.), Wilmette, Glencoe, Ravinia Park (special trains on concert nights), Highland Park, Highwood, Fort Sheridan, Lake Forest, Waukegan, and Zion.

El Train. The **CTA's** Howard line will take you as far as Wilmette, with multiple stops in Evanston. Board it northbound along State Street in the Loop or at Chicago Avenue and State Street in the Near North. Change at Howard for the Evanston shuttle. To reach the Northwestern campus, get off at Foster and walk east to Sheridan Road. The Howard line is not recommended after dark.

Guided Tours

The **Chicago Architectural Foundation** (☎ 312/922–3432) has occasional walking, bicycle, and bus tours of parts of the North Shore. The **office of undergraduate admissions** at Northwestern University (☎ 708/491–7271) offers tours of the campus.

Visitor Information

Call the **Illinois Bureau of Tourism** (100 W. Randolph St., ☎ 312/814–4732) or the **Lake County Illinois Convention and Visitors' Bureau** (☎ 708/662–2700).

THE INDIANA DUNES

Many Chicagoans looking for an escape from the city have discovered the unexpected pleasures of nearby northwest Indiana. This otherwise industrial area on the southern shores of Lake Michigan boasts beaches, wetlands, and the "singing sands" of the Indiana Dunes. The sand here squeaks when you walk on it— one of the world's only beaches with such musical talents. The views across the lake, with the Chicago skyline on the horizon, are spectacular, particularly compared to the surrounding smokestacks and blast furnaces of steel mills. The area is still being developed for weekend travel, but a day trip here to explore the Indiana Dunes State Park is certainly worthwhile.

Exploring

Start at the **Indiana Dunes National Lakeshore Visitor Center,** which is 1 mile west of the Beverly Shores train station on Highway 12. The center has a full range of maps and brochures, a brass-rubbing area for children to make pictures of the wildlife, and a bookstore. It also runs tours and has displays on area flora and fauna. Several walking paths start here as well; some are old Native American trails, and all follow relatively gentle terrain. The park claims to have the fourth most diverse flora in the U.S. park system, and you'll notice a great variety of plant life along the trails. ☎ 219/926–7561, ext. 225. ☺ Daily 9–5, later in summer.

A quarter mile from the visitor center are the **Bailly Homestead** and the **Chellberg Farm,** two restored settlements that give a feeling of what life was like for the area's first European residents, who came to the area as fur traders. The homestead and turn-of-the-century farm host a Maple Sugar Festival each March; included on the grounds are fields, gardens, a petting zoo, a windmill and granary, and a barn built in 1880.

Across Highway 12, toward the lake, is **Cowles Bog.** This inter-dunal pond is bordered by an old stagecoach trail that leads through wildflower fields; marshes of cattails, pussy willows, and skunk cabbage; and woods of fern, oak, and sassafras. You can spot deer and beavers building their dams. Hike old dune ridges farmed 10,000 years ago, when Lake Michigan was at least 25 feet higher.

If you just want to loll about on a clean, beautiful, relatively uncrowded beach, you have several options. Central and Kemil beaches are closest to the attractions above, but **West Beach,** about 6 miles west, is probably the area's best. It has good picnic areas, bathroom facilities, a snack bar, and an information center. West Beach is also the trailhead for a walk that traces the development of the area's ecosystem; hikers start among sand dunes and pass through cottonwoods on their way to an oak forest.

Dining

The area offers few notable restaurants, so a picnic on the beach is the best option. Pick up groceries at the **Jewel Foodstore** (770 Indian Boundary Rd., ☎ 219/926–7172), 4 miles south of the dunes on Highway 49. There are a few local hangouts not too far from the beaches. **Wagner's** (361 Wagner Rd., ☎ 219/926–7614), a casual pub with an impressive beer selection, is famous among locals for its ribs and cheeseburgers. **Wingfield's** (526 Indian Boundary Rd., ☎ 219/926–2200) serves moderately priced fish and pasta dishes, fresh salads, and cold draft beers. **The Spa** (333 N. Mineral Springs Rd., ☎ 219/926–1654) is a more formal spot with a cozy grill room that's inviting for lunch or a cocktail.

The Indiana Dunes Essentials

Getting There

BY CAR

Take I–80/94 East to Indiana. The park exits are at Highway 249 or Highway 49. Both lead to Highway 12, which runs east to the parks. In moderate traffic, it takes about one hour and 15 minutes to reach the dunes from Chicago.

BY TRAIN

The **South Shore Line** (☎ 800/356–2079) runs from the southwest corner of Michigan Avenue and Randolph Street, under the Chicago Cultural Center. In Indiana, the Beverly Shores station puts you closest to the park's visitor center, while the Dunes Park station provides the best access to Cowles Bog and the Bailly/Chellberg settlement. For West Beach, get off at the Ogden Dunes station. The trip takes about an hour and 15 minutes from downtown Chicago, and costs $5.25 one way. Trains leave regularly from 6 AM to 12:45 PM.

Visitor Information

For information on directions, hours, nature programs, and camping facilities, contact **Indiana Dunes National Lakeshore** (1100 N. Mineral Springs Rd., Porter, IN 46304, ☎ 219/926–7561) or **Indiana Dunes State Park** (1600 N. 25 E, Chesterton, IN, 46304, ☎ 219/926–1952).

MILWAUKEE

By Don Davenport

Visitors to Chicago have the exciting option of taking in two sharply different cities on one trip. Milwaukee, in contrast to Chicago's enormity and urbanity, is an enclave of distinctly accessible, even local, pleasures. You can easily make a day trip here, but an overnight jaunt will allow you to sample Milwaukee's beer-ocentric nightlife to the fullest.

Set on the shores of Lake Michigan, just a few hours north of Chicago, Wisconsin's largest city is an international seaport and the state's primary commercial and manufacturing center. A small-town atmosphere prevails in Milwaukee, which is not so much a city as a large collection of neighborhoods. Modern steel-and-glass high-rises occupy much of the downtown area, but the early heritage persists in restored and well-kept 19th-century buildings that share the city skyline. First settled by Potawatomi Indians and later by French fur traders in the late 18th century, the city boomed in the 1840s with the arrival of German brewers, whose influence continues.

Milwaukee has also become known as a city of festivals. The **Summerfest** kicks off each summer's activities on the lakefront. Another annual highlight is the **Great Circus Parade,** a July spectacle that features scores of antique circus wagons from the famed Circus World Museum in Baraboo, Wisconsin. August brings the **State Fair.**

Exploring

Numbers in the margin correspond to points of interest on the Milwaukee map.

Downtown

Milwaukee's central business district is a mile long and only a few blocks wide and is divided by the Milwaukee River. On the east side, the **Iron Block Building** (N. Water St. and E. Wisconsin Ave.) is one of the few remaining ironclad buildings in the United States. Its metal facade was brought in by ship from an eastern foundry and installed during the Civil War. In the 1860s, Milwaukee exported more wheat than any other port in the world, which gave impetus to building the **Grain Exchange Room** in the **Mackie Building** (225 E. Michigan St.). The 10,000-square-foot trading room has three-story-high columns and painted ceiling panels that feature Wisconsin wildflowers.

Milwaukee

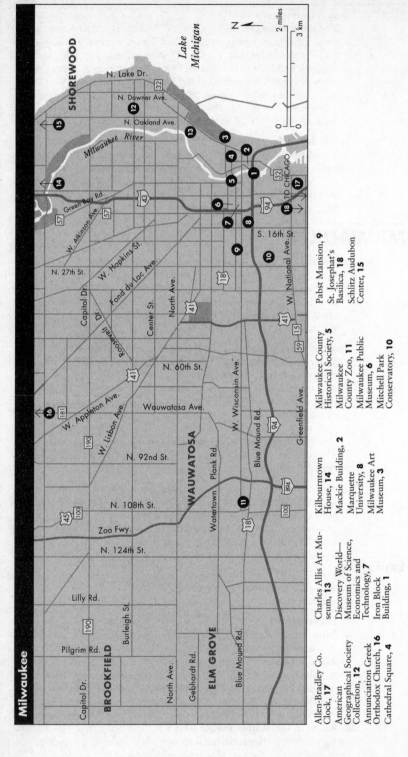

N

2 miles
3 km

SHOREWOOD

Lake Michigan

N. Lake Dr.

N. Downer Ave. ⑫

N. Oakland Ave. ⑬ ③ ②

⑮

Milwaukee River ④

⑭ ⑤ ① 32 TO CHICAGO ⑰

Green Bay Rd. 43 ⑥ 94 ⑱

57 57 W. Atkinson Ave. ⑦ ⑧

S. 16th St.

N. 27th St. W. Hopkins St. ⑨ ⑩

Capitol Dr. Fond du Lac Ave. 18 W. National Ave.

North Ave. 41

Center St.

N. 60th St. 41 15

59

N. 92nd St. Wauwatosa Ave. WAUWATOSA

W. Appleton Ave. 190 W. Wisconsin Ave.

⑯ 181 W. Lisbon Ave. 94 Greenfield Ave.

Plank Rd.

N. 108th St. 894

Zoo Fwy. Watertown ⑪ 18 100

45 100 Blue Mound Rd.

N. 124th St.

BROOKFIELD

Lilly Rd. Burleigh St.

Pilgrim Rd. ELM GROVE

Capitol Dr. 190 North Ave. Gebhardt Rd. Blue Mound Rd.

Allen-Bradley Co. Clock, **17**

American Geographical Society Collection, **12**

Annunciation Greek Orthodox Church, **16**

Cathedral Square, **4**

Charles Allis Art Museum, **13**

Discovery World—Museum of Science, Economics and Technology, **7**

Iron Block Building, **1**

Kilbourntown House, **14**

Mackie Building, **2**

Marquette University, **8**

Milwaukee Art Museum, **3**

Milwaukee County Historical Society, **5**

Milwaukee County Zoo, **11**

Milwaukee Public Museum, **6**

Mitchell Park Conservatory, **10**

Pabst Mansion, **9**

St. Josephat's Basilica, **18**

Schlitz Audubon Center, **15**

❸ The **Milwaukee Art Museum,** in the lakefront War Memorial Center designed by Eero Saarinen, houses notable collections of paintings, drawings, sculpture, photography, and decorative arts. Its permanent collection is strong in European and American art of the 19th and 20th centuries. *750 N. Lincoln Memorial Dr.,* ☏ *414/224–3200.* ☛ *$4 adults, $2 senior citizens, children under 12 free. Closed Mon.*

❹ Returning to the river, stop at **Cathedral Square.** This quiet park (E. Kilbourn Ave. and Jefferson St.) was built on the site of Milwaukee's first courthouse. Across the street, **St. John's Cathedral,** dedicated in 1853, was the first church built in Wisconsin specifically as a Roman Catholic cathedral.

The banks of the Milwaukee River are busy in summer, especially at noon, when downtown workers lunch in the nearby parks and public areas, such as **Père Marquette Park,** on the river at Old World 3rd Street and West Kilbourn Avenue.

❺ Adjacent to the park, the **Milwaukee County Historical Center** (910 N. Old World 3rd St., ☏ 414/273–8288), a museum housed in a graceful bank building, features early fire-fighting equipment, military artifacts, toys, and women's fashions. It also contains a research library with naturalization records and genealogical resources.

The river is also the departure point for cruises of Milwaukee's harbor and lakefront. **Iroquois Harbor Cruises** (Clybourn St. bridge on the west bank, ☏ 414/332–4194) offers harbor cruises aboard a 149-passenger vessel. **Celebration of Milwaukee** (502 N. Harbor Dr., ☏ 414/278–1113) and **Edelweiss Cruise Dining** (1110 N. Old World 3rd St., ☏ 414/272–3625) offer lunch and dinner cruises.

As you cross the river to the west side, notice that the east-side streets are not directly opposite the west-side streets and that the bridges across the river are built at an angle. This layout dates from the 1840s, when the area east of the river was called Juneautown and the region to the west was known as Kilbourntown. The rival communities had a fierce argument over which would pay for the bridges that connected them; so intense was the antagonism that citizens venturing into rival territory carried white flags. The Great Bridge War was finally settled by the state legislature in 1845, but the streets on either side of the river never were aligned.

❻ A few blocks west of the river, the **Milwaukee Public Museum** has the fourth-largest collection of natural history exhibits in the country, as well as outstanding fine arts and Native American, African, and pre-Columbian collections. Walk-through exhibits include the "Streets of Old Milwaukee," depicting the city in the 1890s; a two-story rain forest; and the "Third Planet" (complete with full-size dinosaurs), where visitors walk into the interior of the Earth to learn about its history. *800 W. Wells St.,* ☏ *414/278–2702.* ☛ *$5.50 adults, $4.50 senior citizens, $3.50 children 4–12 and students.* ☉ *Daily 9–5.*

❼ Nearby, **Discovery World—Museum of Science, Economics and Technology,** in the Milwaukee Public Central Library, has a wide range of hands-on exhibits on magnets, motors, electricity, health, and computers. It also features the "Great Electric Show" and the "Light Wave–Laser Beam Show" on weekends. *818 W. Wisconsin Ave.,* ☏ *414/765–9966.* ☛ *$4.50 adults; $2 senior citizens, students, and children over 6.* ☉ *Mon.–Sat. 9–5, Sun. 11–5.*

Farther west, just off Wisconsin Avenue at 16th Street on the central
❽ mall of the **Marquette University** campus, is **St. Joan of Arc Chapel** (☏

414/288–6873), a small, stone, 15th-century chapel moved from its original site near Lyon, France, and reconstructed here in 1964. One of the stones was reputedly kissed by Joan before she went to her death and is said to be discernibly colder than the others. The **Patrick and Beatrice Haggerty Museum of Art** (13th St. and Clybourn St., ☎ 414/288–7290) houses the university's collection of more than 6,000 works of art, including Renaissance, Baroque, and modern paintings; sculpture; prints; photography; and decorative arts. The museum also has changing exhibitions.

Other Attractions

⑨ Away from downtown, the **Pabst Mansion,** built in 1893 for the beer baron Captain Frederick Pabst, is one of Milwaukee's treasured landmarks. The castlelike, 37-room Flemish Renaissance-style mansion has a tan pressed-brick exterior and is decorated with carved stone and terra-cotta ornamentation outside and carved cabinets and woodwork, ornamental ironwork, marble, tile, stained glass, and carved panels inside, all imported from a 17th-century Bavarian castle. *2000 W. Wisconsin Ave.,* ☎ *414/931–0808.* ☞ *$6 adults, $3 children 6–17.* ☉ *Mon.–Sat. 10–3:30, Sun. noon–3:30.*

⑩ Milwaukee's unique **Mitchell Park Conservatory** consists of three modern 85-foot-high glass domes housing tropical, arid, and seasonal plant and flower exhibits; its displays of lilies and poinsettias are spectacular at Easter and Christmas. There are picnic facilities on the grounds. *524 S. Layton Blvd.,* ☎ *414/649–9800.* ☞ *$3 adults, $1.50 senior citizens and children.* ☉ *Daily 9–5.*

⑪ The **Milwaukee County Zoo** displays more than 3,000 wild animals and birds, including many endangered species, in natural environments. It also offers educational programs, a seasonal children's zoo, narrated tram tours, miniature-train rides, picnic areas, and cross-country ski trails. *10001 W. Bluemound Rd.,* ☎ *414/771–3040.* ☞ *$7 adults, $6 senior citizens, $5 children; parking $4.* ☉ *Daily 9–5.*

⑫ North of downtown Milwaukee, the **American Geographical Society Collection,** housed in the Golda Meir Library on the University of Wisconsin–Milwaukee campus (2311 E. Hartford Ave., ☎ 414/229–6282), has an exceptional assemblage of maps, old globes, atlases, and charts, plus 180,000 books and 400,000 journals. The **University of Wisconsin–Milwaukee Art Museum** (3253 N. Downer Ave., ☎ 414/229–5070) displays a permanent collection of Greek and Russian icons and 20th-century European paintings and prints.

⑬ The **Charles Allis Art Museum** (1801 N. Prospect Ave., ☎ 414/278–8295) occupies an elegant Tudor-style house built in 1911 for the first president of the Allis-Chalmers Manufacturing Co. The home has stained-glass windows by Louis Comfort Tiffany and a stunning worldwide collection of paintings and objets d'art, including works by major 19th- and 20th-century French and American painters.

⑭ The Greek Revival cream-color slate **Kilbourntown House** (4400 W. Estabrook Dr., ☎ 414/273–8288), built in 1844, is listed on the National Register of Historic Places and contains an outstanding collection of mid-19th-century furniture and decorative arts.

⑮ The **Schlitz Audubon Center,** 10 miles north of downtown, is a 186-acre wildlife area of forests, ponds, marshland, and nature trails along Lake Michigan. Popular with cross-country skiers and bird-watchers, it has an environmental research and education center. *1111 E. Brown*

Deer Rd., ☎ *414/352–2880.* ☛ *$2 adults, $1 senior citizens and children under 12.* ⊘ *Tues.–Sun. 9–5.*

⑯ The **Annunciation Greek Orthodox Church** (9400 W. Congress St., ☎ 414/461–9400) was Frank Lloyd Wright's last major work; the famed Wisconsin architect called it his "little jewel." Since it opened in 1961, the blue-domed, Byzantine-style church has drawn visitors from all over the world.

⑰ Just south of downtown, the **Allen-Bradley Co. Clock** (1201 S. 2nd St.) is a Milwaukee landmark and, according to the *Guinness Book of World Records,* the largest four-faced clock in the world. Great Lakes ships often use the clock as a navigational reference point.

⑱ Built by immigrant parishioners and local craftsmen at the turn of the century, **St. Josephat's Basilica** (601 W. Lincoln St., at 6th St., ☎ 414/645–5623) has a dome modeled after St. Peter's in Rome. The church is adorned with a remarkable collection of relics, portraits of Polish saints and leaders, stained glass, and wood carvings.

Shopping

Stores range from tiny ethnic and specialty shops to enclosed shopping malls with large department stores. Using the downtown skywalk system, it's possible to browse in hundreds of stores over several blocks without once setting foot outside. Downtown Milwaukee's major shopping street is **Wisconsin Avenue** west of the Milwaukee River. The **Grand Avenue Mall,** the major downtown retail center, spans four city blocks. **Historic Third Ward,** a turn-of-the-century wholesale and manufacturing district on the National Register of Historic Places, is bordered by the harbor, the river, and downtown and offers many unusual shops and restaurants. **Jefferson Street,** stretching four blocks from Wisconsin to Kilbourn avenues, offers upscale shops and stores. The **Lincoln Avenue District,** minutes from downtown off I–94, has specialty shops and ethnic restaurants in a quaint, historic Polish and German neighborhood. On Milwaukee's south side, historic **Mitchell Street** is a multicultural blend of retail shops and diverse ethnic restaurants.

Dining

Milwaukee's culinary style was shaped to a great extent by the Germans who first settled here. Many restaurants—whether or not they are German—offer Wiener schnitzel or the meringue-based desserts called *schaumtortes.* Rye bread, sometimes crusted with coarse salt, is common on Milwaukee tables. Many other ethnic groups have also donated specialties to Milwaukee's tradition of gemütlichkeit (fellowship and good cheer).

Milwaukeeans like to relax and socialize when they eat out. Fashion isn't as important here as it is in faster-paced cities. Jackets and ties are customary at the most expensive restaurants, but only a few actually require them.

Price ranges are the same as those in Chapter 5, Dining.

$$$$ **English Room.** Milwaukee's premier hotel restaurant, in the Pfister Hotel, ★ has a dark, Victorian elegance. The menu has been updated and now features a lighter American cuisine along with its German meat-and-potato dishes. Service is formal. ✕ *424 E. Wisconsin Ave.,* ☎ *414/273–*

8222. *Reservations advised. Jacket required. AE, D, DC, MC, V. No lunch weekends.*

$$$$ **Grenadier's.** Knut Apitz, chef-owner, serves some of the most elegant
★ food in Milwaukee. Imaginative dishes combine classical European style
with Oriental or Indian flavors; offerings include tenderloin of veal with
raspberry sauce and angel-hair pasta. The three small rooms have an
air of matter-of-fact refinement; the handsome, darkly furnished piano
bar also has tables. ✕ *747 N. Broadway St.,* ☎ *414/276–0747. Reservations advised. Jacket required. AE, DC, MC, V. Closed Sun. and holidays. No lunch Sat.*

$$$ **Boder's on the River.** Tieback curtains, fireplaces, and lots of knick-
knacks give the dining rooms in this suburban restaurant a cheerful
country look. The menu offers Wisconsin favorites prepared in a
straightforward manner, including roast duckling and baked whitefish.
✕ *11919 N. River Rd., Mequon,* ☎ *414/242–0335. Reservations advised. AE, D, DC, MC, V. Closed Mon.*

$$$ **Karl Ratzsch's Old World Restaurant.** In the authentic German atmo-
★ sphere of this family-owned restaurant, such specialties as schnitzel,
roast duckling, and sauerbraten are served by dirndl-skirted waitresses
while a string trio schmaltzes it up. The main dining room is decorated
with murals, chandeliers made from antlers, and antique beer steins.
✕ *320 E. Mason St.,* ☎ *414/276–2720. Reservations advised. AE, D, DC, MC, V.*

$$ **Jake's.** Two locations, both with perfectly prepared steaks and heaps
of french-fried onion rings, helped this longtime Milwaukee favorite
earn its reputation. The best menu choices include escargot, roast
duckling, and Bailey's chocolate-chip cheesecake. ✕ *6030 W. North
Ave., Wauwatosa,* ☎ *414/771–0550; 21445 W. Capitol Dr., Brookfield,* ☎ *414/781–7995. No reservations. AE, MC, V. No lunch.*

$$ **Three Brothers Bar & Restaurant.** Set in an 1887 tavern is one of Milwaukee's revered ethnic restaurants, serving chicken paprikash, roast
lamb, Serbian salad, and homemade desserts at old metal kitchen tables. It's about 10 minutes from downtown on the near South Side. ✕
2414 S. St. Clair St., ☎ *414/481–7530. Reservations advised. No
credit cards. Closed Mon. No lunch.*

$ **Benjamin's Delicatessen and Restaurant.** You'll find a wide selection
of such tasty specialties as matzo-ball soup, corned beef sandwiches,
and brisket of beef at this neighborhood deli. There are booths, tables,
and a counter where the TV is usually tuned to the latest sporting event.
✕ *4160 N. Oakland Ave., Shorewood,* ☎ *414/332–7777. MC, V.*

$ **Rudy's Mexican Restaurant.** Located in Walker's Point, an area south
of downtown inching toward gentrification, Rudy's serves fresh standard Mexican fare, including chilies rellenos, enchiladas, and gua-
camole. ✕ *627 S. 5th St.,* ☎ *414/291–0296. AE, D, DC, MC, V.*

Lodging

Milwaukee accommodation options range from cozy small motels to
executive suites overlooking Lake Michigan and the city. Most downtown hotels are within walking distance of the theater district, the Convention Center and Arena, and plenty of shopping and restaurants. In
summer, book well ahead, especially for weekends.

Price ranges are the same as in Chapter 6, Lodging.

$$$$ **Pfister Hotel.** Many of the rooms in Milwaukee's grand old hotel, built
★ in 1893, have been combined to make suites with enlarged bathrooms.
Rooms in the Tower (built 1975) are bright and contemporary with a
Victorian accent, in keeping with the original hotel. A collection of 19th-

century art hangs in the elegant Victorian lobby. 🖅 *424 E. Wisconsin Ave., 53202,* ☎ *414/273–8222 or 800/558–8222;* FAX *414/273–0747. 307 rooms. 3 restaurants, lounge, indoor pool, health club, nightclub. AE, D, DC, MC, V.*

$$$ **Embassy Suites Hotel.** The sweeping atrium lobby with fountains, pot-
★ ted plants, and glass elevators is the focal point of this hotel in the west-
ern suburbs. The two-bedroom suites are decorated in pastels and
earth tones with contemporary furnishings. 🖅 *1200 S. Moorland Rd., Brookfield 53008,* ☎ *414/782–2900;* FAX *414/796–9159. 203 suites. Restaurant, lounge, indoor pool, hot tub, sauna, exercise room. AE, D, DC, MC, V.*

$$$ **Wyndham Milwaukee Center.** Part of the city's growing theater dis-
★ trict, this hotel is next to the Milwaukee Center, by the river. The op-
ulent lobby is tiled with Italian marble; guest rooms are contemporary,
large, pleasant, and have mahogany furnishings. 🖅 *139 E. Kilbourn Ave., 53202,* ☎ *414/276–8686 or 800/822–4200;* FAX *414/276–8007. 221 rooms. Restaurant, lounge, sauna, 2 steam rooms, exercise room, hot tub, health club. AE, D, DC, MC, V.*

$$ **Ramada Inn Downtown.** Rough knotty-pine paneling gives the lobby
of this motor hotel a casual feeling. The maroon-toned rooms are fur-
nished in standard Ramada style. 🖅 *633 W. Michigan St., 53202,* ☎
414/272–8410; FAX *414/272–4651. 154 rooms. Restaurant, lounge, pool, airport shuttle. AE, D, DC, MC, V.*

$$ **Sheraton Mayfair.** This bustling high-rise motor hotel on the west side
is convenient to the County Medical Complex and the Milwaukee
County Zoo. Guest rooms are bright and airy, with traditional fur-
nishings; those near the top have fine views. 🖅 *2303 N. Mayfair Rd., Wauwatosa 53226,* ☎ *414/257–3400 or 800/325–3535;* FAX *414/257–0900. 150 rooms. Restaurant, lounge, indoor pool, sauna. AE, D, DC, MC, V.*

$ **Astor Hotel.** Close to Lake Michigan, the Astor has the not-unpleas-
ant air of a hotel past its heyday. Many of the rooms have been remodeled and furnished with antiques and period reproductions but retain
old bathroom fixtures. 🖅 *924 E. Juneau Ave., 53202,* ☎ *414/271–4220, 800/558–0200, or 800/242–0355 in WI;* FAX *414/271–6370. 96 rooms. Restaurant, lounge, parking. AE, D, DC, MC, V.*

The Arts and Nightlife

Milwaukee Magazine (on newsstands) lists arts and entertainment events. Also check the Arts section of the Sunday *Milwaukee Journal*.

The Arts

Milwaukee's theater district is in a two-block downtown area bounded by the Milwaukee River, East Wells Street, North Water Street, and East State Street. Most tickets are sold at box offices.

Broadway Theater Center (158 N. Broadway Ave., ☎ 414/291–7800) is the new, intimate home of the acclaimed Skylight Opera Theater, the Milwaukee Chamber Theater, and Theater X.

Milwaukee Center (108 E. Wells St., ☎ 414/224–9490) houses the Milwaukee Repertory Theater.

The **Performing Arts Center** (929 N. Water St., ☎ 414/273–7206) serves as a base for the Milwaukee Symphony Orchestra, Milwaukee Ballet Company, Florentine Opera Company, and First Stage Milwaukee.

Riverside Theater (116 W. Wisconsin Ave., ☎ 414/224–3000) and **Pabst Theater** (144 E. Wells St., ☎ 414/286–3663) host touring theater companies, Broadway shows, and other entertainment.

Nightlife

City nightlife includes friendly saloons (about 1,600 at last count) and a varied music scene. The **Safe House** (779 N. Front St., ☎ 414/271–2007), with a James Bond spy hideout decor, is a favorite with young people and out-of-towners. **La Playa** (Pfister Hotel, 424 E. Wisconsin Ave., ☎ 414/273–8222) combines a South American atmosphere with the glamour of a supper club. **Major Goolsby's** (340 W. Kilbourn Ave., ☎ 414/271–3414) is regarded as one of the country's top 10 sports bars by the jocks and occasional major-league sports stars who hang out here. Jazz fans go to **The Estate** (2423 N. Murray Ave., ☎ 414/964–9923), a cozy club offering progressive jazz four nights a week.

Milwaukee Essentials

Getting There

BY CAR

I–94 runs from Chicago into downtown Milwaukee.

BY TRAIN

Amtrak (☎ 800/872–7245) has service from Chicago to Milwaukee. The round-trip fare starts at $38; the ride takes 1½ hours.

BY BUS

Greyhound (☎ 800/231–2222) service connects the two cities. The round-trip fare is $22; the ride takes two hours.

Getting Around

Lake Michigan is the city's eastern boundary; Wisconsin Avenue is the main east–west thoroughfare. The Milwaukee River divides the downtown area into east and west sections. The East–West Expressway (I–94/I–794) is the dividing line between north and south. Streets are numbered in ascending order from the Milwaukee River west well into the suburbs. Many downtown attractions are near the Milwaukee River and can be reached on foot. **Milwaukee County Transit System** (☎ 414/344–6711) provides bus service. **Taxis** can be ordered by phone or at taxi stands; the fare is $1.75 plus $1.50 for each mile. The largest firm is **Yellow Cab** (☎ 414/271–1800).

Visitor Information

Greater Milwaukee: Convention & Visitors Bureau (510 W. Kilbourn Ave., 53203, ☎ 414/273–7222 or 800/231–0903).

9 Portraits of Chicago

CHICAGO

JANUS, THE TWO-FACED god, has both blessed and cursed the city-state Chicago. Though his graven image is not visible to the naked eye, his ambiguous spirit soars atop Sears, Big Stan, and Big John. (Our city is street-wise and alley-hip of the casually familiar. Thus the Standard Oil Building and the John Hancock are, with tavern gaminess, referred to as Big Stan and Big John. Sears is simply that; never mind Roebuck. Ours is a one-syllable town. Its character has been molded by the muscle rather than the word.)

Our double-vision, double-standard, double-value, and double-cross have been patent ever since—at least, ever since the earliest of our city fathers took the Pottawattomies for all they had. Poetically, these dispossessed natives dubbed this piece of turf *Chikagou*. Some say it is Indian lingo for "City of the Wild Onion"; some say it really means "City of the Big Smell." "Big" is certainly the operative word around these parts.

Nelson Algren's classic *Chicago: City on the Make* is the late poet's single-hearted vision of his town's doubleness. "Chicago . . . forever keeps two faces, one for winners and one for losers; one for hustlers and one for squares . . . One face for Go-Getters and one for Go-Get-It-Yourselfers. One for poets and one for promoters. . . . One for early risers, one for evening hiders."

It is the city of Jane Addams, settlement worker, and Al Capone, entrepreneur; of Clarence Darrow, lawyer, and Julius Hoffman, judge; of Louis Sullivan, architect, and Sam Insull, magnate; of John Altgeld, governor, and Paddy Bauler, alderman. (Paddy's the one who some years ago observed, "Chicago ain't ready for reform." It is echoed in our day by another, less paunchy alderman, Fast Eddie.)

Now, with a new kind of mayor, whose blackness is but one variant of the Chicago norm, and a machine—which like the old gray mare ain't what it used to be—creaking its expected way, all bets are off. Race,

though the dominant theme, is but one factor.

It is still the arena of those who dream of the City of Man and those who envision a City of Things. The battle appears to be forever joined. The armies, ignorant and enlightened, clash by day as well as night. Chicago is America's dream, writ large. And flamboyantly.

It has—as they used to whisper of the town's fast women—a reputation.

Elsewhere in the world, anywhere, name the city, name the country, Chicago evokes one image above all others. Sure, architects and those interested in such matters mention Louis Sullivan, Frank Lloyd Wright, and Mies van der Rohe. Hardly anyone in his right mind questions this city as the architectural Athens. Others, literary critics among them, mention Dreiser, Norris, Lardner, Algren, Farrell, Bellow, and the other Wright, Richard. Sure, Mencken did say something to the effect that there is no American literature worth mentioning that didn't come out of the palatinate that is Chicago. Of course, a special kind of jazz and a blues, acoustic rural and electrified urban, have been called Chicago style. All this is indubitably true.

Still others, for whom history has stood still since the Democratic convention of 1968, murmur: Mayor Daley. (As our most perceptive chronicler, Mike Royko, has pointed out, the name has become the eponym for city chieftain; thus, it is often one word, "Maredaley.") The tone, in distant quarters as well as here, is usually one of awe; you may interpret it any way you please.

An English Midlander, bearing a remarkable resemblance to Nigel Bruce, encounters me under London's Marble Arch: "Your mayor is my kind of chap. He should have bashed the heads of those young ruffians, though he did rather well, I thought." I tell him that Richard J. Daley died several years ago and that our incumbent mayor is black. He finds this news somewhat startling.

"Really?" He recovers quickly: "Nonetheless, I do like your city. I was there some 30-odd years ago. Black, is he?"

Yeah, I tell him, much of the city is.

He is somewhat Spenglerian as he reflects on the decline of Western values. "Thank heavens, I'll not be around when they take over, eh?"

I nod. I'm easy to get along with. "You sound like Saul Bellow," I say.

"Who?"

"Our Nobel laureate. Do you realize that our University of Chicago has produced more Nobel Prize winners than any other in the world?"

"Really?"

"Yeah."

He returns to what appears to be his favorite subject: gumption. "Your mayor had it. I'm delighted to say that our lady prime minister has it, too."

I am suddenly weary. Too much Bells Reserve, I'm afraid. "So long, sir. I'll see you in Chicago."

"Not likely; not bloody likely."

In Munich, a student of the sixties, now somewhat portly and balding, ventures an opinion. Not that I asked him. Chicago does that to strangers as well as natives.

"Your Mayor Daley vas bwutal to those young pwotesters, vasn't he?"

Again I nod. Vat could I say?

But it isn't Daley whose name is the Chicago hallmark. Nor Darrow. Nor Wright. Nor is it either of the Janes, Addams or Byrne. It's Al Capone, of course.

I N A BRESCIAN TRATTORIA, to Italy's north, a wisp of an old woman, black shawl and all, hears where I'm from. Though she has some difficulty with English (far less than I have with Italian), she thrusts both hands forward, index fingers pointed at me: *Boom, boom,* she goes. I hold up my hands. We both laugh. It appears that Jimmy Cagney, Edward G. Robinson, and Warner Brothers have done a real job in image making.

Not that Al and his colleagues didn't have palmy days during what, to others, were parlous times. Roaring '20s or Terrible '30s, the goose always hung high for the Boys. I once asked a casual acquaintance, the late Doc Graham, for a résumé. Doc was, as he modestly put it, a dedicated heist man. His speech was a composite of Micawber and Runyon:

"The unsophisticated either belonged to the Bugs Moran mob or the Capone mob. The fellas with talent didn't belong to either one. We robbed both."

Wasn't that a bit on the risky side?

"Indeed. There ain't hardly a one of us survived the Biblical threescore and ten. You see this fellow liquidated, that fellow—shall we say, disposed of? Red McLaughlin was the toughest guy in Chicago. But when you seen Red run out of the drainage canal, you realized Red's *modus operandi* was unavailing. His associates was Clifford and Adams. They were set in Al's doorway in his hotel in Cicero. That was unavailing."

Was it a baseball bat Al used?

"You are doubtless referring to Anselmi and Scalisi. They offended Al. This was rare. Al Capone usually sublet the matter. Since I'm Irish, I had a working affiliate with Bugs Moran. Did you know that Red and his partners once stole the Checker Cab Company? They took machine guns, went up, and had an election. I assisted in that operation."

What role did the forces of law and order play?

"With a bill, you wasn't bothered. If you had a speaking acquaintance with Mayor Thompson, you could do no wrong. Al spoke loud to him." . . .

Chicago is not the most corrupt of cities. The state of New Jersey has a couple. Need we mention Nevada? Chicago, though, is the Big Daddy. Not more corrupt, just more theatrical, more colorful in its shadiness.

It's an attribute of which many of our Respectables are, I suspect, secretly proud. Something to chat about in languorous moments. Perhaps something to distract from whatever tangential business might have engaged them.

Consider Marshall Field the First. The merchant prince. In 1886, the fight for the eight-hour day had begun, here in Chicago. Anarchists, largely German immigrants, were in the middle of it for one reason or another.

There was a mass meeting; a bomb was thrown; to this day, nobody knows who did it. There was a trial. The Haymarket Eight were in the dock. With hysteria pervasive—newspaper headlines wild enough to make Rupert Murdoch blush—the verdict was in. Guilty.

Before four of them were executed, there was a campaign, worldwide, for a touch of mercy. Even the judge, passionate though he was in his loathing of the defendants, was amenable. A number of Chicago's most respected industrialists felt the same way. Hold off the hooded hangman. Give 'em life, what the hell. It was Marshall Field I who saw to it that they swung. Hang the bastards. Johnny Da Pow had nothing on him when it came to power.

Lucy Parsons, the youngest widow of the most celebrated of the hangees, Albert—an ex-soldier of the Confederacy—lived to be an old, old woman. When she died in the forties and was buried at Waldheim Cemetery, my old colleague Win Stracke sang at the services. Though Parsons sang "Annie Laurie" on his way to the gallows, Win sounded off with "Joe Hill." It was a song, he said, that Lucy liked. When I shake hands with Win, I shake hands with history. That's what I call continuity.

The Janus-like aspect of Chicago appeared in the being of John Peter Altgeld. One of his first acts as governor of Illinois in 1893 was an 18,000-word message, citing chapter and verse, declaring the trial a frame-up. He pardoned the three survivors. The fourth had swallowed a dynamite cap while in the pokey.

Though it ended his political life, Altgeld did add a touch of class to our city's history. He was remembered by Vachel Lindsay as Eagle Forgotten. Some kid, majoring in something other than business administration or computer programming, might come across this poem in some anthology. Who knows? He might learn something about eagles.

Eagles are a diminished species today, here as well as elsewhere. On occasion, they are spotted in unexpected air pockets. Hawks, of course, abound, here as well as elsewhere. Some say this is their glory time. So Dow-Jones tells us. Observe the boys and girls in commodities. Ever ride the La Salle Street bus? Bright and morning faces; *Wall Street Journals* neatly folded. The New Gatsbys, Bob Tamarkin calls them. Gracelessness under pressure.

Sparrows, as always, are the most abundant of our city birds. It is never glory time for them. As always, they do the best they can. Which isn't very much. They forever peck away and, in some cockeyed fashion, survive the day. Others—well, who said life was fair? They hope, as the old spiritual goes, that His eye is on all the sparrows and that He watches over them. And you. And me . . .

O**N A HOT SUMMER** day, the lake behaves, the beach is busy, and thousands find cool delight. All within sight of places where ads are created telling you Wendy's is better than Burger King, where computers compute like crazy, and where billions of pages are Xeroxed for one purpose or another, or for no purpose at all. All within one neighborhood. It's crazy and phenomenal. No other city in the world has a neighborhood like this. Visitors, no matter how weary-of-it-all and jaded, are always overawed. You feel pretty good; and, like a spoiled débutante, you wave a limp hand and murmur: It *is* rather impressive, isn't it?...

But those damn bridges. Though I haven't searched out any statistics, I'll bet Chicago has more bridges than Paris. When up they go and all traffic stops, you lean against the railing and watch the boats: pulp paper from Canada for the *Trib* and *Sun-Times,* and ore from where?—the Mesabi iron range?—and all sorts of tugs easing all sorts of lake vessels, bearing all sorts of heavy stuff, big-shouldered stuff. You may not feel particularly chesty, yet there's a slight stirring, a feeling of Chicago's connection with elsewhere.

However—and what an infuriating however—when a lone sailboat comes through with two beautiful people sporting Acapulco or Palm Beach tans, she in a bikini and he in Calvin Klein shorts, and the two, with the casualness and vast carelessness of a Tom and Daisy Buchanan, wave at the held-up secretaries, file clerks, and me, I look around for a rock to throw, only to realize I'm not Walter Johnson, and I settle for a mumbled *sonofabitch* and I'm late for lunch. *Sonofabitch.*

There's no other city like this, I tell you.

And taxi drivers.

When, in eighth-grade geography, Miss O'Brien, her wig slightly askew, quizzed you ferociously on populations of the world's great cities, you had to, with equal ferocity, look them up in the atlas. Thanks to Third World hackies, you can save an enormous amount of time and energy.

You peek up front toward the driver and you see the name Ahmed Eqbal. Naturally, you ask him what's the population of Karachi and he tells you. With great enthusiasm. If his surname is Kim, you'll find out that Seoul is close to 7 million. If the man driving at an interesting speed is Marcus Olatunji, you might casually offer that Ibadan is bigger than Lagos, isn't it? If his name has as many syllables as a Welsh town's, you simply ask if Bangkok has changed much; has its population really experienced an exponential growth?

Of course, all shortcuts to knowledge have their shortcomings. Sometimes he'll whirl around, astonished, and in very, very precise British English ask, "How do you *know* that?" A brief cultural exchange ensues as suddenly you cry out, Watch out! We missed an articulated bus with a good one-tenth of an inch to spare. If it's a newspaper circulation truck, God help the two of us.

Chicago's traffic problem is hardly any problem at all—if you forget about storms, light rains, accidents, and road construction—when compared with other great cities. In contrast to New York's cacophony of honks and curses, ours is the song of the open road. Mexico City is not to be believed. Ever been to Paris where the driver snaps his fingers, frustrated, as you successfully hop back onto the curb? Need we mention the Angeleno freeway? . . .

SO WE'RE REMINISCING about one thing or another, Verne and I. Vernon Jarrett knocks out a *Sun-Times* column: reflections of black life in Chicago and elsewhere. I can't get that Jubilee Night, '38, out of my mind. He tells me of that same celebratory moment in Paris, Tennessee, along the IC tracks. Hallelujah and hope. We see our reflections in the mirror behind the bar and neither of us looks too hopeful. Hallelujah for what?

"The ghetto used to have something going for it," he says. "It had a beat, it had a certain rhythm and it was all hope. I don't care how rough things were. They used to say, If you can't make it in Chicago, you can't make it anywhere. You may be down today; you're gonna be back up tomorrow."

The lyric of an old blues song is rolling around in my head like a loose cannonball:

I'm troubled in mind, baby, I'm so blue,

But I won't be blue always

You know the sun, the sun gonna shine

In my back door someday.

"You had the packinghouses going, you had the steel mills going, you had secondary employment to help you 'get over.' "

Oh, there's still a Back of the Yards, all right, but where are the yards? And Steeltown. Ever visit South Chicago these days? Smokestacks with hardly an intimation of smoke. A town as silent, as dead as the Legionnaires' fortress in *Beau Geste.* Where the executioner's ax fell upon Jefferson and Johnson as upon Stasiak, Romano, and Polowski.

"Now it's a drag," says Verne. "There are thousands of people who have written off their lives. They're serving out their sentences as though there were some supreme judge who said, 'You're sentenced to life imprisonment on earth and this is your cell here.' What do you do if you've got a life sentence? You play jailhouse politics. You hustle, you sell dope, you browbeat other people, you abuse other cell mates, you turn men into weaklings, and girls you overcome.

"If I'm feeling good and want to have my morale lowered, all I have to do is drive out Madison Street on a bright, beautiful day and look at the throng of unemployed young guys in the weird dress, trying to hang on to some individuality. Can't read or write; look mean at each other. You see kids hating themselves as much as they hate others. This is one thing that's contributed to the ease with which gangs kill each other. Another nigger ain't nothin'."

Is it possible that ol' Hightower, the pubcrawling buddy of Dude and me during those Jubilee hours on a June night so long ago, has a signifying grandson among the wretched and lost on some nonsignified corner somewhere on the West Side?

FROM THE YEAR ONE we've heard Lord Acton cited: Power corrupts and absolute power corrupts absolutely. You're only half right, Your Lordship, if that. In a town like Chicago, Johnny Da Pow and a merchant prince and, in our day, a Croation Sammy Glick run much of the turf because of another kind of corruption: the one Verne Jarrett observed. Powerlessness corrupts and absolute powerlessness corrupts absolutely. You see, Lord A knew nothing of Cabrini-Green. Or—*memento mori*—47th and South Parkway, with exquisite irony renamed Martin Luther King, Jr., Drive. Mine eyes haven't seen much glory lately.

However—there's always a however in the city Janus watches over . . .

Somethin's happenin' out there not covered by the six-o'clock news or a Murdoch headline. There is a percolating and bubbling in certain neighborhoods that may presage unexpected somethings for the up-againsters. A strange something called self-esteem, springing from an even stranger something called sense of community.

Ask Nancy Jefferson. It happened at the Midwest Community Council on the West Side. She's director of this grassroots organization. "This morning I had a young man. He had taken some money from us. I didn't think I'd see him again. I spread the warning: 'Watch out; he's a bad egg.'

Today, out of the clear blue sky, he walked into my office. He says, 'I want to pay back my debt at 50 dollars a month. I've gotten a job. I didn't want to see you until I got a job.' I didn't know what made him come back. Was it the spirit of the community?"

In South Chicago, a bit to the southeast, Fast Eddie is finding out about UNO. That's the United Neighborhood Organization. While the alderman was busy giving Harold a hard time, his Hispanic constituents in the Tenth Ward were busy giving Waste Management, Inc., a hard time. The multinational toxic dumper was about to dump some of the vile stuff in the neighborhood. Hold off, big boy, said Mary Ellen Montez, a 26-year-old housewife. So far, she and her neighbors are doing a far better job than Horatio ever did at the bridge.

UNO's grassroots power is being felt in Pilsen, too, where rehabs are springing up without the dubious touch of gentrification. The community folk are there because they're there and that's where they intend to stay. No shoving out in these parts. And no yuppies need apply.

Farther west, the South Austin Community Council, when not challenging joblessness and street crime, has sent housewives and suddenly redundant steelworkers to Springfield as well as to City Hall to lobby for the Affordable Budget, so that gas and electric bills don't destroy those whom God has only slightly blessed with means. They're not waiting for the hacks to fight for it; they're do-it-yourselfers.

Talk about fighting redundancy, the Metro Seniors are among the most militant. Never mind the wheelchairs, crutches, tea, and sympathy. They bang away everywhere, with or without canes and walkers: Keep your grubby hands off Medicare and Social Security. Ever hear of the time they marched into official sanctums with a cake: Cut the cake but not the COLA (cost-of-living adjustment)? The hacks ate that cake more slowly and thoughtfully than ever. There are 7,500 such scrappers in town, the youngest 65. They may not have heard "Me and Bobby McGee," but they sure know the lyric: "Freedom's just another word for nothin' left to lose."

All sorts of new people from Central America and Southeast Asia, together with the more settled have-nots, are at it in Uptown with ONE (Organization of the North East). Tenants' rights, lousy housing, ethnic identity—name it; if it's an elementary right, they're battling for it.

And let's not forget all those nimble neighborhood organizers coming out of Heather Booth's Midwest Academy. Their style is '60s hipness, Saul Alinsky's Actions (political jujitsu, he called it), and eighties hard-earned awareness. They're all over town, astirring.

This is house-to-house, block-by-block, pavement-pounding, church-meeting, all-kinds-of-discussion stuff that may, as we wake up some great gettin'-up morning, reveal a new kind of Chicago. Nick Von Hoffman, who for a time was Alinsky's right arm, said it: "You who thought of yourself, up to that moment, as simply being a number, suddenly spring to life. You have that intoxicating feeling that you can make your own history, that you really count."

Call it a backyard revolution if you want to. It will sure as hell confute the Johnny Da Pows of our day, the merchant princes and the Fast Eddies. And, incidentally, lay the ghost of Lord Acton: less powerlessness that corrupts and more power than may ennoble.

Perhaps mine eyes may yet see the glory.

— Studs Terkel

A writer, a broadcaster, and of late a film actor, Studs Terkel has become virtually synonymous with Chicago. His most recent book is Race: How Blacks & Whites Think & Feel about the American Obsession.

This essay is drawn from Studs Terkel's *Chicago*, which was originally published in 1986, when the late Harold Washington was mayor of Chicago.

NEIGHBORHOODS OF THE SOUTHWEST SIDE

CHICAGO IS PROUD of its ethnic neighborhoods. The "City of the Big Shoulders" is also the city of the blues and the polka, the jig and the tarantella. Tacos, kielbasa, Irish meat pies, and soul food are the sustenance of Chicago beyond the Loop and the highrise towers of the lakefront. On Chicago streets newspapers in Polish, Lithuanian, Arabic, Spanish, German, and Greek are sold alongside the better-known English-language dailies, and a black newspaper, the *Chicago Defender,* makes its voice heard throughout the city. Many of the churches whose spires dot the cityscape can trace their origins to the arrival in Chicago of a particular national group. Schools, hospitals, museums, monuments, even street names (Emerald Avenue, King Drive, Lituanica Street, Pulaski Road) speak to the influence of ethnic groups on the city's history and political life.

As the city grew along with the Industrial Revolution of the 19th century, its neighborhoods became mazes of railroads, mills, factories, and packinghouses that reached across the Illinois prairie. The huge industrial complexes attracted workers from all over the United States, Europe, and Asia. Every major wave of migration that affected the United States after 1825 had a part in transforming Chicago. In recent years Arab, Vietnamese, Mexican, and Chinese immigrants have joined the descendants of the Germans, Irish, Swedes, Poles, Jews, Italians, and black Americans who made earlier journeys in search of peace and prosperity. And each group has left its mark on the city: Hispanic and Vietnamese cultural centers and museums have now joined the long-established Polish Museum on the Northwest Side, the Balzekas Museum of Lithuanian Culture on the Southwest Side, and the DuSable Museum of African American Culture on the South Side.

Chicago's communities have not always lived in harmony. Clashes between white ethnic groups have marked the history of the city, and relationships between whites and blacks exploded in a calamitous race riot in 1919. Although much has changed over the last 30 years, Chicago is still known as the nation's most segregated city. Yet its pluralism remains intact and healthy. Polish, Hmong, Greek, Arabic, and other languages mix freely with English, and summer in Chicago is a time when ethnic and community street fairs attract crowds.

The neighborhoods that lie like a fan to the southwest of the meeting of State Street and Archer Avenue have seen a succession of working-class ethnic populations. Archer Avenue, which runs roughly parallel to the South Branch of the Chicago River and the Chicago Sanitary and Ship Canal, is part of a huge transportation corridor that includes rail lines and the Stevenson Expressway (I–55). On this corridor much of the industrial history of the city took place.

Father Jacques Marquette and the explorer Louis Jolliet, who first arrived in the area in 1673, suggested the construction of a canal to connect Lake Michigan with the Illinois River. Begun in 1836, the monumental task took 12 years to complete. The Illinois–Michigan Canal gave Chicago commercial transportation to the hinterlands, and the canal and the river soon teemed with barges, docks, and factories. The activity quickly brought the railroads as well to the Archer Avenue corridor. By the turn of the century, the larger Chicago Sanitary and Ship Canal had also been constructed.

Irish workers made up a large portion of those who came to dig the Illinois–Michigan Canal, many of them having worked on the Erie Canal. The "canal" Irish tended to settle along the river in the area known originally as Hardscrabble or Lee's

---

The communities described in this essay are shown in the Chicago Neighborhoods map. A note following the essay gives directions and suggestions for visiting these neighborhoods, which are not covered in the tours of Chapter 2.

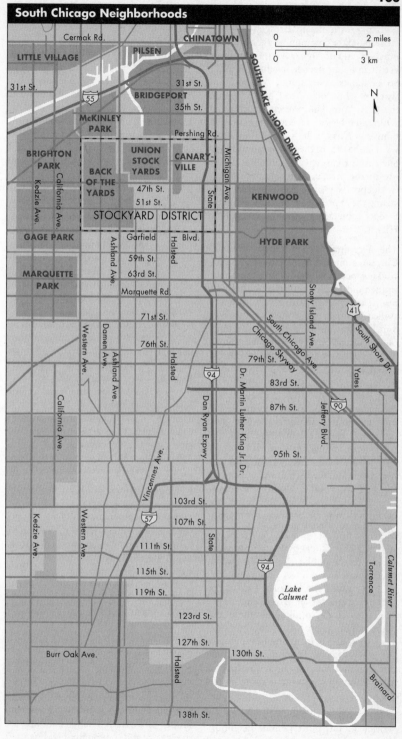

South Chicago Neighborhoods

Farm; the building of the canal brought a change in name to Bridgeport. This working-class community anchored the northern end of Archer Avenue. St. Bridget's Church at Archer Avenue and Arch Street stands as a reminder of the canal workers who flocked to Chicago before the Civil War. The present structure of 1906 resembles a cathedral built by Irish monks in Novara, Italy, in 1170; its survival in the face of the construction of the Stevenson Expressway in 1964 is a tribute to the efforts of its pastor and to Bridgeport's political clout. (Planners swung the expressway directly behind St. Bridget's and its Shrine of Our Lady of the Highway.)

The river and the canal soon attracted Chicago's most famous industry: Meatpacking plants opened along the South Branch and fouled the river with pollution. The packinghouses in turn attracted skilled German and Bohemian butchers and brought more Irish to Bridgeport. On Christmas Day, 1865, the Union Stock Yard opened west of Halsted Street, between Pershing Road (39th Street) and 47th Street, just to the south of Bridgeport. The huge livestock market became the center of the nation's meatpacking industry. In time, an immigrant city grew up around the more than 400 acres of livestock pens, chutes, and railroad yards. Bridgeport's Irish, Germans, and Bohemians found themselves surrounded by Poles, Lithuanians, Slovaks, Italians, French Canadians, black Americans, and others; this was the beginning of the ethnic mélange of the South Side.

In 1905 the Chicago stockyards were rocked by the publication of Upton Sinclair's muckraking novel *The Jungle*. Sinclair portrayed the life of a Lithuanian immigrant family that lived in Back of the Yards, just to the southwest of the stockyards and Bridgeport. The Chicago stockyards soon had an international reputation for unwholesome practices, and it was not the last time the area was looked upon unfavorably in literature or in the press.

In fact, the area contains four of the most written about, most famous neighborhoods in the history of urban America. Bridgeport, McKinley Park, Back of the Yards, and Canaryville surround the old Union Stock Yard. Bridgeport, the oldest settlement, predates the founding of the stockyards; much of its fame rests on its working-class ethnicity and its peculiar brand of politics. Richard J. Daley, its best-known political son, was only one of four Chicago mayors born and raised in Bridgeport, who together ran the city from the death of Anton Cermak in 1933 until the election of Jane Byrne in 1979. For many people, the name Bridgeport still means politics, especially Irish machine politics.

BRIDGEPORT today has more than a dozen resident ethnic groups, some of them the overflow from neighboring communities. Pilsen, to the north, across the Chicago River, was once the center of Chicago's lumber industry; by 1900 it had become the largest Bohemian community outside Chicago; today it is the home of the city's principal concentration of Mexicans. Chinatown, to the northeast, its heart at the intersection of Cermak Road and Wentworth Avenue, was once occupied by Germans and Irish; Italians followed them before the Chinese arrived after 1900. The Chinatown community today is a growing and prosperous one, with a good deal of cohesion, and new immigrants have helped to solidify the Asian presence in the inner city.

Canaryville, to the south of Bridgeport, between Pershing Road and 49th Street, Halsted and the old New York Central Railroad yards, is a largely Irish-American neighborhood with many Mexicans and Appalachian whites. Here, at the corner of 45th Street and Lowe Avenue, is St. Gabriel's, perhaps the most famous church in the Stock Yard District. One of John Root's finest designs, the Romanesque structure was built in 1887–88 with financial help from the packinghouse owners who were close friends of Fr. Maurice Dorney, the founder of the parish in 1880.

The neighborhoods that once surrounded the stockyards have more than 30 Roman Catholic churches and many Protestant houses of worship. Each is a monument to the faith and community-building spirit of an ethnic group that settled in the area. Polish packinghouse workers, who came to the area in large numbers between 1880 and 1920, alone built six of the structures. Today many of the old national parishes are of mixed ethnicity; many have services in the language of their founders, as well as in English and Spanish. Worshipers entering the magnificent church of St. John of God at 52nd Street and Throop, across the street from Sherman Park, are greeted by the flags of Poland, Mexico, the United States, and the Vatican.

The Stock Yard District, once known as Town of Lake, a suburb of Chicago until it was annexed in 1889, behaved in some ways like a city in itself. As its residents moved to the south and west after World War I, out of the core neighborhoods of wooden two-flats and cottages in close proximity to the stockyards and the packinghouses, they created suburbs in the new neighborhoods of the Southwest Side, principally along Archer Avenue. These areas are part of Chicago's "bungalow belt."

DURING THE 1920S bungalows appeared throughout the Southwest, Northwest, and Southeast sides. The single-family dwellings, with their small front and back yards, were the pre-Depression equivalent of suburban sprawl. Today they comprise much of Chicago's second tier of ethnic neighborhoods: Brighton Park, Gage Park, and Marquette Park all owe their existence to the movement away from the stockyard communities of Bridgeport, McKinley Park, Back of the Yards, and Canaryville. And the movements of ethnic groups can be traced across the Southwest Side in the churches and other institutions they left behind.

The Lithuanian community, for example, organized its first church, St. George's, in 1892 in Bridgeport. (The present structure was dedicated in 1902.) A second Lithuanian parish, Providence of God, was founded in 1900, north of St. George's in the Pilsen community. Three more Lithuanian parishes opened in 1904, including Holy Cross in Back of the Yards. Ten years later the Lithuanian community was supporting 10 Roman Catholic parishes, a consequence of the large East European

emigration to America that took place before 1914. These arrivals became part of Chicago's first tier of ethnic neighborhoods.

As Lithuanians settled into better jobs following World War I, many of them decided to move away from the old industrial districts, and they looked to the bungalow belt for newer, more spacious housing. In the 1920s the Marquette Park area near the intersection of Marquette Road and California Avenue attracted Lithuanian Americans. A Lithuanian order of religious sisters had laid the foundation for the community in 1911 by opening the Academy of St. Casimir (later Maria High School). In 1928 ground was broken for a Lithuanian parish, Nativity B.V.M., at 68th Street and Washtenaw, and the parish quickly became a central institution in the Lithuanian community. In the same year the Sisters of St. Casimir opened Holy Cross Hospital near the church and the high school.

The large institutional base drew more Lithuanians to the neighborhood throughout the interwar period. After World War II, another major emigration from Eastern Europe rejuvenated the Lithuanian community, and Marquette Park became its new center. The present Nativity Church, designed by John Mulokas and dedicated on May 12, 1957, is a striking example of Lithuanian architecture. Its dedication to Our Lady of Siluva celebrates the site of a famous Shrine to the Blessed Virgin in Lithuania.

The movement of Lithuanians away from the inner city has been typical of that of ethnic groups that originally settled in the area. By 1988 many of the Marquette Park Lithuanians were relocating in the southwest suburbs near Lemont. Yet the neighborhood they left behind continues to nourish the community; many people and cultural institutions choose to stay in Chicago, and Marquette Park remains the Lithuanian "gold coast."

The Union Stock Yard closed its gates on August 1, 1971, after 105 years of active livestock trading. In reality the meatpacking business had begun to leave the city nearly 20 years earlier, when Wilson and Company announced the closing of its huge Chicago plant. By the early 1960s the big packers had left the city, and

Chicago was facing its first post-industrial crisis. The area west of the Union Stock Yard, formerly the center of one of the nation's great industries, now resembled a ghost town.

Recent years have seen a partially successful attempt to redevelop some of the land the stockyards and packinghouses had occupied. A visit to the Old Stone Gate at Exchange and Peoria, which marks the entrance to the area, will show you industrial buildings mixed with open prairie and abandoned packinghouse buildings. Yet the new industries, important as they are to the city's economic base, employ only a fraction of the number of workers formerly employed by Chicago's most infamous industry. Meanwhile, new immigrants from Poland, Mexico, and elsewhere continue to come to the district in search of employment.

THE ECONOMIC FUTURE of Chicago's Southwest Side looked bleak just a few years ago. Now a resurgent Midway Airport at 55th Street and Cicero and a new rapid transit line that is scheduled to open by 1993 have infused the local economy with optimism. Bridgeport, in part because of its proximity to downtown and an excellent public transportation system that will improve when the Southwest Rapid Transit opens, is already witnessing economic rebirth. Areas a little farther down Archer Avenue should see new development as Midway Airport increases its capacity and the rapid transit line reaches them. The entire area along the canal and the river is now part of the Illinois–Michigan Canal National Heritage Corridor, and there are plans for riverfront parks and other amenities. In the shadow of great economic, cultural, and social change, Chicago's ethnic communities continue to maintain their heritage in the old and the new neighborhoods.

— *Dominic A. Pacyga*

An urban historian who teaches at Columbia College in Chicago, Dominic A. Pacyga is the coauthor of Chicago: City of Neighborhoods.

The Southwest Side is easily accessible by public or private transportation. The Archer Avenue (No. 62) bus, which can be boarded on State Street, makes its way southwest through the corridor. The Dan Ryan Rapid Transit Line will take you to Chinatown (Cermak Avenue) or to Comiskey Park (35th Street), the home of the Chicago White Sox. By automobile, you can take Archer and turn down Halsted Street (800 W), Ashland Avenue (1600 W), Western Avenue (2400 W), or another major street and follow it until you find an interesting side street or attraction to explore. If you continue west on Archer past Kedzie Avenue, stop at the Dom Podhalan or Polish Highlanders Hall at 4808 South Archer Avenue; it is as authentic a Polish mountain chalet as you are likely to see this side of the Odra River. A visit to the Balzekas Museum of Lithuanian Culture at 6500 South Pulaski Road would be worthwhile (*see* Sightseeing Checklists *in* Chapter 2, Exploring Chicago). Wonderful and inexpensive Lithuanian restaurants line 71st Street from Western to California avenues (2600 W). Some of the best Middle Eastern restaurants in Chicago are located along 63rd Street between Western and Central Park avenues (3600 W). While the Northwest Side, along Milwaukee Avenue, is famous for Polish cuisine, the South Side holds its own: Tatra Inn serves a satisfying smorgasbord at 6038 South Pulaski. **Mexican** restaurants abound in Back of the Yards near the intersection of Ashland Avenue and 47th Street and in Pilsen along 18th Street and on Blue Island Avenue. Mi Pueblo, at 2908 West 59th Street, resembles a Mexican hacienda. The Southwest Side Italian community is well represented with restaurants along Oakley Avenue (2300 W), Western just north of 26th Street, and on 63rd Street, where Palermo's at 3715 West 63rd Street and Little Joe's at 63rd Street and Richmond are noteworthy. Many of the churches hereabouts have beautiful interiors, and Sunday is the best time to visit them, when services are scheduled. At other times of the week, you may find the church you want to see closed unless you call in advance of your visit.

THE BUILDERS OF CHICAGO

WHEN MRS. O'LEARY'S cow kicked over the lantern and started the Great Chicago Fire of 1871, she set the scene for the birth of a Modern Architecture that would influence the entire globe. If Chicago today is a world capital of modern architecture landmarks—a city whose buildings embody contemporary architectural history from its beginnings in the 1880s—it is thanks to this cataclysmic fire and a unique set of cultural circumstances that were fueled by the new wealth of the thriving port city. In 1871 Chicago was isolated from European and East Coast opinion. At the same time, it was not uncivilized frontier, nor had it been traumatized by the Civil War. And it was strongly conscious of being the metropolis of the American heartland. Yet it had absolutely no existing architectural tradition; physically and aesthetically, it was wide open.

Because Chicago had been built mainly of wood, it was wiped out by the fire. Virtually the only building left standing downtown, where it still dominates the intersection of North Michigan and Chicago avenues, was the bizarre yellow stone Water Tower of 1869. Oscar Wilde, that infamous aesthete, called it a "monstrosity" when he visited Chicago in 1882. Today, with its fake battlements, crenellations, and turrets, it looks like a transplant from Disneyland rather than a real part of a vibrant and serious city. It serves now as a tourist information center, and even amid the amazingly varied architecture of central Chicago it appears to be an anachronism.

In the years following the fire, many remarkable people flocked to the building opportunity in the city that sprawled for miles along the western shore of Lake Michigan and inland along the branches of the Chicago River. A brilliant engineer named William LeBaron Jenney and a young Bostonian trained at MIT and Paris named Louis Sullivan, who would become a great architect, philosopher, writer, and teacher, were joined by a group of ingenious architects and engineers from diverse parts of America and Europe: Dankmar Adler (from Denmark), William Holabird (from New York), John Wellborn Root, Frank Lloyd Wright (from Wisconsin), Henry Hobson Richardson (from Louisiana via Boston and Paris), Daniel H. Burnham, and Martin Roche, among others. During the 1880s and 1890s in Chicago, these men did nothing less than create the foundations of modern architecture and construction.

The skyscraper was born here. The "curtain-wall," a largely glass exterior surface that does not act as a "wall" supporting the building but is supported on the floors from within, originated here. Modern metal-frame, multistory construction was created here. The Chicago Window—a popular window design used in buildings all over America (until air-conditioning made it obsolete), consisting of a large fixed glass panel in the center, with a narrow operable sash on each side—was developed here. Chicago builders also discovered how to fireproof the metal structures that supported their buildings, which would otherwise melt in fires and bring total collapse: They covered the iron columns and beams with terra-cotta tiles that insulated the structural metal from heat.

Philosophically, the Chicago architects believed they were creating a democratic architecture to express the soul of American civilization, an architecture pragmatic, honest, healthy, and unashamed of wealth and commerce. Louis Sullivan, a philosopher, a romantic, and a prolific writer (his most famous book on architecture, *Kindergarten Chats,* is a Socratic dialogue), originated and propagated the ideas that "form follows function" and "a building is an act." For Sullivan, social purpose and structure had to be integrated to create an architecture of human satisfaction.

Technologically, the Chicago School, as they became known, were aware of the latest developments in European iron structures, such as the great railroad stations. Jenney had his engineering degree from Paris in 1856—he was older than the others, many of whom worked for him—yet he, Richardson, and John Root were the only conventionally well-educated men of the group. At the same time, they had in Chicago a daring and innovative local engineering tradition. Jenney, a strict rationalist, incarnated this no-nonsense tradition and gave romantics like Sullivan and, later on, Sullivan's disciple Wright, the tools with which to express their architectural philosophy.

The term *Chicago School of Architecture* refers to the work of these men, whose offices served as their true school: Jenney and Mundie, Root and Burgee, Adler and Sullivan, Holabird and Roche, Burnham and Root, H.H. Richardson, and Frank Lloyd Wright. In many instances it requires a scholarly effort to figure out precisely who did what, as they worked for and with one another, living in each other's pockets, shifting partnerships, arguing the meaning of what they did as well as how best to do it. Jenney and Adler were essentially engineers uninterested in decoration; with the exception of Richardson's Romanesque motifs, Sullivan's amazing ornament, and Wright's spatial and ornamental forms, these builders did not have distinct, easily discernible "styles." It becomes an academic exercise to try to identify their individual efforts.

THE CHICAGO SCHOOL'S greatest clients were wealthy businessmen and their wives. The same lack of inhibition that led Mrs. Potter Palmer and Mrs. Havemeyer to snap up Impressionist paintings that had been rejected by French academic opinion (and today are the core of the Art Institute collection) led sausage magnates to hire young, inventive, local talent to build their mansions and countinghouses. Chicagoans may have been naive, but history has vindicated their taste.

Although they started building in the 1870s, nothing of note remains from before 1885. The oldest important structure is H.H. Richardson's massive granite Italian Romanesque–inspired Glessner House, with its decorative interiors derived from the innovative English Arts and Crafts

movement. The only Richardson building left in Chicago, the Glessner House is considered by some his highest creation; Wright was influenced by its flowing interior space. At the corner of 18th Street and the Prairie Avenue Historic District, it now houses the offices of the Chicago Architecture Foundation.

Downtown, Richardson designed a Wholesale Building for Marshall Field that was later demolished. An addition to the Field store in the same architectural vocabulary, done by Burnham in 1893 and now part of the Marshall Field block, stands at the corner of Wabash and Washington streets. Burnham completed the block in 1902–1907, but in the airy, open, metal-frame, Chicago Window style.

In 1883 William LeBaron Jenney invented the first "skyscraper construction" building, in which a metal structural skeleton supports an exterior wall on metal shelves. (The metal frame or skeleton, a sort of three-dimensional boxlike grid, is still used today.) His earliest surviving metal-skeleton structure, the Second Leiter Building of 1891, is now Sears, Roebuck and Company, at the southeast corner of State and Van Buren streets in the Loop. The granite-face facade is extremely light and open, suggesting the metal frame behind. The building looks so modern that it comes as a shock to realize it is nearly a century old.

At 209 South La Salle Street, the Rookery Building of 1886, a highly decorated, structurally transitional building by Burnham and Root, employs masonry bearing walls (brick, terra-cotta, and stone) on the two major street facades and lots of iron structure (both cast-iron columns and wrought-iron beams) elsewhere. Here the decoration emphasizes the structural elements—pointing out, for example, the floor lines. Note also how specially shaped bricks are used at the edges of the window openings and to make pilasters. The plan, a freestanding square "donut," was unusual at the time. A magnificent iron and glass skylight covers the lower two stories of the interior courtyard, which was renovated in 1905 by Frank Lloyd Wright, who designed light fixtures and other decorative additions.

The nearby Marquette Building of 1894 at 140 South Dearborn Street, by Holabird and Roche, is almost a prototype for the modern office building, with its skeleton metal frame covered by decorative terra-cotta and its open, cellular facade with Chicago Windows. The marble lobby rotunda has Tiffany mosaic portraits of Indian chieftains and Père Marquette, a hymn to local history.

The most advanced structure from this period, one in which the exterior wall surface is freed of all performance of support, is Burnham's Reliance Building of 1895 at 36 North State Street. Here the proportion of glass to solid is very high, and the solid members are immensely slender for the era. Today the white terra-cotta cladding needs cleaning, and the building's seedy condition mars its beauty; the casual observer would be surprised to learn that most critics consider it the masterpiece of the Chicago School's office buildings.

TO APPRECIATE FULLY the giant leap taken by the architects of the Reliance, look at Burnham and Root's Monadnock Building of 1889–1892, at 53 West Jackson Boulevard. Its 16 stories are supported by conventional load-bearing walls, which grow to 6 feet thick at the base! While elegant in its stark simplicity (the result of a cheap-minded entrepreneur who had all the decoration removed from the plans while Root was traveling), its ponderousness contrasts sharply with the delicate structure and appearance of the Reliance Building. The Monadnock Building may have been the swan song of conventional building structure in Chicago, yet its verticality expressed the aspirations of the city.

Jenney's Manhattan Building of 1890, at 431 South Dearborn Street, with its variously shaped bay windows, was the first tall building (16 stories) to use metal-skeleton structure throughout; it is admired more for its structure than for its appearance. Both it and the equally tall Monadnock would never have come into being without Elisha Otis's elevator invention, which was already in use in New York City in buildings of 9 or 10 stories at most.

The impetus toward verticality was an essential feature of Chicago commercial architecture. Verticality seemed to embody commercial possibility, as in "the sky's the limit!" Even the essential horizontality of the 12-story, block-long Carson Pirie Scott store is offset by the rounded corner tower at the main entrance.

The Chicago School created new decorative forms to apply to their powerful structures, and they derived them largely from American vegetation rather than from classical motifs. The apogee of this lush ornament was probably reached by Sullivan in his Carson Pirie Scott and Company store of 1899–1904 at State and Madison streets. The cast-iron swirls of rich vegetation and geometry surround the ground-floor show windows and the entrance, and they grow to the second story as well, with the architect's initials, LHS, worked into the design. (A decorative cornice that was originally at the top was removed.) The facade of the intermediate floors is extremely simple, with wide Chicago Windows surrounded by a thin line of delicate ornament; narrow vertical and horizontal bands, all of white terra-cotta, cover the iron structure behind.

Terra-cotta plaques of complex and original decoration cover the horizontal spandrel beams (the beams that cover the outer edges of the floors, between the vertical columns of the facades) of many buildings of this era, including the Reliance and the Marquette. Even modest residential and commercial structures in Chicago began to use decorative terra-cotta, which became a typical local construction motif through the 1930s.

Adler and Sullivan's Auditorium Building of 1887–89 was a daring megastructure sheathed in massive granite, the same material Richardson used, and its style derives from his Romanesque forms. Here the shades of stone color and the rough and polished finishes provide contrasts. Built for profit as a civic center at South Michigan Avenue and Congress Street, facing Lake Michigan, the Auditorium Building incorporated a theater, a hotel, and an office building; complex engineering solutions allowed it to carry heavy and widely varying loads. Adler, the engineer, devised a hydraulic stage lift and an early air-conditioning system for the magnificent theater. Sullivan freely decorated the interiors with his distinctive flowing ornamental shapes.

In the spirit of democracy and populism, Adler wanted the Auditorium to be a "people's theater," one with lots of cheap seats and few boxes. It is still in use today as the Auditorium Theater, Adler's belief in the common man having been upheld when thousands of ordinary Chicagoans subscribed to the restoration fund in 1968. The rest of the building is now Roosevelt University.

FRANK LLOYD WRIGHT, who had worked for a year on the Auditorium Building in Adler and Sullivan's office, remained in their employ and in 1892 designed a house for them in a wealthy area of the Near North Side of town. The Charnley House, 1365 North Astor Street, built of long, thin, yellowish Roman brick and stone, has a projecting central balcony and shows a glimmer of Wright's extraordinary later freedom with volumes and spaces. The Charnley House, with its exquisite interior woodwork and the exterior frieze under the roof, has now been completely restored. Soon after the Charnley House project, Wright left Adler and Sullivan to work on his own.

Wright's ability to break apart and recompose space and volume, even asymmetrically, was given full range in the many houses he built in and around Chicago. What became typical of American domestic "open plan" interiors (as opposed to an arrangement of closed, boxlike rooms) derived from Wright's creation, but they could never have been practical without the American development of central heating, which eliminated the need for a fire in each room.

Wright was the founder of what became known as the Prairie School, whose work consisted largely of residences rather than buildings intended for commerce. Its principal characteristic was a horizontality evocative of the breadth of the prairies that contrasted with the lofty vertical shafts of the business towers. Like his teacher Sullivan, Wright also delighted in original decorative motifs of geometric and vegetable design.

The opening of the Lake Street El railway west to the new suburb of Oak Park gave Wright an enormous opportunity to build. In 1889 he went to live there at 951 Chicago Avenue, where he created a studio and a home over the next 22 years. Dozens of houses in Oak Park, of wood, stucco, brick, and stone, with beautiful leaded- and stained-glass windows and carved woodwork, were designed or renovated by him. He was almost obsessional in his involvement with his houses, wanting to design and control the placement of furniture and returning even after his clients had moved in. For Wright a house was a living thing, both in its relationship to the land and in its evolution through use.

Yet Wright's masterpiece in Oak Park is not a house but the Unitarian Unity Temple of 1906, at Kenilworth Avenue and Lake Street, a short walk from the Oak Park Avenue El stop. Because of intense budget limitations, he built it of the daring and generally abhorred material, poured concrete, and with only the simplest details of applied wood stripping. Nevertheless, Wright's serene creation of volume and light endures to this day. It is lit by high windows from above and has operable colored-glass skylights inserted into the "coffers" of the Roman-style "egg-crate" ceiling, intended for ventilation as well as light. The design of the windows and skylights echoes the designs applied to the walls, the door grilles, the hinges, the light fixtures; everything is integrated visually, no detail having been too small to consider.

Unity Temple was built on what became known as an H plan, which consisted of two functionally separate blocks connected by an entry hall. The Unity Temple plan has influenced the planning of public buildings to the present day. Recently restored to its original interior greens and ochers, Unity Temple is definitely worth a pilgrimage.

On the South Side of Chicago is the most famous of all Wright's houses, the Robie House of 1909, now on the University of Chicago campus, at 5757 South Woodlawn Avenue. Its great horizontal overhanging rooflines are echoed by the long limestone sills that cap its low brick walls. Wright designed everything for the house, including the furniture. Wright's stock has soared of late: A single lamp from the Robie House sold at auction recently for three-quarters of a million dollars!

The World's Columbian Exposition of 1893 was held at Midway Park in South Chicago. For complex political reasons, the planning was turned over mainly to eastern architects, who brought the influence of the international Beaux-Arts style to Chicago. A furious Louis Sullivan prophesied that "the damage wrought to this country by the Chicago World's Fair will last half a century." He wasn't entirely wrong in his prediction; the classicist style vied sharply over the next decades with the native creations of the Chicago and Prairie schools, all the while incorporating their technical advances. But the city fathers succumbed to the "culture versus commerce" point of view; thus most of the museums and public buildings constructed before World War II in Chicago were built in classical Greek or Renaissance styles.

MANY OF THESE public buildings are fine works in their own right, but they do not contribute to the development of 20th-century architecture. The most notable of them, the Public Library of 1897, at 78 East Washington Street, by Shepley, Rutan and Coolidge, has gorgeous interiors of white and green marble and glass.

Many of Chicago's museums are situated in Grant Park and along Lake Shore Drive, magnificent points from which to view the city skyline. The park and the drive were built on landfill in the 1910s and 1920s after the tracks of the Illinois Central Railroad along the old lakefront had been bridged over. Lake Shore Drive, with its parks and beaches, seems such an integral part of today's city that it is hard to imagine a Chicago without it. Daniel Burnham called for this development in his "Chicago Plan" of 1909.

In 1922 an important international competition offered a prize of $100,000 for the design of a Tribune Building that would dominate the Chicago River just north of the Loop. Numerous modernist plans were submitted, including one by Walter Gropius, of the Bauhaus. Raymond Hood's Gothic design—some called it Woolworth Gothic—was chosen. The graceful and picturesque silhouette of the Tribune Tower was for many years the symbol of Chicago, not to be overshadowed until general construction resumed, following World War II. More important, the Tribune Building moved the center of gravity of downtown Chicago north and east, causing the Michigan Avenue bridge to be built and opening the Near North Side to commercial development along Michigan Avenue.

The postwar Chicago School was dominated by a single personality who influenced modern architecture around the world: Ludwig Mies van der Rohe. The son of a stonemason, Mies was director of the Bauhaus in Dessau, Germany, the world's leading modern design center, from 1930 until Nazi pressure made him leave in 1937. On a trip to the United States he met John Holabird, son of William, who invited him to head the School of Architecture at the Armour Institute, later the Illinois Institute of Technology. Mies accepted—and redesigned the entire campus as part of the deal. Over the next 20 years he created a School of Architecture that disseminated his thinking into architecture offices everywhere.

Whatever Mies owed to Frank Lloyd Wright, such as Mies's own open-plan houses, his philosophy was very much in the tradition of Chicago, and the roots of Bauhaus architecture can be traced to the Chicago School. Mies's attitudes were profoundly pragmatic, based on solid building techniques, technology, and an appreciation of the nature of the materials used. He created a philosophy, a set of ethical values based on a purist approach; his great aphorisms were "Less is more" and "God is in the details." He eschewed applied ornament, however, and in that sense he was nothing like Wright. All Mies's "decoration" is generated by fine-tuned structural detail. His buildings are sober, sometimes somber, highly orderly, and serene; their aesthetic is based on the almost religious expression of structure.

The campus of IIT was built in 1942–58 along South State Street, between 31st and 35th streets. Mies used few materials in the two dozen buildings he planned here: light cream color brick, black steel, and glass. Quadrangles are only suggested; space is never rigidly defined. There is a direct line of descent from Crown Hall (1956), made of black steel and clear glass, with its long-span roof trusses exposed above the level of the roof, to the great convention center of 1970 on South Lake Shore Drive at 23rd Street, Mc-Cormick Center by C.F. Murphy, with its great exposed black steel space-frame roof and its glass walls.

AGE REQUIREMENTS forced Mies to retire from IIT in 1958, but his office went on to do major projects in downtown Chicago, along Lake Shore Drive, and elsewhere. He had impressed the world in 1952 with his black steel and clear glass twin apartment towers, set at right angles to one another, almost kissing at the corner, at 860–880 North Lake Shore Drive. Later he added another, darker pair just to the north, 900–910.

In 1968 Heinrich and Schipporeit, inspired by "860" and by Mies's Berlin drawings of 1921 for a free-form glass skyscraper, built Lake Point Tower. This dark bronze metal and glass trefoil shaft, near the Navy Pier at East Grand Avenue, is a graceful and dramatic joy of the Chicago skyline. It is one of the few Chicago buildings, along with Bertram Goldberg's Marina City of 1964—twin round concrete towers on the river between State and Dearborn streets—to break with strict rectilinear geometry.

Downtown, Mies's Federal Center is a group of black buildings around a plaza, set off by a bright red steel Alexander Calder stabile sculpture, on Dearborn Street between Jackson Boulevard and Adams Street. The Dirksen Building, with its courthouse, on the east side of Dearborn, was built in 1964; the Kluczynski office building at the south side of the plaza and the single-story Post Office to the west were added through 1975. The north side of the large Federal Plaza is enclosed by the Marquette Building of 1894,

thereby integrating the past with the present.

The IBM Building of 1971, the last office building designed by Mies, is a dark presence north of the river, between Wabash and State streets.

Perhaps the most important spinoff of Miesian thinking was the young firm of Skidmore, Owings & Merrill, which bloomed after the war. Their gem of the postwar period was the Inland Steel Building of 1957, at 30 West Monroe Street, in the Loop. The bright stainless-steel and pale green glass structure, only 18 stories high, with exposed columns on the long facade and a clear span in the short dimension, has uninterrupted interior floor space. It is considered a classic.

SOM became the largest architecture firm in America, with offices in all major cities. In Chicago the firm built, among other works, the immensely tall, tapering brown Hancock Tower of 1965–70, with its innovative exterior crisscross wind-bracing, and the even taller Sears Tower (1970–75), with two of its nine shafts reaching to 1,450 feet, now the tallest structure in the world. SOM may have achieved the epitome of the vertical commercial thrust of the Chicago School.

Meanwhile, Mies's Federal Plaza started a Chicago tradition, that of the outdoor plaza with a focus on monumental art. These plazas are real, usable, and used; they are large-scale city gathering places, not the mingy setbacks of New York office megaliths, and they shape the architectural and spatial character of downtown Chicago.

A string of plazas, featuring sculptures by Picasso and Dubuffet and mosaic murals by Chagall, leads one up Dearborn and Clark streets, to the Chicago River. At the river one finds more outdoor space. The south bank quays, one level down from the street, are a series of imaginatively landscaped gardens. Here one can contemplate the ever-changing light on the river and the 19th-century riveted-iron drawbridges, which prefigure Calder's work. Other monumental outdoor sculpture downtown includes Joan Miró's *Chicago* and Claes Oldenburg's *Batcolumn.*

The Jean Dubuffet sculpture stands before the State of Illinois Building of 1985 at the corner of Randolph and Clark streets. Here there are really two plazas: one outdoors, the other inside the stepped-back, mirrored-glass and pink-paneled irregular donut of a building. This wild fantasy is the work of Helmut Jahn, a German who came to Chicago in the 1960s to study at IIT. His colorful, lighthearted, mirrored Chicago buildings provide a definite counterpoint to the somber Mies buildings of the 1950s and 1960s, and they appear everywhere, influencing the design and choice of materials of the architecture of the 1980s.

Jahn's first important contribution to the Chicago scene was a sensitive addition to the Board of Trade in 1980. The Board of Trade was housed in an architectural landmark at 141 West Jackson Boulevard, at the foot of La Salle Street, a jewel of Art Deco design by the old Chicago firm of Holabird and Root in 1930. Murphy/Jahn's glittering addition echoed numerous features of the original structure. Both parts of the building have sumptuous interior atrium spaces. Marble, nickel, and glass motifs from the earlier edifice are evoked and reinterpreted—but not copied—in the high-tech addition. Within the new atrium, framed by highly polished chromium-plated trusses and turquoise panels, hangs a large Art Deco painting that was found in the older building during renovation. This complex captures the spirit of Chicago architecture: Devoted to commerce, it embraces the present without denying the past.

Next came Jahn's sleek, curving Xerox Center of white metal and reflective glass, at Monroe and Dearborn streets (1980). Mirrored glass, introduced by Jahn, has become one of the favorite materials in new Chicago commercial buildings. It is successful as a foil to the dark Miesian buildings, especially along the river, where it seems to take on a watery quality on an overcast day. His latest accomplishment is the elegant but playful high-tech United Airlines Terminal 1 at O'Hare (1987). The terminal has been praised as a soaring technological celebration of travel, in the same splendid tradition as the 19th-century European iron and glass railroad stations that Jenney had studied.

Two disparate threads of architectural creation are weaving the modern tissue of Chicago, providing aesthetic tension and dynamism, much as in the period following the World's Columbian Exposition of 1893. The solid, muscular past provides an armature that can support diversity and even fantasy without cracking apart. Yet Chicago is a down-to-earth place whose greatest creations have been products of a no-nonsense approach. "The business of Chicago is business"; when Chicago becomes self-consciously "cultural," it fares less well.

Chicago is a city with a sense of continuity, where the traditions of design are strong. Money and technology have long provided a firm support for free and original intellectual thought, with a strong populist local bias. Chicagoans talk of having a "second city" mentality, yet at the same time they have a strong sense of self; perhaps being "second" has indeed freed them to be themselves.

— *Barbara Shortt*

A practicing architect and an architectural historian, Barbara Shortt writes frequently on architecture and travel.

MORE PORTRAITS

Chicago has been celebrated and vilified in fiction and nonfiction. For the flavor of the city a century ago, pick up Theodore Dreiser's *Sister Carrie,* the story of a country innocent who falls from grace in Chicago. Upton Sinclair's portrayal in *The Jungle* of the meatpacking industry's squalor and employee exploitation raised a public outcry.

More recently, native Chicagoan Saul Bellow has set many novels in the city, most notably in *The Adventures of Augie March.* Richard Wright's explosive *Native Son* and James T. Farrell's *Studs Lonigan* depict racial clashes in Chicago from the black and white sides, respectively. The works of longtime resident Nelson Algren—*The Man with the Golden Arm, A Walk on the Wild Side,* and *Chicago: City on the Make*—show the city at its grittiest, as does playwright David Mamet's *American Buffalo.* On a lighter note, two series of detective novels use a Chicago backdrop: Sara Paretsky's V.I. Warshawski novels and the Monsignor Ryan mysteries of Andrew Greeley. Greeley has set other novels in Chicago as well, including *Lord of the Dance.*

Chicago was once the quintessential newspaper town; the play *The Front Page,* by Ben Hecht and Charles MacArthur, is set here. Local reporters have penned some excellent chronicles, including *Fabulous Chicago,* by Emmett Dedmon; *Division Street,* by Studs Terkel; and *Boss,* a portrait of the late Mayor Richard J. Daley, by Mike Royko. Lois Willie's *Forever Open, Clear and Free* is a superb history of the fight to save Chicago's lakefront parks. *Sun-Times* travel editor Jack Schnedler's *Chicago* (Compass American Guides) provides an excellent overview of the city as well as practical information.

If you're an architecture buff, you can choose from among three excellent guidebooks by Ira J. Bach, former director of city development: *Chicago's Famous Buildings, Chicago on Foot,* and *Chicago's Public Sculpture.* David Lowe's *Lost Chicago* is a fascinating and heartbreaking history of vanished buildings.

INDEX

NOTES

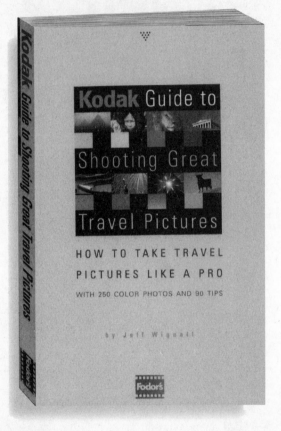

*E*scape to ancient cities and

journey to  exotic islands with

CNN *Travel Guide*, a wealth of valuable advice. *H*ost

Valerie Voss will take you to

all of your favorite destinations,

including those off the beaten

path. Tune-in to your passport to the world.

CNN TRAVEL GUIDE

SATURDAY 12:30 PM ᴇᴛ   SUNDAY 4:30 PM ᴇᴛ

CNN

Fodor's Travel Publications

Available at bookstores everywhere, or call 1–800–533–6478, 24 hours a day.

Gold Guides

U.S.

Alaska

Arizona

Boston

California

Cape Cod, Martha's Vineyard, Nantucket

The Carolinas & the Georgia Coast

Chicago

Colorado

Florida

Hawaii

Las Vegas, Reno, Tahoe

Los Angeles

Maine, Vermont, New Hampshire

Maui

Miami & the Keys

New England

New Orleans

New York City

Pacific North Coast

Philadelphia & the Pennsylvania Dutch Country

The Rockies

San Diego

San Francisco

Santa Fe, Taos, Albuquerque

Seattle & Vancouver

The South

U.S. & British Virgin Islands

USA

Virginia & Maryland

Waikiki

Washington, D.C.

Foreign

Australia & New Zealand

Austria

The Bahamas

Bermuda

Budapest

Canada

Cancún, Cozumel, Yucatán Peninsula

Caribbean

China

Costa Rica, Belize, Guatemala

The Czech Republic & Slovakia

Eastern Europe

Egypt

Europe

Florence, Tuscany & Umbria

France

Germany

Great Britain

Greece

Hong Kong

India

Ireland

Israel

Italy

Japan

Kenya & Tanzania

Korea

London

Madrid & Barcelona

Mexico

Montréal & Québec City

Moscow, St. Petersburg, Kiev

The Netherlands, Belgium & Luxembourg

New Zealand

Norway

Nova Scotia, New Brunswick, Prince Edward Island

Paris

Portugal

Provence & the Riviera

Scandinavia

Scotland

Singapore

South America

Southeast Asia

Spain

Sweden

Switzerland

Thailand

Tokyo

Toronto

Turkey

Vienna & the Danube

Fodor's Special-Interest Guides

Branson

Caribbean Ports of Call

The Complete Guide to America's National Parks

Condé Nast Traveler Caribbean Resort and Cruise Ship Finder

Cruises and Ports of Call

Fodor's London Companion

France by Train

Halliday's New England Food Explorer

Healthy Escapes

Italy by Train

Kodak Guide to Shooting Great Travel Pictures

Shadow Traffic's New York Shortcuts and Traffic Tips

Sunday in New York

Sunday in San Francisco

Walt Disney World, Universal Studios and Orlando

Walt Disney World for Adults

Where Should We Take the Kids? California

Where Should We Take the Kids? Northeast

Special Series

Affordables
Caribbean
Europe
Florida
France
Germany
Great Britain
Italy
London
Paris

Fodor's Bed & Breakfasts and Country Inns
America's Best B&Bs
California's Best B&Bs
Canada's Great Country Inns
Cottages, B&Bs and Country Inns of England and Wales
The Mid-Atlantic's Best B&Bs
New England's Best B&Bs
The Pacific Northwest's Best B&Bs
The South's Best B&Bs
The Southwest's Best B&Bs
The Upper Great Lakes' Best B&Bs

The Berkeley Guides
California
Central America
Eastern Europe
Europe
France
Germany & Austria
Great Britain & Ireland
Italy
London
Mexico

Pacific Northwest & Alaska
Paris
San Francisco

Compass American Guides
Arizona
Chicago
Colorado
Hawaii
Hollywood
Las Vegas
Maine
Manhattan
Montana
New Mexico
New Orleans
Oregon
San Francisco
South Carolina
South Dakota
Texas
Utah
Virginia
Washington
Wine Country
Wisconsin
Wyoming

Fodor's Español
California
Caribe Occidental
Caribe Oriental
Gran Bretaña
Londres
Mexico
Nueva York
Paris

Fodor's Exploring Guides
Australia
Boston & New England
Britain

California
Caribbean
China
Florence & Tuscany
Florida
France
Germany
Ireland
Italy
London
Mexico
Moscow & St. Petersburg
New York City
Paris
Prague
Provence
Rome
San Francisco
Scotland
Singapore & Malaysia
Spain
Thailand
Turkey
Venice

Fodor's Flashmaps
Boston
New York
San Francisco
Washington, D.C.

Fodor's Pocket Guides
Acapulco
Atlanta
Barbados
Jamaica
London
New York City
Paris
Prague
Puerto Rico

Rome
San Francisco
Washington, D.C.

Rivages Guides
Bed and Breakfasts of Character and Charm in France
Hotels and Country Inns of Character and Charm in France
Hotels and Country Inns of Character and Charm in Italy

Short Escapes
Country Getaways in Britain
Country Getaways in France
Country Getaways Near New York City

Fodor's Sports
Golf Digest's Best Places to Play
Skiing USA
USA Today The Complete Four Sport Stadium Guide

Fodor's Vacation Planners
Great American Learning Vacations
Great American Sports & Adventure Vacations
Great American Vacations
National Parks and Seashores of the East
National Parks of the West

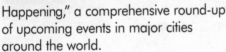

HERE'S YOUR OWN PERSONAL VIEW OF THE WORLD.

Here's the easiest way to get up-to-the-minute, objective, personalized information about what's going on in the city you'll be visiting—before you leave on your trip! Unique information you could get only if you knew someone personally in each of 160 destinations around the world. Everything from special places to dine to local events only a local would know about.

It's all yours—in your Travel Update from Worldview, the leading provider of time-sensitive destination information.

Review the following order form and fill it out by indicating your destination(s)

and travel dates and by checking off up to eight interest categories. Then mail or fax your order form to us, or call your order in. (We're here to help you 24 hours a day.)

Within 48 hours of receiving your order, we'll mail your convenient, pocket-sized custom guide to you, packed with information to make your travel more fun and interesting. And if you're in a hurry, we can even fax it.

Have a great trip with your Fodor's Worldview Travel Update!

Fodor's WORLDVIEW TRAVEL UPDATE

Customized to your interests and dates of travel

Time-sensitive

Insider perspective

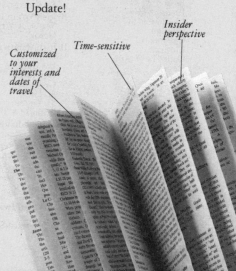

DESTINATIONS

Worldview covers more than 160 destinations worldwide. Choose the destination(s) that match your itinerary from the list below:

Europe
Amsterdam
Athens
Barcelona
Berlin
Brussels
Budapest
Copenhagen
Dublin
Edinburgh
Florence
Frankfurt
French Riviera
Geneva
Glasgow
Lausanne
Lisbon
London
Madrid
Milan
Moscow
Munich
Oslo
Paris
Prague
Provence
Rome
Salzburg
Seville
St. Petersburg
Stockholm
Venice
Vienna
Zurich

United States (Mainland)
Albuquerque
Atlanta
Atlantic City
Baltimore
Boston
Branson, MO
Charleston, SC
Chicago
Cincinnati
Cleveland
Dallas/Ft. Worth
Denver
Detroit
Houston
Indianapolis
Kansas City
Las Vegas
Los Angeles
Memphis
Miami
Milwaukee
Minneapolis/St. Paul
Nashville
New Orleans
New York City
Orlando
Palm Springs
Philadelphia
Phoenix
Pittsburgh
Portland
Reno/Lake Tahoe
St. Louis
Salt Lake City
San Antonio
San Diego
San Francisco
Santa Fe
Seattle
Tampa
Washington, DC

Alaska
Alaskan Destinations

Hawaii
Honolulu
Island of Hawaii
Kauai
Maui

Canada
Quebec City
Montreal
Ottawa
Toronto
Vancouver

Bahamas
Abaco
Eleuthera/
  Harbour Island
Exuma
Freeport
Nassau &
  Paradise Island

Bermuda
Bermuda Countryside
Hamilton

British Leeward Islands
Anguilla
Antigua & Barbuda
St. Kitts & Nevis

British Virgin Islands
Tortola & Virgin
Gorda

British Windward Islands
Barbados
Dominica
Grenada
St. Lucia
St. Vincent
Trinidad & Tobago

Cayman Islands
The Caymans

Dominican Republic
Santo Domingo

Dutch Leeward Islands
Aruba
Bonaire
Curacao

Dutch Windward Island
St. Maarten/St. Martin

French West Indies
Guadeloupe
Martinique
St. Barthelemy

Jamaica
Kingston
Montego Bay
Negril
Ocho Rios

Puerto Rico
Ponce
San Juan

Turks & Caicos
Grand Turk/
  Providenciales

U.S. Virgin Islands
St. Croix
St. John
St. Thomas

Mexico
Acapulco
Cancun & Isla Mujeres
Cozumel
Guadalajara
Ixtapa & Zihuatanejo
Los Cabos
Mazatlan
Mexico City
Monterrey
Oaxaca
Puerto Vallarta

South/Central America
Buenos Aires
Caracas
Rio de Janeiro
San Jose, Costa Rica
Sao Paulo

Middle East
Istanbul
Jerusalem

Australia & New Zealand
Auckland
Melbourne
South Island
Sydney

China
Beijing
Guangzhou
Shanghai

Japan
Kyoto
Nagoya
Osaka
Tokyo
Yokohama

Pacific Rim/Other
Bali
Bangkok
Hong Kong & Macau
Manila
Seoul
Singapore
Taipei

INTERESTS

For your personalized Travel Update, choose the eight (8) categories you're most interested in from the following list:

1.	**Business Services**	Fax & Overnight Mail, Computer Rentals, Protocol, Secretarial, Messenger, Translation Services

Dining

2.	**All-Day Dining**	Breakfast & Brunch, Cafes & Tea Rooms, Late-Night Dining
3.	**Local Cuisine**	Every Price Range — from Budget Restaurants to the Special Splurge
4.	**European Cuisine**	Continental, French, Italian
5.	**Asian Cuisine**	Chinese, Far Eastern, Japanese, Other
6.	**Americas Cuisine**	American, Mexican & Latin
7.	**Nightlife**	Bars, Dance Clubs, Casinos, Comedy Clubs, Ethnic, Pubs & Beer Halls
8.	**Entertainment**	Theater – Comedy, Drama, Musicals, Dance, Ticket Agencies
9.	**Music**	Classical, Opera, Traditional & Ethnic, Jazz & Blues, Pop, Rock
10.	**Children's Activites**	Events, Attractions
11.	**Tours**	Local Tours, Day Trips, Overnight Excursions
12.	**Exhibitions, Festivals & Shows**	Antiques & Flower, History & Cultural, Art Exhibitions, Fairs & Craft Shows, Music & Art Festivals
13.	**Shopping**	Districts & Malls, Markets, Regional Specialties
14.	**Fitness**	Bicycling, Health Clubs, Hiking, Jogging
15.	**Recreational Sports**	Boating/Sailing, Fishing, Golf, Skiing, Snorkeling/Scuba, Tennis/Racket
16.	**Spectator Sports**	Auto Racing, Baseball, Basketball, Golf, Football, Horse Racing, Ice Hockey, Soccer
17.	**Event Highlights**	The best of what's happening during the dates of your trip.
18.	**Sightseeing**	Sights, Buildings, Monuments
19.	**Museums**	Art, Cultural
20.	**Transportation**	Taxis, Car Rentals, Airports, Public Transportation
21.	**General Info**	Overview, Holidays, Currency, Tourist Info

Please note that content will vary by season, destination, and length of stay.

Name _____

Address _____

City _____ **State** ____ **Country** ____ **ZIP** ____

Tel # ( ) - **Fax #** ( ) -

Title of this Fodor's guide: _____

Store and location where guide was purchased: _____

INDICATE YOUR DESTINATIONS/DATES: You can order up to three (3) destinations from the previous page. Fill in your arrival and departure dates for each destination. **Your Travel Update itinerary (all destinations selected) cannot exceed 30 days from beginning to end.**

		Month	Day		Month	Day
(Sample) **LONDON**	From:	**6**	/ **21**	To:	**6**	/ **30**
1	From:		/	To:		/
2	From:		/	To:		/
3	From:		/	To:		/

CHOOSE YOUR INTERESTS: Select up to eight (8) categories from the list of interest categories shown on the previous page and circle the numbers below:

1 2 3 4 5 6 7 8 9 10 11 12 13 14 15 16 17 18 19 20 21

CHOOSE WHEN YOU WANT YOUR TRAVEL UPDATE DELIVERED (Check one):
❏ Please send my Travel Update immediately.
❏ Please hold my order until a few weeks before my trip to include the most up-to-date information.
Completed orders will be sent within 48 hours. Allow 7–10 days for U.S. mail delivery.

ADD UP YOUR ORDER HERE. SPECIAL OFFER FOR FODOR'S PURCHASERS ONLY!

	Suggested Retail Price	Your Price	This Order
First destination ordered	$ 9.95	$ 7.95	$ 7.95
Second destination (if applicable)	$ 6.95	$ 4.95	+
Third destination (if applicable)	$ 6.95	$ 4.95	+

DELIVERY CHARGE (Check one and enter amount below)

	Within U.S. & Canada	Outside U.S. & Canada
First Class Mail	❏ $2.50	❏ $5.00
FAX	❏ $5.00	❏ $10.00
Priority Delivery	❏ $15.00	❏ $27.00

ENTER DELIVERY CHARGE FROM ABOVE: + _____

TOTAL: $ _____

METHOD OF PAYMENT IN U.S. FUNDS ONLY (Check one):
❏ AmEx ❏ MC ❏ Visa ❏ Discover ❏ Personal Check (U. S. & Canada only)
❏ Money Order/International Money Order

Make check or money order payable to: Fodor's Worldview Travel Update

Credit Card _/_/_/_/_/_/_/_/_/_/_/_/_/_/_/ **Expiration Date:** _/_

Authorized Signature _____

SEND THIS COMPLETED FORM WITH PAYMENT TO:
Fodor's Worldview Travel Update, 114 Sansome Street, Suite 700, San Francisco, CA 94104

OR CALL OR FAX US 24-HOURS A DAY
Telephone **1-800-799-9609** • Fax **1-800-799-9619** (From within the U.S. & Canada)
(Outside the U.S. & Canada: Telephone 415-616-9988 • Fax 415-616-9989)

(Please have this guide in front of you when you call so we can verify purchase.)
Code: FTG   Offer valid until 12/31/97